A Roadmap to Reducing
Child Poverty

Committee on Building an Agenda to Reduce the
Number of Children in Poverty by Half in 10 Years

Greg Duncan and Suzanne Le Menestrel, *Editors*
Board on Children, Youth, and Families
and
Committee on National Statistics
Division of Behavioral and Social Sciences and Education

A Consensus Study Report of

The National Academies of
SCIENCES · ENGINEERING · MEDICINE

THE NATIONAL ACADEMIES PRESS
Washington, DC
www.nap.edu

THE NATIONAL ACADEMIES PRESS   500 Fifth Street, NW   Washington, DC 20001

This activity was supported by contracts and grants between the National Academy of Sciences and the Doris Duke Charitable Foundation, Inc. (2017032); the Foundation for Child Development (NAS-03-2017); the Joyce Foundation (17-37856); the Russell Sage Foundation (83-18-04); Office of the Assistant Secretary for Planning and Evaluation, the U.S. Department of Health and Human Services (HHSP233201400020B, Order No. HHSP2337058); the William T. Grant Foundation (187516); and the W.K. Kellogg Foundation (P0130499). Any opinions, findings, conclusions, or recommendations expressed in this publication do not necessarily reflect the views of any organization or agency that provided support for the project.

International Standard Book Number-13: 978-0-309-48398-8
International Standard Book Number-10: 0-309-48398-0
Library of Congress Control Number: 2019945735
Digital Object Identifier: https://doi.org/10.17226/25246

Additional copies of this publication are available for sale from the National Academies Press, 500 Fifth Street, NW, Keck 360, Washington, DC 20001; (800) 624-6242 or (202) 334-3313; http://www.nap.edu/25246.

Suggested citation: National Academies of Sciences, Engineering, and Medicine. (2019). *A Roadmap to Reducing Child Poverty*. Washington, DC: The National Academies Press. doi: https://doi.org/10.17226/25246.

The National Academies of
SCIENCES · ENGINEERING · MEDICINE

The **National Academy of Sciences** was established in 1863 by an Act of Congress, signed by President Lincoln, as a private, nongovernmental institution to advise the nation on issues related to science and technology. Members are elected by their peers for outstanding contributions to research. Dr. Marcia McNutt is president.

The **National Academy of Engineering** was established in 1964 under the charter of the National Academy of Sciences to bring the practices of engineering to advising the nation. Members are elected by their peers for extraordinary contributions to engineering. Dr. C. D. Mote, Jr., is president.

The **National Academy of Medicine** (formerly the Institute of Medicine) was established in 1970 under the charter of the National Academy of Sciences to advise the nation on medical and health issues. Members are elected by their peers for distinguished contributions to medicine and health. Dr. Victor J. Dzau is president.

The three Academies work together as the **National Academies of Sciences, Engineering, and Medicine** to provide independent, objective analysis and advice to the nation and conduct other activities to solve complex problems and inform public policy decisions. The National Academies also encourage education and research, recognize outstanding contributions to knowledge, and increase public understanding in matters of science, engineering, and medicine.

Learn more about the National Academies of Sciences, Engineering, and Medicine at **www.nationalacademies.org**.

The National Academies of
SCIENCES · ENGINEERING · MEDICINE

Consensus Study Reports published by the National Academies of Sciences, Engineering, and Medicine document the evidence-based consensus on the study's statement of task by an authoring committee of experts. Reports typically include findings, conclusions, and recommendations based on information gathered by the committee and the committee's deliberations. Each report has been subjected to a rigorous and independent peer-review process and it represents the position of the National Academies on the statement of task.

Proceedings published by the National Academies of Sciences, Engineering, and Medicine chronicle the presentations and discussions at a workshop, symposium, or other event convened by the National Academies. The statements and opinions contained in proceedings are those of the participants and are not endorsed by other participants, the planning committee, or the National Academies.

For information about other products and activities of the National Academies, please visit www.nationalacademies.org/about/whatwedo.

Acknowledgments

The U.S. Congress asked the National Academies of Sciences, Engineering, and Medicine to provide a nonpartisan, evidence-based report that would provide its assessment of the most effective means for reducing child poverty by half in the next 10 years. The National Academies appointed the Committee on Building an Agenda to Reduce the Number of Children in Poverty by Half in 10 Years to address its charge. The committee thanks the following sponsors of this study for their support: the Doris Duke Charitable Foundation; the Foundation for Child Development; the Joyce Foundation; the Russell Sage Foundation; the Office of the Assistant Secretary for Planning and Evaluation, U.S. Department of Health and Human Services; the William T. Grant Foundation; and the W.K. Kellogg Foundation.

This report would not have been possible without the contributions of many people. Special thanks go to the members of the committee who dedicated extensive time, expertise, and energy to the drafting of the report. The committee also thanks the members of the staff of the National Academies for their significant contributions to the report: Suzanne Le Menestrel, Connie Citro, Rebekah Hutton, Chris Mackie, Dara Shefska, and Elizabeth Townsend. We also thank Jennifer Duer, University of California, Irvine, for her invaluable assistance in developing graphics and tables for the report. Pamella Atayi provided key administrative and logistical support and made sure that committee meetings ran smoothly. We also thank Michelle Burbage for her research assistance.

The committee is also grateful to Azzure Beale, Anthony Bryant, and Lisa Alston for their administrative and financial assistance on this project. From the Division of Behavioral and Social Sciences and Education Office of Reports and Communication, Kirsten Sampson Snyder, Viola Horek, Patricia L. Morison, Douglas Sprunger, and Yvonne Wise shepherded the report through the review and production process and assisted with its communication and dissemination. The committee also thanks the National Academies Press staff, Clair Woolley and Holly Sten, for their assistance with the production of the final report; Daniel Bearss and Rebecca Morgan in the National Academies research library for their assistance with fact checking and literature searches; the report's editor, Marc DeFrancis, for his skillful and thoughtful editing; and Jay Christian for his elegant graphic design work. Finally, throughout the project, Natacha Blain, director of the Board on Children, Youth, and Families, Mary Ellen O'Connell, and Monica Feit provided helpful oversight. We also thank Melissa Welch-Ross for her helpful comments.

Many individuals volunteered significant time and effort to address and educate the committee during our public information sessions. Their willingness to share their perspectives, research, and personal experiences was essential to the committee's work. We thank: MaryLee Allen, Children's Defense Fund; Douglas Besharov, University of Maryland; Gary Bonner, Center for Urban Families; Roy Brooks, Tarrant County, Texas; Miles Corak, Graduate Center of the City University of New York; Marla Dean, Bright Beginnings; Jesús Gerena, Family Independence Initiative; Olivia Golden, Center for Law and Social Policy; Richard Hendra, MDRC; Tara Lobin, Fairfax County Public Schools; Nora Morales, Maryland Public Schools; Edgar Olsen, University of Virginia; Anita Sampson, Maryland Public Schools; Isabel Sawhill, Brookings Institution; Kelsey Schaberg, MDRC; Arloc Sherman, Center on Budget and Policy Priorities; Satira Streeter, Ascensions Psychological and Community Services, Inc; Bruce Western, Harvard University; and W. Bradford Wilcox, University of Virginia.

We also thank the researchers who conducted original analyses and prepared commissioned papers for the committee: Randall Akee, University of California, Los Angeles and the Brookings Institution; Rosemary Hyson, Dahlia Remler, and Sanders D. Korenman, City University of New York; Thierry Kruten and Teresa Munzi, Cross-National Data Center in Luxembourg; Emilia Simeonova, Johns Hopkins University; and Christopher Wimer, Columbia University. The committee would also like to extend a special acknowledgement to the Transfer Income Model Version 3 project team at The Urban Institute for their expert analyses, patience, thoroughness, and attention to detail: Linda Giannarelli, Joyce Morton, Kevin Werner, and Laura Wheaton.

The committee also thanks the following individuals for their contributions to this study and the final report: Brian Baird, David Britt, Dorothy Duncan, Camille Gamboa, David H. Greenberg, Jeff Hutchinson, Arthur Lupia, Nancy McArdle, Clemens Noelke, Sheri Roder, Adam Thomas, and James Ziliak. Many individuals also submitted memos for the committee's consideration; a listing of these individuals can be found in Appendix C in this report.

This Consensus Study Report was reviewed in draft form by individuals chosen for their diverse perspectives and technical expertise. The purpose of this independent review is to provide candid and critical comments that will assist the National Academies in making each published report as sound as possible and to ensure that it meets the institutional standards for quality, objectivity, evidence, and responsiveness to the study charge. The review comments and draft manuscript remain confidential to protect the integrity of the deliberative process.

We thank the following individuals for their review of this report: Eloise Anderson (retired), Department of Children and Families, State of Wisconsin; Lenette Azzi-Lessing, School of Social Work, Boston University; Robert Doar, Morgridge Fellow in Poverty Studies, American Enterprise Institute; Kenneth A. Dodge, Sanford School of Public Policy, Duke University; Kathryn J. Edin, Department of Sociology, Princeton University; Gary W. Evans, College of Human Ecology, Cornell University; Wade F. Horn, Health and Human Services Marketplace Leader, Deloitte Consulting, LLC; Sara Rosenbaum, Department of Health Policy and Management, Milken Institute School of Public Health, The George Washington University; H. Luke Schaefer, Poverty Solutions and Gerald R. Ford School of Public Policy, University of Michigan; Diane Whitmore Schanzenbach, Institute for Policy Research, Northwestern University; Michael R. Strain, John G. Searle Scholar, American Enterprise Institute; Scott Winship, Manhattan Institute for Policy Research and The University of Chicago; and Barbara L. Wolfe, Institute for Research on Poverty, University of Wisconsin–Madison.

Although the reviewers listed above provided many constructive comments and suggestions, they were not asked to endorse the conclusions or recommendations of this report nor did they see the final draft before its release. The review of this report was overseen by V. Joseph Hotz, Department of Economics, Duke University, and Joseph P. Newhouse, Harvard University. They were responsible for making certain that an independent examination of this report was carried out in accordance with the standards of the National Academies and that all review comments were carefully considered. Responsibility for the final content rests entirely with the authoring committee and the National Academies.

One of the pleasures of serving on a National Academies committee such as ours is that it provides opportunities to strike up friendships with individuals with very different interests and viewpoints. It also allows us to share in the joys and sorrows of fellow committee members. We dedicate this report to the memory of Joseph Smeeding, a bright young doctoral student at the University of Arizona and son of committee member Timothy Smeeding. He died on January 12, 2018, after a 2-year battle with glioblastoma multiforme.

Greg Duncan, *Chair*
Committee on Building an Agenda to Reduce
the Number of Children in Poverty by Half in 10 Years

Contents

Summary   1

1   Introduction   19
The Committee's Charge, 21
Temporal and Other Considerations Associated with the
    Statement of Task, 23
How the Committee Selected Programs to Review, 24
Considerations in Estimating Policy and Program Impacts, 26
Organization of the Report, 28
References, 30

2   A Demographic Portrait of Child Poverty in the United States   33
Measuring U.S. Child Poverty, 33
A Demographic Portrait of U.S. Child Poverty in 2015, 41
Historical Trends in Child Poverty, 1967–2016, 55
Child Poverty in the United States and Other English-Speaking
    Developed Countries, 57
References, 62

3   Consequences of Child Poverty   67
Why Childhood Poverty Can Matter for Child Outcomes, 68
Correlational Studies, 71
The Impact of Child Poverty, 73
Macroeconomic Costs of Child Poverty to Society, 89
References, 91

xiii

4   How the Labor Market, Family Structure,
    and Government Programs Affect Child Poverty   97
    Forces that Shape Child Poverty, 97
    The Changing Role of Government Taxes and Transfers, 106
    Child-Related Income Transfers and Tax Benefits, 112
    Effects of Income Transfers and Tax Benefits on Child Poverty
        in 2015, 116
    Effects of Government Benefits on Child Poverty in the
        United States and Other English-Speaking Countries, 120
    References, 128

5   Ten Policy and Program Approaches to Reducing Child Poverty, 133
    Program and Policy Options in 10 Areas, 134
    Modifications Examined for 10 Policy and Program Areas, 137
    Impacts on Poverty, Cost, and Employment, 152
    References, 168

6   Packages of Policies and Programs That Reduce Poverty
    and Deep Poverty Among Children   173
    A Work-Based Poverty-Reduction Package, 174
    A Work-Based and Universal Supports Poverty-Reduction
        Package, 176
    A Means-Tested Supports and Work Poverty-Reduction
        Package, 182
    A Universal Supports and Work Poverty-Reduction
        Package, 183
    Simulating the Impacts of the Four Program Packages, 185
    References, 194

7   Other Policy and Program Approaches to
    Child Poverty Reduction   195
    Family Planning, 196
    Family Composition, 200
    Paid Family and Medical Leave, 204
    Mandatory Employment Programs, 207
    Block Grants, 210
    The TANF Program, 213
    Health, Health Insurance, and Measuring Poverty, 214
    Policies Toward American Indian and Alaska Native
        Children, 217
    References, 220

8   Contextual Factors That Influence the Effects of Anti-Poverty
    Policies and Programs   227
    Why Context Matters, 227
    Six Major Contextual Factors, 228
    Income Stability and Predictability, 229
    Equitable and Ready Access to Programs, 233
    Racial/Ethnic Discrimination, 237
    Criminal Justice System Involvement, 239
    Neighborhood Conditions, 242
    Health and Disability, 245
    References, 248

9   Recommendations for Research and Data Collection   257
    Priority Areas for Research, 259
    Improvements in Data Collection and Measurement, 265
    Continued Monitoring and Program Evaluation, 270
    Coordinating Research and Data Priorities Across
        Departments, 271
    References, 273

APPENDIXES
Note: Papers commissioned by the committee are available on the
National Academies Press website at http://www.nap.edu/25246.

A   Biosketches of Committee Members and Staff   275
B   Public Session Agendas   285
C   Authors of Memos Submitted to the Committee   289

ON-LINE APPENDIXES (Available: *http://www.nap.edu/25246*
under the Resources tab)

D   Technical Appendixes to Select Chapters   291
    2-1.   A Brief History of Poverty Measurements
           in the United States   291
    2-2.   Types of Income-Based Poverty Measures and the
           Advantages of Using the Adjusted SPM for
           Policy Analysis   293
    2-3.   Consumption-Based Poverty Measures   310
    2-4.   How Equivalence Scales Are Used to Adjust
           Poverty Thresholds   318
    2-5.   Cost-of-Living Adjustments in Poverty Thresholds
           and Benefits   320

2-6.   Differences Between the Resource Measures Used
       by the OPM and SPM Poverty Measures   325
2-7.   Poverty Among American Indian and Alaska
       Native Children   325
2-8.   The Changing Demography of Children,
       Including Children in Poverty   328
2-9.   Distribution of Child Population Across Persistently
       High-Poverty Counties   332
2-10. Anchored and Unanchored Methods of Calculating
       SPM Poverty Over Time   345
2-11. Poverty Measurement Across Countries: Cross-Country
       Poverty Lines and Child Poverty Rates   350
3-1.   Associations Between Poverty and Child Outcomes   362
4-1.   Definitions Pertaining to Chapter 4 from the
       Organisation for Economic Co-operation and
       Development (OECD)   392
4-2.   Government Policies Affecting Child Poverty in
       Australia and Ireland   393
5-1.   Adjusting Estimates of Poverty Reduction for
       Behavioral Effects   411
5-2.   Modifications to the Earned Income Tax Credit   412
5-3.   Modifications to Child Care Subsidies   415
5-4.   Modifications to the Minimum Wage   417
5-5.   Scaling Up WorkAdvance   419
5-6.   Modifications to the Supplemental Nutrition
       Assistance Program (SNAP)   421
5-7.   Modifications to Housing Programs   424
5-8.   Modifications to the Supplemental Security
       Income (SSI) Program   426
5-9.   Introducing a Child Allowance   430
5-10. A Child Support Assurance Program   432
5-11. Changes in Immigrant Policies   434
5-12. Reducing Child Poverty through a Universal
       Basic Income   440
5-13. Construction of Summary Tables 5-1 and 5-2   443

E   TRIM3 Summary Tables   455

F   Urban Institute TRIM3 Technical Specifications:
    Using Microsimulation to Assess the Policy Proposals of the
    National Academies Committee on Reducing Child Poverty   457
    Introduction   457
    The TRIM3 Model and the 2015 Baseline   458

Policy Changes to Reduce Child Poverty   482
Overview of Simulation Assumptions   483
EITC   487
Child Care Expenses   497
Minimum Wage   506
Employment Policy   518
SNAP   523
Housing   534
SSI   538
Child Allowances   541
Child Support Assurance   550
Immigrant Eligibility Policies   557
Basic Income Guarantee   565
Policy Packages   572
Simulations Using 2018 Tax Law   581
Summary and Caveats   584
References   592
About the Urban Institute   594

Summary

The strengths and abilities children develop from infancy through adolescence are crucial for their physical, emotional, and cognitive growth. And that growth in turn enables them to achieve success in school and to become responsible, economically self-sufficient, and healthy adults. Capable, responsible, and healthy adults are the foundation of any well-functioning and prosperous society, yet in this regard the future of the United States is not as secure as it could be. This is because millions of American children live in families with incomes below the poverty line. A wealth of evidence suggests that a lack of adequate family economic resources compromises children's ability to grow and achieve success in adulthood, hurting them and the broader society as well.

Recognizing this challenge to America's future, Congress included in an omnibus appropriations bill that was signed into law in December 2015 a provision directing the National Academies of Sciences, Engineering, and Medicine to conduct a comprehensive study of child poverty in the United States. The heart of this congressional charge is to identify evidence-based programs and policies for reducing the number of children living in poverty in the United States by half within 10 years. This 10-year window meant that the National Academies' study would need to focus on policies that could affect poor parents' resources in the near term, rather than on investments such as improved education for poor children that might well reduce poverty for future generations. Specifically, Congress requested that the committee provide the following:

1. a review of research on linkages between child poverty and child well-being;
2. objective analyses of the poverty-reducing effects of major assistance programs directed at children and families; and
3. policy and program recommendations for reducing the number of children living in poverty—including those living in deep poverty (with family incomes below one-half the poverty line)—in the United States by half within 10 years.

After nearly 2 years of work, the Committee on Building an Agenda to Reduce the Number of Children in Poverty by Half in 10 Years (hereafter, the committee) has completed a review of the research literature and its own commissioned analyses to answer some of the most important questions surrounding child poverty and its eradication in the United States. Moreover, the committee was able to formulate two program and policy packages, described below, that meet the 50 percent poverty-reduction goals while at the same time increasing employment among low-income families.

WHY IS CHILD POVERTY SUCH A SERIOUS PROBLEM?

Although some children are resilient to the adverse impacts of economic poverty, many studies show significant associations between poverty and poor child outcomes, such as harmful childhood experiences, including maltreatment, material hardship, impaired physical health, low birthweight, structural changes in brain development, and mental health problems. Studies also show significant associations between child poverty and lower educational attainment, difficulty obtaining steady, well-paying employment in adulthood, and a greater likelihood of risky behaviors, delinquency, and criminal behavior in adolescence and adulthood.

Because these correlations do not in themselves prove that low income is the active ingredient producing worse outcomes for children, the committee focused its attention on the literature addressing the *causal* impacts of childhood poverty on children. The committee concludes from this review that **the weight of the causal evidence does indeed indicate that income poverty itself causes negative child outcomes, especially when poverty occurs in early childhood or persists throughout a large portion of childhood.**[1] (The full text of this and other conclusions and recommendations included in the Summary are presented in Box S-1.)

The committee also reviewed the much less extensive evidence on the macroeconomic costs of child poverty to measure how much child poverty costs the nation overall. Studies in this area attempt to attach a monetary

---

[1] Conclusion 3-8, Chapter 3.

value to the reduction in adult productivity, increased costs of crime, and increased health expenditures associated with children growing up in poor families. Estimates of these costs range from 4.0 to 5.4 percent of the Gross Domestic Product—roughly between $800 billion and $1.1 trillion annually if measured in terms of the size of the U.S. economy in 2018.[2] As we demonstrate below, outlays for new programs that would reduce child poverty by 50 percent would cost the United States much less than these estimated costs of child poverty.

DO POVERTY-REDUCING PROGRAMS IN THE UNITED STATES PROMOTE CHILDREN'S HEALTHY DEVELOPMENT?

Given the evidence that poverty harms children's well-being, policies designed to reduce poverty by rewarding work or providing safety-net benefits might be expected to have the opposite effect. The committee examined research findings to assess whether that is the case. A number of researchers have studied the effects on children of changes in policies, such as the emerging availability of food stamps across the country in the 1960s and 1970s and expansions of the Earned Income Tax Credit (EITC) Program in the 1990s. Further expansions of some of these policies are obvious candidates for meeting the 50 percent poverty-reduction goal in the committee's statement of task, so it is particularly important to assess the evidence of their past impacts on children. **The committee finds that many programs that alleviate poverty—either directly, by providing income transfers, or indirectly, by providing food, housing, or medical care—have been shown to improve child well-being.**[3]

Specifically, we find that

- periodic increases in the generosity of the Earned Income Tax Credit Program have improved child educational and health outcomes,[4]
- the Supplemental Nutrition Assistance Program (SNAP) has improved birth outcomes as well as many important child and adult health outcomes,[5]
- expansions of public health insurance for pregnant women, infants, and children have led to substantial improvements in child and adult health, educational attainment, employment, and earnings,[6] and

---

[2] This is based on a Gross Domestic Product of $20.41 trillion in the second quarter of 2018. See Table 3, https://www.bea.gov/system/files/2018-09/gdp2q18_3rd_3.pdf.

[3] Conclusion 3-8, Chapter 3.

[4] Conclusion 3-3, Chapter 3.

[5] Conclusion 3-5, Chapter 3.

[6] Conclusion 3-7, Chapter 3.

BOX S-1
Conclusions and Recommendations
Referenced in the Summary

CONCLUSION 3-3: Periodic increases in the generosity of the Earned Income Tax Credit Program have improved children's educational and health outcomes.

CONCLUSION 3-5: The Supplemental Nutrition Assistance Program has been shown to improve birth outcomes as well as many important child and adult health outcomes.

CONCLUSION 3-6: Evidence on the effects of housing assistance is mixed. Children who were young when their families received housing benefits enabling them to move to low-poverty neighborhoods had improved educational attainment and better adult outcomes.

CONCLUSION 3-7: Expansions of public health insurance for pregnant women, infants, and children have generated large improvements in child and adult health and in educational attainment, employment, and earnings.

CONCLUSION 3-8: The weight of the causal evidence indicates that income poverty itself causes negative child outcomes, especially when it begins in early childhood and/or persists throughout a large share of a child's life. Many programs that alleviate poverty either directly, by providing income transfers, or indirectly, by providing food, housing, or medical care have been shown to improve child well-being.

CONCLUSION 4-4: Government tax and transfer programs reduced the child poverty rate, defined by the Supplemental Poverty Measure (SPM), modestly between 1967 and 1993, but became increasingly important after 1993 because of increases in government benefits targeted at the poor and near poor. Between 1993 and 2016, SPM poverty fell by 12.3 percentage points, from 27.9 to 15.6 percent, more than twice as much as market-income-based poverty.

CONCLUSION 5-1: Using a threshold defined by 100 percent of the Supplemental Poverty Measure, no single program or policy option developed by the committee was estimated to meet the goal of 50 percent poverty reduction. The $3,000 per child per year child allowance policy comes closest, and it also meets the 50 percent reduction goal for deep poverty.

CONCLUSION 5-2: A number of other program and policy options lead to substantial reductions in poverty and deep poverty. Two involve existing programs—the Supplemental Nutrition Assistance Program and housing vouchers. The option of a 40 percent increase in Earned Income Tax Credit benefits would also reduce child poverty substantially.

CONCLUSION 5-3: Programs producing the largest reductions in child poverty are estimated to cost the most. Almost all of the committee-developed program options that lead to substantial poverty-reduction cost at least $20 billion annually.

CONCLUSION 5-4: Projected changes in earnings and employment in response to simulations of our program and policy options vary widely, but taken as a whole they reveal a tradeoff between the magnitude of poverty reduction and effects on earnings and employment. Work-based program expansions involving the Earned Income Tax Credit and the Child and Dependent Care Tax Credit were estimated to increase earnings by as much as $9 billion and employment by as many as half a million jobs. Programs such as the child allowances and expansions of the housing voucher program were estimated to reduce earnings by up to $6 billion and jobs by nearly 100,000. The bulk of the remaining program and policy proposals are estimated to evoke more modest behavioral responses.

CONCLUSION 5-5: The 20 program and policy options generate disparate impacts across population subgroups in our simulations. Although virtually all of them would reduce poverty across all of the subgroups we considered, disproportionately large decreases in child poverty occur only for Black children and children of mothers with low levels of education. Hispanic children and immigrant children would benefit relatively less.

CONCLUSION 6-1: Two program and policy packages developed by the committee met its mandated 50 percent reduction in both child poverty (defined by 100% of Supplemental Poverty Measure [SPM]) and deep poverty (defined by 50% of SPM). The first of these packages combines work-oriented policy expansions with increases in benefit levels in the housing voucher and Supplemental Nutrition Assistance Programs. The second package combines work-oriented expansions with a child allowance, a child support assurance program, and elimination of immigrant restrictions on benefits built into the 1996 welfare reforms. Both packages increase work and earnings, and both are estimated to cost between $90 and $111 billion per year.

CONCLUSION 6-2: The committee was unable to formulate an evidence-based employment-oriented package that would come close to meeting its mandate of reducing child poverty by 50 percent. The best employment-oriented package it could design combines expansions of the Earned Income Tax Credit, the Child and Dependent Care Tax Credit, a minimum wage increase, and a promising career development program. Although this package is estimated to add more than a million workers to the labor force, generate $18 billion in additional earnings, and cost the government only $8.6 to $9.3 billion annually, its estimated reductions in child poverty are less than half of what is needed to meet the goal.

continued

BOX S-1 Continued

CONCLUSION 7-1: Increasing both awareness of and access to effective, safe, and affordable long-acting reversible contraception (LARC) devices reduces the incidence of unplanned births, which could in turn reduce child poverty. In contrast, policies that reduce access to LARC by cutting Medicaid, Title X funding of family planning services, or mandated contraceptive coverage appear to increase the number of unintended births and thus also child poverty.

CONCLUSION 7-2: Although increasing the proportion of children living with married or cohabiting parents, as opposed to single parents, would almost certainly reduce child poverty, the impacts of existing social programs designed to promote such a change are uncertain. Evidence from these programs is inconclusive and points to neither strong positive nor negative effects. In the early 2000s, an ambitious attempt to develop programs that would improve couple-relationship skills, promote marriage, and improve child well-being failed to boost marriage rates and achieve most of their other longer-run goals.

CONCLUSION 7-4: There is insufficient evidence to identify mandatory work policies that would reliably reduce child poverty, and it appears that work requirements are at least as likely to increase as to decrease poverty. The dearth of evidence also reflects underinvestment over the past two decades in methodologically strong evaluations of the impacts of alternative work programs.

RECOMMENDATION 9-10: The U.S. Office of Management and Budget (OMB) should convene working groups of appropriate federal program, research, and statistical agencies to assess this report's conclusions about program packages that are capable of reducing child poverty by half within 10 years of adoption. OMB should also convene working groups charged with assessing the report's recommendations for research and data collection to fill important gaps in knowledge about effective anti-child-poverty programs. These working groups should be tasked to recommend action steps, and OMB should work with relevant agencies to draw up implementation plans and secure appropriate resources. The working groups should consult with relevant state agencies and outside experts, as appropriate, to inform their deliberations.

- evidence on the effects of housing assistance is mixed, although children who were young when their families received housing benefits that allowed them to move to low-poverty neighborhoods had improved educational and adult outcomes.[7]

HOW MUCH DO CURRENT PROGRAMS IN THE UNITED STATES REDUCE CHILD POVERTY?

Mindful of the evidence that links childhood poverty with problems in adulthood, as well as studies showing the benefits for children from some of the nation's anti-poverty programs, the committee sought to understand how child poverty has been affected by current programs and policies. In 2015, the latest year for which the committee was able to generate estimates that took full account of benefits from federal tax credits and other safety net programs, more than 9.6 million U.S. children (13.0%) lived in families with annual incomes below a poverty line defined by the Supplemental Poverty Measure (SPM).[8]

That same year, some 2.1 million children (2.9%) lived in "deep poverty," defined as having family resources below one-half of the poverty-based line. Child poverty rates were much higher for Black children (18%) and Hispanic children (22%) than for non-Hispanic White children (8%); for children in single-parent families (22%) than for those in two-parent families (9%); for children in immigrant families (21%) than for those in non-immigrant families (10%); and for children in families with no workers (62%) than for those in families with part-time workers (28%) or with full-time workers (7%). Poverty rates also appear to be much higher among American Indian children; however, precise rates are unavailable.

The committee examined the poverty-reducing impacts of the current set of major federal assistance programs by estimating how child poverty rates would have changed had each of these programs *not* been operating (see Figure S-1).[9] The two refundable tax credits—the EITC and the refundable portion of the Child Tax Credit—are the most successful at alleviating poverty, as shown in Figure S-1. We estimate that the elimination of these

---

[7] Conclusion 3-6, Chapter 3.

[8] The committee's child poverty estimates are lower than those in official statistics. Its estimates were produced by a widely used microsimulation model, TRIM3, which corrects for the underreporting of a number of important sources of income in household surveys. The 2015 SPM poverty lines for two-parent, two-child families were about $22,000 for those owning a home free and clear and about $26,000 for renters and homeowners with a mortgage.

[9] It is important to note that these estimates of the poverty-reducing impact of current programs do not account for the extent to which eliminating a given program might also affect work and other decisions that would in turn affect a family's market income.

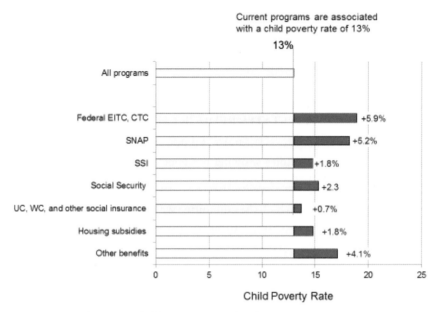

FIGURE S-1 Changes in child poverty rates if each current income support program were eliminated.

NOTE: CTC = Child Tax Credit, EITC = Earned Income Tax Credit, SNAP = Supplemental Nutrition Assistance Program, SSI = Supplemental Security Income, UC = Unemployment Compensation, WC = Workers' Compensation.

SOURCE: Estimates from TRIM3 commissioned by the committee, using the Supplemental Poverty Measure with the Current Population Survey Annual Social and Economic Supplement, with income corrected for underreporting.

tax credits would raise SPM child poverty to 18.9 percent, an increase of 5.9 percentage points or 4.4 million children.

The poverty-reducing benefits from the Supplemental Nutrition Assistance Program (SNAP) are the next largest: In the absence of SNAP benefits, the child poverty rate would have increased to 18.2 percent. In the absence of Social Security benefits, which go to many multigeneration households containing children, the child poverty rate would have been 15.3 percent. Without the Supplemental Security Income (SSI) Program, the child poverty rate would have increased to 14.8 percent.

In contrast to rates of child poverty defined by SPM thresholds, rates of deep poverty (50% of SPM thresholds) are affected very little by refundable tax credits. This is because most families in deep poverty have very low levels of earned income, and all three of the tax benefits are based on earnings. SNAP is by far the single most important federal program for reducing deep poverty; it is estimated that eliminating SNAP would nearly double (from 2.9 to 5.7%) the fraction of children in families with incomes below the deep poverty threshold.

The demographic groups with the highest child poverty rates—Blacks and Hispanics, single-parent families, and families with poorly educated parents—benefit disproportionately from both SNAP and the tax benefit programs. The two exceptions are children in noncitizen families, who benefit less from both programs, and children in families with no workers, who do not benefit from tax-related benefit programs.

IS A GOAL OF 50 PERCENT REDUCTION IN CHILD POVERTY REALISTIC?

Both the U.S. historical record and the experience of peer countries show that reducing child poverty in the United States is an achievable policy goal. Child poverty fell by nearly one-half between 1967 and 2016 (see Figure S-2).[10] Rates of deep child poverty declined as well over that period, both overall and across subgroups of children defined by race and ethnicity.

Historically, macroeconomic growth has fueled growth in wages and employment, which in turn has led to corresponding reductions in poverty. However, during the past several decades economic growth has not been shared equally across the income distribution. Wages have stagnated or declined for lower-skilled male workers since the early 1970s, while the wages of lower-skilled women have stagnated since 2000. **During the 1967–2016 period, child poverty rates varied with both business cycles and changes in social benefit programs. Government tax and transfer programs reduced child poverty modestly between 1967 and 1993, but they became increasingly important after 1993 because of increases in government benefits (mainly the Earned Income Tax Credit) targeted at the poor and near poor. Between 1993 and 2016, SPM poverty fell by 12.3 percentage points, dropping from 27.9 to 15.6 percent.**[11]

The United States spends less to support low-income families with children than peer English-speaking countries do, and by most measures it has much higher rates of child poverty. Two decades ago, child poverty rates were similar in the United States and the United Kingdom. That began to change in March 1999, when Prime Minister Tony Blair pledged to end child poverty in a generation and to halve child poverty within 10 years. Emphasizing increased financial support for families, direct investments in children, and measures to promote work and increase take-home pay,

---

[10] As defined by the U.S. Census Bureau, an SPM-based poverty measure that counts cash income, tax credits, and near-cash benefits (e.g., SNAP benefits) in its measure of household resources.

[11] Conclusion 4-4, Chapter 4.

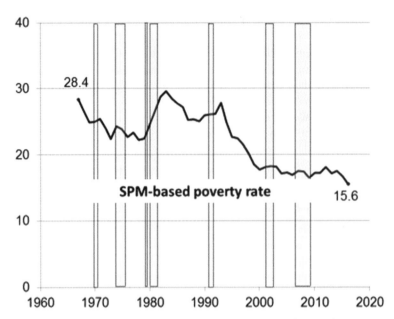

FIGURE S-2 Child poverty rates as measured by the Supplemental Poverty Measure (SPM), 1967–2016, using the Current Population Survey Annual Social and Economic Supplement (CPS ASEC).

NOTE: Shaded areas indicate recession years. Poverty estimates use the SPM with income that is not corrected for underreporting, as it is not feasible to correct income reporting in the CPS ASEC over the entire period shown. Corrections for underreporting account for the bulk of the 13.0% vs. 15.6% poverty rate differences shown in Figures S-1 and S-2.

SOURCE: Analyses commissioned by the committee and conducted by Christopher Wimer (2017).

the United Kingdom enacted a range of measures that made it possible to meet the 50 percent poverty-reduction goal by 2008—a year earlier than anticipated. More recently, the Canadian government introduced the Canada Child Benefit in its 2016 budget. According to that government's projections, the benefit will reduce the number of Canadian children living in poverty by nearly one-half.

REDUCING CHILD POVERTY IN THE UNITED
STATES BY HALF IN 10 YEARS

The heart of the committee's charge is to identify policies and programs that have the potential to reduce child poverty and deep poverty in the United States by half within 10 years. With hundreds of local, state, federal, and international anti-poverty program and policy models to choose from, the committee developed a set of criteria to guide its selection process. These included (1) the strength of the research and evaluation evidence; (2) likely reductions in the number of poor children; (3) the extent of child poverty reduction achievable within the subgroups with the highest child poverty rates; (4) cost; and (5) positive impacts on work, marriage, opportunity, and social inclusion.

The committee examined 10 program and policy options. Four of them are tied to work, three of them modify existing safety net programs, two come from other countries, and the final one modifies existing provisions relating to immigrants. It then formulated two variations for each of the 10 options, yielding 20 scenarios in all. The 10 options are as follows:

Program and policy options tied to work:
1. expanding the EITC;
2. expanding child care subsidies;
3. raising the federal minimum wage; and
4. implementing a promising training and employment program called WorkAdvance nationwide.

Modifications to existing safety net programs:
5. expanding SNAP;
6. expanding the Housing Choice Voucher Program; and
7. expanding the SSI program.

Options used in other countries:
8. introducing a universal child allowance (which, in the U.S. context, can also be thought of as an extension of the federal child tax credit delivered monthly instead of once a year); and
9. introducing a child support assurance program that sets guaranteed minimum child support amounts per child per month.

Modifications to existing provisions relating to immigrants:
10. increasing immigrants' access to safety net programs.

The committee's simulations showed that no single program or policy option that we considered could meet the goal of reducing child poverty by one-half. A $3,000 per child per year child allowance policy would produce the largest poverty reduction, and it would meet the goal of reducing deep poverty (50% of SPM poverty) by one-half.[12] A number of other program and policy options were also estimated to reduce child poverty substantially

---

[12] Conclusion 5-1, Chapter 5.

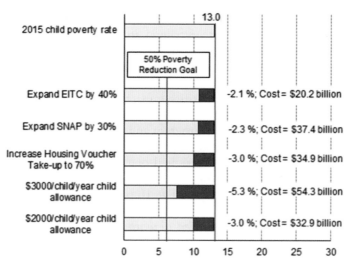

FIGURE S-3 Reductions in child poverty and cost of several policy and program options developed by the committee.

NOTES: Costs are based on provisions of the 2015 tax law applied to income for 2015. Incomes are corrected for underreporting. EITC = Earned Income Tax Credit, SNAP = Supplemental Nutrition Assistance Program.

SOURCE: Estimates from TRIM3 commissioned by the committee.

(see Figure S-3). **Three of them involve modifications to existing programs: the EITC, SNAP, and subsidized housing.**[13]

Policy makers may wish to balance poverty reduction against other policy goals, including boosting employment among low-income families as well as containing costs, keeping in mind the consequences of raising revenues to pay for the policies and programs that reduce the number of children raised in a poor family. As might be expected, **there is a strong positive relationship between cost and the number of children moved out of poverty. Almost all of the committee-developed program options that would lead to substantial poverty reductions were estimated to cost at least $20 billion annually.**[14]

The committee devoted significant effort to estimating how families might change their work effort in response to each of the policy and program options under consideration. It found considerable variation in the changes in employment and earnings resulting from the simulated implementation of the 20 program and policy options. **Work-based program**

---

[13] Conclusion 5-2, Chapter 5.
[14] Conclusion 5-3, Chapter 5.

expansions involving the Earned Income Tax Credit and the Child and Dependent Care Tax Credit were estimated to increase earnings by as much as $9 billion and employment by as many as half a million jobs. Programs such as child allowances and expansions of the housing voucher program were estimated to reduce earnings by up to $6 billion and jobs by nearly 100,000.[15]

The 20 program and policy options the committee examined generated different impacts in different subgroups of the population. **Although virtually all of these options reduced poverty across all of the subgroups considered, there were disproportionately large decreases in child poverty for Black children and children of mothers with low levels of education. Hispanic children and children in immigrant families benefited relatively less.**[16]

PACKAGES OF POLICIES AND PROGRAMS TO REDUCE CHILD POVERTY AND DEEP POVERTY

Since none of the committee's individual policy and program options met both of the 50 percent reduction goals—for both poverty and deep poverty—the committee developed the four program and policy "packages" shown in Table S-1 and assessed their expected impacts.

The *work-oriented package* attempted to capitalize on the fact that gains in steady employment and earnings are among the strongest correlates of escaping poverty. Accordingly, this package was focused exclusively on policies tied to paid employment by combining expansions of two tax credits (the EITC and Child and Dependent Care Tax Credit [CDCTC]) with an increase in the minimum wage and implementing the WorkAdvance Program nationwide. **Although combining these four programs was estimated to add a million workers to the labor force, generate $18 billion in additional earnings, and cost only $8.7 billion, the reduction in child poverty it was estimated to bring about was less than one-half of what is needed to meet the 50 percent poverty-reduction goal.**[17]

It was disappointing to conclude that this work-oriented package would be unable to achieve adequate reductions in child poverty, in light of the often-stated policy goal of moving low-income families from reliance on government assistance and toward greater participation in the labor force. Although states have been testing a number of new work-oriented programs, especially those including work requirements, most states have evaluated the new programs using weak methods that fall far short of the evidentiary standard set by the National Academies for its reports. Some of

---

[15] Conclusion 5-4, Chapter 5.
[16] Conclusion 5-5, Chapter 5.
[17] Conclusion 6-2, Chapter 6.

TABLE S-1 Components of the Four Packages and Their Estimated Costs and Impact on Poverty Reduction and Employment Change

		1. Work-oriented Package	2. Work-based and Universal Supports Package	3. Means-tested Supports and Work Package	4. Universal Supports and Work Package
Work-oriented Programs and Policies	Expand EITC	X	X	X	X
	Expand CDCTC	X	X	X	X
	Increase the Minimum Wage	X			X
	Roll Out WorkAdvance	X			
Income Support-oriented Programs and Policies	Expand Housing Voucher Program			X	
	Expand SNAP Benefits			X	
	Begin a Child Allowance		X		X
	Begin Child Support Assurance				X
	Eliminate 1996 Immigration Eligibility Restrictions				X
	Percentage Reduction in the Number of Poor Children	–18.8%	–35.6%	–50.7%	–52.3%
	Percentage Reduction in the Number of Children in Deep Poverty	–19.3%	–41.3%	–51.7%	–55.1%
	Change in Number of Low-income Workers	+1,003,000	+568,000	+404,000	+611,000
	Annual Cost, in Billions	$8.7	$44.5	$90.7	$108.8

NOTE: CDCTC = Child and Dependent Care Tax Credit, EITC = Earned Income Tax Credit, SNAP = Supplemental Nutrition Assistance Program.

the committee's research recommendations address the need for building a more solid and reliable body of evidence on current programs.

Our second package, the *work-based and universal supports package*, builds on the work-based package by combining expansions of two tax credits (the EITC and CDCTC) with a $2,000 child allowance designed to replace the Child Tax Credit. This package generates an estimated 36 percent reduction in poverty and 41 percent reduction in deep poverty, which also falls short of meeting the full 50 percent reduction goals. However, at a cost of $44.5 billion per year, and with increases of employment and earnings amounting to 568,000 jobs and $10 billion, respectively, it offers a potentially appealing approach to meeting policy goals that are often in competition with one another.

The *means-tested supports and work package* combined expansions of the two tax credits in the work-oriented package with expansions of two existing income support programs: SNAP (formerly known as food stamps) and housing voucher programs. **The committee estimates that this package of programs would in fact meet the goal of reducing both poverty and deep poverty by one-half, at a cost of $90.7 billion per year.** On balance, the work incentives associated with the two tax credits outweigh the disincentives arising from the income support programs: The package is estimated to add about 400,000 workers and generate $2.2 billion in additional earnings.

The *universal supports and work package* was designed to meet the 50 percent poverty-reduction goals by enhancing income security and stability while at the same time rewarding work and promoting social inclusion. The cornerstone of this package is a child allowance, but the package also includes a new child support assurance program, an expansion of the EITC and CDCTC, an increase in the minimum wage, and elimination of the immigrant eligibility restrictions imposed by the 1996 welfare reform. **This package of programs, which also meets the 50 percent poverty-reduction goals, is estimated to cost $108.8 billion.** The net effect of this full package of universal supports and work promotion policies is to increase employment by more than 600,000 jobs and earnings by $13.4 billion.

What Other Policy and Program Approaches Should Be Considered?

The committee considered a number of other program and policy ideas. One involved family planning. **Research evidence suggests that increasing both awareness of and access to effective, safe, and affordable long-acting reversible contraception devices reduces the incidence of unplanned births, which could in turn reduce child poverty.**[18] At the same time, the evidence was not strong enough to support a calculation of the likely magnitude of this poverty-reduction effect for the nation as a whole.

We also examined marriage promotion policies. Although increasing the proportion of children living with married or cohabiting parents, rather than single parents, would almost certainly reduce child poverty, whether and how policy can achieve this goal remains uncertain. Evidence from existing social programs is inconclusive and points to neither strong positive

---

[18] Conclusion 7-1, Chapter 7.

nor negative effects. In the early 2000s, an ambitious attempt to develop programs that would improve couple relationship skills, promote marriage, and improve child well-being failed to boost marriage rates and achieve most of their other longer-run goals.[19]

Similarly, evidence was insufficient to identify mandatory work policies that would reliably reduce child poverty. It appears that work requirements are at least as likely to increase as to decrease poverty. The dearth of evidence on mandatory work policies also reflects an underinvestment over the past two decades in methodologically strong evaluations of the impacts of alternative work programs.[20]

WHICH CONTEXTUAL FACTORS PROMOTE OR IMPEDE ANTI-POVERTY POLICIES AND PROGRAMS?

Any policies aimed at reducing child poverty will necessarily be implemented in complex societal and individual contexts, and these contexts can influence the policies' success. The committee identified six major contextual factors that policy makers and program administrators should consider when designing and implementing anti-poverty programs:

1. *Stability and predictability of income:* Because unstable and unpredictable income makes it difficult for families to juggle their everyday challenges, programs that provide regular income support—whether through tax credits, cash, or vouchers—may be more helpful to families if they provide adequate benefits at well-timed intervals.

2. *Equitable and ready access to programs:* Unnecessarily burdensome administrative procedures can discourage families—especially the most needy families—from applying for the income assistance benefits they are eligible to receive, and thus prevent them from receiving them at all.

3. *Equitable treatment across racial/ethnic groups:* Discrimination in hiring and employment may undermine policies that aim to increase or subsidize wages as well as policies that require beneficiaries to work. Similarly, housing discrimination reduces racial/ethnic minority families' access to and benefits from housing programs.

4. *Equitable treatment by the criminal justice system:* Involvement of a parent or other relative in the criminal justice system harms

---

[19] Conclusion 7-2, Chapter 7.
[20] Conclusion 7-4, Chapter 7.

significant numbers of low-income children, particularly minority children, both economically and in other ways.

5. *Positive neighborhood conditions:* Living in areas of concentrated poverty makes it difficult for parents to lift themselves and their children out of poverty. Supportive, thriving social networks and neighborhood conditions enrich family life, personal connections, and access to opportunities, yet too frequently the poor live in urban areas of concentrated poverty or are widely dispersed in rural areas with limited transportation and little access to employment, poverty-reduction programs, or community resources.

6. *Health and well-being:* Because physical and mental ailments, substance abuse, and domestic violence can undermine parents' ability to make sound decisions, care for their children, gain education, obtain and keep work, and support their households, anti-poverty programs that require participants to be employed in order to maintain eligibility or that have cumbersome eligibility requirements may be less effective for families with these issues.

SUMMARY AND NEXT STEPS

The committee's work has identified two program and policy packages that would enable the nation to meet the ambitious goal of reducing by half the number of poor children and children living in deep poverty. Other packages are also conceivable. **Both of the committee's packages involve combinations of program enhancements, some of which encourage and reward paid employment, while others provide basic income support to help cover the expenses incurred when raising children. Both are also quite costly in an absolute sense. They would require an investment of between $90 and $110 billion per year, although this cost is much lower than the estimated annual macroeconomic cost of child poverty, which is estimated to range from $800 billion to $1.1 trillion.**[21] A third package fell short of the full 50 percent poverty-reduction goal but, at $44.5 billion, cost considerably less and increased work and earnings.

The virtues of bundling work- and supports-oriented policy and program enhancements into packages are clear from the committee's analyses. No single modification we considered met the 50 percent poverty-reduction goals, and those that came close led more people to leave than enter the labor force. And while work-oriented enhancements, such as expanding the EITC or making the CDCTC fully refundable, would reduce child poverty at a relatively low cost, they would be much less effective at reducing the number of children living in deep poverty. The committee found that it is

---

[21] Conclusion 6-1, Chapter 6.

possible to combine the two approaches in a way that would meet both the poverty and deep poverty-reduction goals and, on balance, increase work and earnings among low-income families with children.

Assuming that stakeholders—Congress, federal and state agencies, and the public—agree that further reduction of child poverty is a priority goal for U.S. policy, the committee recommends that a coordinating mechanism be put in place to ensure that its report is followed up and that well-considered decisions are made on priorities for new and improved anti-poverty programs and policies. This mechanism should also ensure that the associated research and data needed for monitoring, evaluating, and further improvement are supported as well.[22]

In the view of the committee, the U.S. Office of Management and Budget (OMB) is the appropriate agency to coordinate the assessment of these conclusions and recommendations and to put together an action plan. It could do this by convening working groups of appropriate federal program, research, and statistical agencies to assess this report's conclusions regarding the program packages capable of reducing child poverty by half within 10 years of adoption. Further, the committee recommends that OMB convene working groups charged with assessing the report's recommendations for research and data collection to fill important gaps in knowledge about programs that are effective at reducing child poverty. A number of additional research recommendations embraced by the committee can be found in Chapter 9 of the report.

Acting on this report's conclusions and recommendations has the potential not only to reduce child poverty, but also to build a healthier and more prosperous nation.

---

[22] Recommendation 9-10, Chapter 9.

1

Introduction

From their infancy to their adolescence, children continuously develop capacities that are crucial for their physical and emotional well-being and their cognitive abilities, which in turn help to promote their success in school, their responsible behavior as adults, their eventual economic self-sufficiency, and lifelong health. These capacities, therefore, are the foundation of a well-functioning and prosperous society. Numerous studies suggest that a lack of adequate resources in childhood compromises the development of these capacities. Accordingly, the widespread poverty among American children today is cause for serious concern.

Using the Supplemental Poverty Measure (SPM) threshold of about $25,000 for a family of four, in 2017 the U.S. Census Bureau counted more than 11 million U.S. children—nearly one-sixth of all our children—living in families with incomes that fell short of that poverty line (Fox, 2018).[1] It also determined that 3.5 million of those children were living in "deep poverty," defined as having family resources less than one-half the SPM poverty line (Fox, 2018). As detailed in Chapter 2 of this report, child poverty rates are much higher for Black, Hispanic, and American Indian children than for White or Asian children. They are also much higher for children in single-parent families than those two-parent families

---

[1]See Tables A-2 and A-4 in *The Supplemental Poverty Measure: 2017* at https://www.census.gov/content/dam/Census/library/publications/2018/demo/p60-265.pdf. The number of children in deep poverty was calculated by multiplying the percentage of people under age 18 with family incomes below 50 percent of the SPM poverty threshold by the number of children under age 18 in the United States (estimated to be 73.7 million in 2017 by the U.S. Census Bureau).

and for children in families with no workers than for those in families with part- or full-time workers. By most measures, poverty among U.S. children is higher than in peer English-speaking countries such as Canada and Australia, and it is much higher than in most other industrialized countries.

A robust research literature (reviewed in Chapter 3) shows that children growing up in poverty fare much worse than other children. Differences favoring children in more affluent families are already evident in toddlers' and preschoolers' language, memory, self-regulation, and socioemotional skills, with corresponding differences observed in neural structure and function in the brain regions that support these skills. Children living in deep poverty have the worst outcomes among all children on important health and development indicators, such as blood lead levels, obesity, and a composite indicator of flourishing that measures children's mood, affection, and resilience (Ekono, Jiang, and Smith, 2016). By the time they reached their 30s, individuals whose families had incomes below the poverty line during early childhood completed two fewer years of schooling and were earning less than one-half as much income, on average, when compared with peers whose family incomes were at least twice the poverty line (Duncan, Ziol-Guest, and Kalil, 2010). Not all these differences can be attributed to poverty *per se*. Nevertheless, our review of the literature on the causal effects of childhood poverty (see Chapter 3) shows that the weight of the evidence indicates that income poverty itself causes negative child outcomes. This is especially the case when poverty begins in early childhood and/or persists throughout a large share of a child's life.

Whether a family's income is above or below a poverty threshold depends on parents' decisions regarding their own schooling, work, and marriage, as well on a host of structural factors such as the availability of work, housing, and public transportation, the prevalence of neighborhood crime, and institutional racism, all of which are well beyond the control of families. However, government programs also matter a great deal. Child poverty rates in the United States would be much higher were it not for programs such as the Supplemental Nutrition Assistance Program (SNAP), which provides nutrition assistance benefits to low-income individuals, the Earned Income Tax Credit (EITC), and the Child Tax Credit (CTC) (see Chapter 4).

If all countries' child poverty rates were measured solely by the earned income of parents, U.S. children would have poverty rates that fell in the middle of the rankings among peer English-speaking countries. Part of what drives our child poverty rates so much higher than those in peer Anglophone and other high-income nations is the much smaller fraction of U.S. Gross Domestic Product that is devoted to redistributive social programs (see Chapter 4). According to *Kids' Share 2018* (Isaacs et al.,

2018), spending on children younger than age 19 accounted for 9 percent of the U.S. federal budget in 2017. This figure, which does not include state spending on education, is projected to fall to 6.9 percent by 2028, while at the same time spending on adults under Social Security, Medicare, and Medicaid, which accounted for 45 percent of the budget in 2017, is projected to rise to 50 percent by 2028.

THE COMMITTEE'S CHARGE

Given the problems generated by child poverty in the United States and the demonstrated effectiveness of many child poverty programs, the omnibus appropriations bill signed into law in December 2015 included a provision directing the National Academies of Sciences, Engineering, and Medicine to conduct a comprehensive study of child poverty in the United States. Specifically, the study was to provide an evidence-based, nonpartisan analysis of the macroeconomic, health, and crime/social costs of child poverty, to study current efforts aimed at reducing poverty, and to propose recommendations with the goal of reducing the number of children living in poverty in the United States by one-half in 10 years.[2] This policy goal mirrors the aims of anti-poverty initiatives that have been undertaken in other English-speaking countries in the past two decades, most notably in the United Kingdom beginning in 1997 (Waldfogel, 2010; see also Chapter 4).

The heart of the charge issued by the U.S. Congress to the National Academies is the goal of reducing the number of children living in poverty in the United States by one-half within 10 years. Congress has requested objective analyses of the existing research on the poverty-reducing effects of major assistance programs directed at children and families and specific policy and program recommendations for accomplishing this goal.

Ad hoc committees appointed by the National Academies are guided by a statement of task that defines and constrains their work.[3] Committee reports are expected to address all of the issues raised in the statements of task but not to go beyond them unless the committee judges it absolutely necessary for carrying out the full scope of the statement of task. The statement of task for the present study is shown in Box 1-1.

In developing its list of policy and program proposals for reducing child poverty by half in 10 years, the committee considered existing federal programs as well as innovative programs developed by states and localities

---

[2] See Consolidated Appropriations Act, 2016, Pub.L. No. 114-113.

[3] This study's statement of task was developed jointly by staff members from Congress, the Office of the Assistant Secretary for Planning and Evaluation within the Department of Health and Human Services, and the National Academies, as well as researchers and policy makers with expertise in the reduction of child poverty.

BOX 1-1
Statement of Task

An ad hoc committee of experts will convene to conduct a consensus study of the costs of child poverty in the United States and the effectiveness of current efforts aimed at reducing poverty. The committee will review available high-quality research on current programs, with emphasis on evaluations that include benefit-cost analysis. Based on these analyses the committee will make recommendations for federal investment aimed at reducing the number of children living in poverty in the United States by one-half within 10 years. The committee will address five specific charges:

1. Briefly review and synthesize the available research on the macro- and microeconomic, health, and social costs of child poverty, with attention to linkages between child poverty and health, education, employment, crime, and child well-being.
2. Briefly assess current international, federal, state, and local efforts to reduce child poverty. The committee will provide an analysis of the poverty-reducing effects of existing major assistance programs directed at children and families in the United States, as well as relevant programs developed in other industrialized countries, such as the United Kingdom, Canada, and Ireland.
3. Identify policies and programs with the potential to help reduce child poverty and deep poverty (measured using the Supplemental Poverty Measure) by 50 percent within 10 years of the implementation of the policy approach.
4. For the programs the committee identifies as having strong potential to reduce child poverty, the committee will provide analysis in a format that will allow federal policy makers to identify and assess potential combinations of policy investments that can best meet their policy objectives.
5. Identify key, high-priority research gaps the filling of which would significantly advance the knowledge base for developing policies to reduce child poverty in the United States and assessing their impacts.

---

and in other countries, such as the United Kingdom and Canada. The scope of the programs the committee considered was broad. In addition to traditional anti-poverty programs, such as cash transfers, food and nutrition programs, and housing programs, the committee considered work support, health insurance, foster youth, juvenile and adult justice, and education and training programs.

For each program and policy option it developed, the committee attempted to estimate what impact it could have on reducing child poverty as defined using the SPM; how its poverty-reducing impacts would be distributed across demographic groups and across groups at three different levels of poverty: those at the poverty level; those in deep poverty; and

those in near poverty; and what would be the annual cost of implementing the program or policy at scale. To the extent possible, the committee
examined the sensitivity of the impacts of its policy or program proposals
to economic conditions, and it also considered other possible benefits the
proposals could provide for government and society, such as improvements
in child health, educational achievement, and welfare.

Because virtually none of the program and policy options we developed,
if considered individually, would meet the 50 percent poverty-reduction
goal, we also considered packages that would combine a number of policy
and program changes to meet that goal. These are presented in Chapter 6.
The task of designing these packages led us to identify interactions among
programs that could result in synergies or redundancies.

TEMPORAL AND OTHER CONSIDERATIONS ASSOCIATED WITH THE STATEMENT OF TASK

Timing is a key element of the committee's statement of task. The
policies and programs identified by the committee are intended to "help
reduce child poverty and deep poverty . . . by 50 percent within 10 years of
the implementation of the policy approach." This relatively brief, decade-
long interval focuses attention on actions that aim to quickly increase the
resources available to the families of poor children—programs and policies
such as tax credits or work requirements. Although programs such as
those that support early childhood education may boost family income by
enabling a mother to work, their main goals are to reduce poverty among
future—rather than current—generations of children. Accordingly, they fall
outside the committee's statement of task, although they may be important
to reducing poverty over the longer term.

Reducing Poverty or Building Children's Capacities and Health?

The concern that growing up in poverty compromises children's
opportunities to develop to their full potential provides a powerful motivation for seeking to reduce or even eliminate child poverty. However,
with children's development in mind, the goal of child poverty reduction
alone, whether in the short or long term, is limiting because it focuses all
our attention on family resources and ignores other important factors in
healthy development. An alternative goal to poverty reduction might be to
promote children's human capital, conceived broadly to include cognitive
and noncognitive capacities as well as physical and mental health, both
during childhood and into the adult years. Poverty reduction will help to
build children's human capital, but so too will attention to a much broader
range of factors that promote children's health and development, both

within the family and in the schools, neighborhoods, and other contexts of children's lives.

For example, a broader goal of human capital development might lead us to favor policies and programs to promote more nurturing homes or more effective school environments over equally costly programs and policies that would benefit children only by improving their material circumstances. This report responds to the committee's short-term poverty-focused congressional charge, but readers should bear in mind that adequate family material resources are but a single, albeit important, input for the healthy long-term development of children.

That said, programs targeting child poverty can build human capital in other ways. As an example, consider food assistance programs. Child poverty, as measured by the SPM, falls when benefits from a program like SNAP boost family resources. But, as explained in Chapter 3, the evidence also indicates that SNAP's predecessor program, food stamps, reduced the incidence of low birth weight among children born into low-income families and, if benefits were received during early childhood, improved that child's cardiovascular health in adulthood as well. When making decisions, policy makers might want to consider these kinds of human capital impacts along with the reductions in shorter-term child poverty that a specific program or policy might achieve. With that in mind, the committee's review of the poverty literature in Chapter 3 includes evidence on programs that both reduce child poverty and promote children's health development.

HOW THE COMMITTEE SELECTED PROGRAMS TO REVIEW

The heart of the committee's charge is to "identify policies and programs with the potential to help reduce child poverty and deep poverty . . . by 50 percent within 10 years." To identify these programs and policies, the committee sought suggestions from its members and invited outside testimony from experts in the field. These included experts from universities, from policy organizations, and from practitioner organizations and represented a diverse array of political perspectives. In addition to holding two public information-gathering sessions, the committee received 25 policy memos, 19 of them from the 40 individuals we invited to submit memos and 6 more that were unsolicited. The committee also drew on the expertise of its own members to develop a list of possible policies and programs that might meet the charge. In addition, the committee commissioned papers from experts in Medicaid and American Indian and Alaska Native (AIAN) children living in poverty.[4]

---

[4] These commissioned papers are available at http://www.nap.edu/25246.

Criteria for Selecting Programs and Policies

With hundreds of local, state, federal, and international anti-poverty program and policy models to choose from, the committee developed a set of criteria to guide its selection and then considered the strengths and weaknesses of each policy or program. The criteria are as follows:

1. Strength of the research and evaluation evidence
2. Magnitude of the reduction in child poverty
3. Child poverty reduction within high-risk subgroups
4. Cost of the program or policy
5. Impacts on the widely held values of work, marriage, opportunity, and social inclusion

The most important criterion was the *strength of the research and evaluation evidence* indicating that, if enacted, the policy would reduce child poverty in the short run. Here the committee gave preference to evidence from random-assignment program evaluations as well as methodologically strong "natural experiments," that is, those that examined the impacts of unanticipated changes in the timing and structure of policies on children and their families. To generate estimates of poverty reduction from the committee's program and policy ideas, it commissioned research from the Urban Institute's Transfer Income Model, Version 3 (TRIM3) microsimulation model.[5]

Second, with a target of reducing child poverty by one-half within 10 years, an obvious guiding criterion was the *magnitude of the reduction in overall child poverty*. The committee's statement of task speaks of reductions in both the number of poor children and the fraction of children whose family incomes are below the poverty line. Since these two indicators may differ slightly in the context of a growing population of children, the committee chose to focus on reductions in the rate of child poverty.

Discussions with study sponsors led the committee to consider the *distribution of poverty-reducing impacts across high-risk groups of children*, defined by such characteristics as race, location, immigration status, and age of parent, who have above-average levels of poverty. Accordingly, the committee assigned importance to anti-poverty programs with relatively larger impacts on the children in these groups.

The fourth criterion was the likely *cost of the program or policy*. We defined cost as the incremental budgetary expense after accounting for all of the secondary impacts of the program or policy change such as

---

[5] For more information, see http://trim3.urban.org/T3Welcome.php.

participation in other programs and changes in taxes paid resulting from changes in employment (for example, payroll taxes).

Fifth, the committee considered whether the program or policy was likely to *promote widely agreed-upon values*. Although not an explicit element of the statement of task, societal values have always figured prominently in debates over the nature of anti-poverty programs in the United States (Lamont and Small, 2008). We focus on four such values: work, marriage, opportunity, and social inclusion. None is without complications or qualifications. In the case of work, for example, expectations that program participants seek paid employment may be suspended in the case of a parent with an infant or a severely disabled child. In the case of marriage, relationship quality is also a criterion, so an abusive or violent relationship, for example, would not be valued. Considerations of social inclusion figure prominently in debates over whether programs should be offered universally rather than targeted to the neediest individuals (Garfinkel, Smeeding, and Rainwater, 2010). Universal programs are obviously more costly, but targeted programs can generate unforeseen incentives for people to qualify for or remain in programs, and recipients of targeted programs can run the risk of being stigmatized and confined to separate programs for the poor. In some cases, targeted programs that reward work, like the EITC, appear to generate a strong sense of social inclusion among recipients (Halpern-Meekin et al., 2015).

In keeping with the spirit of its charge, the committee omitted political feasibility from its list of criteria, although we understood that some policies and programs might be more politically feasible than others. As the charge from Congress directs, the committee endeavored to "provide an evidence-based, nonpartisan analysis."

The committee did not insist that all of the anti-poverty programs and policies it identified meet all of its five criteria. Strong research evidence was vital, but at the same time the committee recognized the inevitable tradeoffs in any policy or program proposal. Some of the approaches it chose were stronger on some criteria and weaker on others. The committee sought to balance the strengths and weaknesses of each proposal in light of the criteria taken as a whole.

CONSIDERATIONS IN ESTIMATING POLICY AND PROGRAM IMPACTS

At first glance, estimating poverty reductions for any given program may appear to be a straightforward calculation. If Program A provides, say, $5 billion in additional benefits to families with children, why not just conduct a simulation in which the incomes of recipient families are increased by the value of the added benefits and then determine how many families are raised above the poverty or deep poverty thresholds by the incremental income? A first complication is that in the course of reducing poverty, anti-poverty policies and programs can produce behavioral responses on the part of parents. For example, programs like the EITC boost the (after-tax) hourly earnings of some low-wage workers, which can induce them to work and earn more, and this would then increase the poverty-reducing impact of the EITC well beyond what is accomplished by the tax credits alone (Hoynes and Patel, 2017). Other programs can discourage work by reducing program benefits when earnings increase, or may discourage marriage by imposing rules that provide fewer benefits to married parents than to single parents. These kinds of behavioral responses are difficult to gauge but, as explained in Chapter 5, the committee, supported by the research literature, attempted to incorporate such responses in its estimates of child poverty reductions.

A second complication in some programs is that not every potential recipient will in fact take up the benefit. Housing vouchers are an obvious example, because a substantial number of families offered vouchers today are not able to use them. As explained in Appendix F, the TRIM3 micro-simulation model the committee used attempts to incorporate adjustments for behavioral responses and incomplete program take-up.

In some cases, the committee concluded that while a program met its criteria, it was not amenable to a quantitative policy simulation. One example is a program to promote the use of long-acting reversible contraception (LARC) devices, which have the potential to reduce poverty by delaying or reducing births into poor families; however, evidence on program take-up and impacts is fragmentary (See Chapter 7 for more information). Indeed, a number of promising small-scale demonstration programs have never been scaled up sufficiently to show whether key program features could be preserved if they were to be implemented across the nation or even across a single state. Expansions of the Medicaid medical insurance program are another example. The committee's literature review in Chapter 3 suggests that health insurance programs can improve child health, but estimating short-run impacts of program expansion on poverty reduction is complicated by the various ways poverty measures handle health care benefits and expenditures.

Therefore, Chapter 5 includes programs and policies for which evidence on behavioral responses, take-up, and other complicating issues is definitive enough to support a reasonably precise set of estimates of child poverty reduction. In Chapter 6, the committee anticipated that programs and policies interact and so they estimated synergies and redundancies across programs and policies in its examination of packages. Chapter 7 discusses programs for which the evidence base was sufficient to suggest considerable promise but not strong enough to support precise estimates of national impacts on child poverty.

Poverty reduction may benefit children in some families more than others. Parents coping with the stresses of unstable work schedules, personal or family illnesses and disabilities, uninvolved partners, neighborhood crime, low-quality schools, or discriminatory workplaces may find it difficult to engage in responsive parenting or longer-run planning on behalf of their children (McLoyd, 1998; Mullainathan and Shafir, 2013). These problems, in turn, may dilute some of the possible benefits of policy-induced increases in material resources. Because these contextual considerations are so important, and most are not part of the simulation model, the committee devotes an entire chapter (Chapter 8) to them and their implications for the committee's conclusions.

Finally, the expertise of committee members spans a wide range of disciplines and includes policy work in state and federal governments as well as in the nonprofit sector. All members share a commitment to the standards of evidence embraced by the National Academies but at the same time brought diverse political orientations to issues surrounding anti-poverty policies. For the programs featured in Chapters 5 and 6, it is important to understand that committee consensus on their inclusion was based *solely on the strength of the evidence base supporting them* and not on individual committee members' endorsements of the policies themselves.

ORGANIZATION OF THE REPORT

The report proper begins in Chapter 2 with a demographic portrait of child poverty in the United States. In this chapter we explain how poverty is measured and why the relatively new SPM, which our statement of task directs us to use, provides a somewhat different view of child poverty than the much older official measure. Child poverty rates are lower with the SPM than with the cash-based Official Poverty Measure (OPM). Over the past half-century, SPM-based child poverty has declined more rapidly than OPM-based poverty. In Chapter 2, we also compare child poverty in the United States and in peer anglophone countries. By and large, the United States has considerably higher rates of child poverty than these other countries, although the concentration of poor children among single-parent and nonworking families is broadly similar.

In Chapter 3, we respond to the first element of the statement of task by reviewing the literature on the consequences of child poverty, including macroeconomic, microeconomic, health, and social costs. The chapter explains how the technical sophistication of these literatures has increased markedly over time, as studies of the consequences of child poverty have progressed from an emphasis on correlational methods to the use of natural experiments that track how measures of child well-being change in response to large changes in policies such as the EITC and SNAP.

Chapter 4 responds to the second element of the statement of task by providing an assessment of current local, state, federal, and international efforts to reduce child poverty. As directed by the statement of task, the committee provides a separate look at poverty lines drawn to distinguish *deep* poverty (defined as below 50% of the SPM poverty line), *conventional* poverty (as defined by the SPM), and *near* poverty (the upper limit of which is defined as 150% of SPM poverty). At the federal level, a noteworthy distinction can be made between program impacts on the poverty of children whose families are near the poverty threshold and impacts on children in families well below the threshold. Tax-based programs such as the EITC move millions of children above the SPM-based poverty line but have much smaller impacts on the economic status of children in families with little taxable income. On the other hand, income-tested programs such as SNAP proved most effective at increasing the economic resources of the families of children in deep poverty.

Peer English-speaking countries provide some interesting examples of efforts to reduce child poverty, most notably the United Kingdom, where the government pledged in 1999 to halve child poverty within a decade and to eradicate it completely within two decades (Waldfogel, 2010). More recently, Canada enacted a very substantial child benefit for low-income families that is estimated to have reduced poverty among Canadian children by 5 to 6 percent within a year of its 2016 enactment (Sherman, 2018). These efforts are also reviewed in Chapter 4.

A crucial element in the committee's charge is to compose a list of promising anti-poverty policies and programs. As discussed above, we did so by drawing on the evaluation research literature as well as on ideas from individuals and groups representing a broad range of political orientations and experiences working in local and county governments, at the local social services and school systems level, and in state and federal government. Chapter 5 details the policy and program proposals that were amenable to a quantitative policy simulation to estimate net impacts. The summary section of Chapter 5 covers several issues that cut across the set of program and policy proposals the committee developed. Several are based on how the various proposals rank based on the selection criteria, for example, ranking proposals based on cost, degree of poverty reduction both overall and in key demographic subgroups, and impacts on employment.

In Chapter 6, the committee presents program packages that are projected to meet the 50 percent poverty-reduction goal set by its authorizing legislation. Chapter 7 describes additional programs and policies that were judged to be promising but for one reason or another were not amenable to precise estimates of impact on child poverty.

The focus of Chapter 8 is on contextual factors that affect child poverty—from program administration to discriminatory behaviors and criminal justice policies and practices. These factors are not typically incorporated in the simulation models, but they can have a profound effect on the success of programs, providing useful infrastructure in some cases and interfering with policy, thereby creating "leaky buckets," in others.

The final chapter (Chapter 9) summarizes the committee's recommendations and outlines a research agenda. Chapter 9 also discusses the importance of implementing high-quality monitoring and evaluation to measure progress and identify further steps.

Appendix A includes biosketches of committee members and project staff and Appendix B provides the agenda for the two public information-gathering sessions. Appendix C lists the individuals and organizations that submitted memos to the committee. Appendix D comprises the appendixes for Chapters 2, 3, 4, and 5. Appendix E includes the TRIM3 summary tables, and Appendix F contains the Urban Institute TRIM3 technical specifications.

Finally, a note on the overall organization of this report: As with all consensus reports produced by the National Academies, we provide evidence supporting all of our conclusions and recommendations. But in contrast to many of those reports, here the bulk of this evidence is presented in online appendixes associated with most of the chapters. Separating the detailed evidence in this way enabled us to write a shorter and, we hope, more accessible presentation of our analyses and conclusions. The online appendixes (D through F) are available on the National Academies Press webpage at http://www.nap.edu/25246 under the Resources tab.

REFERENCES

Duncan, G.J., Ziol-Guest, K.M., and Kalil, A. (2010). Early childhood poverty and adult attainment, behavior, and health. *Child Development, 81*(1), 306–325.

Ekono, M.M., Jiang, Y., and Smith, S. (2016). *Young Children in Deep Poverty*. Columbia University Academic Commons. Available: https://doi.org/10.7916/D86Q1X3.

Fox, L. (2018). *The Supplemental Poverty Measure: 2017*. Current Population Reports, P60-265. Washington, DC: U.S. Census Bureau.

Garfinkel, I., Smeeding, T., and Rainwater, L. (2010). *Wealth and Welfare States: Is America a Laggard or Leader?* New York: Oxford University Press.

Halpern-Meekin, S., Edin, K., Tach, L., and Sykes, J. (2015). *It's Not Like I'm Poor: How Working Families Make Ends Meet in a Post-Welfare World*. Berkeley: University of California Press.

Hoynes, H.W., and Patel, A.J. (2017). Effective policy for reducing poverty and inequality? The Earned Income Tax Credit and the distribution of income. *Journal of Human Resources*. doi: 10.3368/jhr.53.4.1115.7494R1.

Isaacs, J.B., Lou, C., Hahn, H., Hong, A., Quakenbush, C., and Steuerle, C.E. (2018). *Kids' Share 2018: Report on Federal Expenditures on Children Through 2017 and Future Projections*. Washington, DC: Urban Institute.

Lamont, M., and Small, M.L. (2008). How culture matters: Enriching our understandings of poverty. In A. Chih Lin and D.R. Harris (Eds.), *The Colors of Poverty: Why Racial and Ethnic Disparities Persist* (pp. 76–102). New York: Russell Sage Foundation.

McLoyd, V.C. (1998). Socioeconomic disadvantage and child development. *American Psychologist, 53*(2), 185.

Mullainathan, S., and Shafir, E. (2013). *Scarcity: Why Having Too Little Means So Much*. New York: Macmillan.

Sherman, A. (2018). *Canadian-style Child Benefit Would Cut U.S. Child Poverty by More Than Half*. Washington, DC: Center for Budget and Policy Priorities. Available: https://www.cbpp.org/blog/canadian-style-child-benefit-would-cut-us-child-poverty-by-more-than-half.

Waldfogel, J. (2010). *Britain's War on Poverty*. New York: Russell Sage Foundation.

2

A Demographic Portrait of Child Poverty in the United States

In light of the committee's charge to identify programs that would reduce child poverty in the United States by half within a decade, and to set the stage for the program and policy proposals we make later in this report, in this chapter we provide an overview of child poverty in the United States. We begin with a brief explanation of how poverty is defined. Next we offer an overview showing which demographic subgroups of U.S. children suffer the highest poverty rates today and how child poverty rates have changed over time. The chapter's final section compares the extent of child poverty in the United States and in peer English-speaking countries. The impacts of poverty on child development are discussed in Chapter 3, while contextual factors that reinforce poverty among low-income families are discussed in Chapter 8.

MEASURING U.S. CHILD POVERTY

"Poverty" typically refers to a lack of economic resources, but measuring it requires careful consideration of the types of economic resources to be counted as well as agreement on a minimum threshold below which a family's economic resources may be considered insufficient. In the 1960s, the U.S. federal government developed a method for identifying a threshold amount of household cash income below which a given household, and all related individuals living in that household, would be designated as "poor." (See Appendix D, 2-1 for a brief history of poverty measurement in the United States.) This Official Poverty Measure (OPM) of income poverty is still being used to determine social program eligibility as well as to track

BOX 2-1
How Much Child Poverty Is There?

Disagreements over how poverty should be defined and how the definitions should be applied using data from the federal statistical system have generated a wide range of poverty estimates. The Official Poverty Measure (OPM), published by the U.S. Census Bureau, estimates that 20 percent of U.S. children were poor in 2015. The Supplemental Poverty Measure (SPM), also published by the Census Bureau, estimates for the same year that 16 percent of children were poor. Our report uses the SPM, corrected for underreporting of some kinds of income in the Annual Social and Economic Supplement to the Current Population Survey, resulting in an estimated 13 percent child poverty rate in 2015. The rationale for using the SPM corrected for underreporting rather than using the OPM is detailed in Appendix D, 2-2—importantly, the SPM takes account of taxes, in-kind benefits, and nondiscretionary expenses (e.g., child support payments) and so is suited for the kinds of policy analysis that we were charged to undertake, and the corrected SPM accounts more completely for families' resources.

Based on an alternative approach to poverty measurement, using consumption rather than income to determine poverty status, a 2018 Council of Economic Advisers (CEA) report declared that "our War on Poverty is largely over and a success" (Council of Economic Advisors, 2018, p. 29). This alternative measure (based on Consumer Expenditure Survey data) produced just a 5 percent poverty rate for children in 2015, dropping to 4 percent in 2016 (Meyer and Sullivan, 2017, Table 3). While many economists believe that consumption is theoretically a better measure than income in determining how families are actually faring, the committee considered the SPM to be superior to currently available consumption-based poverty measures (see Appendix D, 2-3)—importantly, it is difficult to trace the effects of more generous assistance programs (e.g., a more generous child tax credit) on consumption, whereas it is straightforward to do so for income; also, it is difficult to evaluate the measure cited by the CEA given how its poverty thresholds were derived and updated, which resulted in contemporary thresholds and poverty rates that seem unrealistically low.

There are sources of error in both federal income and expenditure statistics, as well as more work that is needed to improve both income-based and consumption-based poverty measures. The committee concludes that the corrected SPM is the preferred measure for its purposes but also recommends investment in better data and measures (see Chapter 9).

long-term trends in poverty rates. Also available are poverty measures based on consumption instead of income. Nevertheless, the statement of task for our committee directed us to use the Supplemental Poverty Measure (SPM) of income poverty, which we adjusted for underreporting of some types of income in the survey data. Box 2-1 illustrates differences in estimated child poverty among these measures. For the reasons detailed in Appendix D, 2-2 (on income poverty) and Appendix D, 2-3 (on consumption poverty), we consider the adjusted SPM to be currently the best available approach to poverty measurement.[1]

Measuring Poverty with the Supplemental Poverty Measure

For this report, the committee was directed to use the SPM, which bases poverty thresholds on the expenditures U.S. families must make for food, clothing, shelter, and utilities (FCSU) plus a small additional amount for other needs (such as personal care, transportation, and household supplies). Expenditures are measured using the average of 5 years of data from the Consumer Expenditure Survey, with the poverty threshold set at the level of FCSU expenditures for family units with two children, which separates the bottom one-third of such families, ranked by FCSU expenditures, from the top two-thirds. For 2016, thresholds ranged between about $22,000 and $26,000 for two-adult, two-child families, depending on whether the family owned or rented its housing (Fox, 2017). The SPM thresholds are also adjusted for family size, using an equivalence scale, and for local cost-of-living differences in housing.[2]

The household resources considered are the sum of money income from all sources, including earnings and government cash benefits such as Social Security and Unemployment Compensation. A key difference between the OPM and SPM is that SPM-based household resources also include "near-cash" income benefits such as the Supplemental Nutrition Assistance Program (SNAP, formerly called food stamps) and housing subsidies, as well as benefits from many smaller programs. Deducted from household resources are child care and other work expenses, child support payments made, and out-of-pocket medical expenses (including insurance premiums).

Taxes paid, most notably payroll taxes, are also deducted from household resources, while refundable tax credits from programs like the Earned Income Tax Credit, Child Tax Credit, and the Additional Child Tax Credit are added to resources. As we show below, because government spending on tax credits and programs that provide "near-cash" (as opposed to cash) benefits have grown markedly over the past 50 years, conclusions about trends in child poverty largely depend on whether poverty is measured using the OPM or the SPM. Key differences between the official measure and the SPM are summarized in Table 2-1 and in Appendix D, 2-6.

---

[1] The large literature of poverty measurement, in the United States and abroad, addresses types of poverty measures and measurement issues that are not central to our charge—for example, the merits of deprivation indexes compared with income- or consumption-based indexes. We briefly note these other measures and measurement issues in Appendix D, 2-2.

[2] Appendix D, 2-4 provides a detailed explanation of how equivalence scales are used to adjust threshold levels. Appendix D, 2-5 discusses how cost-of-living adjustments (COLAs) are used in the SPM, including how geographic COLAs compensate for differences in the price of rental housing.

TABLE 2-1 Key Differences in Poverty Measure Concepts Between the Official Poverty Measure (OPM) and the Supplemental Poverty Measure (SPM)

Concept	Official Poverty Measure	Supplemental Poverty Measure
Measurement Units	Families (individuals related by birth, marriage, or adoption) or unrelated individuals	Resource units (official family definition plus any co-resident unrelated children, foster children, or unmarried partners and their relatives) or unrelated individuals (who are not otherwise included in the family definition)
Poverty Threshold	Three times the cost of a minimum food diet in 1963	Based on expenditures for food, clothing, shelter, and utilities (FCSU), and a little more
Threshold Adjustments	Vary by family size, composition, and age of householder	Vary by family size and composition, as well as geographic adjustments for differences in housing costs by tenure
Updating Thresholds	Consumer Price Index: all items	5-year moving average of expenditures on FCSU
Resource Measure	Gross before-tax cash income	Sum of cash income, plus noncash benefits that resource units can use to meet their FCSU needs, minus taxes (or plus tax credits), minus work expenses, out-of-pocket medical expenses, and child support paid to another household

SOURCE: Fox (2017).

The Census Bureau has published SPM-based poverty statistics every fall since 2011. Its most recent report (Fox, 2018) indicates that, in 2017, 15.6 percent of children lived in families with incomes below the SPM-based poverty line. That rate is lower than the 18.0 percent rate based on the OPM (Semega, Fontenat, and Kollar, 2017), owing primarily to the SPM's more comprehensive measure of household resources. For certain demographic groups other than children, poverty rates are higher when measured by the SPM as compared with the OPM. An example is the elderly, whose higher out-of-pocket medical payments are deducted from household resources in the SPM but not in the OPM. In addition, the 15.6 percent overall child poverty rate conceals considerable demographic and geographic variation, which we explore in subsequent sections of this chapter and Appendix D, 2-8 and 2-9.

The committee's statement of task directs it to identify programs and policies that reduce both SPM-based poverty and deep poverty by half in

10 years. To address deep poverty, the committee adopted a common definition, namely having resources below 50 percent of those used to define poverty based on the SPM. We also provide data on "near poor" children by including those with household resources below 150 percent of poverty. These three sets of thresholds are used consistently throughout this report.

Indirect Treatment of Health Care Needs and Benefits in the SPM

One important family need that is difficult to incorporate into poverty measurement is health care—both households' medical costs and the extent to which health insurance programs for low-income families help households afford them and shield families from falling into poverty as a result of health shocks. The importance of health care and health insurance has historically been recognized by making health insurance through Medicaid part of the package of benefits offered to low-income families such as those who qualified for Aid to Families with Dependent Children (the program that preceded Temporary Assistance for Needy Families [TANF]).

The OPM takes no account of health care needs or insurance benefits. It was developed before the life-extending advances of the past 50 years in medical treatments, such as treatment for childhood cancer, and before the expansion of health insurance to cover such treatments. However, for reasons detailed in National Research Council (1995; see also Remler, Korenman, and Hyson, 2017, and the discussion in Chapter 7), the SPM takes only a partial step forward. SPM thresholds do not include any estimated expenditure amounts for medical care, but the SPM definition of resources subtracts families' medical out-of-pocket expenditures for any insurance premiums, copayments, deductibles, or bills for uncovered care.[3] This deduction of medical out-of-pocket expenses puts some people below the SPM poverty line whom the OPM would not count as poor.[4] Conversely, reductions in out-of-pocket medical care costs—through Medicaid expansion, for example—will reduce measured SPM poverty rates, all else equal (see, e.g., Summers and Oellerich, 2013).

These adjustments in the SPM, despite being a step forward, still do not account for the full contribution of government health insurance programs to reducing poverty, particularly Medicaid and the Children's Health Insurance Program (CHIP), to the well-being of low-income

---

[3] The reason for subtracting medical out-of-pocket costs is that, unless low-income families receive free care from providers or qualify for insurance (e.g., Medicaid) that does not require the family to contribute toward their care, then obtaining health care will require out-of-pocket expenditures.

[4] For example, see U.S. Census Bureau, Table A-6: Effect of Individual Elements on SPM Poverty Rates: 2016 and 2015, September 21, 2017. Available: https://www.census.gov/library/publications/2017/demo/p60-261.html.

children and their parents. As we discuss in more detail in Chapter 7, one problem with the SPM approach is that families that defer medical care because they cannot afford it will appear to be better off than they really are. On the other hand, families who are covered by Medicaid but have little or no out-of-pocket expenses in a particular year will be appear to be worse off than they really are, because having insurance in case of future illness is much better than having no insurance at all. Nevertheless, both types of families are treated the same in this instance by the SPM. As we discuss in Chapter 7, a conceptually complete approach to the problem, one suggested in a paper by Korenman, Remler, and Hyson (2017) commissioned by the committee is to include the value of a basic health insurance plan in the poverty threshold and to include in resources the amount of government subsidy received by a family for insurance coverage. Korenman, Remler, and Hyson report some new estimates of the impact of Medicaid on poverty using this approach (see Chapter 7).[5]

Adjusting the Supplemental Poverty Measure Using the TRIM3 Model

Both the SPM and the OPM poverty rates are based on annual data from government surveys. To obtain these data, large national samples of households are chosen at random to participate in the Annual Social and Economic Supplement (ASEC) to the Current Population Survey (CPS), which is conducted by the U.S. Bureau of Labor Statistics. Consequently, both poverty rates are subject to bias when households misreport their incomes. The total amount of income that households report receiving from social programs in a given year can be checked against estimates of the total benefits that were paid out based on government administrative data. These comparisons often reveal large discrepancies, which have grown over time (Meyer, Mok, and Sullivan, 2009; Moffitt and Scholz, 2009; Wheaton, 2008). For example, household reports of food stamp income in the 1986 CPS accounted for 71 percent of administrative benefit totals, but in the 2006 CPS they accounted for only 54 percent of administrative benefit totals (Meyer, Mok, and Sullivan, 2009).

---

[5] We discuss the benefits of Medicaid and CHIP in improving child health in Chapter 3. An alternative approach to valuing health care for poor families is to create a medical care financial risk index; this is discussed in Institute of Medicine and National Research Council (2012). This is a useful perspective and adds extra information to how risk varies by income in the population, but it not easily incorporated into a poverty index (Korenman, Remler, and Hyson, 2018).

To address this underreporting, the committee relied on the Transfer Income Model, Version 3 (TRIM3).[6] TRIM3 is a microsimulation model that adjusts benefits from tax and transfer programs across households so that aggregated benefits reported by or assigned to households match the totals shown by administrative records.[7] Imputing or modeling government transfers in this manner increases the estimated incomes of many low-income households, and in some cases it raises them above a poverty threshold. As a result, the SPM-based child poverty rates presented in this chapter and used in the policy simulations in Chapters 4, 5, and 6 are almost always lower than SPM rates reported in Census Bureau publications.

The committee used the most recent version of the TRIM3 model that was available when the bulk of its simulation work was conducted. It is based on incomes in calendar year 2015 as reported in the 2016 ASEC. Importantly, that version of TRIM3 is based on program rules and federal and state tax codes that prevailed in 2015.[8] Given the potential importance of changes in federal income tax rules taking effect in 2018, the committee includes some data in later chapters showing that its key conclusions regarding child poverty reductions associated with program and policy proposals were largely unaffected by the recent changes in the tax code.

Figure 2-1 compares child poverty rates using the OPM and SPM, as well as using our modification of the SPM—labeled "TRIM3-SPM" in the remainder of this report—which is adjusted for underreported income. Some of the differences are stark. Based on the conventional definition of OPM poverty (household income below 100% of the applicable poverty line, with no adjustment for underreporting of income), nearly one-fifth (19.7%) of U.S. children—14.5 million children in all—were poor in 2015.[9] The addition of tax credits, in-kind income, and other adjustments in the

---

[6] TRIM3 is developed and managed by the Urban Institute with primary funding from the U.S. Department of Health and Human Services, Office of the Assistant Secretary for Planning and Evaluation. See http://trim3.urban.org/T3Welcome.php for more details about the TRIM3 model.

[7] TRIM3 corrects underreporting of TANF, SSI, and SNAP only. In the 2001 CPS, just 52% of self-employment income was reported, 59% of dividends, 70% of retirement and disability benefits (excluding Social Security and Workers' Compensation), and 73% of interest income. Unemployment Compensation is also underreported and not corrected by TRIM3. Discussions of these and other estimates are provided in Winship (2016, Appendix 3). In contrast, earnings are actually overreported at the bottom of the CPS earnings distribution when compared to administrative data (Bollinger et al., 2018; Hokayem, Bollinger, and Ziliak, 2015).

[8] TRIM3 baselines for a particular year always involve applying that year's rules to that year's data. The results are aligned and validated using the actual benefit and tax data for that year.

[9] The 19.7% figure for 2015 SPM-based poverty is considerably higher than the 18.0% figure reported above in Fox (2017), because the latter is based on 2016 incomes. Economic growth between 2015 and 2016 increased family income and decreased poverty rates among low-income families.

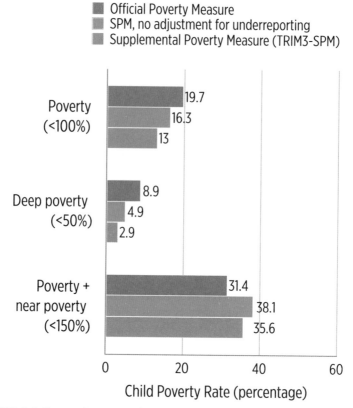

FIGURE 2-1 Rates of poverty, deep poverty, and near poverty for children using three alternative poverty measures, 2015.
NOTE: SPM = Supplemental Poverty Measure.
SOURCE: Commissioned by the committee, estimates are from TRIM3, which include adjustment for underreporting.

SPM drove the poverty rate down to 16.3 percent. Census Bureau publications use the "SPM, no adjustment for underreporting" poverty measure in their reports. But adjustments for underreporting reduced the SPM child poverty rate to 13.0 percent. Such large impacts from adjusting poverty rate estimates for underreporting of income—a 3.3 percentage-point reduction in the case of child poverty in 2015—led the committee to one of its research recommendations, presented in Chapter 9.

Although it produces a poverty count that is one-third lower than the official OPM-based count reported by the Census Bureau, our adjusted SPM-based poverty rate of 13.0 percent still represents 9.6 million U.S. children living in households with economic resources judged by the SPM to be inadequate. The congressional charge to the committee is to identify programs that—either alone or in combination—would lift nearly 5 million of these 9.6 million children out of poverty within 10 years.

A look at rates of deep poverty, defined by the percentage of children whose families' resource levels are less than half the poverty line, shows even more measurement sensitivity to the inclusion of taxes, in-kind income, and adjustments for underreporting. According to the OPM, which makes none of those adjustments, some 8.9 percent of children lived in deep poverty in 2015. When all three adjustments are made, the deep-poverty rate drops by more than two-thirds, to 2.9 percent. This 2.9 percent rate translates into 2.1 million children living in households with grossly inadequate resources. The congressional charge to the committee regarding deep poverty is identifying programs and policies that reduce this 2.1 million figure by more than 1 million children.

By contrast, when poverty is defined to include the "near poor"—those with incomes up to 150 percent of the poverty line—the 31.4 percent rate based on the OPM actually increases: It rises to 38.1 percent with no adjustments for underreporting and to 35.6 percent with adjustments. Substantial numbers of near-poor families pay more in taxes than they receive in tax credits, and they also incur additional work-related expenses. These factors combine to reduce net incomes and push some near-poor families below 150 percent of the SPM poverty line (Short and Smeeding, 2012).

> **CONCLUSION 2-1: The Supplemental Poverty Measure (SPM) has advantages over the Official Poverty Measure (OPM), the most important of which is that it includes government benefits, such as near-cash benefits and tax transfers, which are not included in the OPM. Current estimates of child poverty based on the SPM are substantially lower than those based on the OPM, and lower still when the SPM poverty estimate is adjusted for the underreporting of income in Census Bureau surveys. SPM-based estimates of poverty, combined with underreporting adjustments, indicate that 13.0 percent of U.S. children—more than 9.6 million children in all—were poor in 2015. In the case of deep poverty (defined by 50% of the SPM poverty thresholds), the corresponding rate is 2.9 percent, representing 2.1 million children.**

A DEMOGRAPHIC PORTRAIT OF U.S. CHILD POVERTY IN 2015

Policy makers and researchers share a broad interest in understanding the distribution of poverty as well as the impacts of poverty-reducing programs across demographic groups. In this section, we therefore discuss how child poverty varies according to six demographic factors: race and ethnicity, maternal schooling, family structure, adult work, immigration status, and parent's age. Throughout this section, except where defined otherwise, the poverty rates we cite are based on the TRIM3-SPM measure described in the previous sections.

Note that a complete set of poverty-rate estimates for selected demographic groups and definitions, provided in Appendix D, Table D2-5 and Appendix E, includes demographic breakdowns not discussed in this chapter. Also note that American Indian and Alaska Native status is not included because the ASEC data did not provide a sufficient sample size to support reliable estimates for this group; a discussion of American Indian and Alaska Native child poverty using other sources of data is provided in Appendix D, 2-7 and in a research recommendation in Chapter 9.

Race and Ethnicity

The U.S. population is becoming more racially and ethnically diverse, and the diversity of the child population is increasing even more rapidly than that of the population as a whole. As detailed in Appendix D, 2-8, the proportion of racial/ethnic minority children in the total U.S. child population increased from less than one-third in 1990 to nearly one-half in 2017 (U.S. Census Bureau, 2018). The Hispanic child population has shown especially dramatic growth, increasing from 9 percent in 1980 to 25 percent in 2017 (U.S. Census Bureau, 2018). According to the Census Bureau, as of 2013 racial/ethnic minority groups combined comprised more than 50 percent of the population of children under age 1 (Pew Research Center, 2016). By 2020, the entire child population is projected to include more Hispanics, Blacks, Asians, and other minorities than non-Hispanic Whites (U.S. Census Bureau, 2018).

Concerns over varying rates of child poverty across racial/ethnic groups are long-standing (Eggebeen and Lichter, 1991; Hill, 2018; Lichter, Qian, and Crowley, 2008). These differences are readily apparent in our TRIM3-SPM-based estimates, as shown in Figure 2-2. Hispanic children experience the highest rates of poverty and deep poverty. The poverty rates for Black (17.8%) and Hispanic (21.7%) children were more than double those of non-Hispanic White (7.9%) children.[10] Similar relative disparities are found for rates of deep poverty. If the line is drawn at 150 percent of SPM to include near poverty, more than one-half of all Black (50.6%) and Hispanic (54.6%) children, but less than one in four (22.9%) non-Hispanic White children, are counted as poor or near poor.

---

[10] The TRIM3-SPM poverty rate for children in the Other Races (non-Hispanic) category, which includes American Indian and Alaska Native, Asian and Pacific Islander, and multiracial children, is 11.1%.

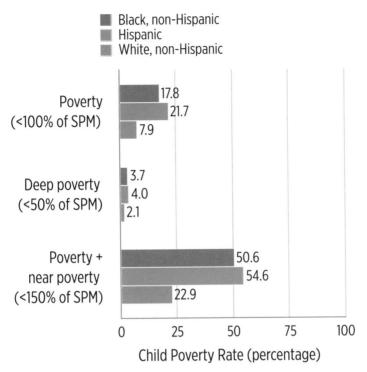

FIGURE 2-2 TRIM3-SPM rates of poverty, deep poverty, and near poverty for children by race and ethnicity, 2015.
NOTES: Based on TRIM3-SPM measurement. Fraction of all children in each group: Black, non-Hispanic–13.9%; Hispanic–24.7%; White, non-Hispanic–51.4%; Other–10.0%. SPM = Supplemental Poverty Measure.
SOURCE: Commissioned by the committee, estimates are from TRIM3, which include adjustment for underreporting.

Another way of describing poverty across racial/ethnic groups is by asking what share of a given poverty group comprises children from specific racial/ethnic categories. Such a breakdown of data is shown in Figure 2-3.[11] Again using our TRIM3-SPM-based estimates, non-Hispanic White children comprise a little more than one-half of all children but only about one-third of children in poverty or in deep poverty. The largest share of poor children are Hispanic. Similar shares of children in deep poverty are Hispanic and non-Hispanic White.

---

[11] Figure 2-3 also shows poverty shares for children living in persistently poor counties. These data are discussed below.

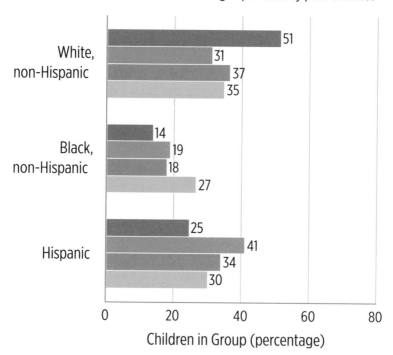

FIGURE 2-3 TRIM3-SPM estimates of the share of children by racial/ethnic category comprising poor children, deeply poor children, and children living in persistently poor counties, 2015.
NOTES: Children in other racial/ethnic groups are not shown. SPM = Supplemental Poverty Measure.
SOURCE: Commissioned by the committee, estimates are from TRIM3, which include adjustment for underreporting.

CONCLUSION 2-2: Poverty rates for children vary greatly by the child's race and ethnicity. Based on our Transfer Income Model, Version 3 Supplemental Poverty Measure poverty estimates, Black and Hispanic children have substantially higher rates of poverty and deep poverty than non-Hispanic White children. Hispanic children constitute the largest share of poor children and nearly as large a share of deeply poor children as non-Hispanic Whites.

Education of Parents

Adults' educational attainment is a strong correlate of their poverty status (National Academies of Sciences, Engineering, and Medicine, 2017; Wood, 2003). Completing more schooling is associated with higher rates of employment, higher earnings, better health, and a greater chance of having a spouse or partner, all of which are in turn associated with higher household income (Child Trends Data Bank, 2016). Figure 2-4 shows that child poverty rates are inversely related to the education level of the parents. Based on the TRIM3 model, one-third of children whose parents dropped

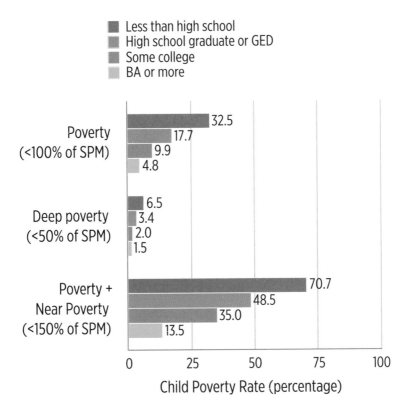

FIGURE 2-4 TRIM3-SPM rates of poverty, deep poverty, and near poverty for children by education level of parents, 2015.
NOTES: Fraction of all children in each group: Less than high school–12.4%; HS grad or GED–24.4%; Some college–29.0%; BA+–33.9%; Other–0.2%. SPM = Supplemental Poverty Measure; BA = Bachelor's degree; GED = General Educational Diploma.
SOURCE: Commissioned by the committee, estimates are from TRIM3, which include adjustment for underreporting.

out of high school are living below the 100 percent SPM poverty line and more than two-thirds (70.7%) of these children are within 150 percent of the SPM poverty line.

Family Composition

Family structure has grown increasingly diverse over recent decades (Furstenberg, 2014); for example, more than 40 percent of children today are born to unmarried parents (Martin et al., 2018) and more than one-half of children will spend some of their childhood not living with both of their biological parents (McLanahan and Jencks, 2015). Although most unmarried biological parents are living together when their child is born, nearly half of these couples will separate before that child's 5th birthday (Kennedy and Bumpass, 2008). Children born to unmarried parents may experience several different family structures over the course of their childhoods, such as living with a step-parent, with a grandparent, or in single-parent households (Manning, Brown, and Stykes, 2014). The proportion of children in single female-headed households is substantially higher for Black children (57%) than for either White (18%) or Hispanic (32%) children (National Center for Education Statistics, 2018).

For children living with both biological parents, our TRIM3 estimates find that poverty rates are less than one-half those of children with other family structures (see Figure 2-5). But even given the economic advantages of having two potential earners in the household, more than one in four (27.5%) children living with their two biological parents have family incomes below the 150 percent (near-poor) poverty line. Children living with a single parent or with neither biological parent (including foster children) have the highest rates of poverty and deep poverty.

Workers in the Household

Nearly four-fifths of all children live in families with at least one full-time working adult and, as shown in Figure 2-6, the TRIM3 SPM poverty rates for these children (6.5%) are correspondingly low. The poverty rates among children living with a part-time, as opposed to full-time, worker are correspondingly higher. By far the highest child poverty rates are observed for the relatively small fraction (6.3%) of children living in households with no workers: nearly one-quarter (22.3%) of these children are in deep poverty, three-fifths (61.5%) are below the poverty line, and the vast majority (90.8%) are below the 150 percent near-poverty line.

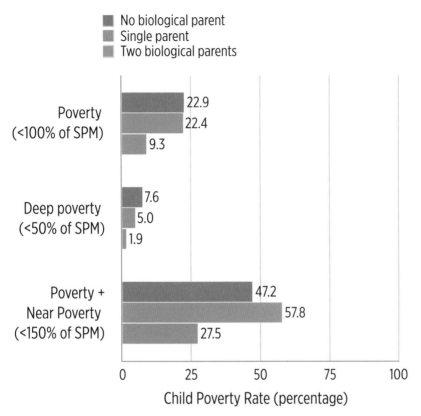

FIGURE 2-5 TRIM3-SPM rates of poverty, deep poverty, and near poverty for children, by family composition, 2015.

NOTES: Fraction of all children in each group: No biological parent–4.6%; Single parent–23.6%; Two biological parents–71.8%; Other–0.1%. SPM = Supplemental Poverty Measure.

SOURCE: Commissioned by the committee, estimates are from TRIM3, which include adjustment for underreporting.

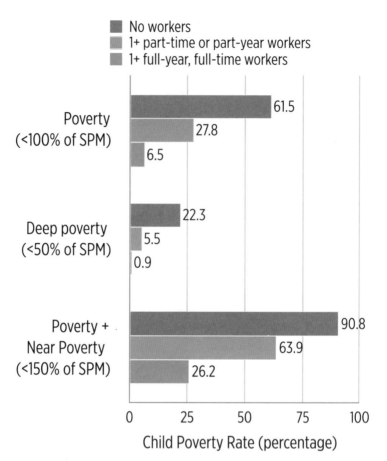

FIGURE 2-6 TRIM3-SPM rates of poverty, deep poverty, and near poverty for children, by number of working adults in household, 2015.
NOTES: Fraction of all children in each group: No workers–6.3%; 1+ part-time or part-year worker–14.1%; 1+ full-year, full-time worker–79.6%. SPM = Supplemental Poverty Measure.
SOURCE: Commissioned by the committee, estimates are from TRIM3, which include adjustment for underreporting.

Immigration Status

Children in immigrant families, defined as those with at least one foreign-born parent, represent about one-quarter of all children (Woods and Hanson, 2016).[12] The TRIM3 SPM poverty rate of children in immigrant families (20.9%) is twice as high as that of children in nonimmigrant families (9.9%) (Appendix D, Table D2-6). The majority of children in immigrant families are U.S. citizens: Some 88 percent of all children in all types of immigrant households are citizens, and 79 percent of children living in households with members who are unauthorized immigrants are citizens. The immigrant status of their families is associated with a higher risk of poverty (Capps, Fix, and Zong, 2016; Migration Policy Institute, 2017; Woods and Hanson, 2016).

The relationship between poverty, citizenship, and immigration status is shown in Figure 2-7 and Appendix D, Table D2-6, again based on the TRIM3-SPM model. Children living in households in which all members are citizens have a poverty rate of 10.2 percent, nearly 3 percentage points below the 13.0 percent overall child poverty rate. By contrast, living in households with noncitizens—particularly unauthorized immigrants—is associated with higher poverty rates, even for children who are themselves U.S. citizens.

Child Citizenship

When the household includes recent or unauthorized immigrants, the poverty rate among noncitizen children is even higher: 31.8 percent and 33.3 percent, respectively. Citizenship for the child appears to buy very little in the way of poverty reduction if other household members are unauthorized: 31.5 percent of citizen children whose households have at least one unauthorized resident are poor, as are 24.7 percent of citizen children whose households have at least one recent immigrant. However, child citizenship is associated with a much lower rate of deep poverty: 6.4 percent versus 15.2 percent, respectively, for citizen versus noncitizen children, in both cases living with unauthorized household members.

---

[12] In the TRIM3 analyses, a child is considered to *have an immigrant parent* if he or she has at least one biological, adoptive, or stepparent that was born in another country. A *recent immigrant* is defined as a person entering as a legal permanent resident within the last 5 years. Children are classified by their own status. For example, in the case of an SPM unit containing unauthorized immigrant parents, an unauthorized immigrant child, and a native-born citizen child, the unauthorized immigrant child would be categorized as "Child is a noncitizen, unit contains unauthorized immigrant" and the native-born child would be classified as "Child is a citizen, unit contains unauthorized immigrant."

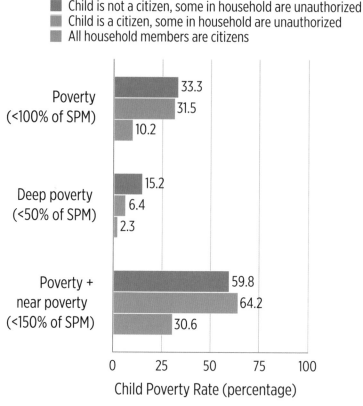

■ Child is not a citizen, some in household are unauthorized
■ Child is a citizen, some in household are unauthorized
■ All household members are citizens

FIGURE 2-7 TRIM3-SPM rates of poverty, deep poverty, and near poverty for children, by citizenship status of child and adults in household, 2015.
NOTE: Fraction of all children in each group: Child is not a citizen, some in household are unauthorized–1.1%; Child is a citizen, some in household are unauthorized–6.9%; All household members are citizens–81.5%; Other–10.0%.
SOURCE: Commissioned by the committee, estimates are from TRIM3, which include adjustment for underreporting.

Age of Parent

Our final demographic dimension is the age of the parent, defined as the age of the biological parent, adoptive parent, or stepparent if present.[13] Children born to younger mothers are more likely to live in poverty (Mather, 2010). On average, maternal age at first birth has been increasing (Mathews and Hamilton, 2016), and over the last three decades births to teen

---

[13] Age of parent is determined first by asking the mother, if present. If the mother is not present, then the biological, adoptive, or stepfather (if present) is asked.

mothers have declined very significantly—by more than 64 percent (Martin, Hamilton, and Osterman, 2017). Despite these trends, in 2015 more than one-quarter of children were born to mothers under age 25, and racial/ethnic minority children were more likely than their White counterparts to be born to young mothers (Martin, Hamilton, and Osterman, 2017).

The poverty risk for living with a younger parent (which we define here as under age 25) is readily apparent in Figure 2-8; nearly one-quarter (23.8%) of children living with a young parent fall below the 100-percent-of-SPM

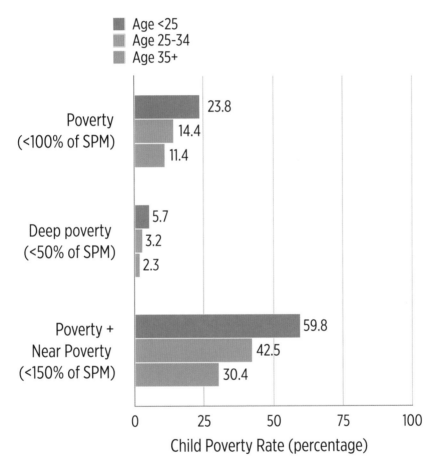

FIGURE 2-8 TRIM3-SPM rates of poverty, deep poverty, and near poverty for children, by age of parent, 2015.
NOTE: Fraction of all children in each group: Age 35+—64.4%; Age 25–34—30.8%; Age <25—4.5%; Other—0.2%.
SOURCE: Commissioned by the committee, estimates are from TRIM3, which include adjustment for underreporting.

poverty line.[14] Nearly three-fifths of children with a young parent live in families with incomes less than 150 percent of the poverty line.

> CONCLUSION 2-3: Poverty rates for children vary greatly depending on other characteristics of parents and households. Higher poverty rates are associated with low levels of parental schooling and with living with a single parent, no parent, or a young parent. Poverty is more prevalent when both children and other family members are not citizens, although these poverty rates improve only a little when children are U.S. citizens but living in households with family members who are unauthorized. Children in families with no workers have by far the highest rates of poverty and near poverty, but even full-time work is insufficient to lift one-quarter of children living with full-time workers above the 150 percent Supplemental Poverty Measure poverty line.

Geographic Distribution of Poverty

Child poverty rates also vary across communities. As documented in Chapter 8, the experience of child poverty in a community with good schools, resources for families, and pathways for economic mobility may be different than the experience in a community that has suffered from persistent poverty for decades.

To examine the geographic distribution of both point-in-time and persistent poverty, we use county data based on the OPM, because SPM county-level estimates are not available (see Appendix D, 2-9).[15] For the point-in-time analyses, we classified counties as poor if 20 percent or more of children under age 18 lived in families with incomes below poverty thresholds in 2015. As shown in Figure 2-9 and Appendix D, 2-9, nearly all counties in the South and Southwest and many counties in the West and the Appalachian region had child poverty rates of 20 percent or higher in 2015. Relative to the total number of children of a given race and ethnicity, the

---

[14] Note this is not the age at birth but the age of the parent at the time of the survey. As shown in the notes to Figure 2.8, only 4.5% of all parents of children less than 18 are to parents of age less than 25.

[15] The committee assessed the lowest geographic disaggregation level that can be achieved with the SPM and found that there are no county or other substate (besides metropolitan area) SPM estimates. This is primarily because the CPS ASEC is the primary dataset used for SPM, and its sample size does not allow estimates for such small geographic areas. Because of its larger sample size, the ACS is the most likely alternate dataset, but it is missing critical variables used in calculating SPM. While there has been some work, primarily Renwick (2015), has experimented with using the CPS ASEC to inform ACS imputations of missing variables so that the ACS can hypothetically be used to estimate substate SPM; in the end those researchers created only state-level (single-year) estimates and reached no conclusions about substate level SPM estimates.

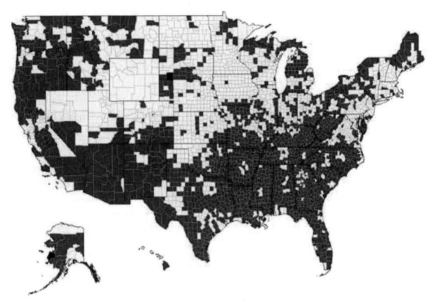

Counties with OPM Point-in-Time Child Poverty Rates 20 Percent or Higher, 2015

FIGURE 2-9 Counties with OPM point-in-time child poverty rates 20 percent or higher, 2015.
NOTE: OPM = Official Poverty Measure.
SOURCE: Estimates by the committee from U.S. Population Estimates, 2016 Vintage, Census Bureau; data as of July 1, 2015. 2015 county child poverty rates from Census Small Area Income and Poverty Estimates (SAIPE) Program data.

risk of residing in a point-in-time poor county is highest among Black children (70.8%), followed by American Indian and Alaskan Native (70.6%), Hispanic (65.0%), and non-Hispanic White children (46%).

We also examined the geographic distribution of persistently high child poverty. A county was classified as having persistently high child poverty if 20 percent or more of its children were classified as OPM-poor over four decades: in the 1980, 1990, and 2000 decennial censuses and in the 2007–2011 American Community Survey 5-year estimates (see Appendix D, 2-9). Some 10.2 million children (13.9% of all children) lived in persistently poor counties in 2015. The 10.2 million figure includes 3.6 million White children, 3.1 million Hispanic children and 2.7 million Black children (refer to Figure 2-3). The risk of living in a persistently poor county is highest among American Indian and Alaska Native children (36%) followed by Black (27%), Hispanic (17.1%), non-Hispanic White (9.4%), and Asian and Pacific Islander (8.2%) children (Appendix D, Figure D2-7).

Persistently high poverty is more geographically concentrated than point-in-time poverty (see Figure 2-10). The South and Northeast regions have the highest proportion of children in persistently poor counties (22.1% and 17.3%, respectively; see Appendix D, Figure D2-9) and account for the vast majority of children (81.3%) living in those counties. Although not readily apparent in Figure 2-10, due to their small land mass the persistently poor counties in the Northeast, which include the cities of New York, Philadelphia, Newark, and Boston, account for 2.1 million children.

CONCLUSION 2-4: Poverty rates for children vary considerably by geographic location. About one in seven children live in counties with persistently high child poverty (Official Poverty Measure child poverty rates always above 20% since 1980). The South and several large metropolitan areas in the Northeast regions have the highest proportions of children in counties with persistently high child poverty.

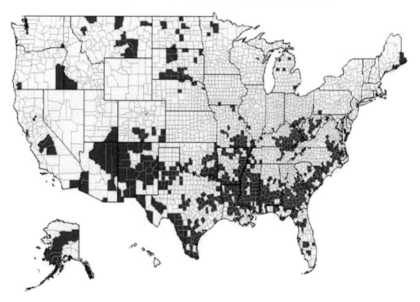

FIGURE 2-10 Counties with Official Poverty Measure (OPM) child poverty rates 20% or higher in 1980, 1990, 2000, and 2008–2012.
SOURCE: Estimates by the committee from U.S. Population Estimates, 2016 Vintage, Census Bureau; data as of July 1, 2015. 2015 county child poverty rates from Census Small Area Income and Poverty Estimates (SAIPE) Program data.

HISTORICAL TRENDS IN CHILD POVERTY, 1967–2016

Historical trends in the OPM are published annually by the Census Bureau. As shown in Figure 2-11, they suggest that virtually no progress has been made in reducing child poverty between the late 1960s and today. If anything, child poverty rates as measured by the OPM were a little higher in 2016 (18.0%) than they had been 50 years before, in 1967 (16.6%; U.S. Census Bureau, 2018, Table 3).

Given the growth in near-cash benefits over this period, it is possible that child poverty rates based on the SPM, which counts most near-cash benefits as income, and the OPM, which does not, may show different trends. A first step in investigating whether this is the case is to construct a consistent time series of SPM-based rates, as shown in Figure 2-11 (Hardy, Smeeding, and Ziliak, 2018).

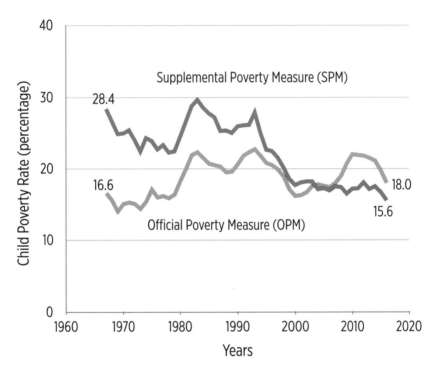

FIGURE 2-11 OPM and SPM child poverty rates, 1967–2016.
NOTE: The SPM poverty measure is anchored in 2012 living standards and adjusted back to 1967 using the Consumer Price Index. Income data are not adjusted for underreporting.
SOURCE: Original analyses commissioned by the committee from Christopher Wimer (2017, October).

Two complications arise. First, because some TRIM3 adjustments are not available for most of the years we examined, the analyses in this section are based on Current Population Survey data that are not adjusted for income underreporting. A second complication is the difficulty of defining SPM-based poverty in a consistent way across the half century between 1967 and 2016. Recall that the SPM uses a poverty threshold based on the 33rd percentile of the distribution of core living expenses. Thus, the poverty threshold in the SPM is tied to changes in the standard of living of this low-income group. In contrast, the OPM poverty thresholds are adjusted over time only by rates of inflation.

Wimer et al. (2013) have estimated annual SPM thresholds going back in time to 1967, using available ASEC historical data. They have also constructed SPM thresholds that are anchored in current living standards and adjusted them backward in time only by inflation, as well as thresholds that are anchored in 1967 and then adjusted forward only by inflation. Though the SPM was designed to be a relative measure, whether to measure poverty in relative or absolute terms for purposes of historical analysis is an unsettled question. We use an anchored SPM (an absolute measure) here and in our analysis in Chapter 4 of the effects of changes in the labor market, family structure, and government programs on child poverty over time, because this measure allows us to abstract from changes in living standards. We anchor the measure in recent (2012) living standards to make it as comparable as possible with the TRIM3-SPM poverty estimates presented elsewhere in this report, which focuses on the current period.[16] Appendix D, 2-10 provides further discussion and illustration of child poverty trends using anchored and unanchored SPM measures.

Figure 2-11 shows both OPM- and anchored SPM-based child poverty rates from 1967 to 2016. As noted before, over this period OPM-based child poverty rates increased from 16.6 percent to 18.0 percent, while the anchored SPM indicates that child poverty actually *decreased by nearly half*—from 28.4 percent to 15.6 percent.[17] SPM poverty rates are higher than OPM poverty rates in the earlier years of the period in part because of the higher SPM threshold and (to a lesser extent) because during that

---

[16] These estimates were taken from a study (Wimer, 2017) commissioned by the committee for this report. Due to the relative nature of the SPM, historical changes in poverty could be at least partly due to changes in poverty thresholds (Wimer et al., 2013). Anchored measures of poverty apply current poverty thresholds to historic data by adjusting for inflation to isolate changes in family resources from changes in living standards. For more information, refer to Wimer et al. (2013).

[17] As explained in Fox et al. (2015), an SPM poverty line anchored in 1967 living standards and subsequently adjusted for inflation annually yields estimates of poverty reduction that are similar to estimates anchored in current living standards and adjusted backward for inflation, like those reported in the figures and text.

period the tax system took more income from poor families with children than these families received from government as in-kind benefits. As we show in Chapter 4, much of the decline in SPM-based child poverty is due to increasingly generous government benefits. Because it does not count benefits from the Earned Income Tax Credit, SNAP, public housing, and housing vouchers, OPM-based child poverty rates include only cash transfers (like Supplemental Security Income [SSI] and the cash portion of TANF) and therefore fail to consider the largest portion of the social safety net. Consequently, trends in the OPM are not useful for drawing conclusions regarding changes in the well-being of children in the United States.

An alternative is to construct SPM poverty thresholds based on changes in living standards rather than inflation; this "historical SPM" also shows a substantial decrease in child poverty, but the decrease is only about half as large, or 25 percent (see Figure 2-15 in Appendix D, 2-10). The decrease in poverty is smaller because living standards at the 33rd percentile of the income distribution have increased over the last half-century by more than the cost of living. Figure 2-12 depicts historical trends in anchored SPM-based child poverty, near poverty, and deep poverty rates. As with the basic (under 100%) SPM poverty measure, shown in Figure 2-11, deep poverty rates had fallen by 2016 to nearly half of their 1967 levels. In the case of the line drawn at 150 percent of SPM, poverty rates fell by nearly 40 percent between 1967 and 2016. Strikingly, most of these three sets of declines occurred prior to the year 2000. It is also worth noting that SPM-based poverty rates declined for all three racial/ethnic groups: for Whites, Blacks, and Hispanics. (Historical trends in OPM- and SPM-based child poverty rates by race and ethnicity between 1970 and 2016 are presented in Appendix D, 2-8.)

CONCLUSION 2-5: When measured by the Official Poverty Measure, poverty rates changed very little between 1967 and 2016; by contrast, when measured by the anchored Supplemental Poverty Measure (SPM), they fell by nearly half over that period, due to the increases in government benefits. SPM-based rates of deep and near child poverty declined as well over the period, both overall and across subgroups of children defined by race and ethnicity.

CHILD POVERTY IN THE UNITED STATES AND OTHER ENGLISH-SPEAKING DEVELOPED COUNTRIES

Over the past several decades, researchers have developed the capacity to analyze child poverty across countries by using comparable microdata. The two most widely used sources of international data are the Luxembourg Income Study (LIS), which allows analysts to work with the microdata, and

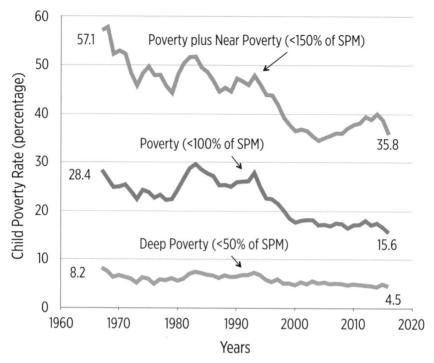

FIGURE 2-12 Trends in Supplemental Poverty Measure (SPM) rates of poverty, deep poverty, and near poverty for children, 1967–2016.
NOTE: The SPM poverty measure is anchored in 2012 living standards and adjusted back to 1967 using the Consumer Price Index. Income data are not adjusted for underreporting.
SOURCE: Original analyses commissioned by the committee from Christopher Wimer (2017, October).

the Organisation for Economic Co-operation and Development (OECD) poverty and income database, which is more up to date but provides only country-level statistics and relative poverty measures.

Early staff and committee discussions with the sponsors of this report revealed a particular interest in comparing child poverty rates across a subset of OECD English-speaking nations: Australia, Canada, Ireland, the United Kingdom, and the United States. These countries have income support systems that differ from those found in central and northern Europe, including Scandinavia (Esping-Anderson, 1990). Three of them are large and diverse nations (Australia, Canada, and the United States), while the other two (Ireland and the United Kingdom), though smaller in size, still exhibit some geographic and ethnic heterogeneity. We gauge the comparative effectiveness of anti-poverty programs across these same countries in Chapter 4.

Most published international poverty comparisons use a poverty line defined by a given fraction of each country's median income, such as 40, 50, or 60 percent.[18] This is a *relative* poverty concept because it measures the fraction of families who have income that is low relative to overall income in the country. Families in a high-income, industrialized country might all have incomes that are higher than the incomes of families in a low-income country, but relative poverty could still be high in the former if the lower-income families there were "further away" from the country's overall median income.[19]

OECD poverty statistics are typically based on a poverty line drawn at 50 percent of median income, a line we will call "OECD-50." For this measure, household resources include money income and near-cash benefits minus taxes (including tax credits). Estimates of child poverty using the OECD-50 for the United States and the four English-speaking comparison countries are shown in the top bars of Figure 2-13 (labeled "Relative Poverty (OECD-50)"). Rates of child poverty using this relative measure are much higher in the United States than in these peer countries—more than twice as high as in Ireland and nearly 5 percentage points higher than in Canada, the country with the second-highest child poverty rates.

To explore the sensitivity of cross-national child poverty rates to the specific definition of child poverty, Figure 2-13 also shows poverty rates using two other measures. The first uses LIS data to set the poverty threshold for each country at the same percentile of the country's income distribution as the SPM threshold in the U.S. income distribution. Since that point is at the 40th percentile of the income distribution, we label this measure "Relative Poverty (LIS-SPM-40)." Drawing the line at the 40th percentile lowers child poverty rates, but the country rankings are similar to those found with the OECD-50 measure of relative poverty.

The third measure is based on what is sometimes called "absolute" poverty. Absolute poverty measures the fraction of families in a country whose incomes fall below some fixed amount, regardless of how affluent the country is. For this reason, high-income countries will tend to have lower absolute poverty rates than lower-income countries. In our case, the dollar levels of the U.S. SPM poverty thresholds are translated into poverty thresholds in other countries using the purchasing power of the dollar relative

---

[18] As explained in Appendix D, 2-2, the income data and thresholds are also adjusted for family size.

[19] The SPM poverty measure is also relative, but it is based on the distribution of expenditures rather than income, and is set at a given (33rd) percentile of the expenditure distribution rather than at a fraction of the median.

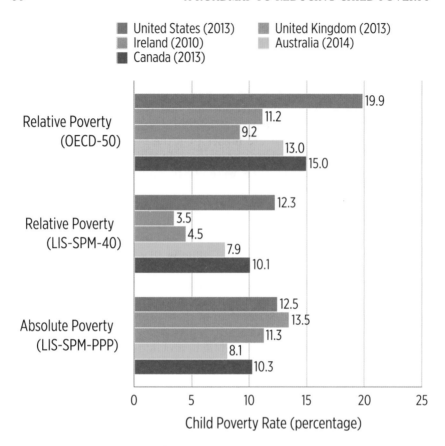

FIGURE 2-13 Child poverty in the United States and four other anglophone countries, using three alternative measures, various years.
NOTES: OECD-50 = Poverty rate defined as 50 percent below each country's median income; LIS-SPM-40 = poverty rate defined as below the 40th percentile in each country's income distribution, based on the Luxembourg Income Study (LIS); LIS-SPM-PPP = poverty rate defined following the SPM definition and adjusted for PPP (purchasing power parity). Data are not adjusted for underreporting.
SOURCE: Original LIS analyses commissioned by the committee from the LIS Cross-National Data Center.

to other countries' currencies.[20] Because the translations are based on purchasing power parity (PPP) data, we label this measure "Absolute poverty (LIS-SPM-PPP)." Appendix D, 2-11 discusses these measures in more detail.

As shown in the bottom panel of Figure 2-13, using an absolute poverty standard changes the country rankings somewhat. The United Kingdom now has the highest absolute poverty rate, followed by the United States, Ireland, Canada, and lastly Australia. The primary reason for this shift in rankings is that living standards are generally higher for U.S. children than for UK children, so a poverty line defined by U.S.-based income cuts the UK income distribution at a higher point than where it cuts the U.S. income distribution.

Finally, we compare rates of deep poverty and near poverty in the United States and these peer countries using the LIS and the absolute SPM poverty measure (see Figure 2-14). At 3.6 percent, the United States has by far the highest rate of deep child poverty, nearly twice the rate seen in the next-ranked nation (Australia, at 1.9%).[21] By contrast, the United States is in the middle of the pack where near poverty is concerned (defining near poverty as 150 percent of the absolute SPM), with a rate of 29.2 percent. This near-poverty rate is considerably lower than what is seen in the United Kingdom (46.4%) and Ireland (37.2%), where the poverty line cuts their distributions at a much higher income level (see Appendix D, Figure D2-3), but it is higher than in countries with absolute living standards most similar to those in the United States: Australia (21.6%) and Canada (27.2%).

Poverty rates for children in single-parent families, in working families (except for the United Kingdom), and in immigrant families are higher in the United States than in the other comparison nations, even using the absolute LIS-SPM-PPP poverty rates. (These rates are shown in Figure 2-13 and Appendix D, 2-11.)

CONCLUSION 2-6: How child poverty rates in the United States rank relative to those in peer English-speaking developed countries depends on how poverty is defined. The United States has much higher rates of child poverty than these peer countries using relative, within-country measures of poverty. However, when an absolute poverty measure is used, child poverty rates in the United States are more similar to rates

---

[20] The 2013 U.S. SPM translates into about $25,550 for two parents and two children. This amount is converted to other currencies using 2011 purchasing power parities (PPP) and national consumer price changes when years differ. The SPM poverty line income, on a household basis, ignoring health care costs and work expenses and other adjustments for COLAs and housing status, is about 40–41 percent of the U.S. median adjusted income on a comparable basis (Fox, 2017; Short, 2013; Wimer and Smeeding, 2017).

[21] These figures are not adjusted for underreporting in any nation. The comparisons by level and composition of poverty are shown in Figures D2-3 and D2-4.

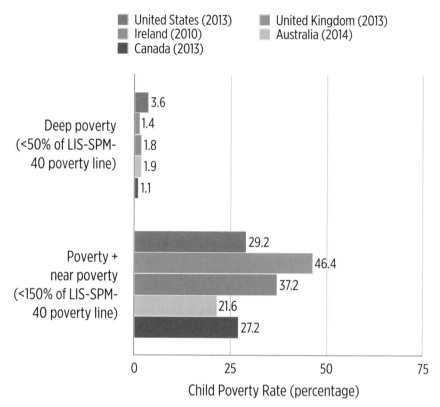

FIGURE 2-14 Deep and near child poverty in the United States and four other anglophone countries, LIS-SPM-40, various years.
NOTES: Poverty lines are absolute and based on the LIS-SPM converted to other countries using purchasing power parities (PPPs). LIS-SPM-40 = poverty rate defined as below the 40th percentile in each country's income distribution, based on the Luxembourg Income Study (LIS). Data are not adjusted for underreporting.
SOURCE: Original LIS analyses commissioned by the committee from the LIS Cross-National Data Center.

in peer countries. Rates of deep poverty, by contrast, are considerably higher for children in the United States than for children in these peer countries, whether absolute or relative measures are used.

REFERENCES

Bollinger, C., Hokayem, C., Hirsch, B., and Ziliak, J. (2018). Trouble in the tails? What we know about earnings nonresponse thirty years after Lillard, Smith, and Welch. *Journal of Political Economy*, December. doi: 10.1086/701807.

Capps, R., Fix, M., and Zong, J. (2016). *A Profile of U.S. Children with Unauthorized Immigrant Parents*. Washington, DC: Migration Policy Institute.

Child Trends Data Bank. (2016). *Educational Attainment: Indicators of Child and Youth Well-Being*. Bethesda, MD: Child Trends. Available: https://www.childtrends.org/wp-content/uploads/2016/12/06_Educational_Attainment.pdf.

Council of Economic Advisors. (2018). *Expanding Work Requirements in Cash Welfare Programs*. Washington, DC: The White House. Available: https://www.whitehouse.gov/wp-content/uploads/2018/07/Expanding-Work-Requirements-in-Non-Cash-Welfare-Programs.pdf.

Eggebeen, D.J., and Lichter, D.T. (1991). Race, family structure, and changing poverty among American children. *American Sociological Review*, 56(6), 801–817.

Esping-Andersen, G. (1990). *The Three Worlds of Welfare Capitalism*. Hoboken, NJ: John Wiley & Sons.

Fox, L. (2017). *The Supplemental Poverty Measure: 2016*. Current Population Reports P60-261. Available: https://www.census.gov/content/dam/Census/library/publications/2017/demo/p60-261.pdf.

Fox, L. (2018). *The Supplemental Poverty Measure: 2017*. Current Population Reports P60-265. Available: https://www.census.gov/content/dam/Census/library/publications/2018/demo/p60-265.pdf.

Fox, L., Wimer, C., Garfinkel, I., Kaushal, N., and Waldfogel, J. (2015). Waging war on poverty: Poverty trends using a historical supplemental poverty measure. *Journal of Policy Analysis and Management*, 34(3), 567–592.

Furstenberg, F.F. (2014). Fifty years of family change: From consensus to complexity. *The ANNALS of the American Academy of Political and Social Science*, 654(1), 12–30. Available: https://doi.org/10.1177/0002716214524521.

Hardy, B., Smeeding, T., and Ziliak, J.P. (2018). The changing safety net for low-income parents and their children: Structural or cyclical changes in income support policy? *Demography*, 55(1), 189–221.

Hill, H.D. (2018). Chapter 6: Trends and divergences in childhood income dynamics, 1970–2010. In J.B. Benson (Ed.), *Advances in Child Development and Behavior* (vol. 54, pp. 179–213). Greenwich, CT: JAI Press.

Hokayem, C., Bollinger, C., and Ziliak, J. (2015). The role of CPS nonresponse in the measurement of poverty. *Journal of the American Statistical Association* 110 (511), 935–945.

Institute of Medicine and National Research Council. (2012). *Medical Care Economic Risk: Measuring Financial Vulnerability from Spending on Medical Care*. Washington, DC: The National Academies Press. https://doi.org/10.17226/13525.

Kennedy, S., and Bumpass, L. (2008). Cohabitation and children's living arrangements: New estimates from the United States. *Demographic Research*, 19, 1663.

Korenman, S., Remler, D.K., and Hyson, R. (2017). *Accounting for the Impact of Medicaid on Child Poverty*. Background Paper for the Committee on Building an Agenda to Reduce the Number of Children in Poverty by Half in 10 Years, Board of Children, Youth and Families of the National Academies of Sciences, Engineering, and Medicine. Available: https://www.nap.edu/resource/25246/Korenman%20Remler%20and%20Hyson.pdf.

Lichter, D., Qian, Z., and Crowley, M. (2008). Poverty and economic polarization among children in racial minority and immigrant families. In D.R. Crane and T. Heaton (Eds.), *Handbook of Families & Poverty*. Thousand Oaks, CA: SAGE.

Manning, W., Brown, S., and Stykes, B. (2014). Family complexity among children in the United States. *The ANNALS of the American Academy of Political and Social Science*, 654(1), 48–65.

Martin, J.A., Hamilton, B.E., and Osterman, M.J. (2017). *Births in the United States, 2016*. Available: https://www.cdc.gov/nchs/products/databriefs/db287.htm.

Martin, J.A., Hamilton, B.E., Osterman, M.J., Driscoll, A.K., and Drake, P. (2018). *Births: Final Data for 2016*. Available: https://www.cdc.gov/nchs/products/databriefs/db287.htm.

Mather, M. (2010). *U.S. Children in Single-Mother Families*. Washington, DC: Population Reference Bureau.

Mathews, T.J., and Hamilton, B.E. (2016). *Mean Age of Mothers Is on the Rise: United States, 2000-2014*. Hyattsville, MD: National Center for Health Statistics.

McLanahan, S., and Jencks, C. (2015). Was Moynihan right? What happens to children of unmarried mothers? *Education Next, 15*(2).

Meyer, B.D., and Sullivan, J.X. (2017). *Consumption and Income Inequality in the U.S. Since the 1960s*. NBER Working Paper No. 23655. Cambridge, MA: National Bureau of Economic Research. Available: http://www.nber.org/papers/w23655.

Meyer, B.D., Mok, W.K.C., and Sullivan, J.X. (2009). *The Under-Reporting of Transfers in Household Surveys: Its Nature and Consequences*. NBER Working Paper No. 15181. Cambridge, MA: National Bureau of Economic Research. Available: http://www.nber.org/papers/w15181.

Migration Policy Institute. (2017). *Children in U.S. Immigrant Families: Number and Share of the Total U.S. Child Population, by Age Group and State*. Washington, DC: Migration Policy Institute. Available: https://www.migrationpolicy.org/programs/data-hub/charts/children-immigrant-families.

Moffitt, R.A., and Scholz, J.K. (2009, November). *Trends in the Level and Distribution of Income Support*. NBER Working Paper No. 15488. Cambridge, MA: National Bureau of Economic Research. Available: http://www.nber.org/papers/w15488.

National Academies of Sciences, Engineering, and Medicine. (2017). *Promoting the Educational Success of Children and Youth Learning English: Promising Futures*. Washington, DC: The National Academies Press. Available: https://doi.org/10.17226/24677.

National Center for Education Statistics. (2018). *The Condition of Education: Characteristics of Children's Families*. Washington, DC: Institute of Education Sciences. Available: https://nces.ed.gov/programs/coe/indicator_cce.asp.

National Research Council. (1995). *Measuring Poverty: A New Approach*. Washington, DC: National Academy Press.

Pew Research Center. (2016). *It's Official: Minority Babies Are the Majority among the Nation's Infants, but Only Just*. Available: http://www.pewresearch.org/fact-tank/2016/06/23/its-official-minority-babies-are-the-majority-among-the-nations-infants-but-only-just.

Remler, D.K., Korenman, S.D., and Hyson, R.T. (2017). Estimating the effects of health insurance and other social programs on poverty under the Affordable Care Act. *Health Affairs, 36*(10), 1828–1837.

Renwick, T. (2015). *Using the American Community Survey (ACS) to Implement a Supplemental Poverty Measure (SPM)*. Working Paper # 2015-09. Washington, DC: U.S. Census Bureau, Social, Economic and Housing Statistics Division.

Semega, J.L., Fontenot, K.R., and Kollar, M.A. (2017). *Income and Poverty in the United States: 2016*. Current Population Reports, P60-259. Available: https://www.census.gov/content/dam/Census/library/publications/2017/demo/P60-259.pdf.

Short, K. (2013). *The Supplemental Poverty Measure: Examining the Incidence and Depth of Poverty in the U.S. Taking Account of Taxes and Transfers in 2012*. Discussion paper. Washington, DC: U.S. Census Bureau.

Short, K., and Smeeding, T. (2012). *Understanding Income-to-Threshold Ratios Using the Supplemental Poverty Measure: People with Moderate Income*. SEHSD Working Paper No. 2012-18. Washington, DC: U.S. Census Bureau.

Summers, B.D., and Oellerich, D. (2013). The poverty-reducing effect of Medicaid. *Journal of Health Economics, 32*, 816–832.

U.S. Census Bureau. (2018). *Annual Estimates of the Resident Population by Sex, Age, Race, and Hispanic Origin for the United States and States: April 1, 2010 to July 1, 2017.* Washington, DC: U.S. Census Bureau.

Wheaton, L. (2008). *Underreporting of Means-Tested Transfer Programs in the CPS and SIPP.* Washington, DC: Urban Institute. Available: https://www.urban.org/research/publication/underreporting-means-tested-transfer-programs-cps-and-sipp.

Wimer, C. (2017). *Child Poverty in the United States: Long-term Trends and the Role of Antipoverty Programs Using the Anchored Supplemental Poverty Measure.* Commissioned by the Committee on Building an Agenda to Reduce the Number of Children in Poverty by Half in 10 Years. The National Academies of Sciences, Engineering, and Medicine, Washington, DC.

Wimer, C., and Smeeding, T. (2017). USA child poverty: The impact of the great recession. In Y.C.B. Cantillon, S. Handa, and B. Nolan (Eds.), *Children of Austerity: The Impact of the Great Recession on Child Poverty in Rich Countries* (pp. 297–331). Oxford: Oxford University Press.

Wimer, C., Fox, L., Garfinkel, I., Kaushal, N., and Waldfogel, J. (2013). *Trends in Poverty with an Anchored Supplemental Poverty Measure.* Columbia University Academic Commons. Available: https://doi.org/10.7916/D8RN3853.

Winship, S. (2016). *Poverty after Welfare Reform.* New York, NY: Manhattan Institute.

Wood, D. (2003). Effect of child and family poverty on child health in the United States. *Pediatrics, 112* (Suppl. 3), 707–711.

Woods, T., and Hanson, D. (2016). *Demographic Trends of Children of Immigrants.* Washington, DC: The Urban Institute.

3

Consequences of Child Poverty

In response to the first element of the committee's statement of task, this chapter summarizes lessons from research on the linkages between children's poverty and their childhood health and education as well as their later employment, criminal involvement, and health as adults. It also provides a brief review of research on the macroeconomic costs of child poverty. Because this research literature is vast, the committee focused its review on the most methodologically sound and prominent studies in key fields, primarily in developmental psychology, medicine, sociology, and economics. All else equal, we also selected more recent studies.

We find overwhelming evidence from this literature that, on average, a child growing up in a family whose income is below the poverty line experiences worse outcomes than a child from a wealthier family in virtually every dimension, from physical and mental health, to educational attainment and labor market success, to risky behaviors and delinquency.

This finding needs to be qualified in two important ways. First, although average differences in the attainments and health of poor and nonpoor children are stark, a proportion of poor children do beat the odds and live very healthy and productive lives (Abelev, 2009; Ratcliffe and Kalish, 2017).

Second, and vital to the committee's charge, is the issue of correlation versus causation. Income-based childhood poverty is associated with a cluster of other disadvantages that may be harmful to children, including low levels of parental education and living with a single parent (Currie et al., 2013). Are the differences between the life chances of poor and nonpoor children a product of differences in childhood economic resources *per se*, or do they stem from these other, correlated conditions? Evidence both on the *causal* (as distinct from correlational) impact of childhood poverty and on which pathways lead to better outcomes is most useful in determining whether child well-being would be best promoted by policies that specifically reduce childhood poverty. If it turns out that associations between poverty and negative child outcomes are caused by factors other than income, then the root causes of negative child outcomes must be addressed by policies other than the kinds of income-focused anti-poverty proposals presented in this report.

That said, most of the scholarly work on poverty and the impacts of anti-poverty programs and policies on child well-being is correlational rather than causal. There is much to be learned from these studies, nevertheless, and it is often the case that evidence derived from experimental designs and that derived from correlational designs lead to similar conclusions. To maintain clarity in our reviews of these two strands in the literature, we have opted to focus this chapter's main text on the results found in the causal literature, while we review the correlational literature in the Chapter 3 portion of Appendix D.

We begin with a brief summary of the mechanisms by which childhood poverty may cause worse childhood outcomes, along with lessons from the vast correlational literature, which is reviewed in depth in this chapter's appendix. We then turn to a review of the causal impacts of policies—income policies as well as anti-poverty policies—on child well-being, derived from both experimental and quasi-experimental (natural experiment) studies. The chapter concludes with a brief review of some of the limited literature on the macroeconomic costs of poverty to society.

Note that virtually all of the available evidence focuses on child poverty as measured by the Official Poverty Measure (OPM) rather than the Supplemental Poverty Measure (SPM) that is used in other chapters of this report. Given the considerable overlap in terms of who is considered poor by both measures, we would expect that the bulk of the lessons from OPM-based studies would carry over to the SPM.

WHY CHILDHOOD POVERTY CAN
MATTER FOR CHILD OUTCOMES

Economists, sociologists, developmental psychologists, and neuroscientists each emphasize different ways poverty may influence children's development. Two main mechanisms have been theorized to describe these processes (see Figure 3-1). One emphasizes what money can buy—in other words, how poverty undermines parents' ability to procure the goods and services that enhance children's development. An alternative mechanism emphasizes the detrimental impact on families of exposure to

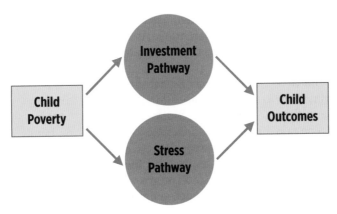

FIGURE 3-1 Hypothesized pathways by which child poverty affects child outcomes.

environmental stressors as a key pathway by which poverty compromises children's development.

As detailed in Chapter 8 and in the appendix to this chapter, low-income parents face steep challenges in meeting basic financial needs. Many poor families are not only cash-constrained but they also have little to no savings and lack access to low-cost sources of credit (Halpern-Meekin et al., 2015; Yeung and Conley, 2008; Zahn, 2006). When faced with income shortfalls, they are often forced to cut back on expenditures, even for essential goods such as food and housing, and to pay high interest rates on loans (McKernan, Ratcliffe, and Quakenbush, 2014). As a result, poverty is linked to material hardship, including inadequate shelter and medical care, food insecurity, and a lack of other essentials (Ouellette et al., 2004).

An "investment" perspective may be adopted in addressing the challenge of poverty reduction by building on an analysis of the foregoing problems, emphasizing that higher income may support children's development and well-being by enabling poor parents to meet such basic needs. As examples, higher incomes may enable parents to invest in cognitively stimulating items in the home (e.g., books, computers), in providing more parental time (by adjusting work hours), in obtaining higher-quality non-parental child care, and in securing learning opportunities outside the home (Bornstein and Bradley, 2003; Fox et al., 2013; Raver, Gershoff, and Aber, 2007). Children may also benefit from better housing or a move to a better neighborhood. Studies of some poverty alleviation programs find that these programs can reduce material hardship and improve children's learning environments (Huston et al., 2001; Morris, Gennetian, and Duncan, 2005).

The alternative, "stress" perspective on poverty reduction focuses on the fact that economic hardship can increase psychological distress in parents and decrease their emotional well-being. Psychological distress can spill over into marriages and parenting. As couples struggle to make ends meet, their interactions may become more conflicted (Brody et al., 1994; Conger et al., 1994). Parents' psychological distress and conflict have in fact been linked with harsh, inconsistent, and detached parenting. Such lower-quality parenting may harm children's cognitive and socioemotional development (Conger et al., 2002; McLoyd, 1990). All of this suggests that higher income may improve child well-being by reducing family stress.

Investing in children and relieving parental stress are two different mechanisms, but they overlap and reinforce each other. For example, both increased economic resources and improved parental mental health and family routines may result in higher-quality child care, more cognitively enriching in-home and out-of-home activities, and more visits for preventive medical or dental care. Better child development, in turn, can encourage more investment and better parenting; for example, more talkative children may trigger more verbal interaction and book reading from their parents, especially if parents can afford to spend the necessary time.

We have focused on parental stress, because reducing poverty may ameliorate this stress and improve parenting, including emotional support for and interactions with children. In addition, a major portion of existing research has focused on this pathway. We recognize that child stress is an important factor leading to negative child outcomes, including effects on early brain development (Blair and Raver, 2016, Shonkoff et al., 2012). We have not included it in the model (refer to Figure 3-1) because it is a more indirect mediator of the effects of other factors of poverty on child outcomes. These other factors include parenting stress, other adverse child experiences, and the negative impacts of underresourced schools and environments in poor neighborhoods. For a more extensive review of both parental and child stress, please see the appendix to this chapter (Appendix D, 3-1).

> **CONCLUSION 3-1:** Poverty alleviation can promote children's development, both because of the goods and services that parents can buy for their children and because it may promote a more responsive, less stressful environment in which more positive parent-child interactions can take place.

The foregoing brief discussion is intended only to provide a framework in which the correlational and causal studies of the impacts of poverty can be understood. We provide a more complete review of the literature about some of these pathways in Chapter 8 and in the appendix to this chapter.

CORRELATIONAL STUDIES

Many studies document that, on average, children growing up in poor families fare worse than children in more affluent families. A study by Duncan, Ziol-Guest, and Kalil (2010) is one striking example (see Figure 3-2). Their study uses data from a national sample of U.S. children who were followed from birth into their 30s and examines how poverty in the first 6 years of life is related to adult outcomes. What they find is that compared with children whose families had incomes above twice the poverty line during their early childhood, children with family incomes below the poverty line during this period completed 2 fewer years of schooling and, as adults, worked 451 fewer hours per year, earned less than one-half as much, received more in food stamps, and were more than twice as likely to report poor overall health or high levels of psychological distress (some of these differences are shown in Figure 3-2). Men who grew up in poverty, they find, were twice as likely as adults to have been arrested, and among women early childhood poverty was associated with a six-fold increase in the likelihood of bearing a child out of wedlock prior to age 21. Reinforcing the need to treat correlations cautiously, Duncan, Ziol-Guest, and Kalil (2010) also find that some, but not all, of these differences between poor and nonpoor children disappeared when they adjusted statistically for

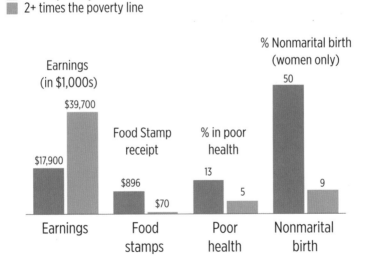

FIGURE 3-2 Adult outcomes for children with lower and higher levels of early childhood income.
SOURCE: Adapted from Duncan, Ziol-Guest, and Kalil (2010).

differences in factors such as parental education that were associated with low childhood incomes.

Neuroscientists have produced striking evidence of the effect of early-life economic circumstances on brain development. Drawing from Hanson et al. (2013), Figure 3-3 illustrates differences in the total volume of gray matter between three groups of children: those whose family incomes were no more than twice the poverty line (labeled "Low SES" in the figure); those whose family incomes were between two and four times the poverty line ("Mid SES"); and those whose family incomes were more than four times the poverty line ("High SES"). Gray matter is particularly important for children's information processing and ability to regulate their behavior. The figure shows no notable differences in gray matter during the first 9 or so months of life, but differences favoring children raised in high-income families emerge soon after that. Notably, the study found no differences in the total brain sizes across these groups—only in the amount of gray matter. However, the existence of these emerging differences does not prove that poverty causes them. This study adjusted for age and birth weight, but not for other indicators of family socioeconomic status that might have been the actual cause of these observed differences in gray matter for children with different family incomes.

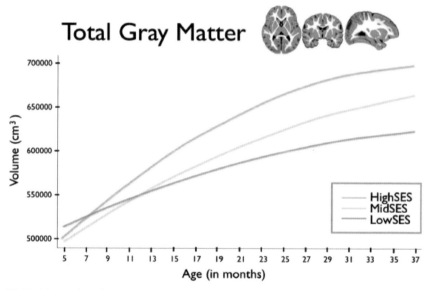

FIGURE 3-3 Total gray matter volume in early life, by socioeconomic group.
SOURCE: Hanson et al. (2013).

Two themes from these two studies characterize much of the child poverty literature: (1) consistent correlations between a child's poverty status and later outcomes and (2) particularly strong associations when poverty status is measured early in childhood. Our review of this correlational literature, which is provided in this chapter's appendix, is organized into the following sections: family functioning, child maltreatment, domestic violence, and adverse childhood experiences; material hardship; physical health; fetal health and health at birth; brain development; mental health; educational attainment; and risky behaviors, crime, and delinquency. Each section discusses the observed relationships between poverty and the outcomes in question. Collectively, they paint a consistent picture, which may be summarized in the following conclusion.

CONCLUSION 3-2: Some children are resilient to a number of the adverse impacts of poverty, but many studies show significant associations between poverty and child maltreatment, adverse childhood experiences, increased material hardship, worse physical health, low birth weight, structural changes in brain development, mental health problems, decreased educational attainment, and increased risky behaviors, delinquency, and criminal behavior in adolescence and adulthood. As for the timing and severity of poverty, the literature documents that poverty in early childhood, prolonged poverty, and deep poverty are all associated with worse child and adult outcomes.

THE IMPACT OF CHILD POVERTY

Policies designed to reduce poverty will promote positive child outcomes to the extent that poverty reduction causes these child outcomes to improve. This section discusses the causal evidence linking poverty and child outcomes. It includes studies that the committee judged to have the strongest research designs, whether purposely experimental or based on natural experiments that can support the estimation of causal linkages.

In experimental approaches to understanding the impacts of poverty reduction, the policy researcher attempts to vary income while holding constant other potentially causative factors. Randomly assigning subjects to large treatment and control groups helps to ensure that the distribution of these other causative factors (e.g., parental education and motivation) will be similar across the two groups. In this case, a poverty reduction "treatment" might be income payments to families for a number of years, with no such payments made to control group families. Comparing the subsequent well-being of children in the two groups would provide strong evidence about the causal impact of poverty reduction on child well-being.

If experimental methods are not feasible, then some nonexperimental methods, in particular "natural experiments," are able to mimic random-assignment experiments. Much of the literature using these kinds of non-experimental designs relies on policy changes or some other unanticipated event that causes family income to change more for one group of children than for another similar group. Our literature review on the causal impacts of poverty reduction on child well-being draws from both experimental methods that use random assignment and natural experiments.

Studies of Increases in Cash Incomes

Family economic resources can be changed in a variety of ways, so researchers have cast a wide net to find circumstances in which families' incomes vary in ways that are beyond their control, which provide an opportunity to relate income changes to changes in child well-being. Examples in which family cash incomes were increased or decreased by policy changes comprise the first part of our review of causal studies. Notably absent from this section are impacts on children of family income changes resulting from legislated changes in the minimum wage; we found no such studies in our review of the literature.

We also do not report on conditional cash transfer programs (CCTs), which condition income on behaviors such as well-baby visits and school attendance. CCTs are prevalent in low- and middle-income countries. These programs, which intend to reduce family economic hardship and stress, typically require families to invest more in their children, especially in their education and health. In the United States, two randomized clinical trials have been conducted of CCTs (Family Rewards 1.0 and 2.0). Both trials found that income increased due to the cash transfers, but that these increases faded after the program ended. Results showed only minimal improvements in children's health and educational outcomes and no impacts on the verified employment or earnings of parents (Aber et al., 2016; Miller et al., 2016; Riccio and Miller, 2016; Riccio et al., 2013).

Negative Income Tax Experiments

The negative income tax experiments initiated under the Nixon administration provided the first random-assignment evidence of income effects on children. A negative income tax is based on a minimum income, or floor, under the tax system; people with incomes above the floor pay taxes, while those with incomes below the floor receive a transfer payment—a kind of negative tax that brings their family incomes up to the floor. The negative tax payment is largest for families with the least income, becoming smaller and smaller as other sources of family income increase.

Large-scale experimental trials of a negative income tax were conducted in seven states between 1968 and 1982. Treatment families, randomly chosen, received payment amounts equivalent to one-third or two-thirds of the federal poverty line. After adjusting for inflation, the largest payments were quite substantial, more than twice the size of current average payments made under the Earned Income Tax Credit (EITC) Program. That these experiments were conducted decades ago limits the value of the lessons they might provide for today's policy discussions. That said, the large negative income tax payments reduced poverty and improved children's birth outcomes and nutrition, but had mixed effects on child outcomes such as school performance (Kehrer and Wolin, 1979; Salkind and Haskins, 1982).

Two of the three experimental sites that measured achievement gains for children in elementary school found significant improvements in treatment-group children relative to control-group children (Maynard, 1977; Maynard and Murnane, 1979). In contrast, the achievement of adolescents in families receiving this income supplement did not differ from the achievement of adolescents in control-group families. Impacts on school enrollment and attainment for youth were more uniformly positive, with both of the sites at which these outcomes were measured producing increases in school enrollment, high school graduation rates, and/or years of completed schooling (Maynard, 1977; Maynard and Murnane, 1979; Venti, 1984).

The Earned Income Tax Credit

The EITC is a refundable federal tax credit for low- and moderate–income working people. A worker's EITC credit grows with each additional dollar of earnings until it reaches a maximum value, and then it flattens out and is gradually reduced as income continues to rise. The dollar value of the EITC payment to a family depends on the recipient's income, marital status, and number of children. As of 2017, 29 states and the District of Columbia had their own EITC programs (Waxman, 2017), supplementing the tax benefits provided by the federal EITC.

Natural-experiment studies of EITC's impact on child outcomes take advantage of the fact that federal EITC benefit levels increased substantially on a number of occasions between the late 1980s and the 2000s. For example, legislation passed in 1993 increased the maximum credit for families with two or more children by $2,160 (in 1999 dollars) compared with an increase in the maximum credit for families with one child of $725 (Hoynes, Miller, and Simon, 2015). Several researchers have used these kinds of expansions, as well as EITC introduction and expansions at the state level, to assess whether child outcomes improved the most for children whose families stood to gain the most from the increased EITC generosity. It is important to bear in mind that the EITC affects family income through the tax credit payment, increases in parental work effort, and, for some families, reductions in other income sources (Hoynes and Patel, 2017). This makes it difficult to separate income effects from the effects of changes in parental employment.

Most of the research on the effects of the EITC focuses on children's school achievement and consistently suggests that boosts in EITC have had positive effects. For example, Dahl and Lochner (2012) link EITC changes to national data tracking children's achievement test scores over time and find that a $1,000 increase in family income raised math and reading achievement test scores by 6 percent of a standard deviation. Chetty, Friedman, and Rockoff (2011) find a similarly sized effect when they look at the test scores of children attending schools in a large urban school district. In the state they study, state and local match rates for the federal EITC increased during the late 1990s and up until 2006. Gains in the children's test scores in math and language arts closely tracked these policy changes. The estimated impact was about 4 percent of a standard deviation in 2003, increasing to about 10 percent of a standard deviation in 2006 and leveling off thereafter. Drawing from the literature estimating the longer-run effects of test scores, they calculate that a typical student would gain more than $40,000 in lifetime income from the initial increase in EITC and its resulting increase in test scores.

Maxfield (2013) uses the same child data as Dahl and Lochner (2012) and finds that an increase in the maximum EITC of $1,000 boosted the probability of a child's graduating high school or receiving a GED by age 19 by about 2 percentage points and increased the probability of completing one or more years of college by age 19 by about 1.4 percentage points. Additionally, Manoli and Turner (2014), using U.S. tax data and variations due to the shape of the EITC schedule, find that a larger EITC leads to an increase in college attendance among low-income families.

A few studies have also examined the effect of EITC increases on infant health. Strully, Rehkopf, and Xuan (2010) find that increases in state EITCs during the prenatal period increased birth weights, partly by reducing maternal smoking during pregnancy. This is consistent with evidence that when an expectant mother receives a larger EITC during pregnancy, this reduces the likelihood that her baby will have low birth weight by 2 to 3 percent (Baker, 2008; Hoynes, Miller, and Simon, 2015). Like Strully, Rehkopf, and Xuan (2010), Hoynes, Miller, and Simon (2015) suggest that a reduction in smoking is partly responsible, but they also find increases in the use of prenatal care by mothers eligible for the higher EITC payments, which in turn might also lead to a reduction in the incidence of infants' low birth weight.

Evans and Garthwaite (2010) find support for a stress and mental health pathway operating in EITC expansions. They use data from the

National Health Examination and Nutrition Survey to estimate whether increased EITC payments were associated with improvements in low-income mothers' health. They find that mothers most likely to receive the increased payments experienced the largest improvements in self-reported mental health as well as reductions in stress-related biomarkers.[1]

Taken together, the robust literature on the impacts of EITC-based increases in family income suggests beneficial impacts on children.

CONCLUSION 3-3: Periodic increases in the generosity of the Earned Income Tax Credit Program have improved children's educational and health outcomes.

Welfare-to-Work Experiments

In the early 1990s, a number of states were granted waivers to experiment with the rules governing welfare payments under the old Aid to Families with Dependent Children (AFDC) Program. A condition for receiving the waiver, for most states, was the use of random assignment to evaluate the effects of changing from "business as usual" AFDC rules to their new programs (Gennetian and Morris, 2003; Morris et al., 2001). Some states implemented welfare reform programs that offered earnings supplements, either by providing working families cash benefits or by increasing the amount of earnings that were not counted as income when calculating the family's welfare benefit. Other state programs provided only mandatory employment services (e.g., education, training, or immediate job search) or put time limits on families' eligibility for welfare benefits and offered no increased income. All of the new programs had the effect of increasing parent employment, relative to the old AFDC programs, but only some of the programs increased family income as well. Because a number of evaluations included measures of child outcomes, these diverse state experiments provided an opportunity to assess the effects of combinations of increased income and parental employment on child and adolescent well-being.

Morris et al. (2001) and Morris, Gennetian, and Knox (2002) examine the effects of these programs on preschool-age and elementary school-age children. Specifically, children were assessed 2 to 4 years after random assignment, and ranged in age from 5 to 12 years old at the time of assessment. The authors find that earnings supplement programs that increased both parental employment and family income produced positive but modest improvements across a range of child behaviors. All the programs had

---

[1] These include measures of inflammation, such as albumin; cardiovascular conditions (e.g., systolic blood pressure); measures of metabolic conditions such as total cholesterol; and other risks (Evans and Garthwaite, 2010).

positive effects on children's school test scores, with impacts ranging from one-tenth to one-quarter of a standard deviation, and some programs also reduced behavior problems, increased positive social behavior, and/ or improved children's overall health. In contrast, programs with work requirements that increased employment but not family income (because participants lost welfare benefits as their earnings increased) showed a mix of positive and negative, but mostly null, effects on child outcomes.

Gennetian et al. (2004) focus on adolescents, ages 12 to 18 years at the time of follow-up surveys. These children had been 10 to 16 years old when their parents entered the experimental programs. In contrast to the positive effects that Morris and colleagues find for younger children's school achievement, Gennetian and colleagues find a number of negative impacts on school performance and school progress, irrespective of the type of policy or program that was tested. Some parents in the experimental group reported worse school performance for their children, a higher rate of grade retention, and more use of special education services among their adolescent children than did parents in the control group. However, overall the sizes of these worrisome negative effects were small, and many of the programs did not produce statistically significant effects.

Why did welfare-to-work programs, particularly those that increase family income, have positive effects on younger children but null or even negative effects on adolescents? Duncan, Gennetian, and Morris (2009) study this question by focusing on children who were ages 2 to 5 when their parents entered the program. Their analysis finds that increased income and the use of center-based child care were key pathways through which programs improved young children's school achievement. These findings are consistent with correlational research linking formal child care to better academic skills among low-income children (National Institute of Child Health and Human Development Early Child Care Research Network and Duncan, 2003). Duncan, Morris, and Rodrigues (2011) conduct a similar analysis using this same set of studies to estimate the causal effect of increases in income on the children's school achievement and standardized test scores 2 to 5 years after baseline. They find modest but policy-relevant effects that began during the preschool years on young children's later achievement. Their estimates suggest that each $1,000 increase in annual income, sustained across an average of 2 to 5 years of follow up, boosts young children's achievement by 5 to 6 percent of a standard deviation.

In contrast, the pattern of negative impacts on adolescents may have been generated by the fact that all of the programs tested increased the amount of parental employment, which in turn led to increases in adolescents' responsibilities for household and sibling care and reduced supervision by adults when parents were working. Those inferences are tentative, however, because several studies lacked the data necessary to explore potential pathways.

CONCLUSION 3-4: Welfare-to-work programs that increased family income also improved educational and behavioral outcomes for young children but not for adolescents. Working parents have less time to supervise their children, which may place more burdens on adolescents in the family.

Pre-AFDC Cash Welfare

Estimating the impacts in adulthood of program benefits received during childhood requires the use of data on children spanning several decades, and consequently it includes children born into general social and economic conditions that often were far worse than conditions prevailing today. One study of a cash assistance program focused on the Mother's Pension Program, which pre-dated the 1935 introduction of the AFDC program and was provided by some states to poor women with children. Aizer et al. (2016) evaluate the long-run effects of this program by comparing the children of women who were granted the pension to those who were rejected. Using data from state censuses, death records, and World War II enlistment records, they find that receiving the pension as a child led to a 1.5 year increase in life expectancy, a 50 percent reduction in the probability of being underweight, a 0.4 year increase in educational attainment, and a 14 percent increase in income in early adulthood. However, these local programs were introduced at a time when few other resources existed for lone mothers, so it may represent an upper bound on what one could expect from cash welfare programs today.

Supplemental Security Income

The Supplemental Security Income (SSI) Program is designed to increase the incomes of low-income families that have adults or children with disabilities. The rationale for assisting families with a severely disabled child is that they face additional expenses, and caregivers may have to reduce their own work hours to care for the child. A family qualifies for full benefits under SSI if its members earn less than about 100 percent of the federal poverty threshold. Benefits phase out altogether for families with incomes above about 200 percent of that threshold. In addition to meeting the income thresholds, eligible children must have a severe, medically documented disability. Currently, SSI benefits cover almost 2 percent of all children, with benefit amounts that average $650 a month, and they raise about one-half of recipient families above the poverty line (Romig, 2017).

Children on SSI are also automatically eligible for public health insurance coverage under the Medicaid program.

There has been relatively little research on the effects of these income supports on child outcomes, in part because benefit levels have not changed as much or as differentially as benefit levels in programs such as the Earned Income Tax Credit. But one SSI program provision provides a natural experiment for estimating the possible benefit of SSI income on child outcomes: babies weighing less than 1,200 grams at birth are eligible for SSI, while babies weighing just over 1,200 grams are not.[2] This eligibility cutoff provides researchers with opportunities to compare the developmental trajectories of children on either side of the cutoff. Guldi et al. (2017) do this, and find that mothers of qualifying children work less but, perhaps as a result, show more positive parenting behaviors than mothers of children whose birth weights placed them just above the cutoff. Most importantly for this chapter, the motor skills of babies with birth weights just below the cutoff improved more rapidly than the motor skills of slightly heavier babies whose parents did not qualify for SSI. Since lower birth weight infants should, all else equal, have more delayed motor skills than infants with higher birth weights, these results are especially consequential.

Levere (2015) takes advantage of a second source of quasi-experimental variation in SSI coverage, in this case occasioned by the 1990 *Sullivan* v. *Zebley* Supreme Court decision, which broadened SSI coverage for children with mental disabilities. Children with mental health conditions who were younger when *Zebley* was handed down became eligible for more years of SSI support than older children. In contrast to the picture of generally positive income effects on children, Levere finds that children who were eligible for more years of SSI support were less likely to work and had lower earnings as adults. This finding is hard to interpret. The negative impact may have to do with more severe mental health problems in those identified in early childhood or factors associated with more prolonged eligibility for SSI that did not help and may have harmed their adult employment prospects.

Supplemental Income Provided by a Tribal Government

In some cases, opportunities to study the causal impacts of income increases on child well-being come from unexpected sources. The Great Smoky Mountains Study of Youth was designed to assess the need for mental health services among Eastern Cherokee and non-Indian, mostly

---

[2] A specific description of disability evaluation under Social Security is available at https://www.ssa.gov/disability/professionals/bluebook/ChildhoodListings.htm. Guldi et al. (2017) note that Social Security Administration low birth weight criteria are more limiting than the medical community's criteria in order to target infants at risk of long-term disability.

White, children living in Appalachia (Costello et al., 2003). When the study began in 1993, children in the study were 9 to 13 years old, and they and their families were then interviewed periodically over the next 13 years. In the midst of the study, a gambling casino owned by the Eastern Cherokee tribal government opened on the tribe's reservation. Starting in 1996, all members of the Eastern Cherokee tribe received an income supplement that grew to an average of approximately $9,000 by 2006 (Costello et al., 2010). Over the study period, payments produced roughly a 20 percent increase in income for households with at least one adult tribal member, excluding the children's cash transfers, which were not available to the families until the child reached maturity (Akee et al., 2010). The fact that incomes increased for families with tribal members relative to families with no tribal members provided researchers with an opportunity to assess whether developmental trajectories were more positive for tribal children than for nontribal children.

The income supplements produced a variety of benefits for children in qualifying families. There were fewer behavioral problems such as conduct disorders, perhaps due to increased parental supervision (Costello et al., 2003). At age 21, the children whose families had received payments for the longest period of time were significantly less likely to have a psychiatric disorder, to abuse alcohol or cannabis, or to engage in crime (Akee et al., 2010; Costello et al., 2010). Reductions in crime were substantial: Four more years of the income supplement decreased the probability of an arrest for any crime at ages 16 to 17 by almost 22 percent and reduced the probability of having ever been arrested for a minor crime by age 21 by almost 18 percent.

Beneficial impacts on educational attainment were also found. Having 4 more years of this income supplement increased a Cherokee youth's probability of finishing high school by age 19 by almost 15 percent. Akee and colleagues (2010) found that annual payments equaling approximately $4,000 often resulted in 1 year of additional schooling for American Indian adolescents living in some of the poorest households. Additionally, Akee et al. (2018) find that the income supplements led to large beneficial changes in children's emotional and behavioral health.

In sum, studies of casino payments provide opportunities to estimate causal impacts of income on adolescent and young adult outcomes. They show strong positive impacts on emotional, behavioral, and educational outcomes, and reduced drug and alcohol use and criminal behavior. As with other studies, younger children and children with longer exposures to higher income had better outcomes.

Cash Payments: International Evidence from Canada

Although many countries have experimented with cash payments to low-income families (Fiszbein et al., 2009), few share the living standards that prevail in the United States. Canada, on the other hand, shares many characteristics with the United States and provides several examples of policy studies of income effects. For example, Milligan and Stabile (2011) take advantage of the fact that the benefit amounts of child benefits in Canada changed in different provinces at different times to investigate whether benefit increases were associated with improvements in child well-being. They find that higher benefits do improve measures of both child and maternal mental health, and also that they increase child math and vocabulary test scores. The effect size is similar to that found in Dahl and Lochner's (2012) EITC study. Among the low-income families most likely to receive the benefits, Milligan and Stabile (2011) also find declining rates of hunger and obesity, an increase in height among boys, and a decrease in physical aggression among girls.

"Near-Cash" Benefits: Supplemental Nutrition Assistance Program (SNAP) and Housing Subsidies

In addition to work on cash transfers of various kinds, there has been a great deal of research into the causal effects of what are sometimes called "near-cash" programs, especially those offering nutrition assistance and housing subsidies. These programs are referred to as near cash because while their benefits must be spent on food or housing, they free up a household's money that would otherwise have been spent on food and housing. The freed-up money can then be spent on other goods or services and may also decrease parental stress. Health insurance has not traditionally been viewed as one of these near-cash programs because of difficulties in assigning a dollar value to health coverage. However, see the appendix to this chapter (Appendix D, 3-1) for a discussion of the effects on child and adult outcomes stemming from expansions of public health insurance for poor pregnant women and children.

Supplemental Nutrition Assistance Program (SNAP)

Serving more than 44 million Americans at a cost of $70.9 billion (in fiscal 2016), the SNAP program (formerly known as the Food Stamp Program) is by far the nation's largest near-cash program (Food and Nutrition Service, 2018a). To be eligible, households must have a gross monthly income of less than 130 percent of the poverty line, net income (after deductions) of less than the poverty line, and assets of less than an asset limit (Food and Nutrition Service, 2018b). Benefits can be used to purchase most foods available in grocery stores, with exceptions such as vitamins and hot foods for immediate consumption. Benefits are delivered in the form of an Electronic Benefit Transfer card that functions much like a debit card.

Given the substitution possibilities between income from SNAP and other sources, it is not surprising that research studies estimate that with a $100 increase in SNAP benefits, households increase their food consumption by quite a bit less than $100. The review of Hoynes and Schanzenbach, (2015) places the increase in food consumption at around $30 per $100 in benefits. While these families do spend all their SNAP benefits on food, the benefits allow them to spend less of their own income on food. The review by Hoynes and Schanzenbach finds that for every $100 in SNAP benefits, households have $70 of their own income that they no longer need to spend on food. Families can then use these household funds for additional resources for their children.

Hoynes and Schanzenbach (2015) also provide a summary of the literature examining causal links between SNAP participation and the nutrition and health outcomes of infants, children, and adults. Many (but not all) of the methodologically strongest studies show SNAP benefits having positive impacts on health. Given the interest in the longer-run impacts of poverty reduction on child health and attainment, in the following we provide more details about two studies that took advantage of the fact that the SNAP (then known as food stamps) program rolled out gradually between the late 1960s and mid-1970s. Notably, the rollout occurred on a county by county basis, which resulted in many instances in which the families of children born in the same state at the same time may have had different access to program benefits.[3]

This slow rollout enabled Almond, Hoynes, and Schanzenbach (2011) to estimate causal effects of participation during pregnancy on infant health and, in a later study (Hoynes, Schanzenbach, and Almond, 2016) to investigate the effects on adult health of the availability of food stamps at different points in childhood. The infant health study found that food stamp availability reduced the incidence of low birth weight—a result similar to one found in a more recent study of birth weight surrounding changes in rules for immigrant eligibility for food stamps beginning in the mid-1990s (East, 2016). In a related paper using the same policy variation, East (2018) finds that more exposure to SNAP at ages 0 to 4 leads to a reduction in poor health and school absences in later childhood. Using variations in the

---

[3] A look at the long-term impact of program participation in childhood on adult health requires that the affected cohorts be followed for decades. A caveat with any such study is that conditions facing children today may be different from those decades ago, hence the effect of program participation may also differ.

price of food across areas of the United States, Bronchetti, Christensen, and Hoynes (2018) find that increases in the purchasing power of SNAP lead to improvements in child school attendance and compliance with physician checkups.

In their 2016 study of possible long-term effects of food stamp coverage in early childhood on health outcomes in adulthood, Hoynes, Schanzenbach, and Almond focus on the presence or absence of a cluster of adverse health conditions known as metabolic syndrome. In the study, metabolic syndrome was measured by indicators for adult obesity, high blood pressure, diabetes, and heart disease. Scores on these indicators of emerging cardiovascular health problems increased (grew worse) as the timing of the introduction of food stamps shifted to later and later in childhood (see Figure 3-4). The best adult health was observed among individuals in counties where food stamps were already available when these individuals were conceived. Scores on the index of metabolic syndrome increase steadily until around the age of 5.

It is impossible to determine the extent to which the adult health benefits of food stamp availability in very early childhood were generated by the nutritional advantages of the extra spending on food or by the more general

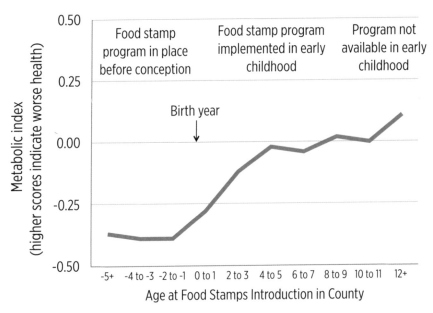

FIGURE 3-4 Impact of food stamp exposure on metabolic syndrome index at age 25 and above.
SOURCE: Adapted from Hoynes, Schanzenbach, and Almond (2016).

increase in economic resources freed up for spending on other family needs. And while these studies of the food stamp rollout offer the best available evidence of the long-term effects of food benefits, the food landscape facing Americans has arguably changed a great deal since that period.

Another possible cause of health benefits is the fact that SNAP benefits appear to cushion unexpected changes in household income: Both Blundell and Pistaferri (2003) and Gundersen and Ziliak (2003) show that the SNAP program substantially reduces the volatility of income.

CONCLUSION 3-5: The Supplemental Nutrition Assistance Program has been shown to improve birth outcomes as well as many important child and adult health outcomes.

Housing Subsidies

By reducing housing costs, housing subsidy programs can provide a substantial transfer of economic resources to recipient households. The main types of assistance available are public housing, voucher-based rental assistance under the Housing Choice Voucher (formerly called Section 8) Program, and subsidized privately owned housing, including the Low Income Housing Tax Credit (Olsen, 2008). All three programs aim to limit the housing expenses of low-income households to 30 percent of their income.

Given their large size and the length of time they have been operating, it is surprising that relatively little research has been conducted concerning the impacts on children of the in-kind resources these programs provide (Collinson, Ellen, and Ludwig, 2015). Some of the best-known studies of housing vouchers—the Moving to Opportunity demonstration is the best known example—involve offering housing vouchers to families that are already living in subsidized public housing. And even when studies compare households receiving housing subsidies with those receiving no housing assistance, it is difficult to separate the benefits to children that stem from improved housing quality occasioned by program benefits from the benefits they experience due to the freeing up of their families' economic resources for spending on other needs.

Nevertheless, whether the resource-enhancing benefits of housing subsidies improve the well-being of children is best seen in studies that contrast children in families that do and do not receive housing subsidies. Jacob, Kapustin, and Ludwig (2015) compare children in families that won the lottery allocating Section 8 housing vouchers in Chicago with children in families that lost that lottery. Examining a 14-year period following the lottery, they find virtually no differences across a range of outcomes in educational attainment, criminal involvement, and health care utilization. On the other hand, Carlson et al. (2012a, 2012b) study a large group of Section 8 recipients in Wisconsin and find small positive effects on the earnings and employment of older children.

A second type of comparison is between children in families that do and do not receive subsidized public housing units. Currie and Yelowitz (2000) take advantage of the fact that two-child families with children of different genders are entitled to larger units and are therefore more likely to "take up" the program and live in public housing. They find that living in public housing reduced the probability that boys would be held back in school and, as well, improved the family's housing quality.

In the case of public housing demolitions, children whose families were displaced from soon-to-be demolished public housing and given housing vouchers may be compared with children living in the same housing projects whose units were not demolished. Since both groups received housing subsidies, the contrast does not involve large differences in economic resources provided by housing subsidies. Jacob (2004) finds no differences in the school achievement of the two groups. Using longer-run data, Chyn (2018) finds improvements in the affected children's labor-market outcomes, namely that young adults who were relocated to less disadvantaged neighborhoods were more likely to be employed than those who lived in the public housing that was not demolished.

The housing policy research that has received much interest focuses on the evaluation of the Moving to Opportunity Program. Moving to Opportunity was a large-scale randomized experiment that provided residents of public housing projects with either "regular" Section 8 housing vouchers or with vouchers that could only be used in a neighborhood with a poverty rate of less than 10 percent (Orr et al., 2003). Those in the latter group also received assistance to find a new residence. In addition to the two treatment groups, a control group of public housing residents remained eligible to stay in their existing public housing. In this experiment, all three groups received housing subsidies, but most families in the two treatment groups moved away from public housing while many in the control group remained.

Focusing first on the comparison between control-group children and children in families receiving the conventional housing vouchers (which were renamed Housing Choice Vouchers during the intervening period), Gennetian and colleagues (2012) find no differences across a range of schooling, health, and behavioral outcomes measured 10 to 15 years after the study began. The longer-run examination of college and labor market outcomes by Chetty, Hendren, and Katz (2015) also failed to find statistically significant outcomes, even for those children who were younger (under age 13) when they entered the study. These results, when combined with those reported in Jacob, Kapustin, and Ludwig (2015), suggest that these programs may reduce child poverty but provide little reason to expect that expanding the existing Housing Choice Voucher Program would lead to better child and youth outcomes.

However, some children in Moving to Opportunity families who received vouchers that could only be used if they moved to low-poverty neighborhoods did have better outcomes. When compared with their control-group counterparts, female (but not male) youth experienced better mental health outcomes (Gennetian et al., 2012). Chetty, Hendren, and Katz (2015) focus on children who were younger than age 13 when their families moved to lower-poverty neighborhoods and find that children who moved to lower-poverty neighborhoods through Moving to Opportunity acquired more education and, as adults, earned more and were less likely to be receiving disability or welfare payments. No such benefits were found for older youth, a result also found in Oreopoulos's (2003) study of families moving into public housing in more advantaged and less advantaged parts of Toronto.

CONCLUSION 3-6: Evidence on the effects of housing assistance is mixed. Children who were young when their families received housing benefits enabling them to move to low-poverty neighborhoods had improved educational attainment and better adult outcomes.

Medicaid

Controversy over the Medicaid expansions included in the Affordable Care Act has obscured public understanding of the sheer scale of the earlier expansions of public health insurance for pregnant women, infants, and children. In 2009, 45 percent of all births in the United States were covered by public health insurance (Markus et al., 2013). Between 1986 and 2005, the share of children eligible for Medicaid/Children's Health Insurance Program (CHIP)[4] increased from a range of 15 to 20 percent of children (depending on the age group) to a range of 40 to 50 percent of children (Currie, Decker, and Lin, 2008). Because the Medicaid expansions were phased in in a staggered way, they have created natural experiments in the value of health insurance for low-income people.

Currie and Gruber (1996a) show that the 30 percent increase in the eligibility of pregnant women during the 1980s and early 1990s was associated with a 7 percent decline in the infant mortality rate. The roughly 15 percent increase in Medicaid eligibility for children that occurred over the same period reduced the probability that a child went without any doctor visits during the year by 9.6 percent (Currie and Gruber, 1996b). Aizer (2007)

---

[4] CHIP was signed into law in 1997. See https://www.medicaid.gov/about-us/program-history/index.html for more information about its history.

and Dafny and Gruber (2005) find that increases in eligibility for Medicaid as well as in Medicaid enrollments reduced preventable hospitalizations among children, also indicating that those children gained access to necessary preventive care. Collectively, these results suggest that as many as 6 million children gained access to basic preventive care as a result of the Medicaid expansions. (See Howell and Kenney, 2012, for a review of research studies.)

Several recent papers look at the long-term effects of the expansions of child Medicaid coverage (Brown, Kowalski, and Lurie, 2015; Cohodes et al., 2016; Currie, Decker, and Lin, 2008; Miller and Wherry, 2018; Wherry and Meyer, 2015; Wherry et al., 2015). These studies all show that cohorts who received Medicaid coverage in early childhood are more likely to work, to have higher earnings, to have more education, and to be in better health in adulthood (using self-reported health, mortality, and hospitalization rates as outcomes) than cohorts who were not covered by the Medicaid/CHIP expansions.

For example, Miller and Wherry (2018) show that early-life access to Medicaid stemming from these expansions is associated with lower rates of obesity and fewer preventable hospitalizations in adulthood. Levine and Schanzenbach (2009) find long-run effects of Medicaid on child educational attainment. Examining the performance of different cohorts of children on the National Assessment of Educational Progress, a nationally representative assessment of U.S. students' knowledge and ability in various subject areas, they find higher scores in states and cohorts where larger numbers of children were covered at birth. East and colleagues (2017) find that women who were covered by Medicaid as infants because of the expansions in the late 1980s and early 1990s have grown into mothers who give birth to healthier children today.

A few studies use historical data about the staggered rollout of Medicaid across the states in the late 1960s to measure its long-term effects. Goodman-Bacon (2018) notes that regulations mandating Medicaid coverage of all cash-welfare recipients led to substantial variations across states in the share of children who became eligible for Medicaid. He finds that after the introduction of Medicaid, mortality fell more rapidly among infants and children in states with bigger Medicaid expansions. Among non-White children, mortality fell by 20 percent. Goodman-Bacon (2016) also looks at the longer-term effects of these increases in coverage and finds that eligibility in early childhood reduced adult disability and increased labor supply up to 50 years later. Boudreaux, Golberstein, and McAlpine (2016) also find that access to Medicaid in early childhood is associated with long-term improvement in adult health, as measured by an index that combines information on high blood pressure, diabetes, heart disease, and obesity.

Currie and Schwandt (2016) argue that the expansions in public health insurance for children have dramatically reduced mortality among poor children, and especially among poor Black children. The result is that socioeconomic inequality in mortality has been falling among children since 1990, even while it has increased for adults. Baker, Currie, and Schwandt (2017) provide comparisons to Canada and show that while mortality remains lower in Canada than in the United States at all ages, the child mortality rate in the United States converged toward the Canadian rate between 1990 and 2010 following the rollout of public health insurance for all poor U.S. children.

> CONCLUSION 3-7: Expansions of public health insurance for pregnant women, infants, and children have generated large improvements in child and adult health and in educational attainment, employment, and earnings.

Summary of Studies on the Causal Impact of Poverty

Causal studies of the effect of poverty on later child well-being often (but not always) find negative impacts, while causal studies of the impact of anti-poverty programs on child well-being consistently find positive impacts. The general pattern may be summed up by this conclusion:

> CONCLUSION 3-8: The weight of the causal evidence indicates that income poverty itself causes negative child outcomes, especially when it begins in early childhood and/or persists throughout a large share of a child's life. Many programs that alleviate poverty either directly, by providing income transfers, or indirectly, by providing food, housing, or medical care, have been shown to improve child well-being.

MACROECONOMIC COSTS OF CHILD POVERTY TO SOCIETY

The first element of the committee's Statement of Task also calls for a review of evidence on the macroeconomic costs of child poverty in the United States. Procedures for estimating these costs are very different from the experimental and quasi-experimental methods adopted in studies of the microeconomic costs of poverty, reviewed above. Holzer et al. (2008) base their cost estimates on the correlations between childhood poverty (or low family income) and outcomes across the life course, such as adult earnings, participation in crime, and poor health. These correlations come from the kinds of studies reviewed in this chapter's appendix (Appendix D, 3-1). Their estimates represent the average decreases in earnings, costs associated with participation in crime (e.g. property loss, injuries, and the justice system), and costs associated with poor health (additional expenditures on health care and the value of lost quantity and quality of life associated with early mortality and morbidity) among adults who grew up in poverty.

Holzer and colleagues (2008) reason that these outcomes are costly to the economy because the overall volume of economic activity is lower than it would have been in the absence of policies that reduced or eliminated poverty. Their procedures lead to a very broad interpretation of the causal effects of childhood poverty—the impacts not only of low parental incomes but also of the entire range of environmental factors associated with poverty in the United States and all of the personal characteristics imparted by parents, schools, and neighborhoods to children affected by them.

At the same time, Holzer and colleagues (2008) make a number of very conservative assumptions in their estimates of earnings and the costs of crime and poor health. For all three, they subtract from their estimates the potential "genetic" (as opposed to environmental) component of the cost.[5] When making calculations, they use those at the lower end of credible estimates in published studies. The earnings data include only those workers who are at least marginally in the labor force; data from families whose household heads are not in the workforce because of incarceration or disability or for other reasons are not captured, nor are government expenditures related to disability included. Additionally, the authors' estimates of the cost of crime include only "street crime" and not other crimes, such as fraud, and they assume that the cost of police, prisons, and private security is unchanged as a result of increases in crime due to child poverty. Finally, they only measure costs related to earnings, crime, and health; there are probably other societal costs that are not measured. All of these analytic choices make it likely that these estimates are a lower bound that understates the true costs of child poverty to the U.S. economy.

The bottom line of the Holzer and colleagues (2008) estimates is that the aggregate cost of conditions related to child poverty in the United States amounts to $500 billion per year, or about 4 percent of the Gross Domestic Product (GDP). The authors estimate that childhood poverty reduces productivity and economic output in the United States by $170 billion per year, or by 1.3 percent of GDP; increases the victimization costs of crime by another $170 billion per year, or by 1.3 percent of the GDP; and increases health expenditures, while decreasing the economic value of health, by $163 billion per year, or by 1.2 percent of GDP.

McLaughlin and Rank (2018) build on the work of Holzer and colleagues (2008) by updating their estimates in 2015 dollars and adding other categories of the impact of childhood poverty on society. They include

---

[5] Holzer et al. (2008) refer to this as the "possible genetic contributions to the intergenerational transmission of disadvantage" (p. 45). For example, the authors recognize that genes can have an important effect on a person's height, weight, and physical and mental health.

increased corrections and crime deterrence costs, increased social costs of incarceration, costs associated with child homelessness (such as the shelter system), and costs associated with increased childhood maltreatment in poor families (such as the costs of the foster care and child welfare systems). Their estimate of the total cost of childhood poverty to society is over $1 trillion, or about 5.4 percent of GDP. This compares to the approximately 1 percent of GDP constituted by direct federal expenditures on children (Isaacs et al., 2018).

These calculations do not reveal which anti-poverty programs are likely to be most effective, nor whether it is sensible to try to reduce poverty in 10 years rather than adopting programs that improve childhood outcomes over a longer time period. They do make it clear that there is considerable uncertainty about the exact size of the costs of child poverty. Nevertheless, whether these costs to the nation amount to 4.0 or 5.4 percent of GDP— roughly between $800 billion and $1.1 trillion annually in terms of the size of the U.S. economy in 2018[6]—it is likely that significant investment in reducing child poverty will be very cost-effective over time.

REFERENCES

Abelev, M.S. (2009). Advancing out of poverty: Social class worldview and its relation to resilience. *Journal of Adolescent Research, 24*(1), 114–141. doi: https://doi.org/10.1177/074355840832844.

Aber, J.L., Morris, P.A., Wolf, S., and Berg, J. (2016). The impact of a holistic conditional cash transfer program in New York City on parental financial investment, student time use and educational processes and outcomes. *Journal of Research on Educational Effectiveness, 9*(3), 335–363. Available: http://dx.doi.org/10.1080/19345747.2015.1107925.

Aizer, A. (2007). Public health insurance, program take-up, and child health. *Review of Economics and Statistics, 89*(3), 400–415.

Aizer, A., Eli, S., Ferrie, J., and Lleras-Muney, A. (2016). The long-run impact of cash transfers to poor families. *American Economic Review, 106*(4), 935–971.

Akee, R.K., Copeland, W.E., Keeler, G., Angold, A., and Costello, E.J. (2010). Parents' incomes and children's outcomes: A quasi-experiment. *American Economic Journal: Applied Economics, 2*(1), 86–115.

Akee, R., Copeland, W., Costello, E.J., and Simeonova, E. (2018). How does household income affect child personality traits and behaviors? *American Economic Review, 108*(3), 775–827.

Almond, D., Hoynes, H.W., and Schanzenbach, D. (2011). Inside the war on poverty: The impact of food stamps on birth outcomes. *Review of Economics and Statistics, 93*(2), 387–403.

Baker, K. (2008). *Do Cash Transfer Programs Improve Infant Health: Evidence from the 1993 Expansion of the Earned Income Tax Credit.* Notre Dame, IN: University of Notre Dame. Available: https://pdfs.semanticscholar.org/a664/5edfe78e6156914ff49a9bd36b975d735c6b.pdf.

---

[6] This is based on a GDP of $20,412 trillion in the second quarter of 2018. See Table 3, https://www.bea.gov/system/files/2018-09/gdp2q18_3rd_3.pdf.

Baker, M., Currie, J., and Schwandt, H. (2017). *Mortality Inequality in Canada and the U.S.: Divergent or Convergent Trends?* Cambridge, MA: National Bureau of Economic Research.

Blair, C., and Raver, C.C. (2016). Poverty, stress, and brain development: New directions for prevention and intervention. *Academic Pediatrics, 16*(3 Suppl), S30–S36.

Blundell, R., and Pistaferri, L. (2003). Income volatility and household consumption—The impact of food assistance programs. *Journal of Human Resources, 38*, 1032–1050.

Bornstein, M.H., and Bradley, R.H. (Eds.). (2003). *Socioeconomic Status, Parenting, and Child Development.* Mahwah, NJ: Lawrence Erlbaum Associates.

Boudreaux, M.H., Golberstein, E., and McAlpine, D.D. (2016). The long-term impacts of Medicaid exposure in early childhood: Evidence from the program's origin. *Journal of Health Economics, 45*, 161–175.

Brody, G.H., Stoneman, Z., Flor, D., McCrary, C., Hastings, L., and Conyers, O. (1994). Financial resources, parent psychological functioning, parent co-caregiving, and early adolescent competence in rural two-parent African-American families. *Child Development, 65*(2 Spec No), 590–605.

Bronchetti, E., Christensen, G., and Hoynes, H. (2018). *Local Food Prices, SNAP Purchasing Power, and Child Health.* NBER Working Paper No. 24762. Cambridge, MA: National Bureau of Economic Research.

Brown, D., Kowalski, A., and Lurie, I. (2015). *Medicaid as an Investment in Children: What Is the Long-term Impact on Tax Receipts?* Cambridge, MA: National Bureau of Economic Research.

Carlson, D., Haveman, R., Kaplan, T., and Wolfe, B. (2012a). Long-term earnings and employment effects of housing voucher receipt. *Journal of Urban Economics, 71*(1), 128–150.

_____ (2012b). Long-term effects of public low-income housing vouchers on neighborhood quality and household composition. *Journal of Housing Economics, 21*(2), 101–120.

Chetty, R., Friedman, J.N., and Rockoff, J. (2011, November). *New Evidence on the Long-Term Impacts of Tax Credits.* Cambridge, MA: National Bureau of Economic Research.

Chetty, R., Hendren, N., and Katz, L. (2015). *The Effects of Exposure to Better Neighborhoods on Children: New Evidence from the Moving to Opportunity Experiment.* Cambridge, MA: National Bureau of Economic Research.

Chyn, E. (2018). Moved to opportunity: The long-run effect of public housing demolition on children. *American Economic Review, 108*(10), 3028–3056.

Cohodes, S.R., Grossman, D.S., Kleiner, S.A., and Lovenheim, M.F. (2016). The effect of child health insurance access on schooling: Evidence from public insurance expansions. *Journal of Human Resources, 51*(3), 727–759.

Collinson, R., Ellen, I.G., and Ludwig, J. (2015). *Low-income Housing Policy.* Cambridge, MA: National Bureau of Economic Research.

Conger, R.D., Ge, X., Elder, G.H., Jr., Lorenz, F.O., and Simons, R.L. (1994). Economic stress, coercive family process, and developmental problems of adolescents. *Child Development, 65*(2 Spec No), 541–561.

Conger, R.D., Wallace, L.E., Sun, Y., Simons, R.L., McLoyd, V.C., and Brody, G.H. (2002). Economic pressure in African American families: A replication and extension of the family stress model. *Developmental Psychology, 38*(2), 179–193.

Costello, E.J., Compton, S.N., Keeler, G., and Angold, A. (2003). Relationships between poverty and psychopathology: A natural experiment. *Journal of the American Medical Association, 290*(15), 2023–2029.

Costello, E.J., Erkanli, A., Copeland, W., and Angold, A. (2010). Association of family income supplements in adolescence with development of psychiatric and substance use disorders in adulthood among an American Indian population. *Journal of the American Medical Association, 303*(19), 1954–1960.

Currie, J., and Gruber, J. (1996a). Saving babies: The efficacy and cost of recent changes in the Medicaid eligibility of pregnant women. *Journal of Political Economy, 104*(6), 1263-1296.

_____. (1996b). Health insurance eligibility, utilization of medical care, and child health. *Quarterly Journal of Economics, 111*(2), 431–466.

Currie, J., and Schwandt, H. (2016). Inequality in mortality decreased among the young while increasing for older adults, 1990–2010. *Science, 352*(6286), 708–712.

Currie, J., and Yelowitz, A. (2000). Are public housing projects good for kids? *Journal of Public Economics, 75*(1), 99–124.

Currie, J., Decker, S., and Lin, W. (2008). *Has Public Health Insurance for Older Children Reduced Disparities in Access to Care and Health Outcomes?* Cambridge, MA: National Bureau of Economic Research.

Currie, J., Zivin, J.S.G., Meckel, K., Neidell, M., and Schlenker, W. (2013). *Something in the Water: Contaminated Drinking Water and Infant Health*. Cambridge, MA: National Bureau of Economic Research.

Dafny, L., and Gruber, J. (2005). Public insurance and child hospitalizations: Access and efficiency effects. *Journal of Public Economics, 89*(1), 109–129.

Dahl, G.B., and Lochner, L. (2012). The impact of family income on child achievement: Evidence from the Earned Income Tax Credit. *American Economic Review, 102*(5), 1927–1956.

Duncan, G., Gennetian, L., and Morris, P. (2009). Parental pathways to self-sufficiency and the well-being of younger children. In C.J. Heinrich and J.K. Scholz (Eds.), *Making the Work-Based Safety Net Work Better: Forward-looking Policies to Help Low-Income Families*. New York: Russell Sage Foundation.

Duncan, G.J., Morris, P.A., and Rodrigues, C. (2011). Does money really matter? Estimating impacts of family income on young children's achievement with data from random-assignment experiments. *Developmental Psychology, 47*(5), 1263–1279.

Duncan, G.J., Ziol-Guest, K.M., and Kalil, A. (2010). Early-childhood poverty and adult attainment, behavior, and health. *Child Development, 81*(1), 306–325.

East, C.N. (2016). *The Effect of Food Stamps on Children's Health: Evidence from Immigrants' Changing Eligibility*. University of Colorado Denver. Available: http://cneast.weebly.com/uploads/8/9/9/7/8997263/east_jmp.pdf.

East, C.N. (2018). The effect of food stamps on children's health: Evidence from immigrants' changing eligibility. *Journal of Human Resources*. Available: https://www.chloeneast.com/uploads/8/9/9/7/8997263/east_fskids_r_r2.pdf.

East, C., Miller, S., Page, M., and Wherry, L. (2017). *Multi-generational Impacts of Childhood Access to the Safety Net: Early Life Exposure of Medicaid and the Next Generation's Health*. Cambridge, MA: National Bureau of Economic Research.

Evans, W., and Garthwaite, C. (2010). *Giving Mom a Break: The Impact of Higher EITC Payments on Maternal Health*. Cambridge, MA: National Bureau of Economic Research.

Fiszbein, A., Schady, N., Ferreira, F.H.G., Grosh, M., Keleher, N., Olinto, P., and Skoufias, E. (2009). *Conditional Cash Transfers: Reducing Present and Future Poverty*. World Bank Policy Research Report. Washington, DC: World Bank. Available: https://openknowledge.worldbank.org/bitstream/handle/10986/2597/476030PUB0Cond101Official-0Use0Only1.pdf?sequence=1&isAllowed=y.

Food and Nutrition Service. (2018a). *SNAP Annual Participation Rates*. Washington, DC: U.S. Department of Agriculture. Available: https://www.fns.usda.gov/pd/supplemental-nutrition-assistance-program-snap.

_____. (2018b). *Income Eligibility Standards*. Washington, DC: U.S. Department of Agriculture. Available: https://www.fns.usda.gov/snap/income-eligibility-standards.

Fox, L., Han, W.J., Ruhm, C., and Waldfogel, J. (2013). Time for children: Trends in the employment patterns of parents, 1967–2009. *Demography, 50*(1), 25–49.

Gennetian, L.A., and Morris, P.A. (2003). The effects of time limits and make-work-pay strategies on the well-being of children: Experimental evidence from two welfare reform programs. *Children and Youth Services Review, 25*(1-2), 17–54.

Gennetian, L.A., Duncan, G., Knox, V., Vargas, W., Clark-Kauffman, E., and London, A.S. (2004). How welfare policies affect adolescents' school outcomes: A synthesis of evidence from experimental studies. *Journal of Research on Adolescence, 14*(4), 399–423.

Gennetian, L.A., Sanbonmatsu, L., Katz, L.F., Kling, J.R., Sciandra, M., Ludwig, J., Duncan, G.J., and Kessler, R.C. (2012). The long-term effects of Moving to Opportunity on youth outcomes. *Cityscape, 14*(2), 137–167.

Goodman-Bacon, A. (2016). *The Long-Run Effects of Childhood Insurance Coverage: Medicaid Implementation, Adult Health, and Labor Market Outcomes*. Cambridge, MA: National Bureau of Economic Research.

_____. (2018). Public insurance and mortality: Evidence from Medicaid implementation. *Journal of Political Economy, 126*(1), 216–262.

Guldi, M., Hawkins, A., Hemmeter, J., and Schmidt, L. (2017). *Supplemental Security Income and Child Outcomes: Evidence from Birth Weight Eligibility Cutoffs*. Cambridge, MA: National Bureau of Economic Research. Available: http://www.nber.org/papers/w24913.

Gundersen, C., and Ziliak, J.P. (2003). The role of food stamps in consumption stabilization. *Journal of Human Resources, 38*, 1051–1079.

Halpern-Meekin, S., Edin, K., Tach, L., and Sykes, J. (2015). *It's Not Like I'm Poor: How Working Families Make Ends Meet in a Post-Welfare World* (first edition). Oakland, CA: University of California Press.

Hanson, J.L., Hair, N., Shen, D.G., Shi, F., Gilmore, J.H., Wolfe, B.L., and Pollak, S.D. (2013). Family poverty affects the rate of human infant brain growth. *PLoS ONE, 8*(12), e80954.

Holzer, H.J., Schanzenbach, D.W., Duncan, G.J., and Ludwig, J. (2008). The economic costs of childhood poverty in the United States. *Journal of Children and Poverty, 14*(1), 41–61.

Howell, E.M., and Kenney, G.M. (2012). The impact of the Medicaid/CHIP expansions on children: A synthesis of the evidence. *Medical Care Research Review, 69*(4), 372–396.

Hoynes, H.W., and Patel, A.J. (2017). Effective policy for reducing poverty and inequality? The Earned Income Tax Credit and the distribution of income. *Journal of Human Resources, 53*(4), 859–890.

Hoynes, H., and Schanzenbach, D.W. (2015). *U.S. Food and Nutrition Programs*. Cambridge, MA: National Bureau of Economic Research.

Hoynes, H., Miller, D., and Simon, D. (2015). Income, the Earned Income Tax Credit, and infant health. *American Economic Journal-Economic Policy, 7*(1), 172–211.

Hoynes, H., Schanzenbach, D.W., and Almond, D. (2016). Long run impacts of childhood access to the safety net. *American Economic Review 106*(4), 903–934. Available: http://dx.doi.org/10.1257/aer.20130375.

Huston, A.C., Duncan, G.J., Granger, R., Bos, J., McLoyd, V., Mistry, R., Crosby, D., Gibson, C., Magnuson, K., Romich, J., and Ventura, A. (2001). Work-based antipoverty programs for parents can enhance the school performance and social behavior of children. *Child Development, 72*(1), 318–336.

Isaacs, J.B., Lou, C., Hong, A., Quakenbush, C., and Steuerle, C.E. (2018). *Kids' Share 2018: Report on Federal Expenditures on Children through 2017 and Future Projections*. Washington, DC: Urban Institute. Available: https://www.urban.org/research/publication/kids-share-2018-report-federal-expenditures-children-through-2017-and-future-projections.

Jacob, B.A. (2004). Public housing, housing vouchers, and student achievement: Evidence from public housing demolitions in Chicago. *American Economic Review, 94*(1), 233–258.

Jacob, B.A., Kapustin, M., and Ludwig, J. (2015). The impact of housing assistance on child outcomes: Evidence from a randomized housing lottery. *Quarterly Journal of Economics, 130*(1), 465–506.

Kehrer, B.H., and Wolin, C.M. (1979). Impact of income maintenance on low birth weight: Evidence from the Gary experiment. *Journal of Human Resources, 14*(4), 434–462.

Levere, M. (2015). *The Labor Market Consequences of Receiving Disability Benefits During Childhood.* Princeton, NJ: Mathematica Policy Research.

Levine, P.B., and Schanzenbach, D. (2009). The impact of children's public health insurance expansions on educational outcomes. *Forum for Health Economics & Policy, 12*(1).

Manoli, D., and Turner, N. (2014). *Cash-on-Hand & College Enrollment: Evidence From Population Tax Data and Policy Nonlinearities.* Cambridge, MA: National Bureau of Economic Research.

Markus, A.R., Andres, E., West, K.D., Garro, N., and Pellegrini, C. (2013). Medicaid covered births, 2008 through 2010, in the context of the implementation of health reform. *Women's Health Issues, 23*(5), e273–e280.

Maxfield, M. (2013). *The Effects of the Earned Income Tax Credit on Child Achievement and Long-Term Educational Attainment.* Job Market Paper, Michigan State University, East Lansing, MI. Available: https://msu.edu/~maxfiel7/20131114%20Maxfield%20EITC%20Child%20Education.pdf.

Maynard, R.A. (1977). The effects of the rural income maintenance experiment on the school performance of children. *The American Economic Review, 67*(1), 370–375.

Maynard, R.A., and Murnane, R.J. (1979). The effects of a negative income tax on school performance: Results of an experiment. *The Journal of Human Resources, 14*(4), 463.

McKernan, S.-M., Ratcliffe, C.E., and Quakenbush, C. (2014). *Small-Dollar Credit: Consumer Needs and Industry Challenges.* Washington, DC: Urban Institute. Available: https://www.urban.org/sites/default/files/publication/33716/413278-Small-Dollar-Credit-Consumer-Needs-and-Industry-Challenges.PDF.

McLaughlin, M., and Rank, M.R. (2018). Estimating the economic cost of childhood poverty in the United States. *Social Work Research, 42*(2), 73–83.

McLoyd, V.C. (1990). The impact of economic hardship on Black families and children: Psychological distress, parenting, and socioemotional development. *Child Development, 61*(2), 311–346.

Miller, C., Miller, R., Verma, N., Dechausay, N., Yang, E., Rudd, T., Rodriguez, J., and Honig, S. (2016). *Effect of a Modified Conditional Cash Transfer Program in Two American Cities.* New York: MDRC. https://www.mdrc.org/publication/effects-modified-conditional-cash-transfer-program-two-american-cities.

Miller, S.M., and Wherry, L.R. (2018). The long-term health effects of early life Medicaid coverage. *The Journal of Human Resources.* doi:10.3368/jhr.54.3.0816.8173R1.

Milligan, K., and Stabile, M. (2011). Do child tax benefits affect the well-being of children? Evidence from Canadian child benefit expansions. *American Economic Journal: Economic Policy, 3*(3), 175–205.

Morris, P., Gennetian, L., and Duncan, G. (2005). Long-term effects of welfare and work policies on children's school achievement: A synthesis from policy experiments conducted in the 1990s. *Social Policy Report, 19*(2), 3–17.

Morris, P., Gennetian, L.A., and Knox, V. (2002). *Welfare Policies Matter for Children and Youth: Lessons for TANF Reauthorization.* New York: MDRC.

Morris, P.A., Huston, A.C., Duncan, G.J., Crosby, D.A., and Bos, J.M. (2001). *How Welfare and Work Policies Affect Children: A Synthesis of Research.* New York: MDRC. Available: http://dev.mdrc.org/sites/default/files/full_392.pdf.

National Institute of Child Health and Human Development Early Child Care Research Network and Duncan, G.J. (2003). Modeling the impacts of child care quality on children's preschool cognitive development. *Child Development, 74*(5), 1454–1475.

Olsen, E.O. (2008). *Getting More from Low-Income Housing Assistance.* Washington, DC: Brookings Institution.

Oreopoulos, P. (2003). The long-run consequences of living in a poor neighborhood. *Quarterly Journal of Economics, 118*(4), 1533–1575.

Orr, L., Feins, J., Jacob, R., Beecroft, E., Sanbonmatsu, L., Katz, L.F., Liebman, J.B., and Kling, J.R. (2003). *Moving to Opportunity: Interim Impacts Evaluation.* Washington, DC: U.S. Department of Housing and Urban Development, Office of Policy Development and Research. Available: https://scholar.harvard.edu/files/lkatz/files/moving_to_opportunity_interim_impacts_evaluation.pdf.

Ouellette, T., Burstein, N., Long, D., and Beecroft, E. (2004). *Measures of Material Hardship: Final Report.* Washington, DC: U.S. Department of Health and Human Services, Office of the Assistant Secretary for Planning and Evaluation.

Ratcliffe, C., and Kalish, E. (2017). *Escaping Poverty: Predictors of Persistently Poor Children's Economic Success.* U.S. Partnership on Mobility from Poverty. Washington, DC: Urban Institute. Available: https://www.mobilitypartnership.org/publications/escaping-poverty.

Raver, C.C., Gershoff, E.T., and Aber, J.L. (2007). Testing equivalence of mediating models of income, parenting, and school readiness for White, Black, and Hispanic children in a national sample. *Child Development, 78*(1), 96–115.

Riccio, J.A., and Miller, C.A. (2016). *Conditional Cash Transfers in NYC: What Worked and Didn't Work.* New York: MDRC. Available: https://www.mdrc.org/publication/new-york-city-s-first-conditional-cash-transfer-program.

Riccio, J.A., Dechausay, N., Miller, C., Nuñez, S., Verma, N., and Yang, E. (2013). *Conditional Cash Transfers in New York City: The Continuing Story of the Opportunity NYC–Family Rewards Demonstration.* New York: MDRC. Available: https://www.mdrc.org/publication/conditional-cash-transfers-new-york-city.

Romig, K. (2017). *SSI: A Lifeline for Children with Disabilities.* Washington, DC: Center on Budget and Policy Priorities.

Salkind, N.J., and Haskins, R. (1982). Negative income tax—The impact on children from low-income families. *Journal of Family Issues, 3*(2), 165–180.

Shonkoff, J.P., Garner, A.S., Siegel, B.S., Dobbins, M.I., Earls, M.F., Garner, A.S., McGuinn, L., Pascoe, K., Wood, D.L., Committee on Psychosocial Aspects of Child and Family Health, Committee on Early Childhood, Adoption, and Dependent Care, and Section on Developmental and Behavioral Pediatrics. (2012). The lifelong effects of early childhood adversity and toxic stress. *Pediatrics, 129*(1), e232–e246.

Strully, K.W., Rehkopf, D.H., and Xuan, Z. (2010). Effects of prenatal poverty on infant health: State Earned Income Tax Credits and birth weight. *American Sociological Review, 75*(4), 534–562.

Venti, S.F. (1984). The effects of income maintenance on work, schooling, and non-market activities of youth. *The Review of Economics and Statistics, 66*(1), 16–25.

Waxman, S. (2017). *State EITC Wins Help Spread Prosperity.* Available: https://www.cbpp.org/blog/state-eitc-wins-help-spread-prosperity.

Wherry, L.R., and Meyer, B.D. (2015). Saving teens: Using a policy discontinuity to estimate the effects of Medicaid eligibility. *Journal of Human Resources, 51*(3), 556–588.

Wherry, L.R., Miller, S., Kaestner, R., and Meyer, B.D. (2015). Childhood Medicaid coverage and later life health care utilization. *Review of Economics and Statistics, 100*(2), 287–302.

Yeung, W.J., and Conley, D. (2008). Black-white achievement gap and family wealth. *Child Development, 79*(2), 303–324.

Zhan, M. (2006). Assets, parental expectations and involvement, and children's educational performance. *Children and Youth Services Review, 28*(8), 961–975.

4

How the Labor Market, Family Structure, and Government Programs Affect Child Poverty

In response to the second element of the committee's statement of task and to provide guidance for the committee's deliberations on new initiatives that can reduce child poverty, in this chapter, we discuss how demographic factors, the labor market and economy, and major government assistance programs affect all child poverty in the United States. We begin with a brief review of the role that demographic factors, particularly single-parent family structure, play in child poverty, followed by an analysis of employment-related factors. We then focus on a key element of our statement of task: the structure and role of current federal government assistance programs as they affect child poverty. We close the chapter with a comparison of the poverty-reducing impact of assistance programs in the United States and in the four English-speaking countries whose selection was discussed in Chapter 2: Australia, Canada, Ireland, and the United Kingdom.

FORCES THAT SHAPE CHILD POVERTY

Three broad sets of forces affect child poverty: demographics, the economy and its labor markets, and government policy. Demographic factors include parental age, education, race, and ethnicity; number of children in the family; and family structure, such as single or married parent. For example, older and more educated parents generally command higher wages, leading to lower levels of family poverty. The presence of two parents in the household would be expected to reduce poverty because of higher earnings and the possibility of specialization as one partner focuses on work and the other on family responsibilities (Becker, 1981). Additionally, whether it is headed by two parents or one, a household with fewer children is likely to experience less poverty because of the higher ratio of potential adult earners to children as well as the fact that the poverty line is lower for a smaller family. The patterns of child poverty across demographic groups shown in Chapter 2 are consistent with these expectations.

Labor market factors include the amount of parental work and the wages earned for every hour worked. Employment and earnings are influenced by secular forces such as macroeconomic growth, labor market forces such as technological change and globalization, and labor market factors such as minimum wage levels and unionization, as well as by cyclical forces such as unemployment.

The third factor is the primary focus of this chapter: government policies, such as tax and transfer programs. These three broad sets of factors are not independent of one another. A change in tax or transfer policy, for example, can affect work patterns and decisions about family structure.

To frame the discussion of the role of these three broad factors, Figure 4-1 illustrates how child poverty rates have evolved over the last five decades (1967 to 2016). The lower line in the figure reproduces the Supplemental Poverty Measure (SPM)-based poverty trend data shown in Figure 2-8. Periods of economic downturn are shown as shaded columns.[1] As discussed in Chapter 2, because some Transfer Income Model, Version 3 (TRIM3) adjustments are unavailable for this entire historical period, the SPM trend in Figure 4-1 (and throughout this chapter) is not adjusted for underreporting of government programs.[2]

The upper trend line in Figure 4-1 illustrates what SPM-based child poverty *would have* been if market income (but no other source of income) were counted as family resources.[3] Market income includes only earnings and income from savings and investments; it does not include any of the government tax and transfers that are included in the SPM resource measure. Importantly, these are "all else equal" poverty rate estimates; these

---

[1] Recession dates are from the National Bureau of Economic Research at http://www.nber.org/cycles.html.

[2] Consistent underreporting adjustments are not possible because TRIM3 data are available only for years 2012, 2014, and 2015. Consequently, the rates reported here are somewhat higher than they would be after such adjustments. The figures are drawn from original analyses commissioned by the committee and conducted by Christopher Wimer (2017, October). The SPM threshold is anchored in 2012 living standards and adjusted back to 1967 using the Consumer Price Index. The Census SPM threshold is not available for years prior to 2009.

[3] Market income was calculated by taking total SPM resources and removing total taxes (tax credits and taxes paid), SNAP, WIC, School Lunch, LIHEAP, housing subsidies, TANF, SSI, Social Security, Unemployment Insurance, and a few smaller government insurance payments such as veterans' assistance. For more on definitions of income, see Gornick and Smeeding (2018).

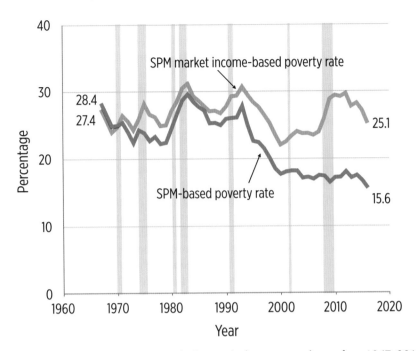

FIGURE 4-1 Child poverty rates, before and after taxes and transfers, 1967–2016.
NOTES: The SPM poverty measure is anchored in 2012 living standards, adjusted back to 1967 using the CPI, and does not adjust for underreporting. Shaded areas indicate recession periods as determined by the NBER Business Cycles Dating Committee. SPM market income-based poverty rate includes labor market income but no other sources of income in its measure of family resources. SPM = Supplemental Poverty Measure, CPI = Consumer Price Index, NBER = National Bureau of Economic Research.
SOURCE: Original analyses commissioned by the committee from Christopher Wimer (2017).

data assume no change in market income (e.g., no change in labor market behavior) in response to the unavailability of tax and transfer income. As we discuss in greater detail below, eliminating pro-work government policies such as the Earned Income Tax Credit (EITC) could reduce market income and thereby increase market-based income poverty, while eliminating means-tested transfers such as food stamps (SNAP) could have the opposite effect.

Figure 4-1 shows that poverty is strongly related to the economy and business cycles, falling during periods of economic growth and rising during recessions and often for another year or two after the official end of a downturn. Many studies document this inverse relationship between unemployment rates and poverty.[4] It is clear from the trends shown in Figure 4-1 that market-income poverty is more cyclical than SPM poverty.[5] Indeed, Figure 4-1 reveals that the Great Recession led to a 3.4 percentage point increase in market-income poverty (between 2008 and 2010), while SPM poverty fell slightly (by 0.2 percentage points). As discussed later in this chapter, this suggests that the tax and transfer programs included in SPM calculations were very successful at mitigating the negative impacts of the economic cycle on child poverty (Bitler and Hoynes, 2010; Bitler, Hoynes and Kuka, 2017; Blank, 1989; Blank and Blinder, 1986; Cutler and Katz, 1991; Freeman, 2001; Gunderson and Ziliak, 2004; Hoynes, Page, and Stevens, 2006; Meyer and Sullivan, 2011).

More generally, Figure 4-1 shows that there is no clear secular, long-term trend in market-income-based child poverty: Child poverty rates based solely on market income have improved only slightly over the 50-year period, falling from 27.4 percent in 1967 to 25.1 percent in 2016. This lack of improvement is particularly notable given that general living standards, as indicated by per-capita Gross Domestic Produce (GDP), more than doubled between the late 1960s and today.[6] Holding other factors constant, market-income-based poverty rates should have fallen substantially if the improved economy had indeed boosted the financial situation of people living in poverty.

The lack of long-term declines in market-based poverty also implies that policy changes since the 1990s that were aimed at reducing poverty by increasing work and earnings—including the welfare reform of the 1990s, the EITC, and expanded access to child care, to name three changes—have not reduced child poverty rates, on net and in combination with changes in the economy. Disentangling the effects of these policy changes from changes in the economy over the period is difficult. To take one of these policy changes as an example, what evidence we have on 1990s welfare reform shows that it did have some short-term effects in reducing poverty rates and thus made a contribution to the decline in market-based poverty in the second half of the 1990s, as shown in Figure 4-1 (see Chapter 7 for a discussion of this evidence). However, the lower SPM child poverty rate in 2015 compared to that in 1996, for example, is almost entirely due to an increase in tax credits and transfers, not due to an increase in work and earnings.

---

[4] Bitler and Hoynes (2010, 2015); Bitler, Hoynes, and Kuka (2017); Blank (1989, 1993); Blank and Blinder (1986); Blank and Card (1993); Cutler and Katz (1991); Freeman (2001); Gunderson and Ziliak (2004); Hoynes, Page, and Stevens (2006); Meyer and Sullivan (2011).

[5] Recent work by Bitler, Hoynes, and Kuka (2017) documents this using data from 2000 to 2014.

[6] See data provided by the Federal Reserve Bank of St. Louis, at https://fred.stlouisfed.org/tags/series?t=gdp%3Bper+capita.

> **CONCLUSION 4-1:** Despite economic growth over the past half century, child poverty rates calculated using only labor market income have remained high—ranging between 22 and 32 percent.

Many aspects of children's demographic circumstances have undergone dramatic changes in the past four or five decades (Social Capital Project, 2017). For example, among children whose mothers had lower levels of education, the share of those living with a married parent has declined sharply (see Figure 4-2). Trends in women's educational attainment (Appendix D, Figure D4-2) and fertility (Appendix D, Figure D4-3) show that there has been a steady increase in attainment since 1962 as well as a steady decrease in fertility among women overall since 1976. Linking some of these demographic changes to child poverty, we would expect the increasing incidence of single parenthood to push up rates of child poverty,

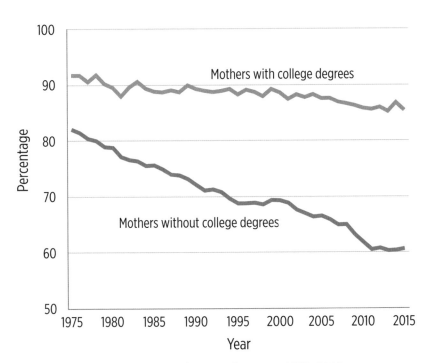

FIGURE 4-2 Share of children with married parents, 1975–2015.
NOTES: Calculations based on Current Population Survey Annual Social and Economic Supplement 1976–2016. Data are restricted to mothers ages 25–54.
SOURCE: Adapted from Hoynes and Schanzenbach (2018).

while the increase in maternal education and the reduction in the number of children should lower them.[7]

There have also been important changes in the parental connections to the labor market. Large numbers of both single and married mothers have joined the workforce since 1975 (see Figure 4-3). The increase in employment among single mothers was particularly dramatic in the 1990s, and was accompanied by a rise in the amount of the EITC and in other work supports in the wake of welfare reform.[8] Male employment, on the other hand, trended downward over this period (Appendix D, Figure D4-1). The increase in employment among single parents, particularly between the early 1990s and 2000, would also be expected to reduce child poverty over that period.

A number of studies have used a "what-if" approach to distinguish between the roles of demographic factors and the labor market in explaining trends in the Official Poverty Measure (OPM). Using poverty rates across different subgroups, such as married/single-parent families or working/nonworking parents, these decomposition studies calculate how overall child poverty rates would have changed if each group had experienced the observed poverty trend but the overall composition of the population (e.g., the share of children living with a single parent) had not changed. This approach is distinct from asking "does family structure matter" at any given point in time, and instead seeks to understand which factors explain *changes* in poverty over time.

Decomposition studies based on data from before the mid-1990s generally find that changes in family structure, most notably the increase in single parenthood, explain a large share of the observed increase in child (official) poverty between the 1970s and the mid-1990s (Danziger and Gottschalk, 1995; Lerman, 1996). After the employment of single mothers began to rise in the early 1990s, however, their families' exposure to labor market fluctuations began to increase. The decomposition studies applied to poverty trends beginning in the 1990s have found that changes in employment, rather than in family structure, are the most important factor in explaining recent (official) poverty trends (Cancian and Reed, 2009; Chen and Corak, 2008; Lichter and Crowley, 2004; Nichols, 2013). This does not mean that family structure has no influence on child poverty, but rather that changes in family structure do not explain changes in child poverty during this later time period.

The shifting influence of family structure versus employment is evident in Nichols' (2013) analyses of data spanning the period from 1975

---

[7] Because of rising educational attainment among women (Appendix D, Figure 4-2) the composition of women in lower-education groups is changing over time. This should be kept in mind when examining trends for various low-education groups over time as in Figure 4-2.

[8] Since 2000, the labor force participation of single mothers has been nearly identical to that of childless women (Black, Schanzenbach, and Breitwieser, 2017; not shown in Figure 4-3).

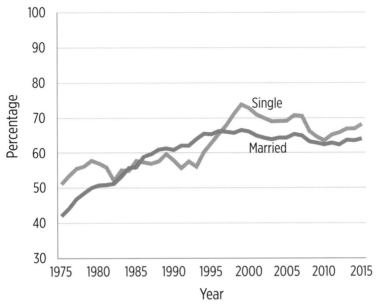

FIGURE 4-3 Share of children with a working mother, 1975–2015.
NOTES: Calculations based on the Current Population Survey Annual Social and Economic Supplement 1976-2016. Data are restricted to mothers ages 25 to 54.
SOURCE: Adapted from Hoynes and Schanzenbach (2018).

to 2011. Nichols (2013) finds that a large fraction of the trend in child (official) poverty between 1975 and 1993 is explained by changes in family structure (single parenthood, number of family members, multigenerational households) and age, while trends in child poverty between 1993 and 2011 are largely explained by increases in employment. This finding holds true for different subgroups of children, including White, Black, and Hispanic children (Appendix D, Figure D4-4). For example, Nichols (2013) shows that for White children, changes in family structure (and age of children) account for 85 percent of the actual change in child poverty between 1975 and 1993, and that changes in employment account for over 70 percent of the change between 1993 and 2011. Among Black children, the role of family structure was particularly important in the early period, explaining more than all of the actual increase in child poverty between 1975 and 1993.[9]

---

[9] Baker (2015) reaches a similar conclusion using a different approach, one that focuses on the changing associations between work, marriage, and poverty over time. Her work shows that the magnitude of the negative association between marriage and child poverty has declined, while the positive association between work and child poverty has increased.

CONCLUSION 4-2: The decline in two-parent family structure is the single biggest factor associated with the increase in child (official) poverty between the mid-1970s and the early 1990s. However, child poverty has fallen since the early 1990s, despite continuing increases in single parenthood. This more recent decline in child poverty is most strongly associated with increases in maternal employment.

To further explore the role of the labor market, the economy, and employment in explaining trends in poverty, Chen and Corak (2008) undertake a decomposition to examine the comparative roles of employment and earnings. They find that between 1991 and 2000, labor market factors reduced poverty. More than one-half of that reduction stemmed from the mother's annual earnings (conditional on work), with the remainder of the effect split between the employment status of the father (20%), the employment status of the mother (17%), and the annual earnings of the father (less than 10%). That is, almost 70 percent of the reduction in poverty owing to labor market effects during the 1991–2000 period resulted from the increased employment and earnings of mothers.

Figure 4-4 provides a summary of the broader trends in earnings, plotting real median weekly wages between 1963 and 2012 for women working full time throughout the year, by education level (Autor, 2014). The 1963 earnings of each group serve as the baseline as the graph tracks the ratio of earnings in a given year relative to 1963 earnings. Women with no more than a high school education experienced much slower wage growth than women with more schooling. (The inflation-adjusted earnings of men with low levels of schooling, as shown in Appendix D, Figure D4-5, were actually *lower* at the end of the period than at the beginning.)

Beginning in the early 1980s, the wage patterns fan out and reflect increasing wage inequality across education levels.[10] In the 5 years following 2012 (after the end of the series in Figure 4-4), inflation-adjusted wages started to increase, showing real gains for the lowest quintile of workers. This growth resulted from both continued recovery from the recession and increases in state minimum wages (Shambaugh et al., 2017). The main forces in the economy that have contributed to wage stagnation for low-skilled workers and higher wages as skills increase include skill-biased technological change (Juhn, Murphy, and Pierce, 1993; Katz and Murphy, 1992), globalization (Autor, Dorn, and Hanson, 2013), the decline in

---

[10] This fanning out is even more dramatic if we include weekly wages for those with education beyond a college degree (Autor, 2014). Note, however, that the share of workers with a high school degree or less has declined over this time period, which may affect the composition of the group with low levels of education over time.

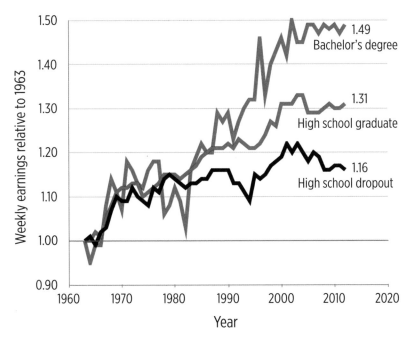

FIGURE 4-4 Changes in median weekly earnings of full-time, full-year female workers, 1963–2012.
NOTES: Data for other education levels and for men are contained in the chapter appendix. Conversion to real 2012 dollars using CPI-U-Research Series.
SOURCE: Autor (2014).

unions (Farber et al., 2018), and the decline in the real value of the federal minimum wage (Autor, Manning, and Smith, 2016).

> **CONCLUSION 4-3:** The earnings of more highly skilled workers have grown substantially in the past 50 years. By contrast, the earnings of men with a high school education or less have stagnated or declined since the early 1970s, and the earnings of women with a high school education or less have stagnated since 2000. Because the large majority of poor parents have completed less schooling than higher-income parents, this stagnation has meant that market income has not reduced child poverty over this period as much as it might otherwise have. Moreover, the stagnation of annual earnings for lower-skilled mothers has been among the most important factors in slowing the decline in market-based child poverty over the last two decades.

THE CHANGING ROLE OF GOVERNMENT
TAXES AND TRANSFERS

The divergence between the 50-year child poverty trend based on a market-income measure and that based on the SPM measure, which is illustrated in Figure 4-1, underscores the increasing importance of government taxes and transfers in reducing child poverty. In this section, we detail the changing role of such taxes and transfers in reducing poverty. The section begins with a brief description of trends in federal spending on children and a review of major changes in policy during this period. This is followed by an analysis of the effects of government tax and transfer policy, based on an examination of the difference between trends in market-income child poverty rates and SPM child poverty rates.

Drawing on Isaacs et al. (2018), Figure 4-5 shows the trend between 1960 and 2017 in inflation-adjusted federal spending on programs that benefit children, most of which are counted as income in the SPM-based poverty measure (see also Appendix D, Table 4-1).[11] The eight-fold growth in real spending between 1960 and 2010 is striking, and it is many times larger than the 15 percent increase in the number of children in the population.

It is little wonder that the trend in child SPM poverty, which is based on a conception of resources that subtracts taxes paid, adds tax credits such as the EITC and includes income from transfer programs such as the Supplemental Nutrition Assistance Program (SNAP) depicted in Figure 4-1, diverges steadily from the market-income-only poverty trend, especially after 1980. In 1960, spending was largely limited to cash assistance from the Aid to Families with Dependent Children (AFDC) and Social Security programs. The next five decades saw the introduction or expansion of major programs benefiting children. Food stamps (now called SNAP) and Medicaid—two major in-kind benefit programs serving children in low-income families—were rolled out in the 1960s and 1970s. Supplemental Security Income (SSI) was also introduced during this period; originally, the program provided cash benefits for low-income disabled and elderly individuals. Now the program also serves children meeting disability requirements.

Transfer programs changed markedly in the 1990s with the expansion of the EITC as well as federal welfare reform (in 1996), which eliminated the entitlement of cash welfare. The Child Tax Credit was introduced in

---

[11] This includes cash transfers, nutrition programs (SNAP, WIC, and child nutrition programs), public housing benefits, tax credits, and other child-related tax benefits. Medicaid spending on children is also included in Figure 4-5 but is not counted in calculating SPM-based poverty.

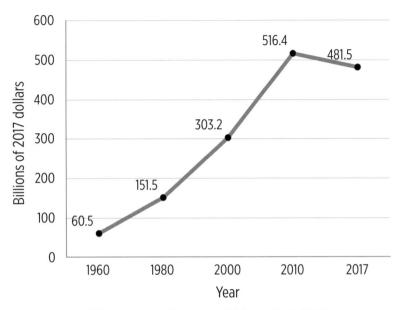

FIGURE 4-5 Total federal expenditures on children, 1960–2017.
NOTE: In billions of 2017 dollars.
SOURCE: Isaacs et al. (2018, Table 3).

1997 and then expanded in the first decade of the 2000s.[12] The spending decline between 2010 and 2016 was largely due to the decrease in transfers during the economic recovery that followed the Great Recession, coupled with the fact that no major new program initiatives directed at children were introduced or expanded during this period.

A comparison of Figure 4-1 and Figure 4-5 reveals that secular SPM poverty trends track expenditure patterns quite closely. In the late 1960s, the net effect of government transfers and the tax system was to *increase* poverty—on balance, the poor paid more in taxes than they received in benefits. In later decades, however, the benefits paid through the tax system have continued to grow; for example, between 1980 and 2000 there was a 10-fold increase in the inflation-adjusted value of refundable tax credits (see Appendix D, Table 4-1). Those benefits, combined with benefits received

---

[12] Spending on Medicaid (for children) and the State Child Health Insurance Program expanded dramatically between 1980 and 2000 as a result of federal and state legislation (Gruber, 2003). But these expansions affect SPM poverty only through their effects on out-of-pocket medical expenses. In Chapter 7 we discuss possible changes to the SPM to better capture the resources provided through public insurance.

through income-tested programs, have been the major factor driving rates of SPM-based poverty as low as they are today.

While market-income poverty rates fell by 8 percentage points between 1993 and 2000, it is also apparent that the booming economy during that period played a substantial role in the 10-percentage point decline in SPM poverty rates over this period. But government policy changes during this period, which included the expansion of the EITC (1994–1996) and federal welfare reform (passed in 1996), also mattered. Indeed, it is the combination of the EITC expansion, welfare reform, and a strong labor market that contributed to a dramatic increase in employment for single mothers (Blank, 2006; Blank and Haskins, 2001; Grogger, 2003; Meyer and Rosenbaum, 2001; refer to Figure 4-3) and a consequent reduction in market-income and SPM poverty.

The role of policy in reducing poverty over and above labor-market earnings began to grow again in 2000, owing mainly to the introduction and expansion of the Child Tax Credit (Hoynes and Rothstein, 2017) and the expansion in eligibility for SNAP (Ganong and Liebman, 2013). Figure 4-1 also shows that government benefits effectively cushioned families from the effects of the Great Recession, since market-income-based poverty rates increased sharply between 2008 and 2010 but SPM-based poverty, which includes transfers, actually fell slightly. SNAP figured prominently as a source of countercyclical income protection during this period, as did temporary measures contained in the 2008 and 2009 stimulus packages (Bitler and Hoynes, 2016; Bitler, Hoynes, and Kuka, 2017).

In the final stage of this historical period—from 2011 to 2016—the combination of expanding employment and added work hours for those already employed pushed market-income-based poverty down sharply for families with children. The effects of refundable tax credits and SNAP were also substantial; for most low-income families with children, work alone was not enough to lift them out of poverty (Hardy, Smeeding, and Ziliak, 2018).

Children in all three of the largest racial/ethnic groups (Whites, Blacks, and Hispanics) have experienced declines in market-income poverty rates over the past 50 years.[13] This is evident in Appendix D, Figures D4-6, D4-7, and D4-8, taken from Wimer (2017), which show market-income and SPM-income child poverty rates from 1967 to 2016. Children in all three groups have also experienced larger declines in SPM poverty rates than

---

[13] These declines are larger than the overall decline in market child poverty rates shown in Figure 4-1 because the demographic composition of American children has changed; the share of White children has decreased and the share of those at greater risk for poverty has grown. Put another way, the changing racial/ethnic composition of American children obscures long-term progress within all three racial/ethnic groups.

in market-income poverty rates, and this difference has become especially large in the past 15 years.

Similarly, poverty rates have declined over this period for children regardless of family composition. Appendix D, in Figures D4-9, D4-10, and D4-11, also taken from Wimer (2017), shows market-income and SPM child poverty rates from 1967 to 2016, separately for single, cohabiting, and married parents. Although both market-income and SPM poverty rates are quite different for these three groups—highest for single parents and lowest for married parents—all three groups show similar trends, with a particularly large decline in SPM poverty for single-parent families. In short, from 1993 onwards the tax and transfer system was increasingly effective at reducing child poverty rates for all racial/ethnic groups and all family types, with especially large effects during the 2000–2016 period.

> **CONCLUSION 4-4: Government tax and transfer programs reduced the child poverty rate, defined by the Supplemental Poverty Measure (SPM), modestly between 1967 and 1993, but became increasingly important after 1993 because of increases in government benefits targeted at the poor and near poor. Between 1993 and 2016, SPM poverty fell by 12.3 percentage points, from 27.9 to 15.6 percent, more than twice as much as market-income-based poverty.**

Figure 4-6 depicts the trends in deep child poverty (below 50 percent of the poverty line) based on market-income poverty and on SPM poverty. Like market-income poverty drawn at the 100 percent SPM line, market-income-based deep poverty is cyclical, rising in economic downturns and falling when the economy expands. Although there was a dramatic decline in SPM poverty (refer to Figure 4-1), less progress was made in reducing SPM deep poverty over this period.[14] In 1967, 8.2 percent of children were in deep SPM poverty, compared with 4.5 percent in 2016.[15] A large reduction was observed between 1967 and 1974, when AFDC benefits were increased and the Food Stamp Program was introduced, and again in the late 1990s because of a strong labor market, welfare reform, and the expansion of the EITC. There has been almost no net change in the deep poverty rate since that time. The impact of government programs on deep poverty (as measured by the difference between market-income deep poverty and SPM deep poverty) declined substantially in the 1990s,

---

[14] Some of this lack of progress fighting SPM poverty may reflect the rising rates of underreporting in the Current Population Survey (Meyer and Mittag, 2015; Meyer, Mok, and Sullivan 2009).

[15] The 5.0 percent rate of deep poverty differs from the 2.9 percent rate presented in Chapter 2 because it does not reflect adjustments for underreporting. It has proved impossible to make a consistent set of underreporting adjustments across the entire 1967–2016 period.

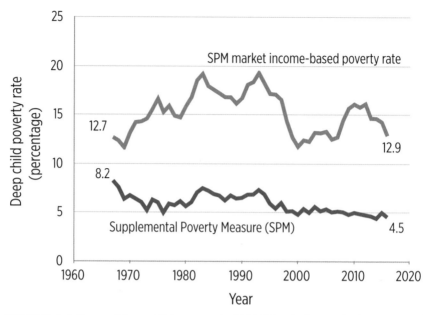

FIGURE 4-6 Rates of deep child poverty (< 50% SPM) before and after taxes and transfers, 1967–2016.

NOTE: The SPM poverty measure is anchored in 2012 living standards, adjusted back to 1967 using the Consumer Price Index, and does not adjust for underreporting. SPM market income-based poverty rate includes labor market income but no other sources of income in its measure of family resources.

SOURCE: Original analyses commissioned by the committee from Christopher Wimer (2017).

following welfare reform and the drop in cash assistance. In 1993, the tax and transfer system reduced deep poverty by 12 percentage points (from 19% for market-income deep poverty to 7% after taxes and benefits), and in 2000 it lowered deep poverty rates by only 7 percentage points. During the Great Recession, market-income deep child poverty rose sharply, but the safety net fully offset that increase.

A major shift occurred in the 1990s, as cash assistance declined (because of welfare reform) and work-dependent assistance (the EITC and, later, the Child Tax Credit) increased. Since about 2000, federal spending on the non-working poor and the deep poor has remained stable or increased modestly; in contrast, spending on the working poor and those above the level of deep poverty has increased more substantially. Overall, then, spending has shifted away from the nonworking/deep poor and toward the working poor (Hoynes and Schanzenbach, 2018; Moffitt, 2015; Moffitt and Pauley, 2018).

Moreover, since the Great Recession the poorest individuals have experienced a sharp drop in support as temporary expansions of programs like SNAP expired, returning almost to pre-recession levels. The trend toward spending more on the working poor and proportionately less on the non-working/deep poor has therefore continued to widen since the Great Recession (Moffitt and Pauley, 2018).

An examination of near poverty among children—drawing the poverty line at 150 percent of the SPM poverty line—shows a remarkable decline in SPM near poverty over the period in question. As shown in Figure 4-7, SPM near poverty fell from nearly 60 percent in 1967 to 36 percent in 2016. However, a comparison of market-income near poverty and SPM near poverty reveals a very different picture of the impacts of the tax and transfer system. Taxes (net of transfers) on the near poor exceeded government benefits during most of the past 50 years, and this pushed the rates of SPM-based near poverty for children *above* the near-poverty rates

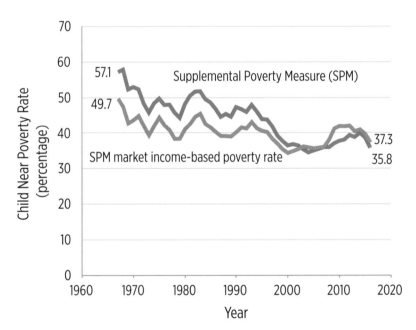

FIGURE 4-7 Rates of child near poverty (< 150% SPM) before and after taxes and transfers, 1967–2016.
NOTE: The SPM poverty measure is anchored in 2012 living standards, adjusted back to 1967 using the Consumer Price Index, and does not adjust for underreporting. SPM market income-based poverty rate includes labor market income but no other sources of income in its measure of family resources.
SOURCE: Original analyses commissioned by the committee from Christopher Wimer (2017, October).

based solely on market income. The gap between the two rates narrows in the mid-1990s with the expansion of the EITC, and again in 1997 and 2000 with the introduction and expansion of the Child Tax Credit. During the Great Recession, market-income near poverty increased sharply, and the safety net partially offset this increase. By the end of the period, the fraction of children with total family resources below 150 percent of SPM poverty was nearly identical to rates based solely on market income, which suggests that, on balance, taxes and transfers had little net impact on the near-poverty thresholds among children.

CONCLUSION 4-5: Increasingly, anti-poverty programs have been geared toward working families. Increased government benefits have been less effective at reducing deep poverty (below 50% of the Supplemental Poverty Measure [SPM]) than at reducing poverty (100% of SPM), because fewer employment-based program benefits reach very low-income families with children. In the case of near poverty (income less than 150% of SPM), the net impact of government taxes and transfers on market income is now neutral, rather than negative, thanks to the expansion of work-based benefits for families above the 100 percent poverty line.

CHILD-RELATED INCOME TRANSFERS AND TAX BENEFITS

In this section, the committee addresses a key element of the statement of task: to provide an analysis of the poverty-reducing effects of the current set of major assistance programs directed at children and families in the United States. We begin with an overview of these programs and then analyze how child poverty rates in 2015 would have changed in the absence of each of these programs.

Although programs like SNAP and Temporary Assistance to Needy Families (TANF) may be among the most visible federal programs for children in low-income families, they are not the largest child-focused programs. The most comprehensive recent accounting of federal expenditures on all children is provided by Isaacs et al. (2018) and summarized in Figure 4-8 for 2017.[16] It includes programs supported by federal budget expenditures as well as "spending" programs that take the form of tax reductions benefiting families with children. Some of the programs, most notably the dependent tax exemption, the deduction for employer-sponsored health

---

[16] Only benefits or services provided either entirely or in some portion directly to children were counted. For benefits such as Medicaid and SSI that serve different age groups, the authors calculated the percentage of expenditures that goes to children (Isaacs et al., 2018).

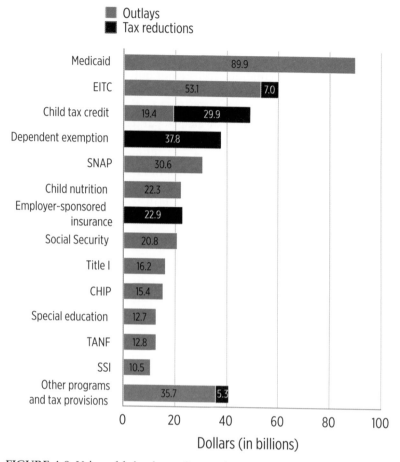

FIGURE 4-8 Value of federal spending outlays and tax reductions with the highest expenditures on children, 2017 (in billions of dollars).
NOTES: Amounts in 2017 dollars. EITC = Earned Income Tax Credit, SNAP = Supplemental Nutrition Assistance Program, CHIP = Children's Health Insurance Program, TANF = Temporary Assistance for Needy Families, SSI = Supplemental Security Income.
SOURCE: Isaacs et al. (2018).

insurance, and (to a lesser extent) the Child Tax Credit, provide considerably more benefits to middle- and high-income families with children than to poor families. Accordingly, they are less likely than benefits targeted toward the low-income population to reduce child poverty. Indeed, Isaacs et al. (2018) estimates that more than one-third (37%) of federal expenditures directed at children go to programs such as the Child Tax Credit and income tax exemption for children, which do not restrict benefits to families with low incomes.

The Medicaid program, with expenditures of nearly $90 billion directed at children, is the federal program that spends the most on children. In 2017, low-income children received not only $90 billion in federal Medicaid payments, but also $15 billion from the government through the Children's Health Insurance Program (CHIP), which provides health insurance to children through Medicaid as well as separate programs negotiated by states with the federal government. Total federal spending for health insurance for all children (including the $23 billion in tax expenditures for the deductibility of employer-provided health insurance, most of which benefits children in middle- and higher-income families) amounts to $128 billion. This amount represents 23 percent of all federal expenditures on children. Despite the crucial importance of health care spending for the future development of poor children, this spending has virtually no impact on SPM-based poverty because of the ways in which SPM-based poverty is defined (see Chapters 2 and 7).[17]

The second-, third-, and fourth-largest expenditures on children relate to provisions in the federal income tax: the EITC, the Child Tax Credit, and tax exemptions for dependent children living in a household (Isaacs et al., 2018). At $60 billion, the EITC is the largest of the three. Although available only to families with earned income, the EITC is refundable, so when a family's income is too low to generate tax obligations, the family receives a refund from the IRS. In 2017, a single mother with two children who earned between $14,040 and $18,340 (a range that includes the earnings of a full-time, full-year minimum wage worker) would receive the maximum credit of $5,616.[18] For the 2016 tax year, the average EITC for a family with children was $3,176.[19] The EITC is not without flaws, however; Box 4-1 describes issues pertaining to noncompliance and overpayments.

The Child Tax Credit ($49 billion; refer to Figure 4-8) is a partially refundable tax credit for each child a working family is allowed to claim. Prior to the 2018 tax reform, the credit amounted to $1,000 per child; the 2018 reforms doubled that amount.[20] The Child Tax Credit provides important benefits to some low-income families with children, but a substantial share of its federal funding goes to families much higher in the

---

[17] See Chapter 9 for recommendations for incorporating public health insurance expenditures into the poverty measure.

[18] See https://www.irs.gov/credits-deductions/individuals/earned-income-tax-credit/eitc-income-limits-maximum-credit-amounts for 2017 EITC limits.

[19] See https://www.cbpp.org/research/federal-tax/policy-basics-the-earned-income-tax-credit.

[20] For more information about the 2018 reforms, see https://www.irs.gov/newsroom/whats-new-with-the-child-tax-credit-after-tax-reform.

BOX 4-1
The Earned Income Tax Credit (EITC):
Reducing Noncompliance and Overpayments

Administered through the tax system, the EITC provides low- and moderate-income workers with a cash benefit designed to incentivize work, increase income, and reduce poverty. Despite its success and low administrative cost, there are ongoing problems with compliance and enforcement, which stem from overclaiming for the benefit.

Based on audited tax returns from the 2006–2008 period, a recent Internal Revenue Service (IRS) study found that between 43 and 50 percent of tax returns with an EITC claim and between 28.4 and 39.1 percent of all claimed EITC dollars were overclaims (Internal Revenue Service, 2014). This form of noncompliance generally falls into two categories: misclaiming children and misreporting income on tax returns.

Opinions vary as to why noncompliance occurs and whether it is a matter of taxpayer error or fraud. The rules governing the EITC are complicated, particularly with regard to its residency requirement. In light of the complexity of family living situations (divorced or separated parents, multigenerational families living in the same household, moves from one home to another, etc.), there can be confusion as to who has the right to claim a child and misreporting of qualifying children (Greenstein, Warwick, and Marr, 2017; Hoynes and Rothstein, 2017).

Misreporting of income—although it is more common than the misclaiming of children—accounts for a smaller share of overpayment dollars. Most incorrect income reporting can be traced to self-employed taxpayers, suggesting that some filers may be reporting higher incomes than they actually earned in order to maximize the credit (Chetty, Friedman, and Saez, 2013; Rector, 2016; Saez, 2010).

The IRS lacks enforcement authority to address most of the noncompliance and overpayment problems. While it has the authority to audit the EITC, since the benefit is refundable the IRS pays out millions of dollars each year before it has a chance to verify the accuracy of the income reported on returns with EITC claims (Rector, 2016). And despite efforts to equip the IRS with more tools to reduce EITC overpayment, its limited authority to correct erroneous claims when tax returns are processed remains a major barrier to reducing improper payments. Owing to limited resources, the IRS is also unable to address erroneous claims despite having devised methods for reducing overpayments (Greenstein, Warwick, and Marr, 2017).

---

income distribution.[21] In the case of the tax exemption for dependent

---

[21] The refundable portion of the Child Tax Credit (CTC), known as the Additional Child Tax Credit (ACTC), is limited to 15 percent of earned income above $3,000. Here we refer to the combined CTC and ACTC simply as the CTC. In 2017, the $1,000 credit was phased out, starting at incomes of about $80,000 and $120,000 for single- and married-couple families, respectively. The credit was fully phased out at incomes of about $100,000 ($130,000) for single-parent (married-couple) families. Hoynes and Schanzenbach (2018) estimate that as of 2017, 40 percent of CTC spending goes to families with incomes above 200 percent of poverty.

children, little of the $38 billion in benefits from the dependent exemption goes to the families of poor children because of their low levels of taxable income. As shown below, both the EITC and Child Tax Credit target low-income families and play an important role in reducing child poverty.

Spending on nutrition-related programs (SNAP, school breakfast and lunch, food for children attending child care) totaled $58 billion in 2017 (Isaacs et al., 2018). Eligibility for SNAP ($31 billion; Isaacs et al., 2018), which provides vouchers for food assistance, is generally limited to those with gross monthly incomes below 130 percent of the federal poverty line. In 2018, the average monthly SNAP benefit was $125 per person.[22]

Social insurance spending, consisting of Survivors Insurance (part of Social Security) and benefits for child dependents of Disability Insurance beneficiaries, was next in size, at $21 billion (Isaacs et al., 2018). Neither is explicitly targeted at the poor or low-income families, but both benefit children who suffer the loss of a wage earner, thereby reducing the economic insecurity of children from all income classes. Because disability and death are more common among families in the bottom half than in the top half of the income distribution, however, these two forms of social insurance prevent a substantial number of children from falling into poverty.

Expenditures on each of the other programs listed in Figure 4-8 amounted to less than $17 billion. It is noteworthy that federal spending on the key cash assistance program that emerged from the 1996 welfare reforms (the TANF program) totaled only $13 billion in 2017 (Isaacs et al., 2018). SSI is a federal cash assistance program that provides benefits to low-income disabled and elderly persons. Following a court decision in 1990, the definition of disability was expanded to allow more children to receive SSI (Duggan, Kearney, and Rennane, 2016); in 2017 those expenditures totaled $11 billion.

EFFECTS OF INCOME TRANSFERS AND TAX BENEFITS ON CHILD POVERTY IN 2015

The degree to which federal programs reduce child poverty is a function of whether program benefits are counted as resources in the SPM poverty measure and, if they are counted, their overall size and the extent to which their benefits are targeted at the families of poor children.[23] We use the TRIM3 microsimulation model to estimate how much rates of child

---

[22] See https://fns-prod.azureedge.net/sites/default/files/pd/SNAPsummary.pdf.

[23] The largest transfer program omitted from SPM resources is Medicaid, which as we saw above is the child program with the highest federal expenditures. Given the expansions to Medicaid in recent decades, the reductions in SPM poverty shown below would be greater if Medicaid were included. See Chapter 7 for a discussion of incorporating public health insurance expenditures into the poverty measure.

poverty (at 100%, 50%, and 150% of the TRIM3 SPM poverty line) would increase if benefits from each major support program were eliminated. As with the poverty estimates discussed in Chapter 2, these TRIM3 estimates adjust for the underreporting of transfers and apply to 2015.

Importantly, though, our estimates of the poverty-reducing impact of current programs do not account for the extent to which eliminating a given program might also affect work and other decisions that would in turn affect a family's market incomes. As discussed in Chapter 5, these behavioral effects could either push the estimates of child poverty rates up (if the elimination of the EITC and its work incentives caused earnings to fall) or down (if the elimination of an important income source, such as SNAP, led to more work and earnings).

The two refundable tax credits—the EITC and the refundable portion of the Child Tax Credit—are the most successful at alleviating poverty, as shown in Figure 4-9.[24] Starting from the 13.0 percent TRIM3 SPM child poverty rate in 2015, we estimate that the elimination of these tax credits would raise SPM child poverty to 18.9 percent, an increase of 5.9 percentage points, or 4.4 million children. Benefits from SNAP are next largest: In the absence of SNAP benefits, the SPM poverty rate is estimated to rise to 18.2 percent. Without the SSI program, it would rise from 13.0 to 14.8 percent. In the absence of Social Security, it is estimated to rise to 15.3 percent. The importance of Social Security in lowering child poverty stems mainly from the numbers of low-income children living in households with retired or disabled members.

An examination of the effects of program elimination on deep poverty reveals a different pattern of effects (see Figure 4-10). In contrast to their effects on 100 percent SPM poverty, tax credits play only a minor role in reducing deep poverty. This is consistent with the fact that families with incomes below 50 percent of the poverty line lack substantial earned income. SNAP is by far the single most important tax and transfer program for reducing deep poverty; our simulations indicate that eliminating SNAP would nearly double the fraction of children in deep SPM poverty (from 2.9 to 5.7%). Social Security has the next largest effect in reducing deep poverty; eliminating it would increase deep poverty from 2.9 to 4.3 percent.

Finally, an analysis of near poverty (150% of the SPM) shows that tax credits are by far the most important component in reducing near poverty among children (see Figure 4-11).

The most disadvantaged demographic groups—Blacks and Hispanics, single parents, and young and poorly educated parents—benefit disproportionately from both SNAP (Appendix D, Figure D4-12) and tax benefit programs (Appendix D, Figure D4-13). However, children who are not

---

[24] See Appendix D, Table 4-2 for more information.

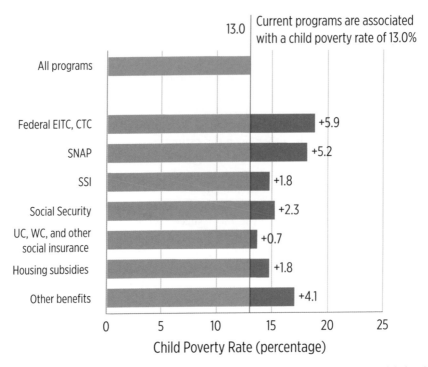

FIGURE 4-9 "What-if" child poverty rates with the elimination of selected federal programs.

NOTES: Poverty defined as below 100 percent of the TRIM3 SPM poverty line. Estimates are for 2015 and adjust for underreporting but not for behavioral effects. Other benefits include Temporary Assistance for Needy Families, solely state-funded assistance, means-tested veterans benefits, means-tested education assistance, the Low Income Home Energy Assistance Program, the National School Lunch Program, and the Special Supplemental Nutrition Program for Women, Infants, and Children. EITC = Earned Income Tax Credit, CTC = Child Tax Credit, SNAP = Supplemental Nutrition Assistance Program, SSI = Supplemental Security Income, UC = Unemployment Compensation, WC = Workers' Compensation.

SOURCE: Estimates from TRIM3 commissioned by the committee.

citizens benefit less from both programs, and children who live in families with no workers do not benefit at all from tax-related benefit programs.

> **CONCLUSION 4-6: The Earned Income Tax Credit, the Child Tax Credit, the Supplemental Nutrition Assistance Program (SNAP), and to a lesser extent Social Security are the most important programs for reducing Supplemental Poverty Measure (SPM)-based child poverty.**

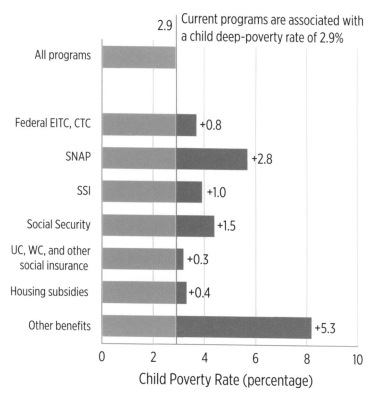

FIGURE 4-10 "What-if" child deep poverty rates with the elimination of selected federal programs.
NOTES: Deep poverty defined as below 50% of the TRIM3 SPM poverty line. Estimates are for 2015 and adjust for underreporting but not for behavioral effects. Other benefits: See note to Figure 4-9. EITC = Earned Income Tax Credit, CTC = Child Tax Credit, SNAP = Supplemental Nutrition Assistance Program, SSI = Supplemental Security Income, UC = Unemployment Compensation, WC = Workers' Compensation.
SOURCE: Estimates from TRIM3 commissioned by the committee.

SNAP and Social Security are the most important programs for reducing deep poverty among children. Tax credits are the most important means of keeping children above near poverty (150% of SPM poverty). Health care programs account for more than one-third of total federal expenditures on children but are not properly accounted for in the SPM poverty measure.

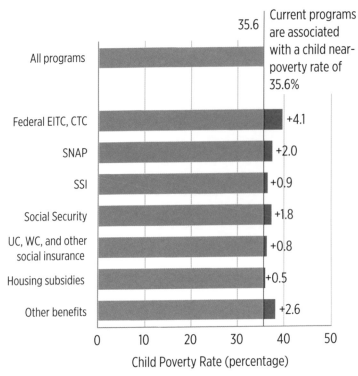

FIGURE 4-11 "What-if" child near-poverty rates with the elimination of selected federal programs.
NOTES: Near poverty is defined as below 150% of the TRIM3 SPM poverty line. Estimates are for 2015 and adjust for underreporting but not for behavioral effects. Other benefits: See note to Figure 4-9. EITC = Earned Income Tax Credit, CTC = Child Tax Credit, SNAP = Supplemental Nutrition Assistance Program, SSI = Supplemental Security Income, UC = Unemployment Compensation, WC = Workers' Compensation.
SOURCE: Estimates from TRIM3 commissioned by the committee.

EFFECTS OF GOVERNMENT BENEFITS ON CHILD POVERTY IN THE UNITED STATES AND OTHER ENGLISH-SPEAKING COUNTRIES

All nations allocate a portion of their budgets to programs that benefit children. Total family-related spending on financial supports, expressed as a percentage of a country's Gross Domestic Product (GDP), is plotted in Figure 4-12 for Australia, Canada, Ireland, the United Kingdom, and the

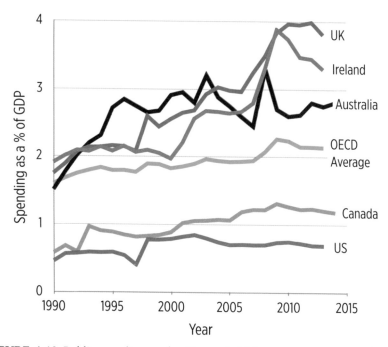

FIGURE 4-12 Public spending on families and children as a percentage of Gross Domestic Product, United States, OECD average, and four peer anglophone countries, 1990–2015.
SOURCE: OECD, Social Expenditure database (see https://data.oecd.org/socialexp/family-benefits-public-spending.htm); and OECD (2017).

United States annually from 1990 through 2015.[25] Although government spending on health and housing also assists families, it is not included in the figure. And while some state and even local governments in the United States spend significant amounts on child-specific programs, these amounts, too, are not included in the following figures.

Peer anglophone nations can be divided into those that spend relatively larger fractions of their national incomes on these family-related programs (Australia, Ireland, and the United Kingdom) and those that spend smaller fractions (Canada and the United States). Increases in spending over the 25-year period show a similar pattern: Spending rose from less than

---

[25] These data come from OECD (2017) and use a spending measure based on the aggregate category of "public spending on family benefits, including financial support that is exclusively for families and children" used by OECD. See Appendix D, 4-1 for an explanation of how the OECD defines its spending categories.

2 percent of GDP in all countries to nearly 3 percent in Australia and more than 3 percent in Ireland and the United Kingdom. In contrast, spending on families never exceeded 1 percent of GDP in the United States over this period, and it rose to slightly over 1 percent in Canada. Although Canada and the United States have always remained below the OECD average, Canada planned to increase the share of its expenditures on families with children that is targeted specifically to children to 1.25 percent of GDP over the following 2 years (in 2017 and 2018), following the passage of its new Child Benefit[26] (see Box 4-2).

The United Kingdom's dramatic increase in spending beginning in the late 1990s was the result of its "War on Poverty" (see Box 4-3). The United Kingdom managed to fight child poverty effectively and consistently and was able to cut its poverty rate by one-half under an umbrella of policies designed both to promote work (with high-quality "sure start" child care readily available) and to make work more attractive than the cash welfare system. The cash welfare system remains available, and its scope was not reduced as much as the TANF system in the United States. However, since 2010 the United Kingdom has been retrenching and implementing cuts in benefits, capping the amount of benefits nonworking families could receive and cutting other benefits (United Kingdom, Department for Work and Pensions, 2015).

Government Spending and Its Effect on Child Poverty Rates

How has this public spending affected child poverty rates in peer English-speaking countries? To find out, we use an SPM line converted to other currencies using purchasing power parities (PPP). Figure 4-13 shows the effects of the tax and transfer system on child poverty based on the latest Luxembourg Income Study (LIS) data and defined in the same way as the absolute poverty (LIS-SPM-PPP) measure used in Chapter 2.

The far-right ends of the bars in Figure 4-13 show that the extent to which families' market income alone is sufficient to raise a child above this poverty threshold varies widely across the five English-speaking OECD nations. With a 23.0 percent child poverty rate based on market income only, the United States is in the middle of the pack—with a poverty rate higher than that in Canada and Australia but much lower than that in the United Kingdom and Ireland.

As explained below, the types of transfers used for Figure 4-13 are broken down into two types: *social insurance* benefits, such as unemployment and Social Security benefits, along with universal benefits such

---

[26] Authors' calculations are based on https://www.fin.gc.ca/afr-rfa/2017/report-rapport-eng. asp#_Toc492557458.

BOX 4-2
The Canada Child Benefit:
A Cash Benefit to Families with Children

Nearly three decades after the Canadian House of Commons passed an all-party resolution committing the federal government to "seek to eliminate child poverty by the year 2000,"[a] the government took a major step toward achieving this goal by introducing the Canada Child Benefit in its 2016 budget. This program took effect in July 2016 and represents a major revamping of cash support to families with children. According to government projections, the Canada Child Benefit—after just 1 full year of implementation—will reduce the number of Canadian children living in poverty by nearly half (Corak, 2017; Sherman, 2018).[b,c]

The new Child Benefit represents an increase in benefits over the three programs that it replaces—the Universal Child Care Benefit, the Canada Child Tax Benefit, and the National Child Benefit Supplement. Eligibility for the benefit, which is distributed monthly and tax free, is determined on the basis of annually reported family income, making annual income tax filing its only eligibility requirement.[d] The amount of the benefit distributed to families is determined both by the age of the child/children and net family income. Families earning less than $30,000 per year receive $6,400 per year per child ages 0 to 6 and $5,400 per year per child ages 6 to 17. For families above the $30,000 threshold, the amount of the benefit is phased out at a relatively moderate rate. The Canada Child Benefit is expected to increase cash support to families by $4.3 billion in its first full fiscal year of implementation, but that amount will decline to $2.5 billion by 2020 and to current levels of support by 2024—and below current levels thereafter—since it is not indexed to inflation[e] (Canada, Office of the Parliamentary Budget Officer, 2016). However, indexing is expected to begin in 2020 (Corak, 2017).

---

[a] Government of Canada, Hansard, November 24, 1989.

[b] Based on 2013 reported poverty levels, which were the most recently available data at the time of the announcement. The government estimates that there were 755,000 children in poverty during 2013, and it was suggested that the Canada Child Benefit would lower this to 471,000 in 2017.

[c] In addition to the efforts of the federal government, 8 out of Canada's 10 provinces have adopted their own poverty-reduction strategies, which include reforms to existing income support programs as well as significant advances in the delivery of cash and non-cash benefits.

[d] This eligibility requirement may be of concern to some First Nations populations, where rates of income tax filing are below the national average and where the need for income supports may be greater.

[e] All dollar figures in this box are in Canadian dollars.

---

as child allowances that are not means tested; and targeted *means-tested* tax and transfer programs. The combined reduction in poverty they bring about is shown by the gray and blue bars. Poverty rates after accounting for taxes and transfers are represented by the white portion of the bars. After accounting for the tax and transfer system, and as already seen in

BOX 4-3
The United Kingdom's War on Poverty

In March 1999, Prime Minister Tony Blair pledged to end child poverty in a generation and to halve child poverty in 10 years (Waldfogel, 2010). When Prime Minister Blair called for this war on child poverty, one in four UK children was living in poverty. Between 2000–2001 and 2007–2008, absolute poverty[a] fell by 50 percent. In 2000–2001, the early years of the policy, absolute child poverty rates were about the same in the United Kingdom and the United States. But while child poverty in the United Kingdom then dropped by one-half, in the United States the official measure of child poverty rose (Smeeding and Waldfogel, 2010).

Some of the policies introduced in the United Kingdom were similar to those that the United States implemented, including an emphasis on employment and making work pay; employment-focused welfare reforms; a national minimum wage; and a tax credit for working families that was similar to the EITC but paid throughout the year (Smeeding and Waldfogel, 2010). However, the United Kingdom's reforms also included policies that were not part of the U.S. reforms, including raising income for families with children regardless of the parents' work status (Waldfogel, 2010). The United States made such income support dependent on parental employment, while Britain's reforms provided for a universal Child Benefit. This benefit is paid to the mother on a regular basis, is intended to help families cover the costs of raising children, and provides extra amounts for younger children (Waldfogel, 2010). While spending on these anti-poverty initiatives for children increased over the 10 years of 1999–2009, spending on working-age adults without children did not. Thus, social spending for children in Britain was prioritized. Over time, some spending was shifted to public services for the middle class, but new investments in children increased by 1 percent of GDP by 2009 (Waldfogel, 2010).

---

[a] Absolute poverty is most comparable to the U.S. SPM measure, as it is based on after-tax and transfer income, but without adjustments for work-related costs or medical expenses, and uses an anchored poverty line that is adjusted for price changes over time (see Chapter 2 and Smeeding and Waldfogel, 2010).

Figure 2-12, the United States has the second-highest child poverty rate (12.5%), which is one percentage point below the UK rate of 13.5 percent, a little over a percentage point above Ireland's rate, and much higher than the rates in Australia and Canada.

As a comparison of the combined widths of the gray and blue bars in Figure 4-13 shows, the United States is notable in that its government tax and transfer policies are the least successful at reducing poverty. Canada ranks next lowest in this regard, although its new Child Benefit (refer to Box 4-2) is expected to substantially reduce its child poverty rate; according to one estimate, it will cut child poverty by one-half (Corak, 2017). If Canada's Child Benefit program meets expectations, the country's child

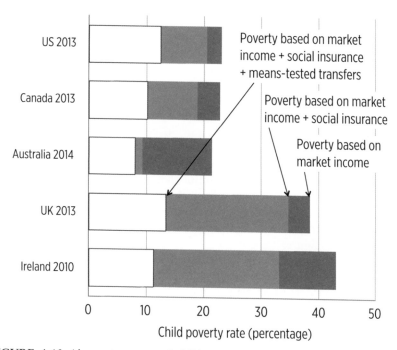

FIGURE 4-13 Alternative rates of child poverty, depending on the inclusion of social insurance and means-tested transfers, United States and four peer anglophone countries, 2013–2014.

NOTES: The blue portion represents reductions in child poverty from social insurance and universal programs. Additional reductions from means-tested transfers, minus direct taxes (including refundable tax credits) are represented by the gray portion. Data are not adjusted for underreporting.

SOURCE: Original Luxembourg Income Study (LIS) analyses commissioned by the committee from the LIS Cross-National Data Center.

poverty rate will fall to the neighborhood of 5 to 6 percent, among the lowest rates in the entire OECD and the lowest among the anglophone nations shown in Figure 4-13. Moreover, it has been estimated that, if the Canadian Child Benefit were implemented in the United States as a replacement for the Child Tax Credit, U.S. child poverty would fall by more than one-half (Sherman, 2018). According to estimates from the TRIM3 model, a similar Child Benefit in the United States would reduce U.S. (SPM-based) child poverty by more than one-half and deep poverty (<50 percent SPM poverty) by more than two-thirds.

Australia has succeeded in reducing poverty more than Canada and the United States, while the United Kingdom and Ireland have achieved the highest level of poverty reduction. Not surprisingly, the poverty-reduction rankings are similar to the spending rankings displayed in the previous figure.

Looking now at the relative importance of social insurance and universal benefits plus income-tested programs in Figure 4-13, it is evident that both types of programs have significant poverty-reducing effects in all countries. Most notable is the uniquely small role of social insurance programs (shown in blue) in the U.S. anti-poverty package. Social insurance programs in the United States reduce child poverty by only 2.5 percentage points, about one-quarter of the total reduction in U.S. poverty. Australia is at the other end of the continuum; in that country virtually all poverty reduction can be attributed to universal (social insurance) programs. In contrast, the United Kingdom and Ireland rely on both types of programs, and especially on income-tested programs, to reduce poverty in the years observed in this figure.

Figure 4-14 is constructed in the same fashion as Figure 4-13 but shows the effects of the safety net on deep child poverty and near child poverty in these same countries, using 50 percent of the same absolute SPM poverty line. Market incomes sufficient to raise family income out of deep poverty are more common in the United States than in other countries. In the United States, the 11.5 percent deep-poverty rate based on market income is somewhat lower than the corresponding rates in Canada and Australia and substantially lower than those in Ireland and the United Kingdom. But in the United States, the small relative amount of means-tested and, especially, social insurance transfers that go to children with very low family incomes translate into the highest rate of children in deep poverty (3.6%). After accounting for targeted benefits as well, all other nations have deep poverty rates that are under 2 percent. The U.S. finding is consistent with recent research showing that the U.S. safety net is increasingly likely to help the working poor while it excludes or minimizes spending on the deeply poor (Hoynes and Schanzenbach, 2018; Moffitt and Pauley, 2018).

Finally, Australia and Ireland are the only countries whose safety nets have an impact on near poverty (see Figure 4-15). The U.S. near-poverty line is very high relative to the income distributions in the United Kingdom and Ireland but fixed at about the same fraction of median income as in Canada and Australia. At these income levels, taxes paid tend to increase and targeted benefits tend to phase out. In Ireland and Australia, however, social insurance and universal transfers are strong enough to make a substantial impact.

CONCLUSION 4-7: The United States spends a somewhat smaller proportion of its Gross Domestic Product on child and family tax and transfer benefits than Canada does, and a much smaller proportion

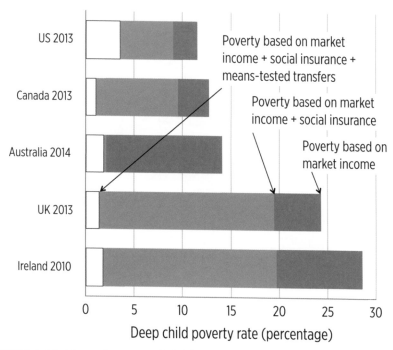

FIGURE 4-14 Alternative rates of child deep poverty depending on inclusion of social insurance and means-test transfers, United States and four peer anglophone countries, 2013–2014.

NOTES: Deep poverty defined as below 50 percent of poverty. The blue portion represents reductions in child poverty from social insurance and universal programs. Additional reductions from means-tested transfers, minus direct taxes (including refundable tax credits), are represented by the gray portion. Data are not adjusted for underreporting.

SOURCE: Original Luxembourg Income Study (LIS) analyses commissioned by the committee from the LIS Cross-National Data Center.

than Australia, Ireland, and the United Kingdom do. Consequently, government transfers do less to reduce poverty in the United States than in Canada and much less than in Australia, Ireland, and the United Kingdom. While U.S. benefits targeted at the poor and near poor reduce child poverty substantially, the United States does the least for children through the use of universal benefits like child allowances and social insurance programs such as Unemployment Compensation and Social Security survivors benefits. Such benefits have much bigger effects on child poverty in Australia, Ireland, and (with its new Child Benefit) Canada.

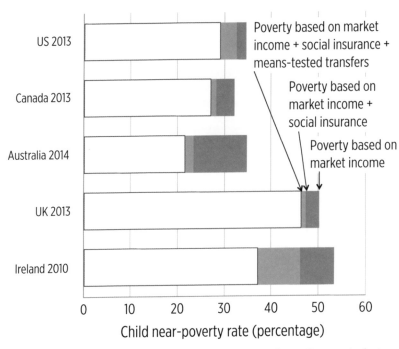

FIGURE 4-15 Alternative rates of child near poverty depending on inclusion of social insurance and means-test transfers, United States and four peer anglophone countries, 2013–2014.

NOTES: Near-poverty is defined as below 150 percent of poverty. The blue portion represents reductions in child poverty from social insurance and universal programs. Additional reductions from means-tested transfers, minus direct taxes (including refundable tax credits) are represented by the gray portion. Data are not adjusted for underreporting.

SOURCE: Original Luxembourg Income Study (LIS) analyses commissioned by the committee from the LIS Cross-National Data Center.

REFERENCES

Autor, D.H. (2014). Skills, education, and the rise of earnings inequality among the "other 99 percent." *Science, 344*(6186), 843–851.

Autor, D., Dorn, D., and Hanson, G. (2013). The China syndrome: Local labor effects of import competition in the United States. *American Economic Review, 103*(6), 2121–2168.

Autor, D., Manning, A., and Smith, C.L. (2016). The contribution of the minimum wage to U.S. wage inequality over three decades: A reassessment. *American Economic Journal: Applied Economics, 8*(1), 58–99.

Baker, R.S. (2015). The changing association among marriage, work, and child poverty in the United States, 1974–2010. *Journal of Marriage and Family, 77*(5), 1166–1178.

Becker, G.S. (1981). Altruism in the family and selfishness in the market place. *Economica*, New Series, *48*(189), 1–15. Available: https://www.jstor.org/stable/pdf/2552939.pdf.

Bitler, M., and Hoynes, H. (2010). The state of the safety net in the post-welfare reform era. *Brookings Papers on Economic Activity*, 2(Fall), 71–127.

_____. (2015). Heterogeneity in the impact of economic cycles and the great recession: Effects within and across the income distribution. *American Economic Review Papers and Proceedings, 105*(5), 154–160.

_____. (2016). The more things change, the more they stay the same? The safety net and poverty in the Great Recession. *Journal of Labor Economics*, *34*(S1, Part 2).

Bitler, M., Hoynes, H., and Kuka, E. (2017). The Great Recession and child poverty. *Journal of Policy Analysis and Management*, *36*(2), 358–389.

Black, S.E., Schanzenbach, D.W., and Breitwieser, A. (2017). The recent decline in women's labor force participation. In D.W. Schanzenbach and R. Nunn (Eds.), *The 51%: Driving Growth Through Women's Economic Participation* (pp. 5-18). Washington, DC: The Brookings Institution. Available: https://www.brookings.edu/wp-content/uploads/2017/10/es_10192017_the51percent_ebook.pdf#page=10.

Blank, R. (1989). Disaggregating the effect of the business cycle on the distribution of income. *Economica*, *56*(2), 141–163.

_____. (1993). Why were poverty rates so high in the 1980s? In D. Papadimitriou and E. Wolff (Eds.), *Poverty and Prosperity in the Late Twentieth Century* (pp. 21–55). New York: St. Martin's Press.

_____. (2006). Was welfare reform successful? *The Economists' Voice*, *3*(4), Article 2. Available: https://www.usi.edu/BUSINESS/cashel/331/welfare%20reform.pdf.

Blank, R., and Blinder, A. (1986). Macroeconomics, income distribution, and poverty. In S. Danziger and D. Weinberg (Eds.), *Fighting Poverty: What Works and What Doesn't* (pp. 180–208). Cambridge, MA: Harvard University Press.

Blank, R., and Card, D. (1993). Poverty, income distribution and growth: Are they still related? *Brookings Papers on Economic Activity*, 2. Washington, DC: Brookings Institution.

Blank, R., and Haskins, R. (Eds.). (2001). *The New World of Welfare*. Washington, DC: Brookings Institution.

Canada, Office of the Parliamentary Budget Officer. (2016). *Fiscal Analysis of Federal Children's Benefits, September 1*. Ottawa, ON: Office of the Parliamentary Budget Officer.

Cancian, M., and Reed, D. (2009). Family structure, childbearing, and parental employment: Implications for the level and trend in poverty. In M. Cancian and S. Danziger (Eds.), *Changing Poverty, Changing Policies*. New York: Russell Sage Foundation.

Chen, W.-H., and Corak, M. (2008). Child poverty and changes in child poverty. *Demography*, *45*(3), 537–553.

Chetty, R., Friedman, J., and Saez, E. (2013). Using differences in knowledge across neighborhoods to uncover the impacts of the EITC on earnings. *American Economic Review*, *103*(7), 2683–2720.

Corak, M. (2017). *Innovation in Cash Benefits to Families with Children: The Canada Child Benefit*. Memo prepared for the Committee on Building an Agenda to Reduce the Number of Children in Poverty by Half in 10 Years.

Cutler, D., and Katz, L. (1991). *Macroeconomic Performance and the Disadvantaged*. Brookings Papers on Economic Activity, 1. Washington, DC: Brookings Institution.

Danziger, S., and Gottschalk, P. (1995). *Unequal America*. New York: Russell Sage Foundation.

Duggan, M., Kearney, M.S., and Rennane, S. (2016). The Supplemental Security Income program. In R. Moffitt (Ed.), *Economics of Means-Tested Transfer Programs in the United States, Volume 2*. Chicago: University of Chicago Press.

Farber, H.S., Herbst, D., Kuziemko, I., and Naidu, S. (2018). *Unions and Inequality over the Twentieth Century: New Evidence from Survey Data.* NBER Working Paper No. 24587. Cambridge, MA: National Bureau of Economic Research. Available: http://www.nber.org/papers/w24587.

Freeman, R. (2001). The rising tide lifts . . .? In S. Danziger and R. Haveman (Eds.), *Understanding Poverty.* Cambridge, MA: Harvard University Press.

Ganong, P., and Liebman, J.B. (2013). *The Decline, Rebound, and Further Rise in SNAP Enrollment: Disentangling Business Cycle Fluctuations and Policy Changes.* Cambridge, MA: National Bureau of Economic Research. Available: http://www.nber.org/papers/w19363.

Gornick, J., and Smeeding, T.M. (2018). Redistributional policy in rich countries: Institutions and impacts in non-elderly households. *Annual Review of Sociology, 43.*

Greenstein, R., Warwick, J., and Marr, C. (2017). *Reducing Overpayments in the Earned Income Tax Credit.* Washington, DC: Center on Budget and Policy Priorities. Available: https://www.cbpp.org/research/federal-tax/reducing-overpayments-in-the-earned-income-tax-credit.

Grogger, J. (2003). The effects of time limits, the EITC, and other policy changes on welfare use, work, and income among female-headed families. *Review of Economics and Statistics, 85*(2), 394–408.

Gruber, J. (2003). Medicaid. In R. Moffitt, (Ed.), *Means-Tested Transfer Programs in the United States* (pp. 15–78). Chicago: University of Chicago Press.

Gundersen, C., and Ziliak, J. 2004. Poverty and macroeconomic performance across space, race, and family structure. *Demography, 41*(1), 61–86.

Hardy, B., Smeeding, T., and Ziliak, J. (2018). The changing safety net for low-income parents and their children: Structural or cyclical changes in income support policy? *Demography 55*(1), 189–221.

Hoynes, H., and Rothstein J. (2017). Tax policy toward low-income families. In A.J. Auerbach and K. Smetters (Eds.), *The Economics of Tax Policy.* Oxford: Oxford University Press.

Hoynes, H., and Schanzenbach, D. (2018). *Safety Net Investments in Children. Brookings Papers on Economic Activity, Conference Draft.* Washington, DC: Brookings Institution. Available: https://www.brookings.edu/bpea-articles/safety-net-investments-in-children.

Hoynes, H., Page, M.E., and Stevens, A.H. 2006. Poverty in America: Trends and explanations. *Journal of Economic Perspectives, 20*(1), 47–68.

Internal Revenue Service. (2014). *Compliance Estimates for the Earned Income Tax Credit Claimed on 2006–2008 Returns.* Research, Analysis & Statistics Report Publication 5162. Washington, DC: Internal Revenue Service. Available: https://www.irs.gov/pub/irs-soi/EITCComplianceStudyTY2006-2008.pdf.

Isaacs, J.B., Lou, C., Hahn, H., Ovalle, J., and Steuerle, C.E. (2018). *Kids' Share 2018: Report on Federal Expenditures on Children Through 2017 and Future Projections.* Washington, DC: Urban Institute. Available: https://www.urban.org/sites/default/files/publication/98725/kids_share_2018_0.pdf.

Juhn, C., Murphy, K.M., and Pierce, B. (1993). Wage inequality and the rise in returns to skill. *Journal of Political Economy, 101*, 410–442.

Katz, L., and Murphy, K.M. (1992). Changes in relative wages, 1963–1987: Supply and demand factors. *Quarterly Journal of Economics, 107*, 35–78.

Lerman, R.I. (1996). The impact of the changing US family structure on child poverty and income inequality. *Economics,* New Series, *63*(250), S119-S139. Available: https://www.jstor.org/stable/pdf/2554812.pdf.

Lichter, D.T., and Crowley, M.L. (2004). Welfare reform and child poverty: Effects of maternal employment, marriage, and cohabitation. *Social Science Research, 33*, 385–408.

Meyer, B.D., and Mittag, N. (2015). *Using Linked Survey and Administrative Data to Better Measure Income: Implications for Poverty, Program Effectiveness, and Holes in the Safety Net.* NBER Working Paper No. 21676. Cambridge, MA: National Bureau of Economic Research. Available: http://www.nber.org/papers/w21676.

Meyer, B.D., and Rosenbaum, D.T. (2001). Welfare, the Earned Income Tax Credit, and the labor supply of single mothers. *Quarterly Journal of Economics, 116*(3), 1063–1114.

Meyer, B.D., and Sullivan, J. (2011). Consumption and income poverty over the business cycle. *Research in Labor Economics, 32,* 51–82.

Meyer, B.D., Mok, W.K.C., and Sullivan, J.X. (2009). *The Under-Reporting of Transfers in Household Surveys: Its Nature and Consequences.* NBER Working Paper No. 1581. Cambridge, MA: National Bureau of Economic Research. Available: http://www.nber.org/papers/w15181.

Moffitt, R. (2015). The deserving poor, the family, and the U.S. welfare system. *Demography, 52*(3), 729–749.

Moffitt, R.A., and Pauley, G. (2018). *Trends in the Distribution of Social Safety Net Support after the Great Recession.* Palo Alto, CA: Stanford Center on Poverty and Inequality.

Nichols, A. (2013). *Explaining Changes in Child Poverty Over the Past Four Decades: Low-Income Working Families.* Discussion Paper No. 2. Washington, DC: Urban Institute. Available: http://webarchive.urban.org/UploadedPDF/412897-Explaining-Changes-in-Child-Poverty-Over-the-Past-Four-Decades.pdf.

Organisation for Economic Co-operation and Development. (OECD). (2017). *Basic Income as a Policy Option: Can It Add Up?* Policy Brief on the Future of Work. Paris: OECD Publishing.

Rector, R. (2016). *Reforming the Earned Income Tax Credit and Additional Child Tax Credit to End Waste, Fraud, and Abuse and Strengthen Marriage.* Available: https://www.heritage.org/welfare/report/reforming-the-earned-income-tax-credit-and-additional-child-tax-credit-end-waste.

Saez, E. (2010). Do taxpayers bunch at kink points? *American Economic Journal: Economic Policy 2,* 180–212. Available: https://eml.berkeley.edu//~saez/course/SaezAEJ.pdf.

Shambaugh, J., Nunn, R., Liu, P., and Nantz, G. (2017). *Thirteen Facts About Wage Growth.* Washington, DC: The Hamilton Project, Brookings Institution. Available: https://www.brookings.edu/wp-content/uploads/2017/09/thp_20170926_thirteen_facts_wage_growth.pdf.

Sherman, A. (2018). *Canadian-style Child Benefit Would Cut U.S. Child Poverty by More Than Half.* Washington, DC: Center for Budget and Policy Priorities. Available: https://www.cbpp.org/blog/canadian-style-child-benefit-would-cut-us-child-poverty-by-more-than-half.

Smeeding, T.A., and Waldfogel, J. (2010). Fighting poverty: Attentive policy can make a huge difference. *Journal of Policy Analysis and Management, 29*(2), 401–407.

Social Capital Project. (2017). *Love, Marriage and the Baby Carriage: The Rise in Unwed Childbearing.* SCP Report No. 3-17. Available: https://www.lee.senate.gov/public/index.cfm/2017/12/love-marriage-and-the-baby-carriage https://www.lee.senate.gov/public/index.cfm/2017/12/love-marriage-and-the-baby-carriage.

United Kingdom Department for Work and Pensions. (2015, May). *Policy Paper: 2010 to 2015 Government Policy: Welfare Reform.* Available: https://www.gov.uk/government/publications/2010-to-2015-government-policy-welfare-reform/2010-to-2015-government-policy-welfare-reform.

Waldfogel, J. (2010). *Britain's War on Poverty.* New York: Russell Sage Foundation.

Wimer, C. (2017). *Child Poverty in the United States: Long-term Trends and the Role of Anti-poverty Programs Using the Anchored Supplemental Poverty Measure.* Commissioned by the Committee on Building an Agenda to Reduce the Number of Children in Poverty by Half in 10 Years, The National Academies of Sciences, Engineering, and Medicine, Washington, DC.

5

Ten Policy and Program Approaches to Reducing Child Poverty

The core of the committee's congressional charge is to "identify policies and programs with the potential to help reduce child poverty and deep poverty (measured using the Supplemental Poverty Measure or SPM) by 50 percent within 10 years of the implementation of the policy approach." Our analyses and conclusions regarding these policy and program proposals are presented in the next three chapters.

The current chapter summarizes our ideas in 10 different program and policy areas, all of which could be simulated using the Transfer Income Model, Version 3 (TRIM3) microsimulation model. Chapter 6 presents four policy and program packages containing two or more of the options presented in this chapter. We find considerable merit to a "package" approach to child poverty reduction because it provides an opportunity to combine options that generate complementary impacts on poverty reduction, work incentives, and other important criteria. Chapter 7 provides a discussion of potentially meritorious policies and programs that, for various reasons, could not meet the high evidentiary standard set by the committee for its simulations.

As explained in Chapter 1, the committee identified possible policies and programs by reviewing the evaluation literature and soliciting ideas from individuals and groups representing a broad range of political orientations and experiences in communities and in state and federal government (see Appendix C for a list of memo authors). As the committee sifted through dozens of policy and program ideas, it applied five key criteria to assess each policy or program it considered: (1) the strength of the research and evaluation evidence indicating whether the policy or program would in fact reduce poverty; (2) the size and magnitude of any poverty reduction suggested by the evidence; (3) the policy's or program's success in reducing child poverty within high-risk subgroups; (4) its cost; and (5) its impact on work, marriage, opportunity, and social inclusion. As throughout this report, we focus on packages of policies and programs that could produce short-run reductions in child poverty, owing to the 10-year window dictated by the committee's Statement of Task. Programs such as early childhood education and child development savings accounts therefore fell outside the committee's purview.

The high evidentiary standard set by the committee played an important role in determining which program and policy ideas should be included in the current chapter and which should be relegated to Chapter 7 (which describes program areas the committee considered but did not simulate). To take a few examples, concerning marriage promotion, family planning, paid family and medical leave, block grants, and mandatory employment programs, the committee judged the evaluation evidence to be insufficient for estimating impacts on child poverty (see Chapter 7). In the case of expanding programs such as the Temporary Assistance for Needy Families (TANF) Program, evidence was lacking on the impacts of the freedom granted to states to spend their block grant funding in many different ways, and as a result we were unable to formulate options for enhancing TANF's impacts on family income and child poverty. In the case of Medicaid, the committee was constrained primarily by the difficulty of incorporating health insurance into poverty measurement (see Chapter 7).

The scope of the current policy evaluation literature also limited our choice of options in the current chapter. In the case of the minimum wage, for example, there is a fairly robust research consensus concerning the impacts of modest changes to the minimum wage (U.S. Congressional Budget Office, 2014), but there is less agreement about the effects of some of the much larger increases now being implemented in a number of cities (Jardim et al., 2017). Accordingly, we identified minimum wage options that incorporated relatively small increases.

PROGRAM AND POLICY OPTIONS IN 10 AREAS

After reviewing a large number of program and policy options, the committee chose two program options in each of 10 program and policy areas. On the basis of research findings and other information on each program, the committee concluded that all 20 met at least some of its 5 criteria. All 20 could also be simulated with the TRIM3 microsimulation model.

The committee was guided by a number of considerations in setting benefit levels and other features of its programs and proposals. First, in many cases its benefit levels and other parameters had been suggested by outside experts. Second, as mentioned above, the committee avoided benefit levels that far exceeded the ranges examined in the behavioral effects research literature. This was done out of a concern that the estimated poverty reductions, employment responses, and budgetary costs would be unreliable. Third, the committee used expected budgetary cost as a criterion when choosing generosity levels. It should be emphasized, however, that the committee chose its generosity levels before it was informed of the poverty reductions, budgetary costs, and other results generated by the TRIM3 simulations. Finally, to gauge the sensitivity of estimated poverty reduction and other impacts to program design features, the committee developed two options within each program proposal, differentiated mostly by level of benefits and therefore by cost.

Of the 10 general program areas selected by the committee, 4 of them focus on policies tied to work, namely:

1. Modifications to the Earned Income Tax Credit (EITC)
2. Modifications to child care subsidies
3. Changes in the federal minimum wage
4. A scale-up of a promising training and employment program called WorkAdvance

Three other program and policy areas involve modifications to existing safety net programs:

5. Supplemental Nutrition Assistance Program (SNAP)
6. Housing Choice Voucher Program
7. Supplemental Security Income (SSI) Program

Two program ideas come from other countries:

8. A child allowance (which can also be thought of as an extension of the federal child tax credit)
9. A child support assurance program

Policy area (10) involves modifications to existing immigrant provisions in safety net programs. Finally, given recent interest in a Universal Basic Income policy, we also investigated two versions of this policy; these are discussed in Appendix D, 5-12.

Following our statement of task, at the heart of this chapter are estimates of the poverty-reducing impacts of these policies and programs, including impacts on the levels of 100 percent SPM poverty and 50 percent SPM poverty ("deep" poverty). We also present estimates for impacts on the level of 150 percent SPM poverty ("near poverty"). Our estimates account for both the resource-enhancing impact of the policies and pro-grams themselves as well as the families' likely labor-supply responses to them (see Box 5-1).

Labor-supply responses can either magnify or lessen the poverty-reducing potential of programs and policies. An example of the former is the EITC: the policy acts as an earnings subsidy that is eventually phased out. The amount of the earnings subsidy is large—currently providing a 40 percent boost in earned income for a family with two children in the subsidy range. At the same time, the EITC's structure decreases the credit amount as earnings increase for higher-income earners in the phase-out range. For some nonworkers, the earnings subsidy makes the monetary difference between working and not working large enough to induce them to begin

---

BOX 5-1
What Are Behavioral Effects?

The term *behavioral effects* refers to changes in household behavior in response to a change in policy. The most common behavioral effects associated with the kinds of programs and policies considered in this report take the form of increases or decreases in employment or, in the case of employed individuals, in the number of hours worked. Most often, these effects are the result of voluntary decisions made by household members, but they may also result from hiring and layoff decisions made by firms. Behavioral responses will blunt the poverty-reducing impact of a policy change if the expansion of benefits reduces work and therefore also family earnings. Conversely, behavioral responses will reinforce poverty reduction if they increase work and earnings.

Behavioral responses also include changes in marital status and living arrangements, as well as changes in childbearing, that may result from changes in policy. The potential effects of tax and transfer programs on marriage and fertility are more complex than the effects they may have on labor market behavior. For example, the EITC, like the broader tax system, provides marriage subsidies for some recipients and marriage penalties for others. This is a result of a progressive tax system based on family income (Eissa and Hoynes, 2000). Generally, income-tested transfers based on family income lead to marriage penalties, since some families are likely to lose eligibility for the benefit when the incomes of two earners are combined.

The direction of the childbearing incentives is less ambiguous because many programs provide benefits only to families with children, and most provide higher benefits to families with more children. In theory, these incentives could lead to additional childbearing, though in practice families must weigh the large costs of having children against such potential fertility-related increases in benefits. We focus on behavioral effects on labor supply, because research finds only very small and/or statistically insignificant evidence of program effects on marriage and fertility (see Appendix D, 5-1).

working. The research literature suggests that, on balance, the increases in work associated with the EITC are larger than the decreases (Hoynes and Rothstein, 2017; Nichols and Rothstein, 2016). The increase in earnings (along with the credit amount) therefore magnifies the poverty-reducing impact of the initial increase in income and can therefore, in some cases, bring a family over the poverty line.

On the other hand, programs like SNAP reduce benefits in response to additional earnings, which may lead some families to cut back on work hours or drop out of the labor market altogether. This response would lower families' earnings, offsetting some of the initial increase in household resources that the program provided, thereby lessening the initial poverty-reducing impact. A more general explanation of the nature of work-related behavioral responses is provided in Appendix D, 5-1, with details on the relevant behavioral assumptions made for each of the 10 policy and program areas discussed elsewhere in Appendix D and in Appendix F. Complete details on the magnitude of behavioral responses are provided in Appendix E.

For each of our 10 programs, we surveyed the existing research literature and assessed the evidence on behavioral responses and their magnitudes. We first used TRIM3 to simulate the poverty reduction, cost, and other impacts of each policy, not taking into account behavioral responses. Then, based on estimates from the literature, we repeated these simulation taking into account likely labor supply responses. Featured in this chapter are the estimated impacts on poverty, employment, and budgetary cost that account for the estimated behavioral responses generated for the 10 program areas.

MODIFICATIONS EXAMINED FOR 10 POLICY AND PROGRAM AREAS

In this section, we describe proposed changes in the 10 different policy and program areas that we investigated.

1. Modifications to the Earned Income Tax Credit (EITC)

We examined two expansions of the EITC. One modification expands the schedule for the lowest earners, while the second increases the generosity of EITC payments across the entire schedule while maintaining the current range of the phase-out region:

EITC Policy #1: Increase payments along the phase-in and flat portions of the EITC schedule.

EITC Policy #2: Increase payments by 40 percent across the entire schedule, keeping the current range of the phase-out region.

Details on these EITC-based policy options are provided in Appendix D, 5-2.

The EITC is a refundable federal tax credit for low- and moderate-income workers. It was introduced under the Tax Reduction Act of 1975 and has since enjoyed bipartisan support, with expansions passed under each president beginning with Ronald Reagan. The EITC program has been highly successful at encouraging single parents to work[1] and at reducing poverty. Our TRIM3-based simulations in Chapter 4 show that, in the absence of behavioral responses, the child poverty rate of 13.0 percent would have been 5.9 percentage points higher if EITC and other tax credits had not been distributed to qualifying families. Additionally, as described in Chapter 3, expansions of the EITC program appear to improve the longer-term health and human capital of children in families receiving the program benefits. All told, the EITC is one of the nation's most popular and effective poverty-reduction programs.

The EITC has the potential to reduce child poverty in two ways: by supplementing the household incomes of low-earning parents and by encouraging work and thereby increasing the earned income of parents. For workers with low earnings, the value of the EITC grows with each additional dollar of earnings, which creates an incentive for people to enter employment and, for low-wage workers, to increase their work hours.

Our first option was proposed in Giannarelli et al. (2015), based on 2011 data. We adapt their proposal to our 2015 data. The revised credit would have a higher phase-in rate, reach the "plateau" region (where the credit does not increase with earned income) at an earlier point, and begin decreasing at a lower level of earnings (but at the same marginal tax rate). Our second option was chosen to gauge the poverty-reduction impacts of a substantial and uniform expansion of the credit.

2. Modifications to Child Care Subsidies

We examined two expansions of federal programs providing child care assistance, one involving the Child and Dependent Care Tax Credit

---

[1] A large body of research shows that the presence (or the expansion) of the EITC leads to increases in employment rates of single mothers. For example, see reviews by Eissa and Hoynes (2006), Hotz and Scholz (2003), and Nichols and Rothstein (2016) and studies by Eissa and Liebman (1996), Hoynes and Patel (2017), and Meyer and Rosenbaum (2000, 2001). For example, Meyer and Rosenbaum (2001) find that the EITC raised annual labor force participation by 7.2 percentage points for single women with children relative to single women without children.

(CDCTC) and the other focused on the Child Care and Development Fund (CCDF):

Child Care Policy #1: Convert the CDCTC to a fully refundable tax credit and concentrate its benefits on families with the lowest incomes and with children under the age of 5.

Child Care Policy #2: Guarantee assistance from CCDF for all eligible families with incomes below 150 percent of the poverty line.

Details on these policy options are provided in Appendix D, 5-3.

Child care expenses can be an immovable barrier to employment for low-income parents, particularly when their children are too young to enroll in elementary school. In the United States, the cost of child care for children under age 5 averages about $8,600 per year (Child Care Aware of America, 2017a). This average cost masks considerable variation among states and among regions in what parents actually pay for child care (Child Care Aware of America, 2017b; NASEM, 2018). Costs also vary by age of child (infant care is more expensive than care for older children) and type of care (center-based, home-based, relative or informal care). Between 2012 and 2016, poor families with children under age 6 who paid for child care spent about 20 percent of their income on child care—more than double the national average (Mattingly, Schaefer, and Carson, 2016).

The federal government defrays the cost of child care to working families through two major programs, the CDCTC and the CCDF. The CDCTC is a nonrefundable tax credit that reimburses a portion of the qualifying child care expenses of working parents with children under age 13. Although the fraction of expenses that can be claimed with this credit declines as income increases, there is no income cap for eligibility. And because it is nonrefundable, the credit affects only tax filers with a positive precredit tax liability. In 2013, the largest average benefits of the CDCTC were received by families with annual incomes between $100,000 and $200,000 (Maag, 2013).

The federal CCDF helps to defray child care costs for approximately 1.4 million children and 823,600 families every month (Administration for Children and Families, 2016a). States have the flexibility to determine eligibility criteria, family copay, and provider payment levels, so the costs to families further vary by state. The CCDF comprised two funding sources: discretionary funding provided to states for child care assistance, most of which goes to families with parents working at low-wage jobs (the Child Care and Development Block Grant), and mandatory funding provided outside the annual appropriations process (Administration for Children and Families, 2018).

Existing research on child care programs suggests that any expansion of child care subsidies and vouchers would reduce child poverty, both because child care assistance adds to family resources and because that assistance can make it possible for families to increase their employment and earnings. In fact, higher child care subsidy expenditures by states are associated with increases in labor force participation rates among low-income mothers (Enchautegui et al., 2016), particularly in the case of mothers with young children (Morrissey, 2017) (other references to the research literature showing positive effects of child care subsidies on employment are included in Appendix D, Chapter 5 appendixes). In choosing its levels of expansion, the committee was influenced by proposals suggested by outside experts.

3. Modifications to the Minimum Wage

The committee simulated two minimum wage policy options:

Minimum Wage Policy #1: Raise the current $7.25 per hour federal minimum wage to $10.25 (moving from the current level over the course of 3 years, 2018–2021, and indexing it to inflation after that).

Minimum Wage Policy #2: Raise the federal minimum wage to $10.25 *or* the 10th percentile of the state's hourly wage distribution, whichever is lower, and index it to inflation after that.

Details on these two policy options are provided in Appendix D, 5-4.

Increases in the minimum wage have the potential to boost the earned income of low-skilled workers, some of whom reside in families with children and below-poverty household incomes. But by raising the cost of low-skilled workers, minimum wage increases are generally predicted to reduce overall employment and thus also employment opportunities for some workers.

The federal minimum wage was set at $7.25 in 2009, but 30 states (or localities within states) now have higher minimum wages (U.S. Department of Labor, 2019). In 27 of these 30 states, the minimum wage exceeds $10 an hour (Neumark, 2017, Fig. 1). After studying the impact of raising the minimum wage to $10.10, in 2014 the Congressional Budget Office projected employment reductions, although the aggregate earnings losses from this loss of employment would be more than offset by the aggregate earnings gains of higher wages (U.S. Congressional Budget Office, 2014). Once a $10.10 federal minimum was fully implemented, the study projected that it would reduce total employment by about 500,000 workers, or 0.3 percent. But among workers whose earnings would increase to the $10.10 level, most of them—about 16.5 million workers in all—would experience earnings increases totaling approximately $31 billion annually by the end of 2016.

Because of the untargeted nature of current minimum wage policies, it is difficult to draw conclusions about the distribution of impacts among workers in low- and higher-income families. Several recent trends, however, suggest a relative increase in impacts for workers in lower-income families. First, the share of lower-wage workers who are in their teens has fallen and, at the same time, the average age of low-wage workers has risen, having increased by 2.6 years between 1979 and 2011 (Schmitt and Jones, 2012). In addition, as shown in Chapter 4, there has been growth in the number of unmarried parents in the labor market who are supporting children.

A higher minimum wage could also reduce the federal cost of supporting people who are poor, because higher earnings would reduce outlays on SNAP and housing programs while increasing payroll and income taxes. Conversely, a higher minimum wage could increase the cost of programs like the EITC. The impact of the minimum wage also depends on the overall state of the economy. In tight labor markets, labor shortages and immigration restrictions can push the wages of low-skilled workers above legislated minimum levels. On the other hand, raising the minimum wage too much or too quickly in areas not yet at full employment would likely increase job losses and reduce wage gains.

When determining the level of minimum wage expansion, the committee largely chose to follow the general range of increase suggested by the Congressional Budget Office (U.S. Congressional Budget Office, 2014), which argued that research shows the strongest evidence for that level of expansion. Higher minimum wages have been suggested and have, in fact, been implemented in a number of cities, but the effects of such larger increases are much more uncertain (e.g., Jardim et al., 2017). The minimum-wage levels chosen were also influenced by other factors detailed in Appendix D, Chapter 5 appendixes.

4. Scaling Up the WorkAdvance Program

WorkAdvance is perhaps the leading example of the new "sectoral" training approach, in which program staff work closely with employers to place disadvantaged individuals with moderate job skills into training programs for specific sectors that have a strong demand for local workers.[2] We examine two policy options for scaling up the WorkAdvance Program to a national level. Because the research evidence on WorkAdvance is much stronger for adult men than for adult women, our proposals and policy simulations focus on men, with the understanding that actual policy would

---

[2] See https://www.mdrc.org/project/workadvance#overview.

offer the program more broadly. Specifically, our simulations apply the program to all male heads of families with children and income below 200 percent of the poverty line.

> **WorkAdvance Policy #1**: All male heads of families with children and income below 200 percent of the poverty line would be eligible for WorkAdvance programming. Training slots would be created for 10 percent of eligible men.

> **WorkAdvance Policy #2**: All male heads of families with children and income below 200 percent of the poverty line would be eligible for WorkAdvance programming. Training slots would be created for 30 percent of eligible men.

Details on these policy options are provided in Appendix D, 5-5.

As shown by the rates of "market-income poverty" discussed in Chapter 4 (refer to Figure 4-1), earnings alone are insufficient for many families to lift themselves out of poverty. While one strategy for boosting the incomes of low-income working families focuses on benefit programs such as the EITC and the Child Tax Credit, another involves training and employment programs designed to increase the job skills and employability of low-skilled workers, thereby boosting the market wages they can earn.

Aside from programs that provide work incentives in the form of benefit payments, most governmental efforts at increasing work have involved training and employment programs, some associated with the receipt of benefits from a welfare program and some not (Barnow and Smith, 2016; Lalonde, 2003). The two best known among these programs are the Workforce Investment Act (WIA; now superseded by the Workforce Innovation and Opportunity Act, WIOA) and the Job Corps Program. Evaluations have shown that many of these programs have modest but positive impacts on employment and earnings among both youth and adults, but that neither the programs nor the evaluations focus on low-income parents with children.

The Career Academies Program was developed more than 40 years ago to keep high school students engaged in school and prepare them for postsecondary education and careers.[3] Evaluations of the Career Academies Program have shown positive earnings impacts, but here again the program does not focus on the group of interest to this report—low-income families with children—and there are also doubts as to whether the Career Academies Program can be scaled up to be a national program (Schaberg, 2017).

---

[3] For more information about MDRC's evaluation of Career Academies, see https://www.mdrc.org/project/career-academies-exploring-college-and-career-options-ecco#overview.

Apprenticeship programs have frequently been mentioned in recent policy debates, but virtually none of them has been evaluated in a rigorous way. Mandatory employment programs for welfare recipients have been evaluated rigorously, but only in the context of the now-defunct Aid to Families with Dependent Children Program (see Chapter 7 for a more extensive discussion).

Despite that paucity of evidence, the committee judged that for one employment program—called WorkAdvance—the evaluation evidence was sufficiently encouraging that we could feature an expansion of it as one of the program and policy options in this chapter. The outside experts consulted by the committee recommended simulating the effects of implementing WorkAdvance.

The random-assignment evaluation of WorkAdvance showed that it increased work and earnings across most of its sites (Hendra et al., 2016; Schaberg, 2017; see details in Appendix D, 5-5). The evaluations of Work-Advance tracked the outcomes for enrolled men in all four sites, but for significant numbers of women in only one of the four sites. Moreover, the earnings impacts for men in the training site that also included women were very different from the impacts among men enrolled at the other three sites. The results for women were therefore considered too statistically unreliable to be featured in this report. We have no evidence-based reason to want to limit the chapter's program options to men, but the nature of the evidence required us to do so.

5. Modifications to the Supplemental Nutrition Assistance Program (SNAP)

We examine two alternative expansions of the current SNAP program.

SNAP Policy #1: Increase SNAP benefits by 20 percent for families with children, make adjustments for the number of children age 12 and above in the home ($360 more per teenager per year), and increase the Summer Electronic Benefit Transfer for Children (SEBTC) ($180 more per child per summer in prekindergarten through 12th grade).

SNAP Policy #2: Increase SNAP benefits by 30 percent, make adjustments for the number of children age 12 and above in the home ($360 more per teenager per year), and increase the Summer Electronic Benefit Transfer for Children (SEBTC) ($180 more per child per summer in prekindergarten through 12th grade).

Details on these two policy options are provided in Appendix D, 5-6.

Evidence reviewed in Chapter 3 suggests that receipt of benefits from SNAP (and its predecessor program, Food Stamps) improves outcomes for children, adults, and families in their nutrition, food security, and health. Child health outcomes show improvements right away, while adult health shows improvements in the longer term. Additionally, as shown in Chapter 4, SNAP lifts more children out of deep poverty than any other program, and only the EITC (and other tax credits) lifts more children out of 100 percent poverty than SNAP. SNAP is therefore of central importance for reducing child poverty.

The committee considered three policy elements regarding SNAP: adequacy of benefits, adjustment for ages of children, and children's extra food needs in the summer months. Here we provide a brief review of these elements; a more complete literature review is provided in Appendix D, 5-6.

A growing body of evidence suggests that SNAP benefit levels are inadequate to provide most recipient families with food security. In 2017, more than one-half (58%) of families receiving SNAP reported food insecurity (Coleman-Jensen et al., 2018), and many families exhaust their SNAP benefits before the end of the month. A second rationale for increasing benefit levels is that the time required for food preparation is too burdensome for working families. SNAP benefit levels are based on the USDA's "thrifty food plan," which research has shown requires between 13 and 16 hours per week of food preparation (Ziliak, 2016).[4] This is impossibly high for adults who are working full time; in fact, almost no parents currently spend anywhere close to that amount of time on food preparation. Adults who work must instead economize on their time, and this means purchasing more expensive, processed foods.

A second policy issue is that as currently designed, SNAP adjusts benefits to account for the age of the children in the home (Ziliak, 2017). Dietary requirements for teenagers are almost as high as for adults, and food insecurity has been shown repeatedly to be higher among families with teenagers (Nord, 2009). Anderson and Butcher (2016) suggest that an additional $30 SNAP benefit per month per teenager would meet those needs.

SNAP's SEBTC is designed to address food gaps for children during the summer, when they lack access to school-based food assistance programs. USDA pilot tests have found that a $60 per eligible child per month increment in benefits reduced food insecurity among children by 26 percent (Collins et al., 2016).

The committee chose its levels of SNAP expansion based on several criteria. First, several outside experts recommended increasing the general range we had proposed, and much of the research literature on the positive

---

[4] For more information about USDA's food plans, see https://www.cnpp.usda.gov/USDAFoodPlansCostofFood.

effects of SNAP focused on increases within the proposed range. Another factor was expected budgetary cost; the committee believed that this should be considered in constraining the scope of our proposal increases. We also considered the range of behavioral responses estimated in the research literature, which the committee felt would not be sufficiently reliable at levels considerably higher than those it chose. The levels we ultimately chose were similar to those proposed to the committee by Ziliak (2017). Further considerations used in choosing the levels are detailed in Appendix D, Chapter 5 appendixes.

6. Modifications to Housing Programs

We examine two expansions of the Housing Choice Voucher Program:

Housing Voucher Policy #1: Increase the number of vouchers directed to families with children so that 50 percent of eligible families not currently receiving subsidized housing would use them.

Housing Voucher Policy #2: Increase the number of vouchers directed to families with children so that 70 percent of eligible families not currently receiving subsidized housing would use them.

Details on these two policy options are provided in Appendix D, 5-7.

The cost of housing plays a key role in the calculation of the SPM poverty thresholds, because adequate housing is essential to having an adequate standard of living for low-income families. Among low-income renters in the United States, 67 percent of their income went toward rent in 2012 (Collinson, Ellen, and Ludwig, 2016, Table 2.4), and such rising housing costs for poor families have resulted in a high rate of eviction and housing displacement among families with children (Desmond, 2016).

Despite the dozens of federal programs designed to help meet the housing needs of low-income families, only one-quarter of eligible households participate in them (U.S. Congressional Budget Office, 2014), the three largest being the Housing Choice Voucher Program, public housing, and the Low-Income Housing Tax Credit (LIHTC). Although public housing has been declining for many years, in terms of both the number of recipients and expenditures, the housing voucher program has been expanding. The housing voucher program served a little more than 2 million families with expenditures of $18 billion in 2014. The LIHTC has also increased in size, with almost 2 million units placed in service at a tax expenditure cost of $7 billion in 2014 (U.S. Congressional Budget Office, 2014).

The most vexing feature of housing programs is that only a fixed number of vouchers, public housing units, and LIHTC-built units are

available. This has led to long waiting lists for assistance from these housing programs—particularly in the case of housing vouchers—to the extent
that in some cases the waiting lists have had to be closed to additional
applicants. In 2012, 4.9 million households were on waiting lists for housing vouchers and 1.6 million households were on waiting lists for public
housing (Collinson, Ellen, and Ludwig, 2016). About three-quarters of
families who qualify for benefits do not receive them.

We limit the voucher take-up rate to 70 percent in Housing Voucher
Policy #2, in keeping with a report by the U.S. Department of Housing and
Urban Development (HUD), showing that a maximum of 70 percent of
families who are offered vouchers end up finding an apartment and actually
using the vouchers (Finkel and Buron, 2001). Our 50 percent simulation
(Policy #1) is simply a smaller and less expensive version of the 70 percent
policy. For both simulations, current income eligibility limits and rent payment formulas would remain as they were in 2015.

The committee chose to model expansions of voucher availability
rather than other modifications, such as an increase in the level of housing
subsidies, primarily because most experts agree that limited availability
is currently the primary barrier preventing subsidized housing programs
from having a larger impact on poverty reduction. As noted above, the
70 percent take-up rate chosen for simulation by the committee represents
the maximum take-up rate possible, and hence no higher level could be
simulated. In addition, there is as yet no consensus among researchers as
to whether existing housing subsidy levels set by the government are sufficiently aligned with true market rents faced by low-income families; as a
result, a simulation of changes in subsidy levels would produce uncertain
results. The committee was also influenced by the recommendations of
outside experts with respect to levels, as detailed in Appendix D, Chapter 5
appendixes.

7. Modifications to the Supplemental
Security Income (SSI) Program

We examine two child-focused modifications to the SSI program, both
of which involve increases to current child benefit levels:

SSI Policy #1: Increase by one-third the maximum child SSI benefit (to
$977 per month from a current baseline of $733).

SSI Policy #2: Increase by two-thirds the child SSI benefit (to $1,222
from a current baseline of $733).

Details on these two policy options are provided in Appendix D, 5-8.

SSI is a federal assistance program designed for three categories of low-income individuals: the elderly, disabled nonelderly adults, and disabled children. In 2016, about 1.2 million children under age 18 received benefits from SSI, with an average monthly payment of $649.58 (U.S. Social Security Administration, 2017). As seen in Chapter 4, the SSI program plays a noteworthy role in alleviating both child poverty and deep child poverty.

Child SSI benefit levels are low relative to the additional out-of-pocket costs families incur when providing care for a disabled child (Kuhlthau et al., 2005). Families who care for a child with special health care needs also incur significant costs in the form of their own lost earnings. For instance, Romley and colleagues (2017) estimate that families provided 1.5 billion hours of health care annually to children with special health care needs, which in turn reduced their earnings by $17.6 billion (in 2015 dollars), or $3,200 per child per year.

Child SSI recipients are among the nation's most vulnerable children, with diagnoses such as intellectual disability, Down Syndrome, cerebral palsy, and blindness (see Appendix D, Table 5-2, for a list of diagnostic groups of 2016 child SSI recipients). Only 1.7 percent of all children receive SSI benefits; to qualify, children need to meet stringent medical eligibility criteria based on a physician's functional assessment (Romig, 2017).[5] Moreover, family incomes need to be below 100 percent of the federal poverty line for a child to qualify for full benefits. Benefits decline as earnings rise, with eligibility phasing out completely at about 200 percent of the federal poverty level (Romig, 2017).[6] In addition, family assets can be no higher than $2,000, if the child lives with one parent, and $3,000, if the child lives with two parents.

The levels of the benefit increases chosen by the committee are based on the recognition that current income eligibility levels in the child SSI program are only slightly above those for families without disabled children. Consequently, at present the program implicitly assumes that families with disabled children need very little in additional resources to care for such children. Increases in benefit levels would address that concern.

---

[5] Child SSI eligibility rules have undergone several important changes in its history, including major changes in congressional legislation in the 1990s, that have generated extensive discussion regarding whether eligibility determinations should be altered (Daly and Burkhauser, 2003; Duggan, Kearney, and Rennane, 2016). We confine our recommendations to changes in benefit levels and do not consider possible change in eligibility rules, which would be quite complex.

[6] This varies by a number of factors including whether it is a one- or two-parent family, the number of children in the family, and by earned or unearned income.

8. A Child Allowance Program

A child allowance is a monthly cash payment to families for each child living in the home. We consider two child allowance options:

Child Allowance Policy #1: Pay a monthly benefit of $166 per month ($2,000 per year) per child to the families of all children under age 17 who were born in the United States or are naturalized citizens. In implementing this new child allowance, we would eliminate the Child Tax Credit and Additional Child Tax Credit as well as the dependent exemption for children. The child allowance benefit would be phased out under the same schedule as the Child Tax Credit.

Child Allowance Policy #2: Pay a monthly benefit of $250 per month ($3,000 per year) per child to the families of all children under age 18 who were born in the United States or are naturalized citizens. (As with Child Allowance Policy #1, we would eliminate the Child Tax Credit and Additional Child Tax Credit as well as the dependent exemption for children.) The child allowance benefit would be phased out between 300 and 400 percent of the poverty line.

Details on these two policy options are provided in Appendix D, 5-9.

A child allowance is a monthly cash payment to families for each child living in the home. When offered universally (to all families with children), child allowances do not stigmatize low-income beneficiaries, but instead have the potential to integrate them into the social mainstream (Garfinkel, Smeeding, and Rainwater, 2010; Kumlin and Rothstein, 2005; and Rainwater, 1982). Because child allowance benefits are not reduced as earnings increase (at least not until incomes reach 300 percent of the poverty line in our Policy #2), they provide a more secure floor than means-tested benefits, one that does not penalize intermittent work. At least 17 rich nations (including all of the English-speaking countries discussed in Chapters 2 and 4, other than the United States) have some form of a child allowance.

The U.S. federal tax system's current $2,000 child tax credit (up from $1,000 beginning in 2018) is akin to a once-a-year child allowance. Most families with children benefit from its $2,000 per child reduction in taxes. But these benefits are not universal: Families with no or very low incomes (and the very rich) are not eligible. We effectively convert the current Child Tax Credit into a nearly universal child tax credit by extending eligibility to receive the same ($2,000 per year) amount per child to include those with low or no earnings. Further, we convert the nearly universal child tax credit to a nearly universal child allowance by paying the benefit on a monthly basis, because doing so enhances a family's economic security (see Chapter 8).

When determining the appropriate level of the child allowance, it is important to balance poverty reduction and expected cost (Schaefer et al., 2018). The levels we specify are modest relative to those in many other countries and are intended to limit budgetary costs. We propose two alternative levels and gauge their impact on the poverty reduction and cost.

9. A Child Support Assurance Program

The committee simulated two variants of a policy option proposed by Cancian and Meyer (2018):

Child Support Assurance Policy #1: Set guaranteed minimum child support of $100 per month per child.

Child Support Assurance Policy #2: Set guaranteed minimum child support at $150 per month per child.

Details on these two policy options are provided in Appendix D, 5-10.

More than one-half of today's children will likely spend some time living with a single parent (Bumpass and Raley, 1995), mostly with a single mother (Vespa, Lewis, and Kreider, 2013), and increasingly with mothers who have never been married (Child Trends, 2016). Child support—financial support provided by the nonresident parent (most often the father)—is an important source of income for custodial parents (Administration for Children and Families, 2016b). However, the potential anti-poverty effectiveness of child support is undermined by the unstable employment of many nonresident parents and their failure to comply fully with child support orders. Our proposals here are for a publicly financed minimum child support benefit.

Single-mother households, and never-married mothers in particular, are much more likely to be poor than two-parent households (McLanahan, 2009). Children in single-parent families are disadvantaged compared with children in two-parent families precisely because there is only one parent and hence only one potential earner. In the United States, individual states and the federal government have already substantially strengthened enforcement of noncustodial child support orders (Garfinkel, 1994a). Enforcing private support is important because it reinforces social norms regarding the obligations of parents to provide financial support for their children.

As an anti-poverty tool, child support enforcement is inherently limited, because child support from fathers with low and irregular incomes tends to be low and irregular. This is not to say that all fathers of the children who live with low-income mothers are themselves poor or near poor or that child support enforcement has no role to play. In 2015, private child support reduced the number of poor children by nearly 800,000 (Renwick and Fox, 2016). Despite improvements in child support enforcement over the last 40 years, however, it is still the case that fewer than one-half of all custodial parents who are supposed to receive child support receive all the support that is due to them, and more than a quarter receive nothing in a given year (Grall, 2018). An "assured child support benefit" would increase the amount and regularity of child support and also would likely reduce the dependence of single mothers on TANF and other safety net programs.

Drawing from the experience of Sweden (Garfinkel, 1994b), a publicly financed minimum child support benefit—one that is conditional on the custodial parent being legally entitled to receive private child support—reduces the poverty and insecurity of single mothers and their children. It also increases mothers' incentives to cooperate in identifying the fathers of their children, establishing paternity, and securing a child support award (Cancian and Meyer, 2018; Garfinkel et al., 1990; Garfinkel, Meyer, and Sandefur, 1992; Schroeder, 2016). It may also reduce the father's incentive to pay child support. Little is known about the magnitudes of these incentive effects.

The $150 guaranteed minimum per child we propose is based on Cancian and Meyer (2018), who argue that it would provide a minimum level of support for families with children, enabling them to meet monthly expenses in the absence of the same amount of support from noncustodial parents, but it would exceed the level of support based on other criteria. Cancian and Meyer also propose requiring a certain standard of support from noncustodial parents, but that part of their proposal is not directly related to our focus: the poverty rate of families with children. We also choose an alternative—slightly lower—level of minimum support, $100 per child, to gauge the effect of the level on costs and poverty reduction.

10. Modification to Immigrant Policies

Given the demographic importance of children of immigrants and restricted program eligibility for unauthorized and nonqualified immigrants, the following changes were simulated:

Immigrant Policy #1: Restore program eligibility for nonqualified legal immigrants. This option would eliminate eligibility restrictions for nonqualified parents and children in the SNAP, TANF, Medicaid, SSI, and other means-tested federal programs.

Immigrant Policy #2: Expand program eligibility for all noncitizen children and parents. This option would eliminate eligibility restrictions for all noncitizen parents and children in the SNAP, TANF, Medicaid, SSI, and other means-tested federal programs.

Details on these two policy options, as well as more information on the policy background regarding immigrant eligibility for anti-poverty programs, are provided in Appendix D, 5-11.

Nearly one-quarter (24.7% as of 2014) of U.S. children live in an immigrant family, defined as a family where at least one parent is foreign-born and/or the child is foreign-born, and 10.2 percent of children live in noncitizen families, defined as families where at least one parent and/or child is not a U.S. citizen (Urban Institute, Children of Immigrants database). While the vast majority of children in the United States are themselves U.S. citizens, living in a mixed family (one where other members are not citizens) may affect children's receipt or level of benefits, because noncitizen immigrants are ineligible for various programs.

The Personal Responsibility and Work Opportunity Reconciliation Act of 1996 (PRWORA) established restrictions to immigrant eligibility, such as requiring U.S. residence for at least 5 years, for various categories of immigrants lawfully residing in the United States (National Research Council, 1999; Siskin, 2016). (See Appendix D, Chapter 5 appendixes for details on immigrant eligibility before PRWORA and additional changes associated with PRWORA, such as the expanded definition of "public charge.") Several of these restrictions were eliminated soon after welfare reform, but others remain (Singer, 2004). The programs affected are SNAP, TANF, Medicaid, SSI, and in general means-tested federal programs. Even when immigrants are eligible, they may fail to apply for benefits because of their limited awareness of their eligibility or due to a fear of deportation or of compromising their ability to apply for citizenship if they become a "public charge" (e.g., Alsan and Yang, 2018; Watson, 2014).

With children in immigrant families representing one-fourth of the U.S. child population and having higher poverty rates than children in nonimmigrant families, the committee proposed two changes to immigrant program eligibility with considerable potential for reducing poverty among children in immigrant families. These proposals were also chosen to address another criterion the committee set for itself: social inclusion. Under the current policy regime, restrictions to legal immigrants' eligibility may increase poverty rates among children in immigrant families, the vast majority of whom are U.S. citizens. Additionally, some groups of legal immigrants who are income eligible are currently denied access to programs solely on the basis of their immigrant status.

IMPACTS ON POVERTY, COST, AND EMPLOYMENT

With two options for each of 10 program and policy areas, we have offered many different ideas for reducing child poverty. Several key questions remain: If implemented, how successful would they likely be at achieving that goal? How do the costs of the various programs compare? And what would be their impacts on earnings and employment?

This final section provides a summary of the projected impacts of these approaches along three key dimensions: (1) child poverty reduction; (2) budget cost; and (3) earnings and jobs. We conclude with a summary and comparison of each of these impacts for all 10 of our program areas, including information on social inclusion, which was part of one of the criteria identified in Chapter 1. Details on our simulation assumptions and results are provided in Appendixes E and F.

Child Poverty Reduction

The core of the committee's statement of task is poverty reduction. Which of the program and policy options, individually or in combination, would reduce child poverty by one-half in 10 years? The committee has considered three poverty lines, all defined using the SPM: 100 percent of SPM ("poverty"), 50 percent of SPM ("deep poverty"), and 150 percent of SPM ("near poverty"). As with the data presented in prior chapters, our estimates of poverty reduction are based on the TRIM3 simulation model, which adjusts for underreporting of a number of important income sources.[7]

Figure 5-1 shows percentage point reductions in child poverty defined by 100 percent of the SPM threshold. While the committee's goal of reducing child poverty by one-half would require a 6.5 percentage point drop (from 13.0 to 6.5%), it is clear that none of the program and policy options we discuss was estimated to achieve this goal on its own. The more substantial child allowance option, which would replace the child tax credit and child tax exemption with a universal $3,000 payment per child per year, comes closest. It would generate a 5.3 percentage point reduction in poverty. The less substantial child allowance option (with a $2,000 annual payment, lower maximum eligibility age, and different phase-out) is estimated to produce a 3.4 percentage-point poverty reduction.

Funding housing vouchers to the point that 70 percent of eligible nonparticipating families with children would receive them would produce a

---

[7] Our poverty-reduction estimates are based on annual income. We therefore ignore issues related to the timing of income and benefits within the year as well as other administrative and implementation details surrounding each policy. See Chapter 8 for a discussion of the importance of intra-year income instability and of cumbersome enrollment procedures.

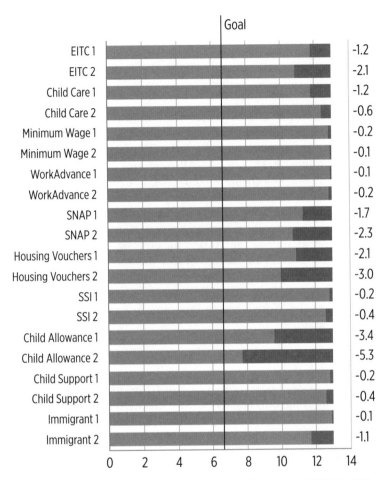

FIGURE 5-1 Simulated child poverty rates using 100 percent TRIM3 SPM under proposed programs.
NOTE: EITC = Earned Income Tax Credit; SNAP = Supplemental Nutrition Assistance Program; SSI = Supplemental Security Income.
SOURCE: Estimates from TRIM3 commissioned by the committee.

3.0 percentage-point poverty reduction, while the less substantial housing voucher program and the more substantial EITC and SNAP policy options would each reduce poverty by at least 2 percentage points. The less substantial proposals for expanding the EITC, SNAP, the Child and Dependent Care Tax Credit, and immigration eligibility would all reduce child poverty by at least 1 percentage point.

These differential effects reflect the varying size of the proposed increases in benefits for the programs in question, the varying breadth of program coverage, and behavioral effects. The larger effects achieved by the child allowance, EITC, and SNAP programs result in part from the significant increases in benefits in our program proposals. Those benefit increases are much larger than the increases proposed in the child support assurance proposal or the earnings increases that would accrue from a higher minimum wage. But the greater poverty-reducing impacts of these three proposals, as well as the 70 percent housing voucher program, also reflect their near-universal coverage of low-income families with children. Much smaller fractions of the target population—children living in low-income families—would be affected by an increase in the minimum wage, an expansion of the WorkAdvance Program, or our proposed expansions of the SSI program.

In the case of deep (under 50% of SPM) poverty (see Figure 5-2), the $3,000 child allowance option is estimated to produce the biggest impact by far. Reducing deep poverty by 1.4 percentage points would cut the estimated rate of deep poverty by one-half (from its initial level of 2.9%), thus all but meeting our mandated 50 percent reduction goal for deep poverty. The SNAP and housing voucher proposals, as well as the less generous child allowance proposal, would reduce deep poverty by at least one-half of a percentage point. The EITC and child care proposals have much smaller comparative impacts on deep poverty than on 100 percent poverty, because those programs are targeted toward workers, and families in deep poverty have less connection to the labor market. The minimum wage, WorkAdvance, SSI, and immigrant policy proposals would have little impact on the number of children living in deep poverty.

Figure 5-3 shows the impacts of the program on near poverty, defined as below 150 percent of the SPM. For the majority of the programs we have proposed, the reduction in poverty at this level is smaller than the reduction based on a 100 percent poverty line (and sometimes substantially so) because the income eligibility thresholds for the proposals are rarely much higher than 100 percent of SPM poverty. The programs with impacts on families living under 100 percent and under 150 percent of poverty that differ the least are the two child allowance proposals, both of which have high income thresholds and hence relatively large impacts on near poverty.

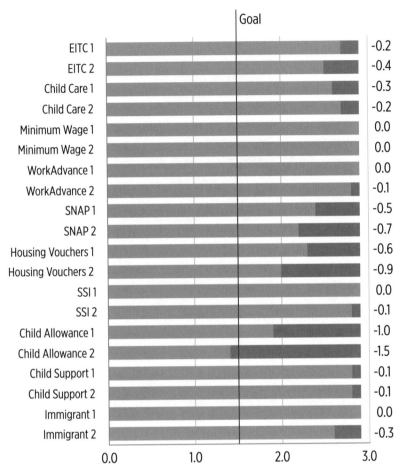

FIGURE 5-2 Simulated child poverty rates using 50 percent TRIM3 SPM under proposed programs.
NOTE: EITC = Earned Income Tax Credit; SNAP = Supplemental Nutrition Assistance Program; SSI = Supplemental Security Income.
SOURCE: Estimates from TRIM3 commissioned by the committee.

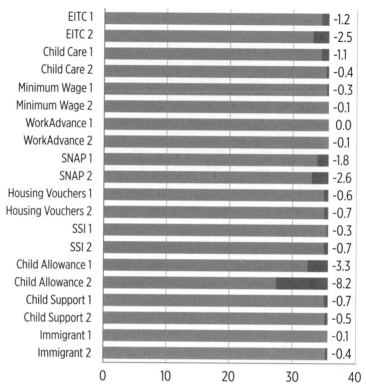

FIGURE 5-3 Simulated child poverty rates using 150 percent TRIM3 SPM under proposed programs.
NOTE: EITC = Earned Income Tax Credit; SNAP = Supplemental Nutrition Assistance Program; SSI = Supplemental Security Income.
SOURCE: Estimates from TRIM3 commissioned by the committee.

CONCLUSION 5-1: Using a threshold defined by 100 percent of the Supplemental Poverty Measure, no single program or policy option developed by the committee was estimated to meet the goal of 50 percent poverty reduction. The $3,000 per child per year child allowance policy comes closest, and it also meets the 50 percent reduction goal for deep poverty.

CONCLUSION 5-2: A number of other program and policy options lead to substantial reductions in poverty and deep poverty. Two involve existing programs—the Supplemental Nutrition Assistance Program and housing vouchers. The option of a 40 percent increase in Earned Income Tax Credit benefits would also reduce child poverty substantially.

Tradeoffs Among Poverty Reduction, Budget Cost, and Employment

The policy and program options we have analyzed present tradeoffs for policy makers to consider. Some options achieve greater reduction in child poverty but at significant budgetary cost, while other options increase employment and earnings but move fewer children out of poverty. We first look at poverty reduction and cost tradeoffs and then consider the tradeoffs between poverty reduction and changes in employment and earnings.

Figure 5-4 shows the poverty reduction/budget cost tradeoffs among the program and policy options developed by the committee by plotting budget cost on the vertical axis and the number of children lifted above the 100 percent SPM poverty line on the horizontal axis. Costs shown in Figure 5-4 are based on the tax code prevailing in 2015; costs using the 2018 tax code

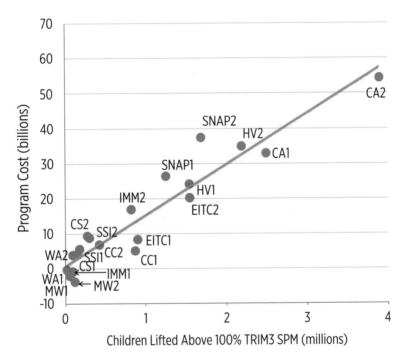

FIGURE 5-4 Simulated number of children lifted out of poverty, by program cost.
NOTE: CA = Child Allowance; CC = Child Care; CSA = Child Support Assurance; EITC = Earned Income Tax Credit; HV = Housing Vouchers; IMM = Immigrant; MW = Minimum Wage; SNAP = Supplemental Nutrition Assistance Program; SSI = Supplemental Security Income; WA = WorkAdvance. Administrative costs are included for WA but not for other programs. Program costs are based on the tax code prevailing in 2015.
SOURCE: Estimates from TRIM3 commissioned by the committee.

are provided in Appendix E and are generally quite similar. The trend line divides programs into those that cost relatively more per child moved out of poverty (above the line) and those with a lower-than-average cost per child (below the line). Program summaries and abbreviations are given in Box 5-2.

As might be expected, there is a strong positive relationship between cost and the number of children moved out of poverty. Using the results across all of our policies and programs, moving a million children out of poverty (which reduces the current rate of 100% of SPM-based child poverty—13.0%—by roughly 1.3 percentage points) costs an average of about $15 billion per year. Some programs, such as the SNAP expansions, lie above the regression line, implying that they have higher-than-average costs per child moved out of poverty. This is due in part to the fact that the behavioral effects of these programs lead to reductions in earnings.

BOX 5-2
Summary of Simulated Programs and Policies

EITC Policy #1: Increase payments along the phase-in and flat portions of the EITC schedule (labeled "EITC1" in the graphs).

EITC Policy #2: Increase payments by 40 percent across the entire schedule, keeping the current range of the phase-out region (EITC2).

Child Care Policy #1: Convert the Child and Dependent Care Tax Credit (CDCTC) to a fully refundable tax credit and concentrate its benefits on families with the lowest incomes and with children under age 5 (CC1).

Child Care Policy #2: Guarantee assistance from the Child Care and Development Fund (CCDF) for all eligible families with incomes below 150 percent of the poverty line (CC2).

Minimum Wage Policy #1: Raise the current $7.25 per hour federal minimum wage to $10.25 and index it to inflation after that (MW1).

Minimum Wage Policy #2: Raise the federal minimum wage to $10.25 *or* the 10th percentile of the state's hourly wage distribution, whichever is lower, and index it to inflation after that (MW2).

WorkAdvance Policy #1: Expand eligibility for WorkAdvance programming to all male heads of families with children and income below 200 percent of the poverty line and create training slots for 10 percent of them (WA1).

WorkAdvance #2: Expand eligibility for WorkAdvance programming to all male heads of families with children and income below 200 percent of the poverty line and create training slots for 30 percent of them (WA1).

SNAP Policy #1: Increase SNAP benefits by 20 percent for families with children, make adjustments for the number of children age 12 and above in the home, and increase the Summer Electronic Benefit Transfer for Children (SNAP1).

SNAP Policy #2: Increase SNAP benefits by 30 percent, make adjustments for the number of children age 12 and above in the home, and increase the Summer Electronic Benefit Transfer for Children (SNAP2).

While Figure 5-4 focuses on the number of children brought above the 100 percent SPM poverty line, we note that our proposed expansions would help to narrow the "poverty gap" of poor children by raising their families' incomes even when the increases are not sufficient to lift them above the poverty line. Most of these proposed expansions would also raise the incomes of many families with incomes between 100 and 150 percent of SPM poverty. Program expansions with higher-than-average costs have different impacts on lower-income families (relative to higher-income families) than other programs have, and as a result they lift relatively fewer family incomes above the poverty line.

The EITC and the Child and Dependent Care Tax Credit expansions (the latter is labeled "CC1" in the figure) lie below the regression line. These programs cost less than average because part of their poverty-reducing

Housing Voucher Policy #1: Increase the number of vouchers directed to families with children so that 50 percent of eligible families not currently receiving subsidized housing would use them (HV1).

Housing Voucher Policy #2: Increase the number of vouchers directed to families with children so that 70 percent of eligible families not currently receiving subsidized housing would use them (HV2).

SSI Policy #1: Increase by one-third the maximum child SSI benefit (SSI1).

SSI Policy #2: Increase by two-thirds the maximum child SSI benefit (SSI2).

Child Allowance Policy #1: Pay a monthly benefit of $166 per month per child to the families of all children under age 17 who were born in the United States or are naturalized citizens. (In implementing this new child allowance, eliminate the Child Tax Credit and additional child tax credit as well as the dependent exemption for children.) (CA1)

Child Allowance Policy #2: Pay a monthly benefit of $250 per month per child to the families of all children under age 18 who were born in the United States or are naturalized citizens. (In implementing this new child allowance, eliminate the Child Tax Credit and additional child tax credit as well as the dependent exemption for children.) Phase out child allowance benefits between 300 percent and 400 percent of the poverty line (CA2).

Child Support Assurance Policy #1: Set guaranteed minimum child support of $100 per month per child.

Child Support Assurance Policy #2: Set guaranteed minimum child support at $150 per month per child.

Immigrant Policy Option #1: Restore program eligibility for nonqualified legal immigrants. (This option eliminates eligibility restrictions for nonqualified parents and children in the SNAP, TANF, Medicaid, SSI, and other means-tested federal programs.) (IMM1)

Immigrant Policy Option #2: Expand program eligibility for all noncitizen children and parents. (This option eliminates eligibility restrictions for all noncitizen parents and children in the SNAP, TANF, Medicaid, SSI and other means-tested federal programs.) (IMM2)

impact comes from the behavioral effects of increased earnings.[8] Taxes paid on these earnings reduce net government costs, while at the same time the increased earnings triggered by work incentives add to family income. Similarly, the two minimum wage policies actually reduce net government expenditures, owing to the fact that they increase earnings, so tax revenues on the earnings increase and expenditures on benefits from transfer programs decrease. At the same time, these minimum wage policies do not lift many children above the poverty line.

The majority of the programs fall under one of two clusters: a cluster of policy and program proposals that not only cost under $10 billion per year but also move relatively few children out of poverty, and a cluster of proposals that not only cost more but also lift more children out of poverty. In the former category are the reforms related to SSI, child care, one of the immigrant reforms, minimum wage expansions, child support assurance reforms, and the less substantial EITC expansion. None of these programs was estimated to lift more than 1 million children out of poverty.

In the second cluster are the SNAP and housing expansions, the more substantial EITC expansion, and the $2,000 per child per year child allowance proposals. These programs would move between 1 to 3 million children out of poverty, at a cost ranging from $20 to $40 billion. The $3,000 per child per year child allowance would move almost 4 million children out of poverty, but it would do so at a cost of $54 billion.

CONCLUSION 5-3: Programs producing the largest reductions in child poverty are estimated to cost the most. Almost all of the committee-developed program options that lead to substantial poverty reduction were estimated to cost at least $20 billion annually.

Policy Tradeoffs with Earnings. Tradeoffs between poverty reduction and annual earnings changes are shown in Figure 5-5.[9] As in Figure 5-4, the horizontal axis shows the number of children brought above the 100 percent SPM poverty line by the given program or policy option, but here the vertical axis shows estimated changes in earned income brought about by the behavioral responses to the introduction of the respective program

---

[8] Details concerning poverty reduction, cost, and employment and earnings changes in the absence or presence of behavioral responses can be found in Appendix E. Some effects are quite substantial. For example, in the case of the first child care policy, which would expand the Child and Dependent Care Tax Credit, the induced employment changes not only increase poverty reduction but also increase government cost by roughly a factor of four but also nearly triple program costs.

[9] As shown in Appendix E, tradeoffs between poverty reduction, earnings, and employment are affected very little by the 2018 tax reforms. Accordingly, only the 2015 tax law simulation results are shown in Figures 5-5 and 5-6.

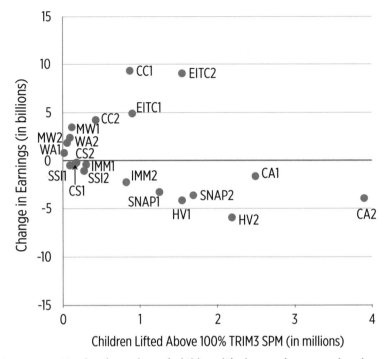

FIGURE 5-5 Simulated number of children lifted out of poverty, by change in earnings.
NOTES: Earnings changes are limited to individuals living in households with incomes below 200 percent of SPM poverty. CA = Child Allowance; CC = Child Care; CSA = Child Support Assurance; EITC = Earned Income Tax Credit; HV = Housing Vouchers; IMM = Immigrant; MW = Minimum Wage; SNAP = Supplemental Nutrition Assistance Program; SSI = Supplemental Security Income; WA = WorkAdvance.
SOURCE: Estimates from TRIM3 commissioned by the committee.

or policy. It is important to note that the earnings and employment changes plotted here are limited to workers in low-income families, defined as having family incomes below 200 percent of SPM poverty. This restriction was imposed because a few of the policy proposals—especially the two involving the minimum wage—would boost the earnings of workers in middle- and even high-income families.[10]

---

[10] In the case of Minimum Wage Policy #1, for example, earnings would increase by more than $12 billion per year overall, but only a quarter of that amount would be gained by workers in low-income households. The committee judged that the behavioral responses among low-income families would be much more relevant to our study than the behavioral responses in other portions of the income distribution.

Earnings changes vary widely—from a nearly $6 billion drop in aggregate earnings in the case of Housing Voucher Policy #2 to more than a $9 billion increase in aggregate earnings in the cases of EITC Policy #2 and Child Care Policy #1. Apart from the minimum wage proposals, proposals for programs and policies that gear benefits to earned income are estimated to produce the greatest increase in earnings, in this case in the $4 billion to $10 billion range. By contrast, SNAP, subsidized housing, and child allowance programs are estimated to reduce earnings by amounts ranging from $1 billion to $6 billion.

An interesting combination of substantial reductions in the number of poor children and substantial earnings increases is projected for Child Care Policy #1, which converts the Child and Dependent Care Tax Credit into a fully refundable tax credit. It would reduce the number of poor children by nearly 1 million and increase total earnings by $9.3 billion, an amount that would exceed the cost of the program (estimated at $5.1 billion).

Policy Tradeoffs with Employment. Tradeoffs between poverty reduction and changes in employment are shown in Figure 5-6. As in Figure 5-5, employment changes plotted here are limited to workers in families with income less than twice the 200 percent SPM poverty line. With one notable exception, the patterns are similar to those found for changes in earnings. In general, work-based programs increase employment and benefits-based programs reduce employment. More notably, our expansions of the CDCTC and the more generous version of the EITC would increase net employment by more than 500,000 jobs.[11] The exception is our minimum wage proposals, both of which increase earnings but are estimated to reduce employment in the 28,000 (MW2) to 42,000 (MW1) range.

> CONCLUSION 5-4: Projected changes in earnings and employment in response to simulations of our program and policy options vary widely, but taken as a whole they reveal a tradeoff between the magnitude of poverty reduction and effects on earnings and employment. Work-based program expansions involving the Earned Income Tax Credit and the Child and Dependent Care Tax Credit were estimated to increase earnings by as much as $9 billion and employment by as many as half a million jobs. Programs such as the child allowances and expansions of the housing voucher program were estimated to reduce earnings by up to $6 billion and jobs by nearly 100,000. The bulk of the remaining program and policy proposals are estimated to evoke more modest behavioral responses.

---

[11] Jobs include full- and part-time jobs. For more details, see Appendix F, the TRIM3 Technical Appendix.

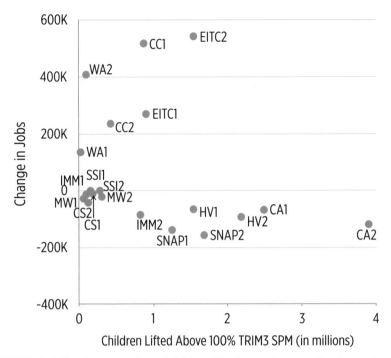

FIGURE 5-6 Simulated number of children lifted out of poverty by change in jobs. NOTES: Job changes are limited to individuals living in households with incomes below 200 percent of SPM poverty. CA = Child Allowance; CC = Child Care; CSA = Child Support Assurance; EITC = Earned Income Tax Credit; HV = Housing Vouchers; IMM = Immigrant; MW = Minimum Wage; SNAP = Supplemental Nutrition Assistance Program; SSI = Supplemental Security Income; WA = WorkAdvance. SOURCE: Estimates from TRIM3 commissioned by the committee.

Impacts Across Demographic Subgroups

With 20 program and policy options and nine demographic subgroups of interest, it is difficult to summarize poverty-reduction patterns in a succinct way. Full details are provided in Appendix D, Tables D5-3, D5-4, and D5-5, and in Appendix E. Perhaps the most important lesson is that all 20 program and policy options reduce child poverty across virtually all groups.

However, the poverty reductions induced by the various policy and program options vary substantially across groups and policies. Table 5-1 provides a summary of poverty reductions by subgroup. The first row of the table repeats the baseline poverty rates for particularly disadvantaged subgroups shown in Chapter 2, which range from about 17 percent for

TABLE 5-1 Simulated Poverty Reduction of Various Programs and Policies Across Demographic Subgroups

	All children	Black	Hispanic	Mother not a HS graduate	No bio parents	Single bio/adoptive parent	No workers	Child not a citizen	Child citizen	Mother < 25 years old
Baseline	13.0%	17.8%	21.7%	32.5%	22.9%	22.4%	61.5%	33.3%	31.5%	23.8%
EITC 1	-9.2%	●	|	|	●	●	●	●	●	●
EITC 2	-16.2%	●	●	|	●	●	●	●	●	●
Child Care 1	-9.2%	●	|	|	●	●	●	●	●	●
Child Care 2	-4.6%	|	|	|	●	●	●	●	|	●
Minimum Wage 1	-1.5%	|	|	|	|	|	●	●	|	|
Minimum Wage 2	-0.8%	|	|	|	|	|	●	|	|	|
WorkAdvance 1	-0.0%	|	|	|	|	|	|	|	|	|
WorkAdvance 2	-0.8%	|	|	|	|	|	|	|	|	|
SNAP 1	-13.1%	|	|	|	●	|	●	|	●	|
SNAP 2	-17.7%	|	●	|	●	●	●	●	|	|
Housing Vouchers 1	-16.2%	●	●	●	●	|	●	●	|	●
Housing Vouchers 2	-22.3%	●	●	●	●	●	●	●	|	●
SSI 1	-1.5%	|	|	|	●	|	|	●	|	|
SSI 2	-3.1%	|	|	|	●	|	|	●	|	|
Child Allowance 1	-26.2%	●	●	|	●	●	●	●	●	●
Child Allowance 2	-40.8%	●	●	●	●	●	|	●	|	|
Child Support 1	-1.5%	|	|	|	●	●	|	●	●	|
Child Support 2	-4.6%	|	|	|	●	●	●	●	|	●
Immigrant 1	-0.8%	|	|	●	|	|	|	●	|	●
Immigrant 2	-8.5%	●	●	●	●	●	●	●	●	●

NOTES: EITC = Earned Income Tax Credit; SNAP = Supplemental Nutrition Assistance Program; SSI = Supplemental Security Income. The vertical dashes indicate that the proportionate poverty reduction was within 1 percent of the overall reduction; green circles indicate that the reduction was more than 1 percent greater than the overall reduction; and red circles indicate that the reduction was more than 1 percent smaller than the overall reduction. SOURCE: Committee created based on commissioned analyses of TRIM3.

Black children to more than 60 percent for children in families with no adult workers. Down the first column of the table are the proportionate reductions in overall child poverty associated with each of the program and policy options. For example, the "–9.4%" entry for the first EITC option indicates our estimate that implementing this policy would reduce the overall number of children with family incomes below the poverty line by 9.4 percent.[12]

The green and red circles and the vertical dashes across the first row indicate whether the percentage reduction in poverty for children from the first EITC option in the given subgroup is larger (green), about the same

---

[12] Table 5-1 mixes percentage-point poverty rates across the top row with proportionate reductions in the number of poor children in each group. Given the very different baseline rates of poverty across groups, it made the most sense to show proportionate reductions in the number of poor children within a group.

(vertical dashes), or smaller (red) than the 9.2 percent reduction among all poor children.[13] The table shows that the first EITC option, which expands the phase-in and flat portions of the EITC schedule, produces disproportionately large poverty reductions for Black children, children living with single parents, and children with relatively younger mothers. It reduces poverty relatively less for immigrant children, children not living with biological parents and—unsurprisingly, given the earnings orientation of the policy—children living in families with no adult workers.

A broader look at Table 5-1 provides several general lessons. First, some groups—Black children and children living with single mothers or young mothers—tend to benefit more than average from many of the program and policy options. On the other hand, other groups—in particular, children in immigrant families (even if the children themselves are citizens) and children in families with no workers—tend to benefit proportionately less. This is particularly worrisome, given that the poverty rates of these groups (shown in the first row) are already among the highest in the table. These patterns reflect the fact that many of our program and policy ideas are oriented toward working families, and in only one case (the second immigration option) are benefits extended to noncitizens.

A second general lesson is that few of the program and policy options provide substantially disproportionate benefits for most of the subgroups listed in the table. Exceptions are the two child allowance proposals, which disproportionately benefit all groups other than noncitizens and Hispanic children.

CONCLUSION 5-5: The 20 program and policy options generate disparate impacts across population subgroups in our simulations. Although virtually all of them would reduce poverty across all of the subgroups we considered, disproportionately large decreases in child poverty occur only for Black children and children of mothers with low levels of education. Hispanic children and immigrant children would benefit relatively less.

Tradeoffs Among All of the Committee's Criteria

In addition to impacts on cost, employment, and reduction in 100 percent SPM poverty, the committee judged it important to consider several other dimensions of possible program impacts. In response to the evidence cited in Chapter 3 regarding the detrimental impacts of growing up in a family whose income is far below the official poverty thresholds, the committee added to its list of criteria reductions in the number of children in deep poverty (under 50% of SPM poverty). To provide a more complete

---

[13] See Appendix D, 5-13, for details.

picture of impacts on the larger group of low-income children, we have also looked at reductions when the poverty threshold is set at 150 percent of the SPM poverty line.

In Chapter 1, we also argued for the importance of promoting social inclusion, for example by reducing the sense of stigma among groups receiving benefits from social programs. We struggled to develop a strong measure of inclusion and, as explained in this chapter's appendix (Appendix D), settled for gauging the extent to which our policy and program options would promote social inclusion by looking at the reduction of poverty rates between groups. Policies that promote social inclusion show a reduction in the gaps in poverty rates between groups.

Table 5-2 provides a summary of the performance of our 20 policy and program options across all of these criteria, most importantly poverty reduction but also cost, work incentives, and social inclusion. Further information on our methods can be found in Appendix D, 5-13, and in Appendix E. As detailed in Appendix D, 5-13, we developed a score for each of the criteria listed across the top and then classified each program and policy option as very strong, strong, neutral, weak, or very weak in meeting the criteria. Light and dark green circles indicate above-average performance in meeting the given criterion, while light and dark red circles indicate the opposite.

For example, the second EITC option, which increases EITC payments by 40 percent, strongly encourages work (as indicated by the additional earnings associated with it). The light green circles for <100 percent and <150 percent SPM poverty reduction indicate modest relative success in reducing poverty under those two definition, while the two light red circles indicate above-average cost and somewhat worse performance in reducing poverty gaps for the demographic subgroups we have been considering.

Drawing from Chapter 3, we indicate in the final column whether the research literature has provided strong evidence that the policy or program in question has been found to improve child well-being. Regardless of their performance on the criteria we have laid out, any policies or programs for which the literature shows such evidence deserve special attention.

Looking across the columns and rows of Table 5-2, it is not surprising that the first four pairs of programs, all of which are oriented toward work, are the most effective at encouraging work. But none of them is particularly effective at reducing deep child poverty, and only the EITC options are above average in reducing poverty—and this comes at a fairly high budget cost.

The three sets of means-tested transfer program options—expansions of SNAP, housing vouchers, and the child allowance—are the most effective at reducing both poverty and deep poverty for children, but all are relatively costly and none encourages work. Most of the other options cost relatively

TABLE 5-2 Simulated Relative Performance of Program and Policy Options Across Committee Criteria

	<100% SPM poverty reduction	<50% SPM deep poverty reduction	<150% SPM poverty reduction	Low Budget	Encourages work	Social Inclusion	Causal evidence on child impacts?
EITC 1	I	●	I	●	●	●	Strong
EITC 2	●	I	●	●	●	●	
Child Care 1	I	●	I	●	●	●	No evidence
Child Care 2	●	●	●	●	●	●	
Minimum Wage 1	●	●	●	●	●	I	No evidence
Minimum Wage 2	●	●	●	●	●	●	
WorkAdvance 1	●	●	●	●	●	I	No evidence
WorkAdvance 2	●	●	●	●	●	●	
SNAP 1	I	●	●	●	●	●	Strong
SNAP 2	●	●	●	●	●	●	
Housing Vouchers 1	●	●	●	●	●	●	Some
Housing Vouchers 2	●	●	●	●	●	●	
SSI 1	●	●	●	●	I	I	No evidence
SSI 2	●	●	●	●	I	I	
Child Allowance 1	●	●	●	●	I	●	Some
Child Allowance 2	●	●	●	●	●	I	
Child Support 1	●	●	●	●	I	●	No evidence
Child Support 2	●	●	●	●	I	●	
Immigrant 1	●	●	●	●	I	●	No evidence
Immigrant 2	I	●	●	I	I	●	

NOTES: EITC = Earned Income Tax Credit; SNAP = Supplemental Nutrition Assistance Program; SSI = Supplemental Security Income. Budget costs for the child allowance proposals are based on the 2018 tax law provisions. See text for explanation of the light and dark green and light and dark red circles.
SOURCE: Committee created based on commissioned analyses of TRIM3.

little but also have little impact on child poverty, which is consistent with the positive slope of the cost/poverty-reduction relationship shown in Figure 5-4.

> **CONCLUSION 5-6:** The work-oriented program and policy options in our simulations would increase employment and earnings but are among the weakest options in reducing child poverty and, especially, deep child poverty. Three sets of means-tested programs—expansions of Supplemental Nutrition Assistance Program benefits, housing vouchers, and a new child allowance—would reduce poverty the most but would also reduce employment and earnings.

> **CONCLUSION 5-7:** Across all of the criteria considered by the committee (poverty reduction, cost, impacts on work, social inclusion, and evidence of positive impacts on child well-being), several of our policy and program proposals stood out:

1. A 40 percent increase in Earned Income Tax Credit benefits would decrease child poverty and strongly encourage work and is also likely to improve child well-being. But it would cost $20 billion annually, have only modest impacts on deep poverty, and fail to promote social inclusion.

2. A $2,000 per year monthly child allowance would strongly reduce child poverty and deep poverty, which most research suggests would promote child development as well as social inclusion. It would also lead to modest reductions in employment and earnings. Its annual cost is $33 billion.

3. Our expansion of the Child and Dependent Care Tax Credit would generate more annual earnings ($9.3 billion) than cost to the budget ($5.1 billion), although its ability to reduce child poverty and deep poverty is relatively modest.

REFERENCES

Administration for Children and Families. (2016a). *CCDF Quick Facts: FY2016 Data*. Washington, DC: U.S. Department of Health and Human Services. Available: https://www.acf.hhs.gov/sites/default/files/occ/fy2016_infographic.pdf.

_____. (2016b). *The Child Support Program Is a Good Investment: The Story Behind the Numbers*. Washington, DC: U.S. Department of Health and Human Services. Available: https://www.acf.hhs.gov/sites/default/files/programs/css/sbtn_csp_is_a_good_investment.pdf.

_____. (2018, May). *Fiscal Year 2018 Federal Child Care and Related Appropriations*. Washington, DC: U.S. Department of Health and Human Services. Available: https://www.acf.hhs.gov/occ/resource/fiscal-year-2018-federal-child-care-and-related-appropriations.

Alsan, M., and Yang, C.S. (2018). *Fear and the Safety Net: Evidence from Secure Communities*. Unpublished manuscript. Palo Alto: Stanford University. Available: https://people.stanford.edu/malsan/sites/default/files/people.stanford.edu/malsan/sites/default/files%20/fearsafetynet_manuscript.pdf.

Anderson, P.M., and Butcher, K.F. (2016). *The Relationships Among SNAP Benefits, Grocery Spending, Diet Quality, and the Adequacy of Low-Income Families' Resources*. Washington, DC: Center on Budget and Policy Priorities.

Barnow, B.S., and Smith, J. (2016). Employment and training programs. In R.A. Moffitt (Ed.), *Economics of Means-Tested Transfer Programs in the United States, Volume II*. Chicago: University of Chicago Press.

Bumpass, L.L., and Raley, R.K. (1995). Redefining single-parent families: Cohabitation and changing family reality. *Demography*, 32(1), 97–109.

Cancian, M., and Meyer, D.R. (2018). Reforming policy for single-parent families to reduce child poverty. *RSF: The Russell Sage Foundation Journal of the Social Sciences*, 4(2), 91–112.

Child Care Aware of America. (2017a). *Parents and the High Cost of Care*. Available: http://usa.childcareaware.org/wp-content/uploads/2017/12/2017_CCA_High_Cost_Report_FINAL.pdf.

_____. (2017b). *Parents and the High Cost of Child Care: County-Level Supplement*. Available: http://usa.childcareaware.org/wp-content/uploads/2018/05/CCA_CountyCosts_2018.pdf.

Child Trends. (2016). *Births to Unmarried Women: Indicators of Child and Youth Well-Being*. Washington, DC: Child Trends DataBank. Available: https://www.childtrends.org/wp-content/uploads/2015/12/75_Births_to_Unmarried_Women.pdf [September 2018].

Coleman-Jensen, A., Rabbitt, M., Gregory, C., and Singh, A. (2018). *Household Food Security in the United States in 2017*. Economic Research Report 256. Washington, DC: Economic Research Service, U.S. Department of Agriculture. Available: https://www.ers.usda.gov/webdocs/publications/90023/err-256.pdf?v=0.

Collins, A.M., Briefel, R., Klerman, J.A., Wolf, A., Rowe, G., Logan, C., and Lyskawa, J. (2016). *Summer Electronic Benefit Transfer for Children (SEBTC) Demonstration: Summary Report No. ae4330d2e5734003bd82df557b62478c*. Washington, DC: Mathematica Policy Research.

Collinson, R. Ellen, I.G., and Ludwig, J. (2016). Low-income housing policy. In R.A. Moffitt (Ed.), *Economics of Means-Tested Transfer Programs in the United States, Volume 2*. Chicago: University of Chicago Press.

Daly, M., and Burkhauser, R. (2003). The Supplemental Security Income Program. In R.A. Moffitt (Ed.), *Means-Tested Transfer Programs in the United States*. Chicago: University of Chicago Press.

Desmond, M. (2016). *Evicted: Poverty and Profit in the American City*. New York: Broadway Books.

Duggan, M., Kearney, M., and Rennane, S. (2016). The Supplemental Security Income Program. In R.A. Moffitt (Ed.), *Economics of Means-Tested Transfer Programs in the United States*, Chicago: University of Chicago Press.

Eissa, N., and Hoynes, H. (2000). Explaining the fall and rise in the tax cost of marriage: The effect of tax laws and demographic trends, 1984–1997. *National Tax Journal, 53*(3, Part 2), 683–712.

_____. (2006). Behavioral responses to taxes: Lessons from the EITC and labor supply. In *Tax Policy and the Economy*. NBER Book Series Volume 20. Cambridge, MA: The MIT Press.

Eissa, N., and Liebman, J.B. (1996). Labor supply response to the earned income tax credit. *Quarterly Journal of Economics, 111*(2), 605–637.

Enchautegui, M.E., Chien, N., Burgess, K., and Ghertner, R. (2016). *Effects of the CCDF Subsidy Program on the Employment Outcomes of Low-Income Mothers*. Washington, DC: U.S. Department of Health and Human Services, Office of the Assistant Secretary for Planning and Evaluation. Available: https://www.researchconnections.org/childcare/resources/33241.

Finkel, M., and Buron, L. (2001). *Study on Section 8 Voucher Success Rates. Volume I. Quantitative Study of Success Rates in Metropolitan Areas*. Prepared by Abt Associates. Washington, DC: U.S. Department of Housing and Urban Development.

Garfinkel, I. (1994a). The child-support revolution. *American Economic Review, 84*(2), 81–85.

_____. (1994b). *Assuring Child Support: An Extension of Social Security*. New York: Russell Sage Foundation.

Garfinkel, I., Robins, P.K., Wong, P., and Meyer, D.R. (1990). The Wisconsin child support assurance system: Estimated effects on poverty, labor supply, caseloads, and costs. *The Journal of Human Resources, 25*(1), 1–31.

Garfinkel, I., Meyer, D.R., and Sandefur, G.D. (1992). The effects of alternative child support systems on Blacks, Hispanics, and non-Hispanic Whites. *Social Service Review, 66*(4), 505–523.

Garfinkel, I., Smeeding, T.M., and Rainwater, L. (2010). *The American Welfare State: Laggard or Leader?* Oxford, UK: Oxford University Press.

Giannarelli, L., Lippold, K., Minton, S., and Wheaton, L. (2015). *Reducing Child Poverty in the U.S.: Costs and Impacts of Policies Proposed by the Children's Defense Fund*. Washington, DC: The Urban Institute.

Grall, T. (2018). *Custodial Mothers and Fathers and Their Child Support: 2015.* Washington, DC: U.S. Census Bureau. Available: https://www.census.gov/content/dam/Census/library/publications/2018/demo/P60-262.pdf.

Hendra, R., Greenberg, D.H., Hamilton, G., Oppenheim, A., Pennington, A., Schaberg, K., and Tessler, B.L. (2016). *Encouraging Evidence on a Sector-Focused Advancement Strategy: Two-Year Impacts from the WorkAdvance Demonstration.* New York: MDRC.

Hotz, V.J., and Scholz, J.K. (2003). The earned income tax credit. In R.M. Moffitt (Ed.), *Means-Tested Transfer Programs in the United States* (pp. 141–197). Chicago, IL: The University of Chicago Press.

Hoynes, H.W., and Patel, A.J. (2017). Effective policy for reducing poverty and inequality? The Earned Income Tax Credit and the distribution of income. *Journal of Human Resources,* 1115–7494 R1.

Hoynes, H., and Rothstein, J. (2017). Tax policy toward low-income families. In A. Auerbach and K. Smetters (Eds.), *Economics of Tax Policy.* New York: Oxford University Press.

Jardim, E., Long, M.C., Plotnick, R., Van Inwegen, E., Vigdor, J., and Wething, H. (2017). *Minimum Wage Increases, Wages, and Low-Wage Employment: Evidence from Seattle.* NBER Working Paper No. 23532. Cambridge, MA: National Bureau of Economic Research.

Kuhlthau, K., Smith Hill, K., Yucel, R., and Perrin, J.M. (2005). Financial burden for families of children with special health care needs. *Maternal and Child Health Journal,* 9(2), 207–218.

Kumlin, S., and Rothstein, B. (2005). Making and breaking social capital: The impact of welfare-state institutions. *Comparative Political Studies,* 38(4), 339–365.

Lalonde, R.J. (2003). Employment and training programs. In R.A. Moffitt (Ed.), *Means-Tested Transfer Programs in the United States* (pp. 517–585). Chicago: University of Chicago Press. Available: http://www.nber.org/chapters/c10261.pdf.

Maag, E. (2013). *Child-related Benefits in the Federal Income Tax.* Washington, DC: The Urban Institute.

Mattingly, M.J., Schaefer, A.P., and Carson, J.A. (2016). *Child Care Costs Exceed 10 Percent of Family Income for One in Four Families.* Carsey School of Public Policy, University of New Hampshire, Scholars' Repository, 288. Available: https://scholars.unh.edu/carsey/288.

McLanahan, S. (2009). Fragile families and the reproduction of poverty. *ANNALS of the American Academy of Political and Social Science,* 621, 111–131.

Meyer, B. D., and Rosenbaum, D.T. (2000). Making single mothers work: Recent tax and welfare policy and its effects. *National Tax Journal,* 53(4, part 2), 1027–1062.

_____. (2001). Welfare, the Earned Income Tax Credit, and the labor supply of single mothers. *The Quarterly Journal of Economics,* 116(3), 1063–1114.

Morrissey, T.W. (2017). Child care and parent labor force participation: A review of the research literature. *Review of Economics of the Household,* 5(1), 1–24. doi: 10.1007/s11150-016-9331-3. Available: https://link.springer.com/content/pdf/10.1007%2Fs11150-016-9331-3.pdf.

National Academies of Sciences, Engineering, and Medicine (NASEM). (2018). *Transforming the Financing of Early Care and Education.* Washington, DC: The National Academies Press. https://doi.org/10.17226/24984.

National Research Council (1999). *Children of Immigrants: Health, Adjustment, and Public Assistance.* Washington, DC: National Academy Press.

Neumark, D. (2017). *The Employment Effects of Minimum Wages: Some Questions We Need to Answer.* NBER Working Paper No. 23584. Cambridge, MA: National Bureau of Economic Research. Available: http://www.nber.org/papers/w23584.

Nichols, A., and Rothstein, J. (2016). The Earned Income Tax Credit. In R.A. Moffitt (Ed.), *Economics of Means-Tested Programs in the United States, Volume I.* Chicago: The University of Chicago Press.

Nord, M. (2009). *Food Insecurity in Households with Children: Prevalence, Severity, and Household Characteristics.* Economic Information Bulletin No. 56. Washington, DC: U.S. Department of Agriculture.

Rainwater, L. (1982). Stigma in income-tested programs. In I. Garfinkel (Ed.), *Income-Tested Transfer Programs: The Case for and Against* (pp. 19–65). New York: Elsevier Academic Press.

Renwick, T., and Fox, L. (2016, September). *The Supplemental Poverty Measure: 2015.* Current Population Reports. Washington, DC: U.S. Census Bureau. Available: https://www.census.gov/content/dam/Census/library/publications/2016/demo/p60-258.pdf.

Romig, K. (2017). *SSI: A Lifeline for Children with Disabilities.* Washington, DC: Center on Budget and Policy Priorities.

Romley, J.A., Shah, A.K., Chung, P.J., Elliott, M.N., Vestal, K.D., and Schuster, M.A. (2017). Family-provided health care for children with special health care needs. *Pediatrics, 139.* doi: 10.1542/peds.2016-1287.

Schaberg, K. (2017). *Can Sector Strategies Promote Longer-Term Effects? Three-Year Impacts from the WorkAdvance Demonstration.* New York: MDRC.

Shaefer, H.L., Collyer, S., Duncan, G., Edin, K., Garfinkel, I., Harris, D., Smeeding, T.M., Waldfogel, J., Wimer, C., and Yoshikawa, H. (2018). A Universal Child Allowance: A plan to reduce poverty and income instability among children in the United States. *RSF: Russell Sage Foundation Journal of the Social Sciences, 4*(2), 22–42.

Schmitt, J., and Jones, J. (2012). *Low-Wage Workers Are Older and Better Educated than Ever.* Washington, DC: Center for Economic and Policy Research. Available: https://www.takeactionminnesota.org/wp-content/uploads/2013/10/Low-wage-Workers-Are-Older-and-Better-Educated-than-Ever.pdf.

Schroeder, D. (2016). *The Limited Reach of the Child Support Enforcement System.* Washington, DC: American Enterprise Institute.

Singer, A. (2004). Welfare reform and immigrants: A policy review. In P. Kretsedemas and A. Aparicio (Eds.), *Immigrants, Welfare Reform, and the Poverty of Policy* (pp. 21–34). Westport, CT: Praeger.

Siskin, A. (2016). *Noncitizen Eligibility for Federal Public Assistance Policy Overview.* Washington, DC: Congressional Research Service.

U.S. Congressional Budget Office (2014). *The Effects of a Minimum-Wage Increase on Employment and Family Income.* Available: https://www.cbo.gov/publication/44995.

U.S. Department of Labor. (2019). *Consolidated Minimum Wage Table.* Available: https://www.dol.gov/whd/minwage/mw-consolidated.htm.

U.S. Social Security Administration. (2017). *SSI Annual Statistical Report 2016.* SSA Publication No. 13-11827. Available: https://www.ssa.gov/policy/docs/statcomps/ssi_asr/2016/ssi_asr16.pdf.

Vespa, J., Lewis, J.M., and Kreider, R.M. (2013). *America's Families and Living Arrangements: 2012.* Washington, DC: U.S. Census Bureau.

Watson, T. (2014). Inside the refrigerator: Immigration enforcement and chilling effects in Medicaid participation. *American Economic Journal: Economic Policy, 6*(3), 313–338.

Ziliak, J.P. (2016, May). *Modernizing SNAP Benefits.* Policy Proposal 2016-06, The Hamilton Project. Washington, DC: The Brookings Institution.

_____. (2017, June). *Memorandum to the Committee on Building an Agenda to Reduce the Number of Children in Poverty by Half in 10 Years: Proposals to Cut Short-Run Poverty by Half.* Lexington: University of Kentucky.

6

Packages of Policies and Programs That Reduce Poverty and Deep Poverty Among Children

As Chapter 5 made clear, none of the policy and program options that the committee identified could, by itself, meet the goal of reducing child poverty by 50 percent. As for reducing deep poverty by 50 percent, the simulations showed that only the more substantial $3,000 per child per year child allowance policy could achieve that goal. The failure of these options to meet our ambitious poverty-reduction goals can be attributed in part to the generally modest scope of the options themselves. Very few were estimated to cost more than $10 billion, and some (e.g., WorkAdvance and increases in the Earned Income Tax Credit [EITC]) were focused on the goal of encouraging paid work at least as much as that of reducing child poverty.

This chapter presents the committee's ideas for ways to achieve our 50 percent child poverty-reduction goal. One approach to achieving that goal would be simply to increase the generosity of some of the individual programs presented in the last chapter. However, the committee instead chose to take an approach of combining programs to form coordinated packages that might achieve the 50 percent goal. A package approach offers some formidable advantages over an individual program approach. Most importantly, program packages are better able to address both poverty reduction and work incentive goals by combining programs that emphasize each of them. As shown in Chapter 5, expansions to income support programs such as the Supplemental Nutrition Assistance Program (SNAP) or housing vouchers were relatively effective at reducing child poverty, but they also reduced employment and earnings. Work support programs such as EITC and the Child and Dependent Care Tax Credit (CDCTC) encouraged work but produced only modest reductions in child poverty. Packages combining these two types of programs have the potential to achieve substantial reductions in child poverty while simultaneously boosting employment and earnings.

Here too, as throughout this report, the 10-year window in the committee's Statement of Task leads us to focus on packages of policies and programs that produce short-run reductions in child poverty. And, as was explained in Chapter 5 and further discussed in Chapter 7, the absence of sufficiently rigorous research evidence led us to omit from our packages policies involving marriage promotion and reforms to the Temporary Assistance for Needy Families (TANF) Program.

Because different packages of programs weight poverty reduction, employment incentives, and other policy goals in different ways, the committee developed four packages, each oriented toward a different mixture of policy goals.

Our first package, the "Work-Based Package," focuses exclusively on paid employment by combining expansions of two tax credits (EITC and CDCTC) with an increase in the minimum wage and a scaling-up of the WorkAdvance Program described in Chapter 5 (see Table 6-1).

Our second package, the "Work-Based and Universal Supports Package," builds on the work-based package by combining expansions of its two tax credits (EITC and CDCTC) with a $2,000 child allowance designed to expand the reach of the Child Tax Credit.

Our third package, the "Means-Tested Supports and Work Package," combines expansions of the two tax credits in the work-oriented package with expansions of two existing income support programs: SNAP and housing voucher programs.

The fourth package, the "Universal Supports and Work Package," seeks to enhance income security and stability, reward work, and promote social inclusion. The cornerstone of this fourth package is a $2,700 per child per year child allowance, but the package also includes a new child support assurance program, an expansion of the EITC and CDCTC, an increase in the minimum wage, and elimination of the immigrant restrictions imposed by the 1996 welfare reforms.

Each package is detailed below along with its rationale. This is followed by our estimates of each package's impacts on poverty and paid employment, as well as its costs.

A WORK-BASED POVERTY-REDUCTION PACKAGE

Our proposed Work-Based Package contains four elements, with the policies numbered as they were in Chapter 5:

TABLE 6-1 Components of the Four Packages

		1. Work-Oriented Package	2. Work-Based and Universal Supports Package	3. Means-Tested Supports and Work Package	4. Universal Supports and Work Package
Work-Oriented Programs and Policies	Expand EITC	X	X	X	X
	Expand CDCTC	X	X	X	X
	Increase the Minimum Wage	X			X
	Roll out WorkAdvance	X			
Income Support-Oriented Programs and Policies	Expand Housing Voucher Program			X	
	Expand SNAP Benefits			X	
	Begin a Child Allowance		X		X
	Begin Child Support Assurance				X
	Eliminate 1996 Immigration Eligibility Restrictions				X

NOTE: CDCTC = Child and Dependent Care Tax Credit, EITC = Earned Income Tax Credit, SNAP = Supplemental Nutrition Assistance Program.

- **EITC Policy #1**: Increase payments along the phase-in and flat portions of the EITC schedule.
- **Child Care Policy #1**: Convert the CDCTC to a fully refundable tax credit and concentrate its benefits on families with the lowest incomes and with children under age 5.
- **Minimum Wage Policy #1**: Raise the current $7.25 per hour federal minimum wage to $10.25 and index it to inflation after it is implemented.
- **WorkAdvance Policy #2**: All male heads of families with children and income below 200 percent of the poverty line would be eligible for WorkAdvance programming. Training slots would be created for 30 percent of eligible men.

We estimate that this package of programs would cost only about $9 billion per year (with tax rules prevailing both before and after the 2018 Tax Cut and Jobs Act). However, our simulations showed that it does not come close to reaching the 50 percent reduction goal for either 100 percent Supplemental Poverty Measure (SPM) poverty or for deep (<50% SPM) poverty.

Rationale for the Work-Based Package

It is widely recognized, and also demonstrated in this report, that low levels of work and earnings are responsible for a substantial portion of the high poverty rates in the United States. As seen in Chapter 4, for example, the sharp increase in single mothers' employment meant that changes in employment, rather than changes in family structure, were the most important factor in explaining recent poverty trends. And in their analysis of differences in total family income between the top two-thirds and bottom one-third of families with an able-bodied head between ages 25 and 54, Sawhill, Rodrigue, and Joo (2016) show that the difference in earned income between the two groups explains the lion's share of the difference in their incomes and plays a much more important role than differences in unearned income (including transfer benefits).

Our Work-Based Package consists of four programs that provide either additional work incentives beyond those currently embedded in the U.S. transfer system or additional supplements to low-income working families, or both. As shown in Chapter 5, expanding the EITC and CDCTC do both, so we include those two programs in this package. As discussed in the WorkAdvance section of Chapter 5, evaluations of that program have shown considerable promise for increasing men's earnings. Finally, while an increase in the minimum wage reduces work to some extent, the major impact of such an increase is to supplement the earnings of unskilled workers.

A WORK-BASED AND UNIVERSAL SUPPORTS POVERTY-REDUCTION PACKAGE

As shown above, the Work-Based Package is unable to make much of a dent in poverty and deep poverty among children, which led the committee to formulate three additional packages, all of which combine work-based and income-support strategies. In the case of our Work-Based Plus Universal Supports package, we combined three policies from Chapter 5 that proved to be unusually cost-effective in either reducing poverty and deep poverty or promoting work:

- **EITC Policy #1**: Increase payments along the phase-in and flat portions of the EITC schedule.
- **Child Care Policy #1**: Convert the CDCTC to a fully refundable tax credit and concentrate its benefits on families with the lowest incomes and with children under age 5.

- **Child Allowance Policy #1**: Pay a monthly benefit of $166 per month ($2,000 per year) per child to the families of all children under age 17 who were born in the United States or are naturalized citizens.

We estimate that this package of programs would cost about $44 billion per year (regardless of whether the pre- or post-2018 tax code is used) and reduce child poverty by about one-third and deep poverty by about 40 percent—both of which fall short of the 50 percent poverty-reduction goals.

Rationale for the Work-Based and Universal-Supports Package

As noted for the first package—the Work-Based Package—two of the policy options detailed in Chapter 5 appeared to be unusually effective at combining strong work incentives and a relatively low budget cost:

- **EITC Policy #1** was estimated to increase employment among adults in low-income families by about 270,000 and earnings by $4.9 billion, at an annual cost of $8.4 billion.[1]
- **Child Care Policy #1** provided even more potent work incentives, increasing employment by more than 500,000 and earnings by around $9 billion. Its annual cost was estimated to be $5.1 billion.

But while both of these policy options performed well on work incentives and cost, their impacts on child poverty (an estimated 1.2 percentage-point reduction in the 13.0 percent child poverty rate and a 0.2 to 0.3 percentage-point reduction in the 2.9 percent rates of children living in deep poverty) fell far short of the committee's mandated 50 percent poverty-reduction goal. The committee therefore coupled these components with a relatively low-cost income support component also presented in Chapter 5:

- **Child Allowance Policy #1**: Pay a monthly benefit of $166 per month ($2,000 per year) per child to the families of all children under age 17, which was estimated to reduce the child poverty rate by 3.0 to 3.4 percentage points and the 2.9 percent rate of deep poverty by 1.0 to 1.1 percentage points, depending on the prevailing tax law. This policy's estimated annual cost was $33 billion.

---

[1] To simplify our discussion of cost, we will use estimates based on the tax code prevailing in 2015, the base year for the report. We will draw attention to instances where cost estimates differ significantly before and after the 2018 Tax Cut and Jobs Act. Details on the costs of all of the programs and program packages we present at provided in Tables 6-2 and 6-3 as well as Appendix E.

TABLE 6-2 Simulated Poverty Reduction, Cost, and Employment Changes Associated with Four Poverty-Reduction Packages, Based on the 2015 Tax Law

Poverty-Reduction Package	Reduction in Poverty (<100% TRIM3 SPM Poverty)		Reduction in Deep Poverty (<50% TRIM3 SPM Poverty)		Total Change in Government Spending (millions)	Only Families with Incomes < 200% TRIM3 SPM	
						Net Change in Earnings (millions)	Net Change in Jobs
1. Work-Based	-2.5	-18.8%	-0.6	-19.3%	$8,654	$18,395	1,002,959
Expand EITC	-1.2	-9.4%	-0.2	-6.9%	$8,384	$4,910	269,713
Expand CDCTC	-1.2	-9.1%	-0.3	-10.3%	$5,141	$9,342	518,085
Increase minimum wage	-0.2	-1.3%	0.0	0.0%	-$3,688	$3,488	-42,347
Roll out WorkAdvance	-0.1	-1.0%	-0.1	-3.4%	-$801	$2,591	408,148
2. Work–Based and Universal Supports	-4.6	-35.6%	-1.2	-41.3%	$44,536	$9,921	567,722
Expand EITC	-1.2	-9.4%	-0.2	-6.9%	$8,384	$4,910	269,713
Expand CDCTC	-1.2	-9.1%	-0.3	-10.3%	$5,141	$9,342	518,085
Begin a $2,000 child allowance	-3.4	-25.9%	-1.1	37.9%	$32,904	-$1,627	-68,434
3. Means-Tested Supports and Work	-6.6	-50.7%	-1.5	-51.7%	$90,732	$2,188	404,243
Expand EITC	-1.2	-9.4%	-0.2	-6.9%	$8,384	$4,910	269,713
Expand CDCTC	-1.2	-9.1%	-0.3	-10.3%	$5,141	$9,342	518,085
Expand Housing Voucher Program	-3.0	-22.7%	-0.9	-31.0%	$34,916	-$5,923	-93,181
Expand SNAP Benefits by 35%	-2.6	-20.2%	-0.8	-27.6%	$43,075	-$3,812	-164,392

4. Universal Supports and Work	-6.8	-52.3%	-1.6	-55.1%	$108,771	$13,447	611,182
Expand EITC by 40%	-2.1	-16.0%	-0.4	-13.8%	$20,206	$9,065	541,366
Expand CDCTC	-1.2	-9.1%	-0.3	-10.3%	$5,141	$9,342	518,085
Increase minimum wage	-0.2	-1.3%	0.0	0.0%	-$3,688	$3,488	-42,347
Begin a $2,700 child allowance	-4.6	-35.7%	-1.3	-44.8%	$77,901	-$2,649	-103,547
Begin child support assurance	-0.2	-1.9%	-0.1	-3.4%	$5,660	-$190	-10,145
Eliminate 1996 immigration eligibility restrictions	-0.1	-1.0%	0.0	0.0%	$3,933	-$483	-13,183

NOTES: Components do not add to package totals owing to redundancies and other interactions across programs (see Appendix F).
CDCTC = Child and Dependent Care Tax Credit, EITC = Earned Income Tax Credit, SNAP = Supplemental Nutrition Assistance Program, TRIM3 = Urban Institute's Transfer Income Model, version 3 microsimulation model.
SOURCE: Analyses commissioned by the committee using TRIM3.

TABLE 6-3 Simulated Poverty Reduction, Cost, and Employment Changes Associated with Four Poverty-Reduction Packages, Based on the 2018 Tax Law

Poverty-Reduction Package	Reduction in <100% TRIM3 SPM Poverty		Reduction in <50% TRIM3 SPM Poverty		Total Change in Government Spending (millions)	Only Families with Incomes < 200% TRIM3 SPM	
						Net Change in Earnings (millions)	Net Change in Jobs
1. Work-Based	-2.4	-19.2%	-0.5	-17.9%	$9,362	$18,011	987,497
Expand EITC	-1.2	-9.8%	-0.2	-7.1%	$8,522	$4,910	269,713
Expand CDCTC	-1.2	-9.3%	-0.2	-7.1%	$5,465	$9,070	502,982
Increase minimum wage	-0.1	-1.2%	0.0	0.0%	-$3,419	$3,431	-42,347
Roll out WorkAdvance	-0.2	-1.3%	-0.1	-3.6%	-$744	$93	406,179
2. Work-Based and Universal Supports	-4.3	-33.7%	-1.2	-41.3%	$44,278	$10,185	563,000
Expand EITC	-1.2	-9.8%	-0.2	-7.1%	$8,522	$4,910	269,713
Expand CDCTC	-1.2	-9.3%	-0.3	-7.1%	$5,465	$9,070	502,982
Begin a $2,000 child allowance	-3.0	-23.9%	-1.1	-34.5%	$32,553	-$1,088	-60,000
3. Means-Tested Supports and Work	-6.3	-50.3%	-1.5	-53.6%	$90,771	$1,985	393,810
Expand EITC	-1.2	-9.8%	-0.2	-7.1%	$8,522	$4,910	269,713
Expand CDCTC	-1.2	-9.3%	-0.2	-7.1%	$5,465	$9,070	502,982
Expand Housing Voucher Program	-2.8	-22.6%	-0.8	-28.6%	$34,706	-$5,904	-93,181
Expand SNAP benefits by 35%	-2.5	-19.6%	-0.8	-28.6%	$42,969	-$3,760	-161,332

4. Universal Supports and Work	-6.5	-51.3%	-1.5	-53.6%	$111,625	$13,687	613,000
Expand EITC by 40%	-2.0	-16.0%	-0.4	-14.3%	$20,446	$9,298	546,747
Expand CDCTC	-1.2	-9.3%	-0.2	-7.1%	$5,465	$9,070	502,982
Increase minimum wage	-0.1	-1.2%	0.0	0.0%	-$3,419	$3,431	-42,347
Begin a $2,700 child allowance	-4.3	-34.5%	-1.3	-46.4%	$85,469	-$2,329	-98,000
Begin child support assurance	-0.3	-2.0%	-0.1	-3.6%	$5,650	-$189	-10,145
Eliminate 1996 immigration eligibility restrictions	-0.2	-1.4%	0.0	0.0%	$4,844	-$483	-13,183

NOTES: Components do not add to package totals owing to redundancies and other interactions across programs (see Appendix F). Simulations are based on the Federal Income Tax provisions prevailing in 2018. CDCTC = Child and Dependent Care Tax Credit, EITC = Earned Income Tax Credit, SNAP = Supplemental Nutrition Assistance Program, TRIM3 = Urban Institute's Transfer Income Model, Version 3 microsimulation model.

SOURCE: Analyses commissioned by the committee from TRIM3.

The principal rationale for a child allowance paid on a monthly basis is that it would provide a steady, predictable source of income to counteract the irregularity and unpredictability of market income (as described in Chapter 8). Because the child allowance would be available to both low-income and middle-class families, it would carry little stigma and would not be subject to the varying rules and administrative discretion of a means-tested program, thereby promoting social inclusion. As we saw in Chapter 5, the incremental cost of our proposed version of a $2,000 per child per year child allowance would be $32.9 billion using either the 2015 or 2018 tax law. In addition there would be the administrative costs from having the Social Security Administration pay the monthly benefits.

Although this second package—Work-Based and Universal Supports—failed to reach the 50 percent poverty-reduction goals, its combination of substantial child poverty reduction, positive impacts on employment and earnings, and cost led the committee to judge it to be of sufficient policy interest to include in this report.

A MEANS-TESTED SUPPORTS AND WORK POVERTY-REDUCTION PACKAGE

Our third and fourth policy packages were formulated in ways that fully met the 50 percent poverty-reduction goals set by the committee's charge. Both combined work-based and income support enhancements. We call the third package a Means-Tested Supports and Work Package because it would expand four existing programs:

1. **EITC Policy #1**: Increase payments along the phase-in and flat portions of the EITC schedule.
2. **Child Care Policy #1**: Convert the CDCTC to a fully refundable tax credit and concentrate its benefits on families with the lowest incomes and with children under age 5.
3. A modification of **SNAP Policy #2**: Chapter 5's version of SNAP Policy #2 increases SNAP benefits by 30 percent as well as increasing benefits for older children and would be provided through the Summer Electronic Benefit Transfers for Children. In order to reach the 50 percent poverty-reduction goal, we included in this program package a 35 percent rather than a 30 percent increase in the basic SNAP benefit.
4. **Housing Voucher Policy #2**: Increase the number of vouchers directed to families with children so that 70 percent of eligible families that are not currently receiving subsidized housing would use them.

We estimate that this package of programs would cost $90.7 billion per year and would achieve 50 percent reductions in both poverty and deep poverty for children.

Rationale for the Means-Tested Supports and Work Package

Developing a strategy to reduce child poverty by one-half within 10 years using existing programs provides a number of benefits. First, the congressional authorization, administrative regulations, and administrative implementation procedures for existing programs have been developed and are currently operating. Consequently, changes in these programs could be implemented rapidly and begin to yield reductions in child poverty rates soon after implementation.

It is obvious from a review of the poverty reductions associated with existing programs as set out in Chapter 5 (refer to Figures 5-1 and 5-2) that the largest poverty-reducing impacts result from our modifications to four of them—the EITC, the CDCTC, housing vouchers, and SNAP. Since both the EITC and the CDCTC condition families' receipt of benefits on employment, both have positive impacts on employment and earnings, but at the same time both are relatively less effective in reducing deep poverty (<50% of SPM) than means-tested programs like SNAP. While expanding the housing voucher and SNAP programs would generate disincentives for work, it would also boost the economic resources for children in families with incomes near the thresholds that define both poverty and deep poverty. The committee judged that the combination of the four program expansions included in this income and work supports package would provide a good balance for meeting the 50 percent poverty-reduction goals by combining work-based and income-support program expansions.

A UNIVERSAL SUPPORTS AND WORK POVERTY-REDUCTION PACKAGE

The fourth package we devised and evaluated combines work incentives, economic security, and social inclusion with some existing programs, plus two new programs introduced in Chapter 5:

- **EITC Policy #2:** Increase payments by 40 percent across the entire schedule, keeping the current range of the phase-out region.
- **Child Care Policy #1:** Convert the CDCTC to a fully refundable tax credit and concentrate its benefits on families with the lowest incomes and with children under age 5.

- **Minimum Wage Policy #1:** Raise the current $7.25 per hour federal minimum wage to $10.25 and index it to inflation after it is implemented.
- **Immigration Policy #1:** Restore program eligibility for nonqualified legal immigrants. This option would eliminate eligibility restrictions for nonqualified parents and children in the SNAP, TANF, Medicaid, SSI, and other means-tested federal programs.
- A modification of **Child Allowance Policy #1:** Pay a monthly benefit of $225 per month ($2,700 per year) per child to the families of all children under age 17. Extending beyond citizen children, and consistent with Immigration Policy #1, this child allowance would also be paid to currently nonqualified legal immigrants. To barely reach the 50 percent poverty-reduction goal, we set the monthly benefit level at $225 rather than the $166 or $250 levels included in the Chapter 5 versions of the child allowance policy.
- **Child Support Assurance Policy #1:** Set a guaranteed minimum child support of $100 per month per child.

We estimate that this package of programs would cost $108.8 billion per year under the federal income tax provisions prevailing before 2018, and $111.6 billion per year based on the current tax law. It too would achieve the 50 percent poverty-reduction goals.

Rationale for the Universal Supports and Work Package

Chapter 5 results for individual programs show that the two child allowances would produce the largest impacts on both poverty (<100% SPM) and deep poverty (<50% SPM) for children, but at the same time generate work disincentives. Because supporting work as a long-term solution for child poverty was one of the criteria developed by the committee, our third proposed package combines economic security and work supports in ways that would reduce child poverty and deep child poverty, enhance security and income stability, provide significant incentives for market-based work, and promote social inclusion.

This package provides a child allowance that is similar in value to what most taxpayers now receive for their children through child tax credits and tax exemptions, combined with three work-enhancing features: an expanded EITC and CDCTC and a higher federal minimum wage. To this we add one of the Child Support Assurance policies and an additional feature that promotes equity and social inclusion—an extension of benefits to include immigrant children.

As we saw in Chapter 5, simulations showed that the incremental cost of our proposed version of a $2,000 per child per year child allowance would be $32.9 billion annually. In order to meet its 50 percent poverty-reduction goal, the committee increased child allowance benefit levels in the Universal Supports and Work Package to $2,700, which adds about $45 billion to its annual cost. An assured child support benefit, also paid on a monthly basis, would provide a somewhat larger measure of economic security to single-parent families legally entitled to private child support. With such an assured benefit set at $1,200 per year, coupled with the child allowance it would all but erase deep child poverty, while also reducing economic insecurity and unpredictability.

To increase the incentives for market work, the package also includes a 40 percent increase in EITC benefits, an increase in the CDCTC, and an increase in the minimum wage. Each of these elements rewards those who choose market work, even parents who have young children and cannot work full time. Finally, to further promote inclusivity, we include in the universal supports and work package the restoration of program eligibility for nonqualified legal immigrants.

SIMULATING THE IMPACTS OF THE FOUR PROGRAM PACKAGES

As explained in Appendix F, simulating the impacts of packages of programs is difficult—even more difficult than simulating impacts of individual program and policy changes. For example, the simulation program must model people's movements into and out of the labor force as the result of policy changes. All four of our packages include expansions of both the EITC and the CDCTC, and each of these two policies might induce an individual to enter the labor force. But since an individual can only enter the labor market once in response to the package, both policies cannot be estimated to produce this effect. As explained in Appendix F, the committee sought reliable estimates of package impacts by adopting conservative assumptions about these kinds of duplications. While these assumptions might be expected to produce reasonable estimates of impacts, we caution against attaching too much weight to the precise numbers generated by the simulations.

Comparisons Across the Four Packages

The simulated poverty-reducing impacts of the four packages are shown in Figure 6-1 for 100 percent poverty, in Figure 6-2 for deep poverty, and in Figure 6-3 for near poverty. As elsewhere in our simulations, the poverty definition here is based on SPM poverty, deep poverty is defined as below 50 percent of the SPM poverty line, and near poverty is defined as below 150 percent of the SPM poverty line.

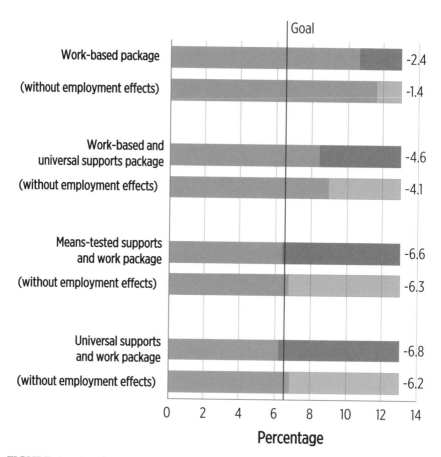

FIGURE 6-1 Simulated reductions in child poverty rates using 100 percent TRIM3 SPM for the four program packages.

NOTES: "Work-oriented package" combines expansions of the Earned Income Tax Credit (EITC), minimum wage, the Child and Dependent Care Tax Credit (CDCTC), and WorkAdvance. "Work-based and universal supports package" combines expansions of the EITC, the CDCTC, and a child allowance. "Means-tested supports and work package" combines expansions of the EITC, the CDCTC, Supplemental Nutrition Assistance Program, and housing vouchers. "Universal supports and work package" combines expansions of the EITC, minimum wage, and the CDCTC with child support assurance, restoration of immigrant program eligibility, and a child allowance.

SOURCE: Estimates from TRIM3 commissioned by committee. The vertical line indicates 50% reduction goal.

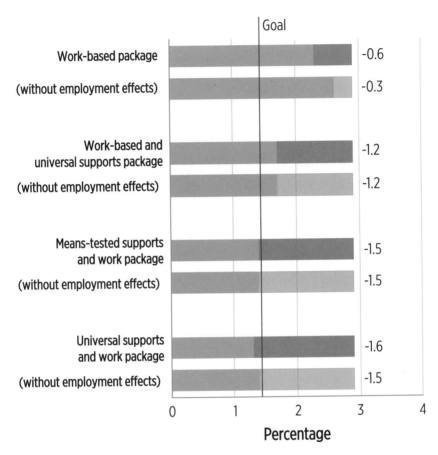

FIGURE 6-2 Simulated reductions in child poverty rates using 50 percent TRIM3 SPM for the four program packages.

NOTES: "Work-oriented package" combines expansions of the Earned Income Tax Credit (EITC), minimum wage, the Child and Dependent Care Tax Credit (CDCTC), and WorkAdvance. "Work-based and universal supports package" combines expansions of the EITC, the CDCTC, and a child allowance. "Means-tested supports and work package" combines expansions of the EITC, the CDCTC, Supplemental Nutrition Assistance Program, and housing vouchers. "Universal supports and work package" combines expansions of the EITC, minimum wage, and the CDCTC with child support assurance, restoration of immigrant program eligibility, and a child allowance. The vertical line indicates 50% reduction goal.

SOURCE: Estimates from TRIM3 commissioned by the committee.

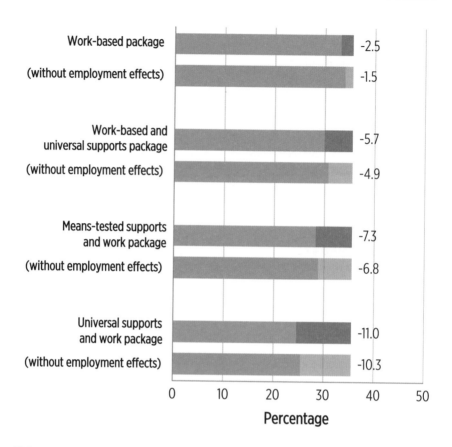

FIGURE 6-3 Simulated reductions in child poverty rates using 150% TRIM3 SPM for the four program packages.
NOTES: "Work-oriented package" combines expansions of the Earned Income Tax Credit (EITC), minimum wage, the Child and Dependent Care Tax Credit (CDCTC), and WorkAdvance. "Work-based and universal supports package" combines expansions of the EITC, the CDCTC, and a child allowance. "Means-tested supports and work package" combines expansions of the EITC, the CDCTC, Supplemental Nutrition Assistance Program, and housing vouchers. "Universal supports and work package" combines expansions of the EITC, minimum wage, and the CDCTC with child support assurance, restoration of immigrant program eligibility, and a child allowance.
SOURCE: Estimates from TRIM3 commissioned by the committee.

Given that some of the components in the third and fourth packages were expressly designed to meet the committee's 50 percent poverty-reduction goal, it is unsurprising that both packages succeeded in doing that. Both the third package, based on means-tested supports and work, and the fourth package, based on universal supports and work, were estimated to reduce the 13 percent SPM child poverty rate by at least 6.6 percentage points (refer to Figure 6-1). By contrast, the first package, which is focused on work alone, falls far short of meeting the reduction goal, achieving only a 2.4 percentage-point reduction in child poverty. The second package, which combines relatively low-cost work-based and universal supports components, would reduce child poverty and deep child poverty considerably but not enough to meet the 50 percent reduction goal.

Figure 6-1 also shows projected poverty reduction in the absence of the employment-related behavioral responses elicited by the program packages. In the case of the work-oriented package, all four components incentivize paid employment, thereby nearly doubling the poverty-reducing impact of the policy package, from –1.4 to –2.4 percentage points. The behavioral impacts of the other three packages are considerably smaller but do boost employment and reduce child poverty. This is because the work-incentivizing effects of the subcomponents that are work-oriented outweigh the work-disincentivizing effects of the purely transfer subcomponents. Employment and earnings increases add more than half a percentage point to the poverty-reducing impacts of the universal supports and work package but only about one-third of a point to the poverty-reducing impacts of the means-tested and work supports package.

Package-induced reductions in deep poverty parallel those found when the line is drawn at 50 percent of poverty (refer to Figure 6-2). Both the means-tested support and work package and the universal supports and work package were estimated to achieve the goal of 50 percent reduction in deep poverty, while the work-oriented package falls far short, even though relatively strong work incentives in the work-oriented package double its ability to reduce deep poverty. Both the third and fourth packages have positive impacts on employment and earnings, but these impacts are relatively small; consequently, the differences in estimated poverty reduction with and without employment effects are small as well. When the threshold is set at 150 percent SPM poverty, the second, third, and fourth packages again outperform the work-oriented package (refer to Figure 6-3).

It is also useful to examine the tradeoffs between poverty reduction and budget cost across the four packages (see Figure 6-4), as we did for the individual packages in Chapter 5. The linear nature of the tradeoffs between program cost and poverty reduction, when the poverty line is drawn at 100 percent of SPM poverty, is quite apparent in Figure 6-4. The first, work-based, package is estimated to cost relatively little ($8.6 to $9.4

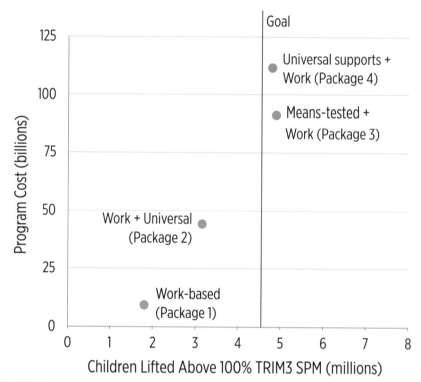

FIGURE 6-4 Simulated program cost, based on the 2015 tax law, by number of children lifted out of 100 percent SPM poverty for the four packages.
SOURCE: Estimates from TRIM3 commissioned by committee.

billion annually, depending on the tax code—refer to Tables 6-2 and 6-3) but lifts only 1.8 million children above the poverty line. The second package adds a $2,000 child allowance to the EITC and CDCTC components of the work-based package, which adds about $35 billion to the cost and lifts an additional 1.6 million children out of poverty. The third and fourth packages bring an additional 1.5 million children out of poverty, but at a marginal cost of about $45 to $67 billion per year.[2]

More details on the estimated impacts on poverty of the four packages are provided in Tables 6-2 (based on the 2015 tax law) and 6-3 (based on the 2018 tax law). The tables show overall package impacts and provide information about the role played by the individual components of each

_____

[2] The costs can be usefully compared to the $481 billion in direct federal expenditures on children in 2017 (Isaacs et al., 2018). The most expensive of our packages, costing $111 billion using the 2018 tax code, represents a 23% increase in that expenditure.

package.[3] The poverty-reduction numbers in the first two columns of these two tables clearly show that for the work-oriented package, expansions of the EITC and CDCTC do much more to reduce child poverty than do expansions of the minimum wage or the WorkAdvance Program rollout. Specifically, the EITC and CDCTC expansions each generate 1.2 percentage point poverty reductions, whereas neither the minimum wage increase nor the WorkAdvance expansion generates more than a 0.2 percentage-point reduction.

The patterns for deep poverty (child poverty less than 50 percent of the SPM) are somewhat different than those for 100 percent of SPM poverty (see Figure 6-5). The work package is not as effective at reducing deep poverty as it is at reducing 100 percent SPM poverty, while the second package, combining the child allowance with work supports, is relatively more effective. As they do for 100 percent SPM poverty, the third and fourth packages both meet the 50 percent poverty-reduction goal for deep poverty.

The final three columns of Tables 6-2 and 6-3 provide information on the simulated cost and labor market impacts. As seen in Figure 6-4, costs vary enormously across the packages, with the work-based package costing around $9 billion per year, the work-based and universal supports package costing $44 billion, and the costs of the third and fourth packages ranging between $90 billion and $110 billion depending on the package and whether the 2015 or 2018 tax law is used to estimate costs.

Despite their different mixtures of income support and work incentives, all four packages are estimated to increase work and earnings for adults living in low-income families (see Figure 6-6). The first, work-oriented package is estimated to add a million low-income workers to the labor force and generate $18 billion in earned income, with the expansion of the CDCTC being the key driver of these changes. The second package, which adds a $2,000 child allowance to the EITC and CDCTC components of the first package, is estimated to add around 550,000 low-income workers to the labor force. The third package, which combines means-test supports with work-oriented provisions, is estimated to add about 400,000 workers and generate about $2 billion in additional earnings.

In the case of the fourth package, which combines universal supports and work-oriented provisions, the work reductions associated with the

---

[3] The data compiled in Table 6-2 are based on simulations with the tax laws that prevailed in 2015 as applied to the 2015 population. Table 6-3 repeats these simulations based on the 2018 tax law but still based on the 2015 population. It is important to point out that the data listed for each component assume that each component acts independently of the others. However, in reality these components interact, and because the interactions are only factored into the package totals, the sum of the component impacts generally exceeds the overall package impacts. Nevertheless, the data for the components provide a general idea of which components matter the most.

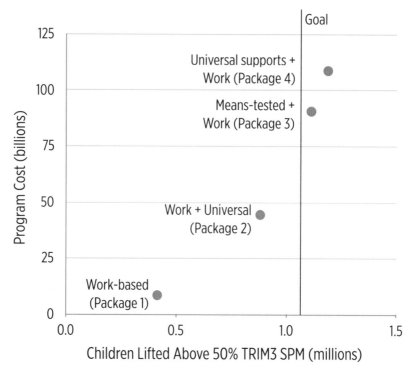

FIGURE 6-5 Simulated program cost, based on the 2015 tax law, by number of children lifted out of deep poverty (<50% SPM poverty) for the four packages. SOURCE: Estimates from TRIM3 commissioned by the committee.

child allowance are more than offset by the gains in employment and earnings associated with the expanded EITC and CDCTC programs. Indeed, the net effect of this full set of policy and program changes is to increase employment among adults living in low-income families by more than 600,000 and earnings by more than $13 billion.

None of these estimated changes in work and earnings is affected very much by the 2018 tax reforms (refer to Table 6-3). These simulations show that a package approach to child poverty reduction can bring children out of poverty and deep poverty while simultaneously inducing hundreds of thousands of their parents and other adults living in their households to enter the paid labor market.

CONCLUSION 6-1: Two program and policy packages developed by the committee met its mandated 50 percent reduction in both child poverty (defined by 100% of the Supplemental Poverty Measure [SPM])

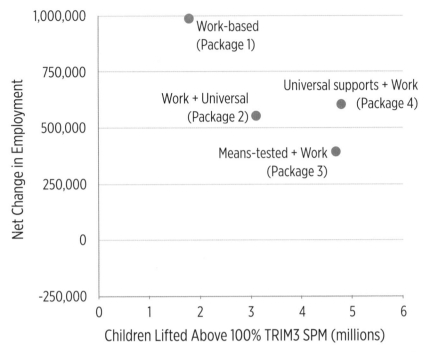

FIGURE 6-6 Simulated net change in employment, based on the 2015 tax law, by number of children lifted out of poverty for the four packages.
NOTE: Changes in employment are limited to individuals living in households with incomes below 200 percent of SPM poverty.
SOURCE: Estimates from TRIM3 commissioned by the committee.

and deep poverty (defined by 50% of SPM). The first of these packages combines work-oriented policy expansions with increases in benefit levels in the housing voucher and Supplemental Nutrition Assistance Programs. The second package combines work-oriented expansions with a child allowance, a child support assurance program, and elimination of immigrant restrictions on benefits built into the 1996 welfare reforms. Both packages increase work and earnings and both are estimated to cost between $90 and $111 billion per year.

CONCLUSION 6-2: The committee was unable to formulate an evidence-based employment-oriented package that would come close to meeting its mandate of reducing child poverty by 50 percent. The best employment-oriented package it could design combines expansions of the Earned Income Tax Credit, the Child and Dependent Care Tax

Credit, a minimum wage increase, and a promising career development program. Although this package is estimated to add more than a million workers to the labor force, generate $18 billion in additional earnings, and cost the government only $8.6 to $9.3 billion annually, its estimated reductions in child poverty are less than one-half of what is needed to meet the goal.

CONCLUSION 6-3: The committee combined two work-based and one income-support policy expansions in a package that was projected to reduce child poverty by one-third and deep child poverty by 40 percent, at an estimated annual cost of $44 billion. This package was estimated to increase employment by 550,000 jobs and earned income by nearly $10 billion.

REFERENCES

Isaacs, J.B., Lou, C., Hahn, H., Ovalle, J., and Steuerle, C.E. (2018). *Kids' Share 2018: Report on Federal Expenditures on Children through 2017 and Future Projections.* Washington, DC: Urban Institute. Available: https://www.urban.org/sites/default/files/publication/98725/kids_share_2018_0.pdf.

Sawhill, I., Rodrigue, E., and Joo, N. (2016). *One-Third of a Nation: Strategies for Helping Working Families.* Washington, DC: The Brookings Institution.

7

Other Policy and Program Approaches to Child Poverty Reduction

Most of the program and policy ideas featured in Chapters 5 and 6 are modifications and combinations of decades-old social programs that have been studied extensively by academic researchers and policy analysts. Their evidence makes it clear who uses these programs, how a given program interacts with other programs to affect child poverty, and how the work effort of parents changes in response to changes in the programs themselves. That knowledge has been incorporated into the Transfer Income Model, Version 3 (TRIM3), which was used to simulate the poverty-reduction effects of changes to the programs and packages of programs presented in Chapters 5 and 6.

This chapter is devoted to evidence-based program and policy ideas that were considered by the committee but, for a variety of reasons, were not chosen for inclusion in Chapters 5 and 6. For most of them, research evidence was not sufficiently strong to support predictions of the magnitude and, in some cases, even the direction of impacts on child poverty rates. In other cases, although the research suggested that a reform was likely to decrease the number of poor children, it was not feasible to simulate the magnitude of the effect.

Some of the programs the committee chose not to simulate relate to families, in particular family planning and structure, including marriage, as well as to paid family and medical leave. For other reforms, such as block grants, mandatory employment programs, and expansion of the Temporary Assistance for Needy Families (TANF) program, the evidence on poverty-reducing impacts is ambiguous or incomplete. For health insurance programs such as Medicaid, we were thwarted by serious poverty measurement issues, which were raised in Chapter 2, are expanded on here, and are the subject of a paper commissioned by the committee (Korenman, Remler, and Hyson, 2017). Finally, we remind readers that many evidence-based program areas such as home visiting and early education may generate benefits that fall outside of the 10-year window dictated by our statement of task. These kinds of programs are not included in this or any other report chapters.

Although it was possible to estimate poverty reductions associated with the various program and policy options and combinations discussed in Chapters 5 and 6 for many demographic subgroups of interest, small sample sizes precluded reliable estimates for certain racial/ethnic groups, such as Asians and Pacific Islanders, American Indians, and Alaska Natives. This is a serious concern, particularly in the case of American Indian and Alaska Native (AIAN) children, whose poverty rates are very high. In the final section of this chapter, we use other sources of data, as well as findings from a paper the committee commissioned (Akee and Simeonova, 2017), to discuss policy issues involving AIAN children.

FAMILY PLANNING

Background

As we will note below, research has shown that unintended births are very common and that they have a high probability of leading to family incomes below the poverty line. Reducing unintended births is therefore an option often raised in discussions of how to reduce poverty. However, before reviewing the research on the issue and discussing the policy implications of that research, the committee considered the question of whether birth control *should* be used as a policy to reduce child poverty. Given the history in the United States of limiting the reproductive freedom of women, particularly low-income women and women of color (Gordon, 1976), any policy that aims to reduce unintended pregnancies may be construed as a policy designed to prevent poor women from having children. The committee strongly condemns any such coercive efforts and considers informed, voluntary access to effective contraception a basic health care right for women and men.

However, research shows large racial/ethnic differences in the implementation of expanded access to effective contraception among women of low socioeconomic status. One study found that low-socioeconomic status African American and Latina women have three times the odds of being offered long-acting reversible contraceptives as do their their low-socioeconomic status White counterparts (Dehlendorf et al., 2010), indicating that reproductive inequities may still exist. Thus, expanding unbiased, voluntary, and informed access to the contraception options that women feel are best for them may be a sound policy objective in and of itself, as long as it is pursued with child poverty reduction as a secondary consequence and not the primary goal.

As background, in the United States, mothers report that nearly one-half of all their pregnancies and over one-third of births are unintended (Guttmacher Institute, 2016; Mosher, Jones, and Abma, 2012). The rate of unintentional births varies considerably by poverty status. Between 2006 and 2010, 46 percent of births to women with household incomes below the federal poverty line were reported as unintended, as compared with 18 percent of births to women with incomes more than four times higher than the poverty line (Mosher, Jones, and Abma, 2012). Furthermore, women who experience an unintended birth are likely to do so again in the future (Rajan et al., 2017).

Recent studies have found that unintended births often limit women's economic mobility and increase the likelihood of poverty-level family incomes. Unintended pregnancies may prevent adolescents and young adults from earning a college degree and make it more difficult for them to obtain and keep stable, well-paying jobs (Sonfield et al., 2013; Waldfogel, 1998). Research also suggests that limited access to and awareness of effective birth control options makes unintended births more frequent, particularly among low-income women.

Might access to effective birth control methods reduce the child poverty rate? Using the FamilyScape 2.0 simulation model, Karpilow and his colleagues (2013) found that if 25 percent of women under age 30 who are not currently using any contraception were to begin using more effective hormonal contraception methods (such as intrauterine devices or implants), the poverty rate among newborns would be reduced by one-half of a percentage point in a single year. They estimate that a sustained 25 percent uptake for each subsequent cohort of younger women would reduce child poverty by at least 2 percentage points over the 10-year period. The reduction in child poverty might be even greater over this timeframe if the indirect effects of delaying pregnancy are considered. For example, if women delay pregnancy until they intend to give birth, they may seek more schooling or have better employment opportunities, which in turn may decrease the likelihood that their child will be born into poverty (Sawhill and Venator, 2015).

Implications for Policy

The research literature on unintended births has established three facts relevant to national policy on birth control methods that would reduce child poverty by allowing women who want to delay births to do so effectively. First, since a disproportionate share of unplanned pregnancies are experienced by women living in poverty, any reduction in the incidence of unplanned pregnancies will lower the child poverty rate.

Second, highly effective means of birth control have been developed over the past two decades. Although the contraceptive pill afforded women and couples greater control over fertility, its impact on pregnancy prevention has been inconsistent, largely because many women have difficulty remembering to take the pill on a regular basis (Bailey, 2013). Intrauterine devices and subcutaneous forms of birth control, collectively referred to as long-acting reversible contraception (LARC), have been found to be 20 times as effective in preventing pregnancy as older methods of birth control, such as contraceptive pills and condoms (Winner et al., 2012).

Third, evidence suggests that increasing access to effective contraception can help reduce the number of unintended births. In 2009, Colorado launched its Colorado Family Planning Initiative with the goal of providing women with no-cost access to and information about the most effective forms of contraception, especially LARC (Colorado Department of Public Health and Environment, 2017). Over a 6-year period, the rate of LARC use quadrupled in Colorado Title X clinics,[1] and the rate of unintended pregnancies declined by 40 percent among teens and by 20 percent among young women ages 20 to 24 (the two groups with the highest rates of unintended pregnancy). The average mother's age at first birth also increased by 1.2 years in the state. In addition, the Colorado Family Planning Initiative saved a total of around $68 million in entitlement program costs (combining federal and state costs) for women ages 15 to 24 and their infants (Colorado Department of Public Health and Environment, 2017).

Training health center staff in proper contraceptive counseling techniques appears to be a promising way of helping women who wish to avoid pregnancy to use voluntary birth control more effectively. A recent national study of family planning clinics in the United States randomly assigned staff in 20 clinics to receive training in providing counseling and inserting IUDs or progestin implants on the same day when women came for advice and counseling about birth control and opted to try these methods; staff in 20 control-group clinics provided standard care. Researchers found that women receiving services from the experimental clinics were less than one-half as likely to become pregnant within the next 12 months (Harper et al., 2015).

In cooperation with local and state governments, Upstream USA[2] trains clinic staff in effective methods for counseling women about available birth

---

[1] Title X clinics are family planning clinics that provide family planning and related preventive health care services to low-income and uninsured individuals. See https://www.hhs.gov/opa/title-x-family-planning/about-title-x-grants/index.html for more information about Title X grants.

[2] For more information on Upstream USA, see https://www.upstream.org.

control options and provides information about how federal programs such as Title X and Medicaid can help clinics finance their operations. Working with Delaware's state government, in 2014 Upstream USA carried out a statewide initiative aimed at increasing access to contraceptives. An evaluation of its efforts showed that among women ages 20 to 39 who were Delaware Title X family planning clients, use of LARC roughly doubled, from 14 to 27 percent, while use of less effective birth control measures, including the pill, the patch, and the ring, decreased substantially. These changes were projected to decrease the rate of unintended pregnancy among this population by 15 percentage points between 2014 and 2016 (Welti and Manlove, 2018).

These studies show that it is possible to increase access to and requests for LARC during a single regular visit to a health clinic, thereby reducing the rate of unintended pregnancy. Although the studies did not provide separate estimates for poor and nonpoor women, the fact that they identified very strong results among women using public clinics suggests that reducing unintended pregnancies might well be effective in reducing the child poverty rate. Research suggests, however, that it is possible for racial bias to influence clinician recommendations in contraceptive counseling sessions (Dehlendorf et al., 2010; Higgins, Kramer, and Ryder, 2016). Thus, the use of patient-centered care practices in health centers could be beneficial in protecting the reproductive autonomy of the women receiving counseling (Higgins, 2014).

In contrast to the positive outcomes that result from increased communication and training, policies that restrict women's access to family planning services have led to reductions in the use of effective contraception and increases in the number of births (Fischer, Royer, and White, 2017; Lu and Slusky, 2016; Stevenson et al., 2016; Woo, Alamgir, and Potter, 2016). Texas provides a valuable case study. Between 2011 and 2014, the Texas state legislature substantially cut funding for women's health programs, eliminated Planned Parenthood from fee-for-service programs, and significantly restricted access to abortion. Because of these policy changes, more than one-half of the abortion-providing women's health clinics and a quarter of publicly funded family planning clinics in the state closed. Stevenson et al. (2016) found that the elimination of Planned Parenthood from the state's family planning program was associated with a one-third reduction in Medicaid claims for LARC and a 1.9 percentage-point increase in Medicaid-related births in Texas (Stevenson et al., 2016).

CONCLUSION 7-1: Increasing both awareness of and access to effective, safe, and affordable long-acting reversible contraception (LARC) devices reduces the incidence of unplanned births, which could in turn reduce child poverty. In contrast, policies that reduce access to LARC by cutting Medicaid, Title X funding of family planning services, or mandated contraceptive coverage appear to increase the number of unintended births and thus also child poverty.

FAMILY COMPOSITION

Background

The poverty rate for children in single-parent families is roughly five times the rate for children in married-couple families (Semega, Fontenot, and Kollar, 2017). Moreover, as detailed in Chapter 4, the rise of single-parent family structures and the increase in the number of births outside marriage played important roles in child poverty trends during the last quarter of the 20th century, although as discussed in earlier chapters they have become less important since 2000. Thus, policies that increase the share of children living in married-couple or other two-parent family structures are likely to reduce child poverty rates (Gibson-Davis, 2016). By the same token, existing policies with provisions that reduce marriage rates, even if unintentionally, are likely to increase child poverty.

Implications for Policy

Social scientists have conducted numerous studies to determine how various social policies might influence the decisions that teens and adults make about family composition (Lopoo and Raissian, 2014). Some of these studies have focused on the impacts on marriage of past and current safety-net policies, while others have evaluated attempts by the George W. Bush administration to increase the share of children living in two-parent households (whether the parents are married or not) (Haskins, 2015).

Much of the rigorous research that has been conducted on the effects of existing programs focuses on the Earned Income Tax Credit (EITC), Medicaid, and the TANF program (Moffitt, 2016). In the case of the EITC, a recent review (Nichols and Rothstein, 2016) describes how low-income couples with one wage earner are incentivized by the EITC to marry, while two-earner couples are effectively penalized for marrying if their joint income brings them above the EITC eligibility level. These kinds of effects are unavoidable in a tax system that taxes income at the family rather than the individual level.

Examining the expansion of the EITC in the 1990s, Eissa and Hoynes (2003) found changes in marriage rates that are consistent with these incentives, increasing marriage rates by 1 to 5 percentage points for families with incomes below $25,000 but reducing marriage rates by 1 percent for families with incomes between $25,000 and $75,000. Other studies have found more uniformly negative impacts on marriage (e.g., Rosenbaum, 2000), while some have found null or very small effects (Dickert-Conlin and Houser, 2002; Ellwood, 2000; Herbst, 2011; Michelmore, 2018). Summarizing this literature, Nichols and Rothstein (2016) conclude only that links between the EITC and marriage are poorly understood.

The limited literature on Medicaid's marriage effects has focused on changes in marriage in response to expansions of Medicaid coverage. Until the mid-1980s, the strong link between Medicaid and the Aid to Families with Dependent Children (AFDC) Program meant that most married couples were ineligible for Medicaid coverage (Buchmueller, Ham, and Shore-Sheppard, 2016). Yelowitz (1998) found that after the Medicaid expansions of the 1980s and 1990s, women whose children were all eligible for Medicaid were slightly (1.5%) more likely to be married than women with at least one ineligible child. However, at least some of that effect may have been due to choices about childbearing, and it is possible that some of the effect is actually accounted for by the EITC expansions (Meyer and Rosenbaum, 2001).

Most studies of the effect of the TANF program on marriage compare it with its predecessor, the AFDC program, which it replaced as part of the welfare reforms of the 1990s. Because TANF is a more restrictive program than AFDC, and because it greatly reduced the program caseload, the effect of the reform can be broadly interpreted as showing the effects of reducing the availability of welfare programs on marriage. Reviews of the literature in this area (Grogger and Karoly, 2005; Ziliak, 2016) find mixed evidence for any effect: A few studies find effects for some subgroups but not others, while other studies find no effects for any group. One of the higher-quality studies, by Dunifon, Hynes, and Peters (2009), highlights the murky nature of program results, finding few consistent effects of welfare policy measures on the likelihood that a child is living with married, cohabiting, or single parents.

Overall, the existing literature on marriage incentives and disincentives provides little reason to believe that current social policies have had a substantial impact.[3] This may be because marriage, cohabitation, and divorce are affected by many economic and noneconomic factors other than transfer programs—including men's employment and earnings levels, women's employment potential, nonmarital birth rates (see above), and levels of community and family support, to name just a few.

In response to evidence suggesting that many low-income couples have a strong desire to marry but often do not because of financial and social

---

[3] We do not cover the effects of child support enforcement programs on marriage and cohabitation, but the results of the literature on that program are also inconclusive (Lopoo and Raissian, 2014).

obstacles (Gibson-Davis, Edin, and McLanahan, 2005), the George W. Bush administration launched an ambitious effort to promote two-parent relationships and provided funding for the Administration for Children and Families to support rigorous evaluations of three different programs.

The Building Strong Families project developed and tested a number of voluntary programs that offered relationship-skills education and other support services to unmarried couples who were expecting or had just had a baby. Over the course of 3 years, more than 5,000 couples living in eight states participated in the evaluation of the Building Strong Families program, at an average program cost of about $11,000 per couple. A random-assignment evaluation found that the project had no overall effects on the quality of couples' relationships, the chances that they would stay together or get married, their coparenting relationships, or their family incomes. Of the two statistically significant effects generated by the programs, one was negative (a reduction in some aspects of father involvement) and one was beneficial (a modest reduction in children's behavioral problems). Couples in one of the eight program sites—Oklahoma City—were more likely to still be living together 3 years after the program began, but that effect did not appear to translate into improved child well-being (Wood et al., 2012).

The Supporting Healthy Marriage Program tested the effectiveness of a skills-based relationship education program designed to help low- and modest-income married couples strengthen their relationships and to support more stable and nurturing home environments. An evaluation showed that the program did not lead more couples to stay together and had little effect on indicators of coparenting, parenting, or child well-being. However, it did find a consistent pattern of modest but sustained positive impacts of the program on the quality of the couples' relationships (Lundquist et al., 2014).

The Community Healthy Marriage Initiative was a community-level effort to improve relationship skills and promote healthy marriages. It brought together multiple stakeholders from a community to develop media campaigns, offer relationship courses, make service referrals, and in other ways attempt to generate a critical mass of community awareness and positive behaviors. An evaluation of the project showed no significant effects on community-level outcomes for parenting measures, awareness of the program, or marriage options and attitudes (Bir et al., 2012).

As compared with the discouraging results from these large-scale studies, a few smaller-scale studies have produced results that some analysts believe to be more hopeful (e.g., Frimmel, Halla, and Winter-Ebmer, 2012). Perhaps the most frequently mentioned is the evaluation of the Parents and

Children Together (PACT) Program (Avellar et al., 2018), which showed beneficial impacts on the participating couples' relationship quality, conflict behavior, coparenting relationship, and marriage rates 1 year after the program ended. Although well conducted, this study has a few limitations. One is that all participating couples were already in long-term (5 years or longer) marital or co-habitation relationships at the beginning of the study, so the marriage impact in the PACT study was one of reducing breakups rather than increasing marriage rates. Also, in contrast to the longer-run follow-ups for the three Bush administration programs, results of the PACT evaluation were obtained after only 1 year of program participation, and it is commonplace for intervention impacts to fade out over time. The committee judged that findings like those from the PACT study, although interesting and potentially important, should not override our conclusions based on the results of well-conducted, longer-term studies like those in the Bush marriage initiative.

At the state level, a related policy initiative in the early 1990s involved the passage of laws streamlining the process of paternity establishment in hospitals at the time of the birth. Rossin-Slater (2017) finds that these laws substantially increased paternity establishment and also increased the amount of time that absent fathers spend with their children and the amount of money they spend with them as well. However, the laws had the unintended effect of *reducing* marriage rates. As a result of the decline in marriage among these mothers, the mothers were more likely to marry or cohabit with men who were older and had higher employment rates than the males with whom they had conceived their baby. Moreover, the fathers who would have married the mothers in the absence of these laws were less involved with the child than they would have been otherwise. Averaged across the entire sample of both married and unmarried parents, the effects of these laws on observable measures of fathers' involvement with their children are either zero or negative.

> CONCLUSION 7-2: Although increasing the proportion of children living with married or cohabiting parents, as opposed to single parents, would almost certainly reduce child poverty, the impacts of existing social programs designed to promote such a change are uncertain. Evidence from these programs is inconclusive and points to neither strong positive nor negative effects. In the early 2000s, an ambitious attempt to develop programs that would improve couple-relationship skills, promote marriage, and improve child well-being failed to boost marriage rates and achieve most of their other longer-run goals.

PAID FAMILY AND MEDICAL LEAVE

Background

The unmet health needs of parents and children can compromise a family's ability to sustain full-time employment and generate earnings sufficient to keep family income above the poverty line. As documented in Chapters 3 and 8, low-income children and adults are more likely than their higher-income counterparts to experience health problems (Case, Lubotsky, and Paxson, 2002; Centers for Disease Control and Prevention, 2013). Further, taking time off from work to care for a sick family member is a challenge for some low-income parents, as some may not be eligible for family and medical leave or have access to paid leave (Joshi et al., 2014; Mathur et al., 2017). When workers lack access to paid leave, families must choose between addressing health needs and continuing to work to earn income (Boushey, 2016). When these individuals do take leave, they forgo wage income, which can put them at risk of falling—or falling deeper—into poverty because of inadequate savings to accommodate financial disruptions (see Chapter 8).

The United States is the only nation among the 34 members of the Organisation for Economic Co-operation and Development (OECD) that does not guarantee paid leave to mothers of infants (Raub et al., 2018b), and it is one of only two OECD nations that does not guarantee leave for personal illness (Raub et al., 2018a). In most OECD countries, benefit levels (as determined by wage replacement rates) provide median wage earners with sufficient income to remain above the poverty line during paid leave, although fewer countries ensure benefits that allow minimum wage earners to remain above the poverty line (Bose et al., 2018).

Current U.S. family and medical leave policy comprises a variety of laws enacted at the federal, state, and local levels to provide for unpaid or paid leave; additionally, in some cases employers have adopted their own policies. The national policy governing family or medical leave is embodied in the Family and Medical Leave Act (FMLA), which entitles eligible employees (roughly one-half of all workers) to take unpaid, job-protected leave for family and medical reasons with continuing group health insurance coverage (Joshi et al., 2014; Klerman, Daley, and Pozniak, 2012). Hispanic workers are less likely to be eligible for unpaid FMLA than other workers, and both Black and Hispanic workers are less likely than other workers to be both eligible for and able to afford unpaid FMLA (Joshi et al., 2014).

Seven states and Washington, D.C., as well as more than 70 municipalities, have established paid family and medical leave for targeted populations (National Partnership for Women and Families, 2018a, 2018b).

Yet in 2016, only 6 percent of low-wage workers had access to employer-provided paid family leave, compared with 25 percent of higher-wage workers (Bureau of Labor Statistics, 2017).

Implications for Policy

Access to paid family and medical leave has the potential to reduce child poverty by increasing employment and improving maternal and child health, although the potential effects of paid family and medical leave on employment and wages are ambiguous (Klerman and Leibowitz, 1994; Olivetti and Petrongolo, 2017). Paid leave might reduce human capital by discouraging employers from hiring, leading to a decline in wages and employment. On the other hand, paid leave might increase job continuity for workers, which could result in higher wages and employment levels.

Likely impacts of paid family and medical leave on child poverty depend on their policy designs. Providing paid leave through a social insurance program could minimize employer costs and prevent wage and employment discrimination against individuals who are perceived as likely to take leave (Mathur et al., 2017). On the other hand, paid family and medical leave provided through an employer mandate might have no net effect on or even increase child poverty because employers might seek to reduce costs by avoiding hiring covered workers or workers they believe are likely to take leave (Mathur et al., 2017).

Some of the best U.S.-based evidence on the impacts of paid leave comes from California, which enacted a paid leave program that began in 2004. Under this program, workers are entitled to a maximum of 6 weeks' leave to care for a newborn, an adopted child, or an ailing family member and are paid about 60 to 70 percent of their normal wages, up to a maximum benefit based on the state's average weekly wage. A tax on all employees finances this program.

Evaluations of California's Paid Family Leave policy have shown that it has generated positive impacts on continued parental employment, when compared with the counterfactual of no provision being made for parental leave.[4] For example, the program made it more likely that mothers would return to work after childbirth (Baum and Ruhm, 2016) and increased labor force attachment around the time of childbirth (Byker, 2016). It increased leave-taking among mothers and fathers (Bartel et al., 2017; Rossin-Slater,

---

[4] In 2016, California increased the weekly wage replacement percentage from approximately 55 percent to approximately 60-70 percent (from $50 to $1,216). The evaluations of California's Paid Family Leave policy included in this chapter represent data collected prior to 2016. For more information on California's Paid Family Leave policy, please see https://www.edd.ca.gov/disability/FAQ_PFL_Benefits.htm.

Ruhm, and Waldfogel, 2013) but also increased work hours for mothers 1 to 3 years after childbirth (Baum and Ruhm, 2016; Rossin-Slater et al., 2013). On the downside, one study of the program found that it was associated with an increase in unemployment among young women, both relative to men and older women in California and relative to young women, men, and older women in states without paid leave (Das and Polachek, 2015). This finding is consistent with Gruber (1994) who found that federal mandates that maternity benefits be included in health insurance plans reduced female employment.

Turning to employers, one study of the California Paid Family Leave policy suggests that it had no burdensome effects on employers' wage costs. After matching paid leave and state disability insurance program data to employee and employer data from the California Employment Development Department, researchers found no evidence that an increase in the share of employees who take leave is associated with an increase in wage costs or a significant rise in employee turnover rates (Bedard and Rossin-Slater, 2016).

The California Paid Family Leave policy also produced changes associated with improved health. In particular, it doubled the average length of time women took for maternity leave, from 3 weeks to between 6 and 7 weeks, which can have a positive impact on infant health (Rossin-Slater et al., 2013). Two California studies found that paid family and medical leave has increased the incidence of breastfeeding relative to other states without such policies (Huang and Yang, 2015) and that children in early elementary school had positive health outcomes, such as a lower probability of being overweight, compared with the period before the introduction of paid leave (Lichtman-Sadot and Bell, 2017).

There are few methodologically strong studies of the direct impact of paid leave policies on child poverty, however. Studies that have examined California's Paid Family Leave policy show positive effects on employment and wages (Baum and Ruhm, 2016; Rossin-Slater, Ruhm, and Waldfogel, 2013) but they have not isolated the effects of the policies on lower-income families.

CONCLUSION 7-3: Evidence suggests that paid family and medical leave increases parents' ability to continue in employment and has positive impacts on children's health, although it might also reduce employment among women potentially eligible for such leave. It is important to continue evaluating the labor market, health, and child-poverty impacts of states' paid-leave laws.

MANDATORY EMPLOYMENT PROGRAMS

Background

Both common sense and a wealth of research, as documented in earlier chapters, point to increases in steady employment, wage rates, and earnings as among the strongest correlates of escaping poverty (Sawhill, Rodrigue, and Joo, 2016). Policies for increasing employment and earnings among the poor in order to help them escape poverty include efforts to build basic skills through education, government-sponsored training programs to help those pursuing specific skills (like the WorkAdvance Program featured in Chapter 5), work-related assistance such as child care subsidies, and purely financial incentives designed to work through the tax system, especially tax credits like the EITC. All of these have the potential to make a difference, and a large body of research evidence shows that many of them generate modest to substantial increases in employment and subsequent reductions in family poverty.[5]

This section focuses on another employment policy approach: *mandatory* employment programs for recipients of government transfers. Mandatory work programs have been attached to the TANF program, apply to some recipients of the Supplemental Nutrition Assistance Program (SNAP), have been tested in public housing in a few areas around the country, and most recently have been adopted in some states for recipients of Medicaid benefits. Mandatory job search requirements have also been a longstanding component of state unemployment-insurance programs in the United States.

Mandatory employment programs have the potential to be more effective than purely voluntary incentive programs at increasing work and earnings among transfer program recipients and, therefore, at reducing poverty. Moreover, they garner considerable public support because they are perceived to reinforce widely accepted social norms about the value of work.

However, while appealingly simple in theory, mandatory employment programs are complex in detail and application. Almost all of them provide for exemptions, and it is difficult to draw the line separating individuals who are from those who are not expected to work, a line that has major implications for the success of such mandates in reducing child poverty.

---

[5] The importance of financial work incentives in increasing employment and reducing poverty is reinforced by several randomized controlled trials conducted in the 1990s that tested major increases in earnings disregards of cash welfare programs. These programs included the Minnesota Family Investment Program, the New Hope program, and the Canadian Self-Sufficiency program. These programs often decreased poverty as well as increasing employment (see Blank, 2002, for a comprehensive review). While these programs reinforce the view that financial incentives can result in poverty reduction, their design is quite different than any program being considered today. The committee's Chapter 5 policy for expansion of the EITC represents its preferred program of this type.

Coupling mandated employment with work supports like child care, job search assistance, and transportation assistance is often the key to success, because, as we discuss in Chapter 8, low-income families face many barriers to work related to these factors. But these supports can be expensive and cumbersome to administer.

Another challenge in implementing mandatory employment programs is determining the amount of time recipients should be given to search for jobs that match their skills and pay at least the minimum wage. Finding the right balance, while also taking into account each recipient's barriers to work, requires skill and experience on the part of job counselors and a supportive administrative structure.

Implications for Policy

The committee sought to develop mandatory employment policy options that could be included in our Chapter 5 simulations. Given the overriding importance of research evidence in the committee's deliberations, we conducted an extensive review of the research on the impacts of mandatory employment programs on poverty. Some of the strongest evidence in support of these programs comes from randomized controlled trials that were published in the 1990s, when a large number of experiments were conducted on a diverse set of mandatory employment programs in several states and localities.[6] Most of these employment-related programs were directed at recipients of benefits from the former AFDC program, most of whom were single mothers, so the bulk of the available evidence relates to that demographic group.

A particularly useful and comprehensive summary of the many randomized clinical trials conducted over that period is provided in Greenberg, Deitch, and Hamilton (2009). The authors divided mandatory employment programs for single mothers into four types, three of which required either (1) work "per se" experience, often with unpaid jobs at nonprofits or government agencies (frequently after a period of job search), (2) an immediate job search, or (3) immediate enrollment in education or training prior to either job search or work. A fourth group included a mixture of mandates, such as (1) through (3), plus work supports such as child care, with recipients' specific mandates based on an assessment of their individual needs. Programs of each type were tested across a number of cities.

---

[6] A randomized controlled trial evaluation of the impact of work requirements in the SNAP program is currently under way. It is being conducted by Mathematica Policy Research, in cooperation with other organizations, with funding from USDA (see https://www.mathematica-mpr.com/our-publications-and-findings/projects/snap-employment-and-training-pilots). Initial findings are expected in 2019, with a final report to be published in 2021.

The results of the clinical trials showed that over a 3- to 5-year period following random assignment, the family incomes of participants in the "work per se" programs rose only minimally, while incomes of participants in the "immediate job search" and "immediate enrollment in education/job training" programs fell because benefit losses exceeded increases in earnings. In contrast, mixed programs tailored to recipients' needs generally produced clear increases in family income (Greenberg, Deitch, and Hamilton, 2009, Table ES.1).

The mixed and tailored program models were therefore the only types that could be expected to increase family income and reduce poverty. In the case of the mixed model, comprehensive programs at five different sites were tested, and the analysis showed net income effects (discounted over a 5-year period) ranging from –$745 to $2,651 (Greenberg, Deitch, and Hamilton, 2009, Table B-11). These 5-year summed effects correspond to an average annual income gain of $340 per year, an amount unlikely to reduce child poverty to any appreciable degree.

A smaller number of randomized clinical trials have assessed impacts on employment and family income for two-parent families. The best-known and most skillfully implemented study evaluated the California Greater Avenues for Independence (GAIN) Program (Riccio, Friedlander, and Freedman, 1994). The GAIN program was a statewide initiative targeted toward increasing employment and self-sufficiency for individuals who received AFDC cash welfare program (Riccio, Friedlander, and Freedman, 1994). The impacts of mandatory work programs on participants in this program (who, unlike the Greenberg et al. [2009] study participants, were not grouped into categories of program types) were generally unfavorable. By the 5th year after random assignment, net family income had fallen by an average of $260 per year, and some sites reported annual income losses exceeding $2,000. While programs implemented at some of the sites did produce substantial gains in household income, the evaluations were unable to identify the program features that made this difference.

Evidence on the impacts of mandatory work programs also comes from the implementation of the Personal Responsibility and Work Opportunity Reconciliation Act of 1996, which required that all states mandate work for most recipients of benefits under the new TANF program. A number of studies have sought to estimate the effects of this legislation on employment, poverty, and other outcomes (Blank, 2002; Grogger and Karoly, 2005; Hamilton, 2002). The most consistent evidence indicates that the legislation reduced welfare receipt and increased employment. But while these work mandates may have generated short-run reductions in poverty, they may have simultaneously increased the number of families with incomes far below the poverty line (Bitler, Gelbach, and Hoynes, 2006). However, it is problematic to draw conclusions about work mandates from this evidence, because impacts on families were generated by multiple features of the legislation, including mandatory work requirements as well as time limits, block grants, and in some cases earnings disregards. Researchers have been unable to identify the relative contributions of mandatory employment and other features to the outcomes that have been observed.[7]

Given that the evidence on the effects of mandatory employment under TANF is inconclusive, the best available evidence on child poverty reduction comes from the experimental evaluations just described, which were conducted in the 1990s. The question remains: Do the increases found in the family incomes of single mothers participating in the mixed programs that were the focus of those evaluations warrant conducting simulations of the impacts of such program for today's transfer recipients? We conclude that they do not.

The AFDC caseload in the early 1990s was very different from the caseloads of major programs today, both in its demographic composition and in the nature of participants' experience and employment-related education. The SNAP program, for example, includes far more nondisabled, nonelderly able-bodied workers than AFDC did, in addition to including large numbers of elderly and disabled individuals. The Medicaid program, with its high income-eligibility levels, covers more workers than AFDC did in the past. The labor market and the availability of other work supports, such as child care and the EITC, are also very different today.

CONCLUSION 7-4: There is insufficient evidence to identify mandatory work policies that would reliably reduce child poverty, and it appears that work requirements are at least as likely to increase as to decrease poverty. The dearth of evidence also reflects underinvestment over the past two decades in methodologically strong evaluations of the impacts of alternative work programs.

BLOCK GRANTS

Background

Block grants provide federal assistance, typically to state governments, for broadly defined functions such as social services. Unlike categorical grants, federal block grants give states considerable flexibility in allocating and spending the allotted funds. In the case of safety-net programs, block

---

[7] See the extensive discussion of this issue in Blank (2002). One study which attempted to separate the work components concluded that "work requirements alone have relatively weak effects on family income and poverty" (Grogger and Karoly, 2005, p. 171).

grants have the potential to affect child poverty rates, and in principle they can be a tool for reducing poverty.

For two key reasons, however, the committee chose not to simulate block grant proposals and reforms in Chapter 5. First, very little evidence concerning the impact of block grants on poverty rates meets the standard of rigor we imposed on the other reforms we simulated. Second, block grants come in a variety of forms, and knowing how they are constructed is crucial in assessing any poverty impacts they might have. Accordingly, there is no simple answer to the question of whether block grants are likely to increase or reduce poverty.

Implications for Policy

Key features of block grants can be gleaned from states' experience with several existing block grants—in particular, the TANF block grant, the Title XX Social Services block grant, and the Child Care and Development block grant.[8] A fundamental feature is the block grant's initial funding level. Ideally, the grant level is geared to a state's level of need, but determining how that compares with the level of funding already received by the state is usually a contentious issue. Generally, block grants require "maintenance-of-effort" provisions to keep total spending at a reasonable level and encourage the recipient state's commitment to program effectiveness and quality. Maintenance-of-effort provisions typically require states to continue to contribute a certain amount of their own funds, and penalties are in place for violating that requirement.

A potentially even more important feature in a block grant's design is how its funding will change over time. Inflation-adjusted expenditures from block grants will fall as time goes by if funding amounts are fixed in nominal dollars and not allowed to change with inflation, unless states make up the shortfall with their own additional funds. Drops in funding for programs directed at children are likely to increase child poverty unless the level of need in the state is also dropping.[9] Additionally, to avoid inequities in federal support over time, block grants also need to adjust to changes in a state's level of need. Recessions are a special case of increased need;

---

[8] There is extensive literature on block grants that discusses in greater detail the issues raised here; see Dilger and Boyd (2014); Finegold, Wherry, and Schardin (2004); and Stenberg (2009).

[9] In the TANF program, the caseload has fallen significantly since the 1990s, so that real spending per recipient has not dropped as much as the drop in real total TANF spending. However, a large share of the block grant is now funding activities other than cash assistance and work supports, and the participation rate of financial eligibles has fallen, demonstrating that the TANF program is now serving a smaller share of the needy population (Bitler and Hoynes, 2016).

without rules stipulating that adjustments are to be made in response to recessions, a block grant is not likely to be effective in reducing poverty during a downturn.

A common argument in favor of block grants is that they enable states to be flexible in addressing the needs of their populations and responding to the will of their voters. However, in some cases that flexibility can allow states to use block-grant funds to finance other, unrelated state activities, contrary to the intent of the grant. As a result, a key challenge in designing block grants is to formulate legislation in a way that constrains states, as intended by Congress, and prevents them from spending funds for unintended purposes. This raises a philosophical question: To what extent should the federal government restrict the states' flexibility? The answer to that, in turn, depends on how much weight should be given to voters' interest in supporting the poor in states other than their own and how important it is to have a uniform floor below which poor families are not allowed to fall.

The TANF block grant is a prime example worth examining, since it allows states considerable flexibility in spending block-grant funding. States vary widely in the amount of money they spend from this grant on cash assistance or a variety of other programs, and they also vary widely in the amounts they allocate per family at different income levels.[10] Unfortunately, we know very little about how states' choices relate to changes in state child-poverty rates.[11] States' reporting requirements under TANF are quite minimal, so federal policy makers and researchers are unable to determine whether the funds are being spent in keeping with the letter or spirit of the block grant.[12] All of these issues illustrate the challenges that are inherent in the design and operation of block grants, which will in turn affect the degree to which these grants are able to reduce the poverty rate.

CONCLUSION 7-5: Block grants that are adequately funded and sustained over time, and that provide for countercyclical relief, may serve local populations well by providing more fiscal flexibility for state

---

[10] See Falk (2016) for a detailed discussion of the TANF block grant. In FY2016, for example, overall, states spent 24% of their block grants on cash assistance, 11% on work-related activities, 20% on early care and education (child care and preschool), and the other 45% on a variety of activities including program management, state EITCs, and child welfare (https://www.acf.hhs.gov/ofa/resource/tanf-financial-data-fy-2016).

[11] Some have suggested that states should be required to put aside some fraction of funds to conduct evaluations of the poverty impacts of their programs. This would provide important information to help states as well as Congress assess the grants' impacts.

[12] Beginning in federal fiscal year 2015, the Administration for Children and Families has required more detailed financial reporting from the states, leading to considerably more detail on spending categories than had been the case in prior years.

and local governments. However, block grants that are inadequately funded, fail to be sustained, or lack provisions for countercyclical adjustment have resulted in reduced support for low-income families and in increased poverty. In addition, most block grants require only limited reporting and almost no evaluation, which decreases the likelihood that their funds will be used for their intended purposes.

THE TANF PROGRAM

Background

On a bipartisan basis, Congress created the TANF program, which was signed into law by President Clinton in 1996. The legislation converted what was previously known as AFDC from a matching grant to a block grant program, introduced work requirements and time limits, and imposed a large number of conditions on the states. Subsequent to the reform, the caseload in the program fell dramatically, and by 2000 it was only a little more than one-half of what it had been in 1995, prior to passage of the TANF legislation (Office of the Assistant Secretary for Planning and Evaluation, 2008). Similarly, expenditures on cash assistance for the affected families dropped by nearly one-half relative to expenditures on cash assistance in 1995 (Falk, 2015).[13]

One of the chief goals of the 1996 law was to increase employment and reduce poverty. Poverty could be expected to decline if the reform led to an increase in earnings and market income that exceeded the decrease in family income triggered by caseload reductions and a consequent drop in benefit receipt. As Figures 4-1 and 4-6 in this report show, market-based poverty fell sharply in the years after 1996, and most of the reduction in the overall poverty rate (including taxes and transfers) in the first 3 or 4 years after 1996 was a result of an increase in market income rather than expansions of transfers (although by 2015 most of the decline in overall poverty could be attributed to increases in transfers rather than increases in market income). However, the years after 1996 were also marked by improvements in the economy and the expansion of the EITC, both of which probably made independent contributions to poverty reduction.

A substantial research literature has attempted to distinguish the various contributions of these forces to poverty reduction. A review examining the short-run poverty impacts of well-evaluated pre-1996 programs

---

[13] Because expenditures in the TANF program have fallen so dramatically, the cash component of the program currently contributes very little to poverty reduction. Eliminating TANF would increase the child poverty rate by about one-half of one percentage point (Wheaton and Haldar, 2018).

resembling TANF, as well as studies of TANF itself, concluded that while evaluations of most of the pre-1996 programs showed no effect on poverty, some of the studies of TANF itself suggested that it did indeed reduce poverty (Grogger and Karoly, 2005, Chapter 7). The review cautioned that after time limits became effective and block grants declined in real value, the program might show different effects. A later review by Ziliak (2016) found less evidence for the poverty-reducing impact of the 1996 legislation, which suggests that the longer-run impacts of TANF on poverty reduction may have been smaller than its short-run impacts.

Implications for Policy

The committee chose not to simulate an expansion of the TANF program or the elimination or removal of any of the provisions of the 1996 law, for several reasons. First, the evidence suggests that the TANF law did in fact reduce poverty in the short run, if not necessarily in the long run, so it is unlikely that the poverty rate would decline if the pre-1996 system were to be reinstated. Furthermore, it would be impossible to simulate changes in work requirements or block grants, for reasons explained in the preceding two sections. All other features of the law held constant, it is impossible to identify the relative contributions of those two components. Based on the available evidence, it would be an impossible task to simulate changes in the many features of state TANF programs and the impacts of these changes on the U.S. child poverty rate.

HEALTH, HEALTH INSURANCE, AND MEASURING POVERTY

Background

Few would disagree with the premise that all children deserve to be healthy and that public policy should enable them to benefit from the dramatic advances in U.S. medical care. Moreover, as documented in Chapter 3, investments in child health provide long-run benefits to society as a whole. Healthier children are more likely to grow up into healthier adults who will, as a consequence, work and earn more (Brown, Kowalski, and Lurie, 2015), experience greater happiness and life satisfaction (Council on Community Pediatrics, 2016), and be more likely to marry (Smith, 2009). Thus, policies aimed at improving child health could significantly reduce future poverty as today's children grow up and start families of their own.

Poverty reduction in the next generation falls outside of the committee's 10-year window. However, we considered how providing health insurance and taking other steps to improve children's health might reduce child poverty in the short run through such mechanisms as reducing families' out-of-pocket medical expenses and allowing parents to work (see Chapter 8). In addition, affordable health insurance may enable parents to seek needed health care for themselves and their children without falling behind on rent or other necessary expenses. Indeed, evidence suggests that good insurance coverage improves parents' mental health, presumably by reducing stress and worry about health-care costs (Baicker et al., 2013; Finkelstein et al., 2016).

Implications for Policy

The United States has always relied on a patchwork health insurance system, one that does not cover everyone and can strain families' ability to afford premiums, copayments, deductibles, and the costs of needed but uncovered care. At the same time, the federal government and the states have made substantial efforts to improve the health of poor children by providing access to medical care through Medicaid and the Children's Health Insurance Program (CHIP).

Abundant evidence suggests that Medicaid and CHIP, which have both grown in size over the years, have had a major positive impact on child health and well-being (see Chapter 3). As documented in Chapter 4, in terms of expenditures Medicaid is by far the largest benefit program for low-income families with children, accounting for expenditures of $180 billion annually. The CHIP program spends an additional $15 billion per year (Centers for Medicare & Medicaid Services, 2017). Yet despite their proven benefits, health insurance programs such as Medicaid and CHIP are not directly reflected in official poverty measures. Consequently, the committee was unable to estimate the full effects on child poverty (as measured by the Supplemental Poverty Measure or SPM) of Medicaid expansion or other improvements in health insurance coverage for low-income families using the TRIM3 simulations (see Chapter 2).

There are two main obstacles to including health care needs and health-insurance benefits in poverty measures. First, families' health care needs vary much more, both within and across years, than other needs such as food and housing. Incorporating these changing needs in poverty thresholds would require constructing a large number of poverty thresholds using, at a minimum, information on people's health conditions and family size. Second, there is no publicly available information on the costs of coverage for many of the different health insurance packages families have.

As detailed in a paper commissioned by the committee (Korenman, Remler, and Hyson, 2017), the SPM takes an indirect approach to these problems. SPM thresholds are based on needs for food, clothing, shelter, utilities, and a few other things, but do not include health care. The SPM resource definition includes nonmedical in-kind benefits but excludes health insurance benefits. Instead, the SPM deducts medical out-of-pocket (MOOP) expenses—for health insurance premiums, copayments, deductibles, and uncovered care—from family resources. When these expenses are deducted, some families that are above the poverty line defined by the Official Poverty Measure (OPM) drop below the SPM poverty line. Conversely, reductions in MOOP as a result of Medicaid expansion, for example, will add to family resources and reduce measured SPM poverty, all else being equal.

Yet the National Research Council (1995, p. 236) has acknowledged that its indirect approach for taking into account medical care benefits and costs (the basis for the SPM) was not fully satisfactory, because ". . . it does not explicitly acknowledge a basic necessity, namely, medical care, that is just as important as food or housing. Similarly, the approach devalues the benefits of having health insurance, except indirectly." In the case of people who defer medically necessary care because they lack affordable insurance or access to free care, the MOOP deduction is too small—consequently, they appear to be better off than they actually are.

In the same paper commissioned by the committee from Korenman, Remler, and Hyson (2017), the authors critique various ways of accounting for health care needs and health insurance benefits in poverty measurement. Their critique covers, among other methods, the SPM indirect approach and the fungible or recipient-value approach of adding a portion of the market value of health insurance to family resources (see, e.g., Winship, 2016, Figure 2). They identify problems in each approach, and conclude by suggesting that health insurance costs, rather than health care needs, should be added to the SPM poverty thresholds and that the benefits from health insurance coverage (net of MOOP) should be included in resources. They name this proposed approach the Health-Inclusive Poverty Measure (HIPM).

Designating health insurance as a fundamental health care need would eliminate the problems of estimating care needs for inclusion in the thresholds, provided that certain conditions were met: Health insurance prices must not vary substantially with health conditions (otherwise, sicker people with higher-cost insurance may seem to be better off than they are), and it must be possible to designate a "Basic Plan"—namely, a plan that covers all health care that is deemed by society to be essential and for which cost-sharing requirements are capped. The Affordable Care Act (ACA) exchange plans make it possible to satisfy these conditions. The ACA-guaranteed issue and community rating regulations allow anyone to purchase health insurance at a price that does not depend on health status and that caps nonpremium MOOP.

As detailed in Korenman, Remler, and Hyson (2017), the HIPM starts with the SPM and then (1) adds health insurance needs to the SPM thresholds, using as the Basic Plan the unsubsidized premium of the second-cheapest Silver Plan available in a household's rating area; (2) adds the health insurance benefits received to resources; and (3) deducts non-premium MOOP for medical care received. Korenman, Remler, and Hyson (2017, Table 1) display SPM thresholds and HIPM thresholds for 2014 by family size and composition. The average threshold for all families with children is $39,745. Of this amount, the average material need (SPM threshold) is $27,662, and the average health insurance need is $12,083, or 30 percent of the HIPM threshold, which makes explicit the importance and high cost to families of obtaining health insurance (in the absence of subsidies). For a family with one adult and two children, the average HIPM threshold is $27,727, of which $6,949 is the health insurance need, constituting 25 percent of the threshold.

Using the HIPM approach, Korenman, Remler, and Hyson (2017, Table 2) estimate that Medicaid reduces child poverty by 5.3 percentage points, compared with a 4.4 percentage point reduction from other means-tested benefits such as SNAP and a 6.5 percentage point reduction from tax credits such as the EITC. To the extent that more states expand Medicaid, child poverty will be further reduced; to the extent that states introduce premiums, copayments, and deductibles for Medicaid, as some are doing under waivers from the federal government, child poverty will increase.

CONCLUSION 7-6: Despite the importance of medical care needs and benefits for both poverty reduction and child health and well-being, these needs and benefits are captured only indirectly by current poverty measures. Thus, by definition, health spending can have little direct short-run impact on child poverty measures. Nevertheless, the significant child-poverty-reducing effects of Medicaid are illustrated by the 2014 results of a Health-Inclusive Poverty Measure, which augments the Supplemental Poverty Measure by considering health insurance needs when setting the thresholds and appropriately treating net medical expenses in measuring family resources.

POLICIES TOWARD AMERICAN INDIAN AND ALASKA NATIVE CHILDREN

Background

AIAN are eligible for the standard programs and services available to all U.S. citizens, and they may also be eligible for additional programs and services offered by their tribes or the U.S. federal government. As mentioned in Appendix D, 2-7, the AIAN population is not only a racial/ethnic group but also recognized by the U.S. government as a political group, which allows individual tribal communities to participate in programs and services designed specifically for them (see Chapter 2 for a discussion of the demographic characteristics of the AIAN population). In addition to federal programs such as TANF and EITC, other programs and policies that have shown promise for reducing poverty in the AIAN population include training and education programs that focus on cultural connections and internal tribal programs and services. The committee's analysis of these policies benefited greatly from a paper we commissioned on the subject (Akee and Simeonova, 2017).[14]

Implications for Policy

Improvements in education and training programs hold promise for reducing poverty in the AIAN adult population, which has lower levels of educational attainment than the U.S. population as a whole (Akee and Taylor, 2014). In particular, programs that incorporate a tribe's values and culture tend to be more effective (Goodluck and Willeto, 2009; HeavyRunner, 2003). The Family Education Model, for example, takes a family-centered approach to education and advocates for a more inclusionary process that takes into account the AIAN students' cultural worldview. This enables them to enroll in, and successfully complete, higher education (HeavyRunner, 2003).

Tribal governments also play an important role in reducing child poverty. In addition to providing direct services and programs to support residents, they are a significant source of employment. Thriving and successful tribal governments are therefore a key component in reducing child poverty among the AIAN population (Jorgensen, 2007). Local political and legal authorities may also play a role in improving incomes on American Indian reservations. For example, Dimitrova-Grajzl, Peter, and Joseph (2014) found that when civil and criminal jurisdiction is removed from tribal control and given to states (U.S.), tribal incomes decrease. Changes in tribal political institutions may come from effective lobbying at the U.S. congressional level as well as the more local level in enacting reforms in tribal constitutions, which many AIAN tribes have been engaged in over the past 25 years (Lemont, 2006).

The Indian Gaming Regulatory Act of 1988, for example, grants federally recognized AIAN tribes the authority to operate casinos on tribal lands, providing a large economic opportunity for tribal communities.[15] Over the past 10 years, the Indian gaming industry has reported annual revenues

---

[14] Papers commissioned by the committee are available on the National Academies Press website, www.nap.edu/25246.

[15] Not all tribal nations operate casinos, and those that do are not all equally successful; revenue generation is dependent primarily on location and proximity to large population centers.

of approximately $28 billion, which may serve as an important means of alleviating child poverty (Akee, Spilde, and Taylor, 2015). Wolfe and colleagues (2012) reported increases in household incomes of about $1,700 for American Indians residing in counties with tribal casinos. Anderson (2013) found that the presence of a casino reduced child poverty rates by 4.6 percent between 1990 and 2000; however, some of that reduction may have been caused by the influx of new residents with more favorable economic characteristics.

One mechanism that might play a direct role in reducing household poverty levels is the use of casino revenues to fund cash transfers. Not all tribes provide this type of transfer, some electing instead to use casino revenues for tribal program operations. Nevertheless, as detailed in Chapter 3, Akee and colleagues (2010) found that these cash transfers result in improved child educational attainment for households that were originally in poverty, and there is no evidence that this additional unearned income reduces the probability that parents will find full- or part-time employment.

Federal programs like EITC and TANF are also important to AIAN households living in poverty. Wagner and Hertel (2008) surveyed individuals in 14 Volunteer Income Tax Assistance areas located on American Indian reservations. When asked how they would spend their tax refunds, respondents overwhelmingly answered that they would spend refunds on basic needs such as groceries, utilities, clothing, and rent or mortgage payments. Only 10 percent of respondents indicated that they would use the refund for savings.

Approximately 70 AIAN tribal governments, serving almost 300 different AIAN tribes and villages, are approved to operate TANF programs.[16] Tribally operated TANF programs are unique in that their participants are exempt from the 5-year lifetime limit on benefits, provided that participants reside on reservations with unemployment rates above 50 percent. As a result, the binding TANF constraint does not apply to a number of AIAN communities and program recipients. Limited evaluation of these programs suggests that tribes that operate their own TANF programs experienced a drop of about 5 percentage points in poverty rates between 1990 and 2010 (Mather, 2017). Yet while TANF recipients on reservations received training and other preparation for jobs, employment opportunities on reservations are scarce, and the few studies that have evaluated TANF programs show that the availability of employment opportunities are the primary determinant of whether an individual is able to leave the TANF program.

---

[16] The U.S. Department of Health and Human Services currently allows federally recognized tribal governments to operate their own TANF programs.

CONCLUSION 7-7: Small sample sizes in population surveys have made it particularly difficult to reliably measure poverty rates among American Indian and Alaska Native children. Moreover, we know little about the effectiveness of a number of important programs and policies—whether provided by the tribes, by the states, or by the federal government—that affect this population. Available evidence does suggest that some federal and tribal programs designed to improve opportunities for educational attainment, boost employment, and increase income have the potential to reduce child poverty.

REFERENCES

Akee, R., and Simeonova, E. (2017). *Poverty and Disadvantage Among Native American Children: How Common Are They and What Has Been Done to Address Them?* Washington, DC: The National Academies Press.

Akee, R., and Taylor, J. (2014). *Social & Economic Change on American Indian Reservations: A Databook of the U.S. Census and the American Community Survey 1990-2010.* Available: http://taylorpolicy.com/us-databook.

Akee, R., Costello, J., Copeland, W., Keeler, G., and Angold, A. (2010). Parents' incomes and children's outcomes: A quasi-experiment with casinos on American Indian reservations. *American Economics Journal: Applied Economics, 2*(1), 86–115.

Akee, R., Spilde, K., and Taylor, J. (2015). The Indian Gaming Regulatory Act and its effects on American Indian economic development. *Journal of Economic Perspectives, 29*(3), 185–208.

Anderson, R.J. (2013). Tribal casino impacts on American Indians' well-being: Evidence from reservation-level census data. *Contemporary Economic Policy, 31*(2), 291–300.

Avellar, S., Covington, R., Moore, Q., Patnaik, A., and Wu, A. (2018). *Parents and Children Together: Effects of four responsible fatherhood programs for low-income fathers.* Washington, DC: Office of Planning, Research, and Evaluation, Administration for Children and Families, U.S. Department of Health and Human Services.

Baicker, K., Taubman, S.L., Allen, H.L., Bernstein, M., Gruber, J.H., Newhouse, J.P., Schneider, E.C., Wright, B.J., Zaslavsky, A.M., Finkelstein, A.N., and Oregon Health Study. (2013). The Oregon experiment: Effects of Medicaid on clinical outcomes. *The New England Journal of Medicine, 368*(18), 1713–1722.

Bailey, M.J. (2013). *Fifty Years of Family Planning: New Evidence on the Long-Run Effects of Increasing Access to Contraception.* Brookings Papers on Economic Activity (Spring 2013). Washington, DC: Brookings Institution Press.

Bartel, A., Rossin-Slater, M., Ruhm, C., Stearns, J., and Waldfogel, J. (2017). Paid family leave, fathers' leave-taking, and leave-sharing in dual-earner households. *Journal of Policy Analysis and Management, 37*(1), 10–37.

Baum, C.L., and Ruhm, C.J. (2016). The effects of paid family leave in California on labor market outcomes. *Journal of Policy Analysis and Management, 35*(2), 333–356.

Bedard, K., and Rossin-Slater, M. (2016). *The Economic and Social Impacts of Paid Family Leave in California.* Washington, DC: U.S. Department of Labor.

Bir, A., Lerman, R., Corwin, E., MacIlvain, B., Beard, A., Richburg, K., and Smith, K. (2012). *The Community Health Marriage Initiative Evaluation.* OPRE Report No. 2012-34A. Washington, DC: Office of Planning, Research and Evaluation, Administration for Children and Families, U.S. Department of Health and Human Services.

Bitler, M.P., and Hoynes, H.W. (2016) *Strengthening Temporary Assistance for Needy Families*. Policy Proposal 2016–04. The Hamilton Project, Brookings.

Bitler, M.P., Gelbach, J.B., and Hoynes, H.W. (2006). What mean impacts miss: Distributional effects of welfare reform experiments. *American Economic Review, 96(4)*, 988–1012.

Blank, R. (2002). Evaluating welfare reform in the United States. *Journal of Economic Literature, 40(4)*, 1105–1166.

Bose, B., Raub, A., Earle, A., and Heymann, J. (2018, June). *Can Working Women and Men in OECD Countries Afford to Take Paid Leave? A Comparative Study of the Extent to Which Paid Leave Benefits Keep Families Out of Poverty*. Paper presented at the Work and Family Researchers Conference. Washington, DC: Work and Family Researchers Network.

Boushey, H. (2016). *Finding Time*. Cambridge, MA: Harvard University Press.

Brown, D., Kowalski, A., and Lurie, I. (2015). *Medicaid as an Investment in Children: What Is the Long-Term Impact on Tax Receipts?* Cambridge, MA: The National Bureau of Economic Research.

Buchmueller, T., Ham, J.C., and Shore-Sheppard, L.D. (2016). The Medicaid program. In R.A. Moffit (Ed.), *Economics of Means-Tested Transfer Programs in the United States, Volume 1* (pp. 21–136). Chicago: The University of Chicago Press.

Bureau of Labor Statistics. (2017). *National Compensation Survey: Employee Benefits in the United States, March 2017*. Washington, DC.

Byker, T. S. (2016). Paid parental leave laws in the United States: Does short-duration leave affect women's labor-force attachment? *American Economic Review, 106(5)*, 242–246.

Case, A., Lubotsky, D., and Paxson, C. (2002). Economic status and health in childhood: The origins of the gradient. *American Economic Review, 92(5)*, 1308–1334.

Centers for Disease Control and Prevention. (2013). CDC health disparities and inequalities report supplement. *Morbidity and Mortality Weekly Report, 62(3)*.

Centers for Medicare & Medicaid Services. (2017). *HHS FY 2017 Budget in Brief*. CMS-CHIP. Available: https://www.hhs.gov/about/budget/fy2017/budget-in-brief/cms/chip/index.html.

Colorado Department of Public Health and Environment. (2017). *Taking the Unintended out of Pregnancy: Colorado's Success with Long-Acting Reversible Contraception*. Denver, CO: The Colorado Department of Public Health and Environment.

Council on Community Pediatrics. (2016). Poverty and child health in the United States. *Pediatrics, 137(4)*.

Das, T., and Polachek, S.W. (2015). Unanticipated effects of California's paid family leave program. *Contemporary Economic Policy, 33(4)*, 619–635.

Dehlendorf, C., Ruskin, R., Grumbach, K., Vittinghoff, E., Bibbins-Domingo, K., Schillinger, D., and Steinauer, J. (2010). Recommendations for intrauterine contraception: A randomized trial of the effects of patients' race/ethnicity and socioeconomic status. *American Journal of Obstetrics and Gynecology, 203(4)*, 319.e1–319.e8.

Dickert-Conlin, S., and Houser, S. (2002). EITC and marriage. *National Tax Journal, 55(1)*, 25–40.

Dilger, R.J., and Boyd, E. (2014). *Block Grants: Perspectives and Controversies*. Washington, DC: Congressional Research Service.

Dimitrova-Grajzl, V., Peter, G., and Joseph, G.A. (2014). Jurisdiction, crime, and development: The impact of Public Law 280 in Indian country. *Law & Society Review, 48(1)*, 127–160.

Dunifon, R., Hynes, K., and Peters, H.E. (2009). State welfare policies and children's living arrangements. *Social Service Review, 83(3)*, 351–388.

Eissa, N., and Hoynes, H. (2003). *Good News for Low-Income Families? Tax-Transfer Schemes, and Marriage*. Mimeograph. Berkeley: University of California, Department of Economics.

_____. (2004). Taxes and the labor market participation of married couples: The Earned Income Tax Credit. *Journal of Public Economics, 88*(9), 1931–1938.

Ellwood, D.T. (2000). The impact of the Earned Income Tax Credit and social policy reforms on work, marriage, and living arrangements. *National Tax Journal, 53*(4), 1063–1065.

Falk, G. (2015). *Temporary Assistance for Needy Family (TANF) Financing Issues.* Washington, DC: Congressional Research Service.

_____. (2016). *The Temporary Assistance for Needy Families (TANF) Block Grant: Responses to Frequently Asked Questions.* Washington, DC: Congressional Research Service.

Finegold, K., Wherry, L., and Schardin, S. (2004). Block grants: Historical overview and lessons learned. In *New Federalism: Issues and Options for States.* Washington, DC: The Urban Institute.

Finkelstein, A.N., Taubman, S.L., Allen, H.L., Wright, B.J., and Baicker, K. (2016). Effect of Medicaid coverage on ED use: Further evidence from Oregon's experiment. *New England Journal of Medicine, 375*(16), 1505–1507.

Fischer, S., Royer, H., and White, C. (2017). *The Impacts of Reduced Access to Abortion and Family Planning Services: Evidence from Texas.* Bonn, Germany: IZA Institute of Labor Economics.

Frimmel, W., Halla, M., and Winter-Ebmer, R. (2012). *Can Pro-Marriage Policies Work? An Analysis of Marginal Marriages.* Germany: IZA.

Gibson-Davis, C.M. (2016). Single and cohabiting parents and poverty. In D. Brady and L. Burton (Eds.), *The Oxford Handbook of the Social Science of Poverty.* New York, NY: Oxford University Press.

Gibson-Davis, C.M., Edin, K., and McLanahan, S. (2005). High hopes but even higher expectations: The retreat from marriage among low-income couples. *Journal of Marriage and Family, 67,* 1301–1312.

Goodluck, C., and Willeto, A. (2009). *Seeing the Protective Rainbow: How Families Survive and Thrive in the American Indian and Alaska Native Community.* Baltimore, MD: Annie E. Casey Foundation.

Gordon, L. (1976). *Woman's Body, Woman's Right: A Social History of Birth Control in America.* New York, NY: Grossman.

Greenberg, D., Deitch, V., and Hamilton, G. (2009). *Welfare-to-Work Program Benefits and Costs: A Synthesis of Research.* New York, NY: MDRC.

Grogger, J., and Karoly, L.A. (2005). *Welfare Reform: Effects of a Decade of Change.* Cambridge, MA: Harvard University Press.

Gruber, J. (1994). The incidence of mandated maternity benefits. *The American Economic Review, 84*(3), 622–641.

Guttmacher Institute. (2016). *Unintended Pregnancy in the United States Fact Sheet.* Washington, DC.

Hamilton, G. (2002). *Moving People from Welfare to Work: Lessons from the National Evaluation of Welfare-to-Work Strategies.* New York: MDRC.

Harper, C.C., Rocca, C.H., Thompson, K.M., Morfesis, J., Goodman, S., Darney, P.D., Westhoff, C.L., and Speidel, J.J. (2015). Reductions in pregnancy rates in the USA with long-acting reversible contraception: A cluster randomised trial. *Lancet, 386*(9993), 562–568.

Haskins, R. (2015). The family is here to stay—or not. *The Future of Children, 25*(2), 129–153.

HeavyRunner, I. (2003). Miracle survivors: Promoting resilience in Indian students. *Tribal College, 14*(4), 14–18. Available: https://tribalcollegejournal.org/miracle-survivors-promoting-resilience-Indian-students.

Herbst, C.M. (2011). The impact of the Earned Income Tax Credit on marriage and divorce: Evidence from flow data. *Population Research and Policy Review, 30*(1), 101–128.

Higgins, J.A. (2014). *Celebration meets caution: LARC's boons, potential busts, and the benefits of a reproductive justice approach.* Contraception, 89(4), 237–241.

Higgins, J.A., Kramer, R.D., and Ryder, K.M. (2016). Provider bias in long-acting reversible contraception (LARC) promotion and removal: Perceptions of young adult women. *American Journal of Public Health, 106*(11), 1932–1937.

Huang, R., and Yang, M. (2015). Paid maternity leave and breastfeeding practice before and after California's implementation of the nation's first paid family leave program. *Economics and Human Biology, 16*, 45–59.

Jorgensen, M. (2007). *Rebuilding Native Nations: Strategies for Governance and Development.* Tucson: University of Arizona Press.

Joshi, P., Geronimo, K., Romano, B., Earle, A., Rosenfeld, L., Hardy, E.F., and Acevedo-Garcia, D. (2014). Integrating racial/ethnic equity into policy assessments to improve child health. *Health Affairs, 33*(12), 2222–2229.

Karpilow, Q., Manlove, J., Sawhill, I.V., and Thomas, A. (2013). *The Role of Contraception in Preventing Abortion, Nonmarital Childbearing, and Child Poverty.* Washington, DC: The Brookings Institution.

Klerman, J.A., and Leibowitz, A. (1994). The work-employment distinction among new mothers. *The Journal of Human Resources, 29*(2), 277–303.

Klerman, J.A., Daley, K., and Pozniak, A. (2012). *Family and Medical Leave in 2012: Technical Report.* Cambridge, MA: Abt Associates.

Korenman, S., Remler, D.K., and Hyson, R. (2017). *Accounting for the Impact of Medicaid on Child Poverty.* Washington, DC: The National Academies Press.

Lemont, E.D. (2006). *American Indian Constitutional Reform and the Rebuilding of Native Nations.* Austin: The University of Texas Press.

Lichtman-Sadot, S., and Bell, N.P. (2017). Child health in elementary school following California's paid family leave program. *Journal of Policy Analysis and Management, 36*(4), 790–827.

Lopoo, L.M., and Raissian, K.M. (2014). U.S. social policy and family complexity. *The ANNALS of the American Academy of Political and Social Science, 654*(1), 213–230.

Lu, Y., and Slusky, D.J. (2016). The impact of women's health clinic closures on preventive care. *American Economic Journal: Applied Economics, 8(3)*, 100–124.

Lundquist, E., Hsueh, J., Lowenstein, A., Faucetta, K., Gubits, D., Michalopoulos, C., and Knox, V. (2014). *A Family-Strengthening Program for Low-Income Families: Final Impacts from the Supporting Healthy Marriage Evaluation.* OPRE Report No. 2013-49A. Washington, DC: Office of Planning, Research and Evaluation, Administration for Children and Families, U.S. Department of Health and Human Services.

Mather, R.A. (2017). *Temporary Assistance with Lasting Effects: A Report on Policies of Self-Determination in Native America.* The University of Minnesota Digital Conservancy.

Mathur, A., Sawhill, I.V., Boushey, H., Gitis, B., Haskins, R., Holtz-Eakin, D., Holzer, H.J., Jacobs, E., McCloskey, A.M., Rachidi, A., Reeves, R.V., Ruhm, C.J., Stevenson, B., and Waldfogel, J. (2017). *Paid Family and Medical Leave: An Issue Whose Time Has Come.* Washington, DC: American Enterprise Institute and Brookings Institution.

Meyer, B.D., and Rosenbaum, D.T. (2001). Welfare, the Earned Income Tax Credit, and the labor supply of single mothers. *The Quarterly Journal of Economics, 116*(3), 1063–1114.

Michelmore, K. (2018). The Earned Income Tax Credit and union formation: The impact of expected spouse earnings. *Review of Economics of the Household, 16*(2), 377–406.

Moffitt, R. (2016). *Economics of Means-Tested Transfer Programs in the United States, Volume I.* Chicago, IL: The University of Chicago Press.

Mosher, W.D., Jones, J., and Abma, J.C. (2012). Intended and unintended births in the United States: 1982-2010. *National Health Statistics Reports, 2012(55)*, 1–28.

National Partnership for Women and Families. (2018a). *Paid Family/Parental Leave Policies for Municipal Employees*. Washington, DC.

_____. (2018b). *State Paid Family Leave Insurance Laws*. Washington, DC.

National Research Council. (1995). *Measuring Poverty: A New Approach*. Washington, DC: National Academy Press.

Nichols, A., and Rothstein, J. (2016). The Earned Income Tax Credit. In R.A.Moffit (Ed.), *Economics of Means-Tested Transfer Programs in the United States, Volume 1* (pp. 137–218). Chicago: University of Chicago Press.

Office of the Assistant Secretary for Planning and Evaluation. (2008). *Indicators of Welfare Dependence: Annual Report to Congress, 2008, AFDC/TANF Program Data*. Available: https://aspe.hhs.gov/report/indicators-welfare-dependence-annual-report-congress-2008/afdctanf-program-data.

Olivetti, C., and Petrongolo, B. (2017). The economic consequences of family policies: Lessons from a century of legislation in high-income countries. *Journal of Economic Perspectives, 31(1)*, 205–230.

Rajan, S., Morgan, S.P., Harris, K.M., Guilkey, D., Hayford, S.R., and Guzzo, K.B. (2017). Trajectories of unintended fertility. *Population Research and Policy Review, 36(6)*, 903- 928.

Raub, A., Chung, P., Batra, P., Earle, A., Bose, B., Jou, J., Chorny, N.D.G., Wong, E., Franken, D., and Heymann, J. (2018a). *Paid Leave For Personal Illness: A Detailed Look at Approaches Across OECD Countries*. Los Angeles, CA: WORLD Policy Analysis Center.

Raub, A., Nandi, A., Earle, A., Chorny, N.D.G., Wong, E., Chung, P., Batra, P., Schickendanz, A., Bose, B., Jou, J., Franken, D., and Heymann, J. (2018b). *Paid Parental Leave: A Detailed Look at Approaches Across OECD Countries*. Los Angeles, CA: WORLD Policy Analysis Center.

Riccio, J., Friedlander, D., and Freedman, S. (1994). *GAIN: Benefits, Costs, and Three-Year Impacts of a Welfare-to-Work Program*. New York: MDRC.

Rosenbaum, D.T. (2000). *Taxes, the Earned Income Tax Credit, and Marital Status*. Chicago: Northwestern University, University of Chicago Joint Center for Poverty.

Rossin-Slater, M. (2017). Signing up new fathers: Do paternity establishment initiatives increase marriage, parental investment, and child well-being? *American Economic Journal: Applied Economics, 9(2)*, 93–130.

Rossin-Slater, M., Ruhm, C.J., and Waldfogel, J. (2013). The effects of California's paid leave program on mothers' leave-taking and subsequent labor market outcomes. *Journal of Policy Analysis and Management, 32(2)*, 224–245.

Sawhill, I.V., and Venator, J. (2015). *Improving Children's Life Chances Through Better Family Planning*. Washington, DC: The Brookings Institution.

Sawhill, I., Rodrigue, E., and Joo, N. (2016). *One Third of a Nation: Strategies for Helping Working Families*. Washington, DC: Center on Children and Families at Brookings.

Semega, J.L., Fontenot, K.R., and Kollar, M.A. (2017). *Income and Poverty in the United States: 2016*. Washington, DC: U.S. Government Printing Office.

Smith, J.P. (2009). The impact of childhood health on adult labor market outcomes. *Review of Economics and Statistics, 91(3)*, 478–489.

Sonfield, A., Hasstedt, K., Kavanaugh, M.L., and Anderson, R. (2013). *The Social and Economic Benefits of Women's Ability to Determine Whether and When to Have Children*. New York, NY: Guttmacher Institute.

Stenberg, C.W. (2009). Block grants and devolution: A future tool? In T.J. Conlan and P.L. Posner (Eds.), *Intergovernmental Management for the 21st Century*. Washington, DC: Brookings Institution Press.

Stevenson, A.J., Flores-Vazquez, I.M., Allgeyer, R.L., Schenkkan, P., and Potter, J.E. (2016). Effect of removal of Planned Parenthood from the Texas women's health program. *The New England Journal of Medicine, 344*(9), 853–860.

Wagner, K., and Hertel, A.L. (2008). *EITC in Indian country: Moving Beyond the Safety Net to Asset Building*. St. Louis, MO: Center for Social Development, Washington University in St. Louis.

Waldfogel, J. (1998). Understanding the "family gap" in pay for women with children. *The Journal of Economic Perspectives, 12*(1), 137–156.

Welti, K., and Manlove, J. (2018). *Unintended Pregnancy in Delaware: Estimating Change After the First Two Years of an Intervention to Increase Contraceptive Access*. Bethesda, MD: Child Trends.

Wheaton, L., and Haldar, S. (2018). *2015 TRIM3 Supplemental Poverty Measure*. Unpublished project memorandum. Washington, DC: The Urban Institute.

Winner, B., Peipert, J.F., Zhao, Q., Buckel, C., Madden, T., Allsworth, J.E., and Secura, G.M. (2012). Effectiveness of long-acting reversible contraception. *The New England Journal of Medicine, 366*(21), 1998–2007.

Winship, S. (2016). *Poverty after Welfare Reform*. New York, NY: Manhattan Institute.

Wolfe, B., Jakubowski, J., Haveman, R., and Courey, M. (2012). The income and health effects of tribal casino gaming on American Indians. *Demography, 49*(2), 499–524.

Woo, C.J., Alamgir, H., and Potter, J.E. (2016). Women's experiences after Planned Parenthood's exclusion from a family planning program in Texas. *Contraception, 93*(4), 298–302.

Wood, R.G., Moore, Q., Clarkwest, A., Killewald, A., and Monahan, S. (2012). *The Long-Term Effects of Building Strong Families: A Relationship Skills Education Program for Unmarried Parents*. Washington, DC: Office of Planning, Research and Evaluation, Administration for Children and Families, U.S. Department of Health and Human Services.

Yelowitz, A.S. (1998). Will extending Medicaid to two-parent families encourage marriage? *The Journal of Human Resources, 33*(4), 833–865.

Ziliak, J. (2016). Temporary Assistance for Needy Families. In R. A. Moffitt (Ed.), *Economics of Means-Tested Transfer Programs, Volume 1*. Chicago: University of Chicago Press.

8

Contextual Factors That Influence the Effects of Anti-Poverty Policies and Programs

WHY CONTEXT MATTERS

A fundamental lesson from the social and the behavioral sciences is that the context of people's lives can affect their behavior in profound ways. Poverty itself is a powerful context because of its economic, physical, social, and psychological dimensions. In Chapter 3, we documented the adverse consequences for children of living in poverty, as well as the severe constraints and stressors that inadequate financial resources place on families. Those constraints and stressors may in turn result in difficult choices and circumstances for both parents and children.

In this chapter, we consider a more general set of contextual factors that can promote or impede the effectiveness of anti-poverty policies and programs. For example, Supplemental Nutrition Assistance Program (SNAP) payments can best promote children's nutrition and health when families have ready access to healthy and affordable food, and families can further benefit more from cash transfers when convenient and receptive banking institutions are available to help them manage their funds. Conversely, a job training program for parents may be less effective if there is racial discrimination in hiring, if there is an absence of employment opportunities, reliable transportation, or affordable child care options, or if parents are too disabled or sick to attend training.

Given the potential for such contextual factors to influence the effectiveness of programs and policies, it is surprising to our committee how little rigorous empirical research has been conducted to test these factors' moderating influence. Nevertheless, a strong empirical case can be made that these contextual factors influence decision-making in low-income families as well as the impact of consequential programs and policies. Note that because the committee's charge is confined to a 10-year period, we refrain from addressing several structural factors—including race and gender attitudes, perceptions of the poor, and the formerly incarcerated—that might generate longer-run impacts on the success and equity of program administration.

SIX MAJOR CONTEXTUAL FACTORS

Through internal discussions, public information-gathering sessions, and a review of the scholarly and policy literatures, the committee identified six major, often co-occurring contextual factors that policy makers and program administrators are advised to consider when designing and implementing anti-poverty programs of the sort discussed in Chapters 5, 6, and 7:

1. *Stability and predictability of income*—Unstable and unpredictable income makes it difficult for families to juggle everyday challenges, diminishes the quality of everyday decisions, and renders the poor vulnerable to financial ruin.
2. *Equitable and ready access to programs*—Because of cumbersome, inconsistent, or demeaning enrollment procedures, or because of other barriers, not all families who qualify for benefits from government programs receive them.
3. *Racial/ethnic discrimination*—Our nation's long and painful history of discrimination persists today in many forms and continues to influence differential access to opportunities and resources to overcome poverty, including employment, education, and housing opportunities.
4. *Equitable treatment by the criminal justice system*—Unequal treatment in legal penalties and law enforcement has disproportionately affected low-income families, especially Black and Hispanic families, in ways that disrupt family and social networks and reduce the economic and psychological resources that people who have been incarcerated could otherwise provide to their families.
5. *Positive neighborhood conditions*—Supportive, thriving social networks and neighborhood conditions enrich family life, personal connections, and access to opportunities, yet too frequently people who live in poverty are concentrated in neglected urban areas or are widely dispersed in rural areas with limited transportation or access to employment, poverty-reduction programs, or community resources.

6. *Health and well-being*—Among parents, physical and mental ailments, substance abuse, and domestic violence can harm their ability to make sound decisions, care for their children, become educated, obtain and keep work, and support their households.

The chapter summarizes why each of these six contextual factors matters, how each of them might affect the administration of anti-poverty policies, and what conclusions the committee has reached. Research recommendations on these contextual factors are provided in the final chapter.

INCOME STABILITY AND PREDICTABILITY

Why It Matters

An adequate and stable monthly family income enables parents to pay bills, meet basic needs, and engage in financial planning. When savings or access to affordable emergency resources are added to that, they can help buffer families against income shortfalls. But low-income families typically lack liquid assets and often pay high interest rates to obtain short-term credit (Barr, 2012). The resulting income instability can generate other kinds of instability—in housing and child care, for example—that in turn may limit families' ability to work (Hahn et al., 2016; McKernan, Ratcliffe, and Vinopal, 2009) and compromise their children's development (Hill et al., 2013). Because the savings and assets of Black and Hispanic families, at all income levels, are often considerably lower than those of White families, these populations are more vulnerable than White families to unpredictable changes in income (Kochhar and Cilluffo, 2017).

Research has provided ample evidence of these differences in financial stability, and of their consequences. For example, the incomes of low earners are more unstable than those of higher earners, and many lower-wage jobs offer little job security, fluctuating work hours, and no paid time off, which makes it difficult to budget and pay for dependable child care (Enchautegui, 2013; Gennetian and Shafir, 2015). Additionally, unexpected financial emergencies are ubiquitous among low-income households (Barr, 2009), and often require deferring bills or cutting spending on basic necessities, such as food. Approximately 9 percent of all children live in households in which one or more child is food insecure. Food security is defined as "access by all people at all times to enough food for an active, healthy life" (Coleman-Jensen et al., 2017, pg. 2).

Another important set of factors creating employment instability is the nature of the low-wage labor market and the difficulties many low-wage workers have in maintaining employment. Many low-wage jobs have high rates of turnover that create frequent periods of unemployment and require looking repeatedly for new jobs. Low-wage jobs are also more likely to have irregular hours and require shift work that low-income parents have difficulty sustaining (Enchautegui, 2013; Enchautegui, Johnson, and Gelatt, 2015). Transportation can pose challenges for low-income parents if they do not live close to work and have to take public transportation, which is unreliable and often includes extremely long commutes (Enchautegui, 2013; Holzer and Wissoker, 2001). Compounding these problems are difficulties in obtaining reliable and flexible child care that can respond to these irregular shifts, long commutes, and high-turnover jobs (Enchautegui, 2013). Taken together, low-income families face a multitude of barriers to work that middle-income families do not face to the same degree (Enchautegui, 2013; Hill et al., 2013).

More than one-half of all low-income families are *asset-poor*, defined as lacking the liquid resources necessary to finance essential consumption for 3 months (Lusardi, Schneider, and Tufano, 2011). Related to this, in recent years, due to their limited financial reserves one in four U.S. households has used at least one alternative financial service, such as a payday, auto title, or refund anticipation loan, during the preceding year—services that are typically subject to very high interest rates (Burhouse et al., 2014; Caskey, 2006). Finally, more than one-half of all low-income families living in rental housing spend more than one-half of their income on housing costs (Desmond, 2016). Most of these problems are worse for racial/ethnic minority families, largely because of differences in wealth or assets minus debt (Kochhar and Cilluffo, 2017; Pew Charitable Trusts, 2015) and more limited options in terms of neighborhoods in which they can live.

The combination of unstable incomes, high fixed expenses, and low savings translates into persistent material hardship for many low-income families, as adverse events challenge their ability to meet basic living needs. These families have little "slack," defined by Mullainathan and Shafir (2013) as the ease with which one can cut down on other expenses to satisfy an unexpected need. When better-off families experience a rough patch of income instability, they typically have discretionary expenses they can cut back on and savings or access to credit to tide them over. In contrast, when low-income families face unanticipated shocks, they first cut back on somewhat less urgent needs, such as certain foods and the bills that are least likely to produce dire consequences if left unpaid. They then must cut back on essentials, which means skipping payments and incurring costly late fees, utility or phone reconnection fees, and eviction threats, and consequently they face a new round of disruptions to work, child care, education, and family life (Barr, 2009; Edin and Lein, 1997; Shipler, 2004).

Relationship to Policy

The unstable circumstances faced by the families of children living in poverty have significant implications for the design of benefit programs. Programs such as SNAP and Housing Choice Vouchers aim to fulfill basic needs by providing monthly benefits. In the case of SNAP, the long, 4-week intervals between benefits, coupled with income instability, lead recipient families to overspend early in the benefit period and run short at the end (Hamrick and Andrews, 2016). Distributing SNAP benefits at weekly intervals might be more helpful to many families. For example, researchers have found lower achievement test scores among children of families receiving SNAP benefits when those tests were taken near the end of the benefit month (Castellari et al., 2017; Gassman-Pines and Bellows, 2018). Experimentation with weekly versus monthly benefit payments would help guide policy in this case. Moreover, although the Earned Income Tax Credit (EITC) can help families pay down debt or purchase needed durables by providing credits annually as a lump sum (Halpern-Meekin et al., 2015; Mendenhall et al., 2012), some families may need the credit to meet basic expenses and may therefore benefit from more frequent payments.[1]

Other program design features to consider are the ease of determining eligibility and the frequency with which renewal is required. For example, when the subsidy authorization period for child care subsidies was expanded from 6 to 12 months, families made use of the subsidies for which they were eligible for 2.5 months longer, on average (Michalopoulos, Lundquist, and Castells, 2010). Other studies have examined the administrative burden on families related to eligibility assessment, documentation, and scheduling and transportation issues. Research has shown that when these burdens are high, unpredictable (yet highly frequent) changes in family circumstances, such as job loss, moving, or a change in child care providers, can lead to a family abruptly losing its child care subsidy (Adams and Rohacek, 2010; Holcomb et al., 2006; Joshi et al., 2018). Abrupt subsidy losses of that kind can make finding or holding a job more difficult.

Programs that provide emergency assistance can help prevent low-income families from falling deeper into poverty when unexpected financial problems occur (Pavetti, Schott, and Lower-Basch, 2011). For example, the Temporary Assistance to Needy Families (TANF) program provides emergency grants so that families at risk of losing the ability to work can repair a vehicle or pay rent without having to turn to public assistance over the longer term. However, in 2013, only 2 percent of TANF spending was on "nonrecurrent short-term benefits" or emergency spending (Schott, Pavetti,

---

[1] For example, see the discussion in Chapter 7 of American Indian families and the discussion in Holt (2015) regarding periodic EITC benefit payments.

and Floyd, 2015). Moreover, the asset limits set on many government assistance programs prohibit parents from saving money for emergencies or purchasing items, such as a reliable car, that can facilitate work and help move their family out of poverty, without the risk of losing the benefit (Campbell, 2014). States have the flexibility to set asset limits for most programs, and across states there is considerable variation in this regard.

Public officials have a responsibility to ensure that families only receive benefits during the time period for which they are eligible, and short renewal periods for programs are a useful mechanism for carrying out that responsibility. However, low-income families' eligibility may change rapidly with a loss or addition of a job or household member. Eligibility periods that are too short may leave families with such fluctuating circumstances more vulnerable than necessary and make it difficult for parents to move out of poverty.

School meal programs have moved to an annual eligibility determination, rather than requiring parents to report any time their income rises above the cutoff. This means that when children become eligible, they remain eligible for the whole school year. In addition, school districts have many options for directly certifying children who, for example, receive SNAP, so that they can also be eligible for the school lunch program without even applying. This sort of streamlining of eligibility requirements and using eligibility for one program as proof of eligibility for another could be a model for other programs (Currie, 2008).[2]

In the context of SNAP, longer periods between recertification have consistently been associated with higher rates of take-up and lower rates of drop-off, among eligible families (Hanratty, 2006; Ratcliffe, McKernan, and Finegold, 2007; Wilde et al., 2000). Research has also shown that simplification of the certification process increases the participation rate (Kaushal and Gao, 2011). Furthermore, replacing paper vouchers with Electronic Benefit Transfer (EBT) cards, which look and operate like prepaid debit cards and, in this way, feel quite mainstream and reduce potential stigma, increased participation (Kabbani and Wilde, 2003; Kaushal and Gao, 2011; Kornfeld, 2002; Wilde et al., 2000).

Another policy consideration related to instability is that participation in public programs can be hindered by income instability. To take maximal advantage of work supports like the EITC and child care subsidies, parents need to be able to sustain steady employment. The barriers to such employment, discussed above, also generate barriers to receiving the public program benefits of work-encouraging programs. Participation in child care

---

[2] For other examples of steps that have been taken to improve access to school meals, see https://www.cbpp.org/research/key-steps-to-improve-access-to-free-and-reduced-price-school-meals.

programs is particularly problematic if child care usage is sporadic and unstable, which typically reduces take-up of child care subsidies.

CONCLUSION 8-1: Income instability, a paucity of savings, and little or no cushion for responding to unexpected financial difficulties are typical for many low-income families, and are more prevalent among Black and Hispanic families than among their White counterparts. Programs that provide regular income support, whether through tax credits, cash, or vouchers, may be more helpful to families if they provide adequate benefits at well-timed intervals. Further, programs that are easily accessible and that facilitate savings or provide emergency cash assistance or credit at a modest cost can help families cope with unexpected emergencies and may prevent them from falling deeper into poverty.

EQUITABLE AND READY ACCESS TO PROGRAMS

Why It Matters

Creating programs to reduce poverty through legislation does not, in itself, ensure equal program access to all families who qualify. If people are to participate in these programs, they need to understand them and then they need to be able to navigate the enrollment process. Often the bureaucratic systems that underpin enrollment are cumbersome, and they vary considerably both by program and even within the same program across different states. The receipt of benefits may even be more a function of where a family lives than of the family's need.

For example, SNAP participation rates vary greatly across states, from an estimated low of 59 percent of eligible families to an estimated high of 100 percent (Gray and Cunnyngham, 2016). Some of this variation has been shown to be a function of enrollment requirements that are easier in some states than in others; 47 states allow families to apply for SNAP online, while the others require the recipient to fill out a paper application at a local office (Currie and Grogger, 2001).[3] Such variation in administrative procedures can lead to considerable variation in participation rates among eligible families for anti-poverty programs across states, and even within states participation rates can differ markedly by the applicant's race, ethnicity, and other characteristics (Moore, Perez-Lopez, and Hisnanick, 2017).

---

[3] Information about SNAP benefits and enrollment requirements is provided on the United States Department of Agriculture's Food and Nutrition Service website, see https://www.fns. usda.gov/snap/facts-about-snap.

The state in which a family lives may also determine the level of benefits families receive. For example, monthly TANF payments to a family vary from a low of $170 in Mississippi to a high of $1,021 in New Hampshire, and these differences are not fully accounted for by the variation in the cost of living across states (Floyd, 2017). Moreover, some states supplement federal programs, whereas others do not; 26 states have their own version of the EITC, increasing the benefit families receive (Internal Revenue Service, 2018b). A study comparing the availability of assistance programs across states following the 1996 federal welfare reforms found that states fell into one of five package-support clusters, which ranged from minimal (with low inclusion rates and below-average support) to integrated (with generous and highly inclusive support packages) (Meyers, Gornick, and Peck, 2001). Naturally, such "contextual" variation can have a profound influence on the potential success of federal programs. Furthermore, there is real concern that the application of programs can be biased—whether intentionally or unintentionally. For example, it has been argued that long-acting, reversible birth control methods like intrauterine devices and implants, as tools for fighting poverty are more likely to be recommended to Black and Latina women of low socioeconomic status than to White women of the same status (Dehlendorf et al., 2010)

In some cases, access for certain groups, such as immigrants or felons, is limited by a program's design. An example can be found in the 1996 welfare reform legislation, the Personal Responsibility and Work Opportunity Reconciliation Act (PRWORA), which was designed to create a separate eligibility regime for legal immigrants to limit their access to means-tested federal programs. Under this law, income-eligible documented immigrants who have been in the United States for less than 5 years are ineligible for the primary federal means-tested programs (SNAP, TANF, Supplemental Security Income [SSI], and Medicaid) unless they have 40 quarters of work history in the United States or have a military connection.

PRWORA also gave states discretion over immigrant eligibility after the 5-year period of ineligibility. Moreover, while citizen children of undocumented immigrants who are income-eligible can receive government benefits, when fears of deportation are high undocumented parents are hesitant to apply for benefits for their American children (Alsan and Yang, 2018; Capps et al., 2004). Even legal immigrants who are income-eligible may be reluctant to apply for anti-poverty programs for themselves or their children due to the fear of being deemed a "public charge," which may jeopardize their ability to become permanent residents or become U.S. citizens (Batalova, Fix, and Greenberg, 2018; Perreira, Yoshikawa, and Oberlander, 2018). Hispanic families bear the brunt of these kinds of restrictions (Child Trends, 2014).

Even if access were not problematic, program participation is often limited because funding is insufficient to provide benefits to all eligible families. For example, the Housing Choice Voucher Program (often called the Section 8 program) is available to only about 15 percent of income-eligible families with children (Joshi et al., 2014). Moreover, the federal Child Care and Development Fund supports only 17 percent of eligible children.[4]

Relationship to Policy

As discussed above, state policies vary widely in the administrative burdens and requirements they impose on parents in anti-poverty programs, and states experience widely differing rates of participation in the programs (e.g., Holcomb et al., 2003). Data compiled by the Center on Budget and Policy Priorities indicate that many states are taking advantage of automated technology so that people can more easily apply for assistance, update relevant information (e.g., changes in earnings), and renew their eligibility online (Wagner and Huguelet, 2016). Florida's public assistance program, Automated Community Connection to Economic Self-Sufficiency (ACCESS), provides an example of a program that increases efficiency in the enrollment process (Cody et al., 2010).[5] Key features of the Florida program include automating the public assistance application process and providing for online submission of applications for TANF, SNAP, and Medicaid (Cody et al., 2010). Other states have also turned to automation to streamline eligibility processes and increase program access, but wide variation in application processes across states and counties remains a significant factor limiting the participation of eligible families in many places (Isaacs, Katz, and Amin, 2016; Loprest, Gearing, and Kassabian, 2016).

Work Support Strategies (WSS), a privately funded multistate initiative, is another example of how automation can improve the uptake of public assistance programs. The WSS initiative, which began in 2011, was developed to determine whether the implementation of technology improvements could better help qualifying families connect to work support programs (Isaacs, Katz, and Amin, 2016; Loprest, Gearing, and Kassabian, 2016). Evaluations suggest that using automated processes to streamline enrollment has resulted in time and money savings for both the applicants and the states. For example, in addition to reductions in lobby wait times in Colorado, Idaho, Illinois, and Rhode Island, individual participants gained an average of $195 annually in benefits, and one state, Idaho, reduced annual administrative costs by an estimated $53,500 (Isaacs, Katz, and Amin, 2016).

---

[4] Congressional Research Service, as reported in the Committee on Ways and Means' Green Book (Congressional Research Service, 2016), Chapter 9, Figure 9.5.

[5] See http://www.myflorida.com/accessflorida for more information on ACCESS Florida.

Training caseworkers to more effectively communicate and work with the families they serve may also improve the chances that parents will obtain steady employment. Caseworker training may also improve the chances that parents are informed about valuable services, such as child care subsidies (Strawn and Martinson, 2000). Federal rules have sought to establish minimum standards for access to information to help eligible families determine which benefits they qualify to receive. For example, SNAP regulations require applications and notices to be available in languages other than English when specific population thresholds are met.[6] How effective such rules are in facilitating access to benefits is not known, however.

Other efforts to increase access to benefits and better coordinate and streamline services have been tried in many states (Annie E. Casey Foundation, 2010; Hoffman, 2006). Rigorous evaluations of the pilot programs would better inform states as to how to ensure that parents who are eligible for programs actually receive the benefits.

One program that has worked to minimize the administrative burden on eligible participants is the EITC. Because it is administered through the tax code rather than through a social services office, it does not require repeated sign-ups throughout the year or a lengthy and complicated application process. Eligible persons must simply fill out their tax returns. Take-up rates have improved over time as commercial tax preparers have increasingly served this market, and more organizations have begun to help lower-income workers file their taxes (Kopczuk and Pop-Eleches, 2007), although commercial tax preparers charge large fees and remove their fees before their clients receive their refunds. The Internal Revenue Service has also provided specific information for tax preparers to help reduce errors (Internal Revenue Service, 2018c).

CONCLUSION 8-2: Unnecessarily burdensome administrative procedures can discourage families from applying for, and thus prevent them from receiving, income assistance program benefits for which they are otherwise eligible. State-by-state variation in the implementation of federal policies can lead to inconsistencies in access among eligible families and to variation in the efficacy of anti-poverty programs.

CONCLUSION 8-3: Federal rules such as limits on the eligibility of documented immigrants and measures that discourage program use (e.g., "public charge" determination) reduce access to means-tested programs for entire groups, even for individuals who meet income-eligibility requirements. These rules may harm both citizen and immigrant children

---

[6] Specifically, Code of Federal Regulations item 7CFR 272.4.

in such families by reducing the benefits available to them, with a disproportionate impact on racial and ethnic minority families.

RACIAL/ETHNIC DISCRIMINATION

Why It Matters

A substantial body of social science research shows that large racial/ethnic disparities persist in U.S. society in access to education, employment, housing, and health care, as well as in equitable treatment in the civil and criminal justice systems (Pager and Shepherd, 2008). Discrimination and unequal access to resources can lead to social policies being less effective for parents who are racial/ethnic minorities.

Employment and housing provide two examples. Discrimination in hiring makes it more difficult for parents from a racial/ethnic minority group to obtain employment and therefore to benefit from policies aimed at supporting low-wage workers or to maintain eligibility for programs that require beneficiaries to work (Bertrand and Mullainathan, 2004; Holzer, Raphael, and Stoll, 2006; Stoll, Raphael, and Holzer, 2004). Discrimination by landlords renders policies to expand housing less effective for parents who are members of racial/ethnic minorities and may expose these families to greater housing instability and the risk of homelessness (Desmond, 2016).

Even for individuals with similar levels of education, racial/ethnic minorities have higher rates of unemployment and lower earnings than Whites (Pew Research Center, 2016), with Black unemployment rates typically twice as high as White unemployment rates (U.S. Bureau of Labor Statistics, 2018a). Black and Hispanic employment is also more vulnerable to downturns in the economic cycle and takes longer to recover (U.S. Bureau of Labor Statistics, 2018b). Moreover, Black and Hispanic families have on average one-sixth of the wealth of their White counterparts (McKernan et al., 2013).

While not all of the racial/ethnic differences in employment, earnings, and asset accumulation can be attributed directly to discrimination, compelling evidence suggests that discrimination plays a continuing role, particularly for employment, and to a lesser degree for wages (Pager and Shepherd, 2008). For example, among job applicants, Whites receive 36 percent more requests to advance in the hiring process (callbacks), on average, than equally qualified Black applicants and 24 percent more callbacks than equally qualified Hispanic applicants (Quillian et al., 2017). Callback rates for Black and Hispanic males without a criminal record are lower than for Whites *with* a criminal record (Pager, Western, and Bonikowski, 2009).

Discrimination against racial/ethnic minorities also persists in housing. Rigorous studies sponsored by the U.S. Department of Housing and

Urban Development (HUD) find that while racial/ethnic discrimination in both rental and sales markets has declined over the past 40 years, Blacks, Hispanics, and Asians seeking housing continue to be informed of and shown fewer housing units than their White counterparts (Turner et al., 2013). For example, one paired-testing study, which sampled 8,000 qualified apartment home-seekers across 28 states, found that for every 25 visits, Black home-seekers were shown one unit fewer than White home-seekers, while Hispanic home-seekers were shown one unit fewer for every 14 visits (Turner et al., 2013).

As discussed above, provisions that limit legal immigrants' eligibility for anti-poverty programs even when they would qualify based on income are discriminatory by program design.

Relationship to Policy

Discrimination against racial/ethnic minorities in the labor and housing markets can limit the effectiveness of anti-poverty programs in several ways. For example, the Housing Choice Voucher program sets a time limit on voucher-subsidized housing searches—typically 60 days (U.S. Department of Housing and Urban Development, 2015). Families unable to locate qualifying housing within that amount of time must return the vouchers. Consequently, if minority families seeking to move are shown fewer units than majority families, as Turner et al. (2013) found, this may result in lower levels of program take-up. Further, if minority families are steered toward housing in neighborhoods with access to fewer job opportunities, then housing subsidy programs will be less successful in promoting economic mobility.

Indeed, research has found that White families receiving Housing Choice vouchers are more likely to find rental units in low-poverty neighborhoods (those with poverty rates under 10%) with higher-performing schools than are Black and Hispanic families seeking the same (Horn, Ellen, and Schwartz, 2014; McClure, Schwartz, and Taghavi, 2015). Therefore, even when different families receive a housing subsidy that is comparable in monetary value, nonmonetary factors such as social ties, reliable information, and housing discrimination (associated with prevailing residential segregation patterns) may reduce the ability of Black and Hispanic families to translate their monetary benefit into better outcomes in employment and well-being.

Discrimination in the operation of anti-poverty programs themselves may also reduce the benefit these programs offer to people who belong to racial/ethnic minorities. In an examination of six types of federal programs (TANF, child care subsidies, Head Start, child support enforcement, programs for homeless and runaway youth, and adolescent pregnancy prevention programs), McDaniel et al. (2017) concluded that employment discrimination, as well as the organization and delivery of the programs themselves, results in racial/ethnic inequities in access to the programs and, consequently, in program outcomes. For example, evidence indicates that TANF case workers are more likely to offer work supports, such as child care, to White TANF recipients than to Black or Hispanic recipients, which may make it more difficult for the latter to find or sustain employment (McDaniel et al., 2017).

CONCLUSION 8-5: Past and current racial/ethnic discrimination have contributed to substantial disparities in access to employment and housing. Discrimination in hiring and employment may undermine policies that aim to increase or subsidize wages and policies that require beneficiaries to work. Housing discrimination reduces racial/ethnic minority families' access to and benefits from housing programs.

CRIMINAL JUSTICE SYSTEM INVOLVEMENT

Why It Matters

As of 2015, some 2.8 percent of the U.S. adult population was either incarcerated (2.2 million adults) or on probation or parole (4.7 million adults) (Kaeble and Glaze, 2016; Kaeble and Bonczar, 2016). Although these figures have declined since their peak in 2007–2008, it remains the case that millions of Americans have close connections to people who are in prison or otherwise involved with the criminal justice system (Kaeble and Glaze, 2016; Kaeble and Bonczar, 2016; Lee et al. 2015).

In 2015, 7 percent of non-Hispanic White children had a parent who was ever incarcerated, compared with 16 percent of Black children and 8 percent of Hispanic children.[7] Such racial/ethnic differences persist even after controlling for parents' educational attainment. For example, among children born in 1990 whose fathers were high school dropouts, the cumulative risk of paternal incarceration by the time the child reached age 14 was 50.5 percent for Black children, but only 7.2 percent for White children (Wildeman, 2009).

Racial/ethnic differences in involvement with the criminal justice system can be attributed to several factors, including disproportionality in school discipline, differential involvement in delinquency, criminal case characteristics, and unequal treatment in the criminal justice system (Donnelly, 2018).

---

[7] For more information, see https://datacenter.kidscount.org/data/tables/9734-children-who-had-a-parent-who-was-ever-incarcerated-by-race-and-ethnicity#detailed/1/any/false/1539/10, 11,9,12,1,13/18995,18996.

In a recent quasi-experimental study, Arnold and colleagues (forthcoming) found that inexperienced and part-time judges in Miami and Philadelphia were more likely to make racially biased prediction errors when imposing bail amounts. Racial/ethnic disparities, however, can be seen throughout the various stages of the criminal justice process (National Research Council, 2014). An example from a recent consensus report issued by the National Research Council is that, for similar crimes, sentences issued for Blacks are more likely to be on the higher end of sentencing guidelines, whereas sentences for Whites tend to be toward the lower end. Further, the report committee found that both Blacks and Hispanics are more likely than Whites to be detained before trial, which has been shown to increase the chances that the defendant will receive a prison sentence (National Research Council, 2014).

According to a recent report by the U.S. Commission on Civil Rights (2017), the fines and fees levied against individuals for even minor crimes can cause low-income families to sink into debt, which can be difficult to escape. The same report also found that these fees were often targeted at communities of color and low-income individuals (U.S. Commission on Civil Rights, 2017).

The net effect of these disparities is that Black and Hispanic children are more vulnerable to the economic, social, and psychological adversities associated with having an incarcerated parent. Reviewing the most rigorous studies on the effect of parental incarceration on children's behavioral problems, academic achievement, and delinquency, Wildeman, Wakefield, and Turney (2013) found that paternal incarceration has consistently negative effects on child well-being and that the effects are greater than if the father were merely absent from the household (e.g., due to divorce).

Research suggests that the effects of maternal incarceration are dependent on the behavior of the mother. For example, if a mother consistently placed her child in dangerous or stressful situations prior to being imprisoned, child outcomes may improve after incarceration. Children who were not exposed to dangerous or stressful situations may experience negative outcomes when the mother is incarcerated (Wildeman and Turney, 2014). Hagan and Foster (2015) have found higher rates of food insecurity and economic insecurity (inability to pay for rent or mortgage, telephone, and utilities) among families with adolescents who were experiencing or had experienced paternal or maternal imprisonment.

Relationship to Policy

Incarcerated parents face challenges in supporting their children economically and psychologically (Turney and Goodsell, 2018). Moreover, the incarceration of one parent puts added stress on the nonincarcerated parent

(National Research Council, 2014). However, the release of an incarcerated parent does not end the adverse effects, because a record of incarceration substantially reduces the parent's ability to work (Looney and Turner, 2018) and to find housing (Keene et al., 2018) and reduces eligibility for public services (Sugie, 2012). The lower levels of educational achievement of parents who enter prison may also reduce their chances of gaining employment after release (Looney and Turner, 2018).

Accordingly, programs that aim to increase or supplement earnings or require beneficiaries to work, such as the EITC, may be less effective for families in which a parent has been incarcerated, unless efforts are made to reduce barriers to employment for these parents. Although the level of evidence in this area is slim, programs for which there is some evidence of effectiveness include training to recognize bias on the part of employers in the recruitment and hiring of staff (Carnes et al., 2015; Devine et al., 2012); readily accessible procedures to expunge records of criminal offenses committed as juveniles (Selbin, McCrary, and Epstein, 2018); and proactive assistance for newly released convicts in obtaining employment (Broadus et al., 2016).

Reforms directed at these problems can sometimes backfire, however. Recently, several states and municipalities have passed laws to "ban the box," meaning they prohibit employers from asking about applicants' criminal history. There is some evidence that employers undercut the effectiveness of such laws by discriminating against all of the applicants in the larger groups that are statistically more likely to have a criminal history. For example, employers may automatically screen out names that appear to be Black or Hispanic (Agan and Starr, 2018; Doleac and Hansen, 2016).

Social policies that exclude felons from receiving benefits may have developed with both punishment and deterrence in mind. A consequence of these policies, however, is that children in these families are (often unintentionally) denied benefits that are extended to other children in otherwise identical economic circumstances. The 1996 welfare reform imposed a lifetime ban on the receipt of TANF and SNAP for individuals with a drug felony conviction, except in states that opt out of the ban. The children of parents with a felony drug conviction are still eligible for SNAP benefits; however, by reducing the total amount of SNAP benefits a family receives as a result of these bans, families living in poverty may not be able to purchase the amount of food needed to maintain good health. To date, 37 states have implemented a full or modified ban on the receipt of TANF benefits for drug felons and 34 states have done so for SNAP benefits as well (Mauer and McCalmont, 2015).

Individuals with a drug conviction also lose their eligibility for college financial aid (U.S. Department of Education, 2019), and Housing Choice Voucher housing assistance is not available to ex-convicts (who are not members of a protected class under anti-discrimination laws) unless local housing authorities choose to allow them to qualify (Curtis, Garlington, and Schottenfeld, 2013). Given the large racial disparity in criminal justice involvement (Lyons and Pettit, 2011), and specifically in drug-related convictions (National Research Council, 2014, pp. 91-97), these reductions in public benefits particularly penalize Black families and limit the ability of incarcerated and previously incarcerated parents to support their children (either privately or through the child support system) or to enable their children to rise out of poverty (Sugie, 2012, pp. 3-4).

CONCLUSION 8-6: Involvement of a parent or other relative with the criminal justice system harms significant numbers of low-income children, particularly minority children, both economically and in other ways. Prior incarceration may render some parents ineligible for benefits that could reduce child poverty and leave them unable to secure housing or work and thus provide for their children.

NEIGHBORHOOD CONDITIONS

Why It Matters

Neighborhood conditions—particularly those associated with high concentrations of families living in poverty—are a potentially important context both for families and children and for the anti-poverty programs that serve them. As the county-based information presented in Chapter 2 makes clear, high-poverty areas—defined as census tracts (neighborhoods of about 4,000 people) with an official poverty rate of 20 percent or more—exist all over the United States. Census data show that the adult residents of these neighborhoods are more likely than residents of low-poverty areas to lack a high school diploma, to be unemployed, to be separated or never-married, to be single parents, and to rent rather than own a home (Bishaw, 2014, Table 2a).

Additionally, levels of child development, educational outcomes, psychological well-being, and health are all worse among children living in high-poverty neighborhoods than among other children (Leventhal, Dupere, and Shuey, 2015). At the same time, as noted concerning the associations between family-based poverty and child outcomes discussed in Chapter 3, it is difficult to disentangle correlation and causation in the associations between neighborhood-based poverty and child outcomes (Gennetian et al. 2012; Sanbonmatsu et al., 2006). Moreover, the effects of neighborhood poverty seem to depend on when children were exposed over the life course (Chetty, 2015).

Neighborhood conditions are associated with a person's ability to move out of poverty. Areas with lower levels of intergenerational mobility are characterized by greater residential segregation by race and income, higher income inequality, poorer quality K–12 schools, weaker measures of social networks and community involvement, and weaker family structures (as measured by the prevalence of single parents) (Chetty et al., 2014).

Lack of intergenerational mobility is highest among Black families living in high-poverty neighborhoods. Chetty et al. (2018) found that White and Hispanic families are more likely than Black families to move up in the income distribution across generations. Moreover, the few geographic areas in which Black-White mobility gaps were found to be relatively small tended to be low-poverty neighborhoods where Whites had low levels of racial bias and Blacks grew up with their fathers present. However, fewer than 5 percent of Black children, as compared with 63 percent of White children, grow up in areas with poverty rates below 10 percent and where more than one-half of fathers are present.

The role of past *de jure* discrimination should not be overlooked. High levels of current racial/ethnic residential segregation have been shaped by historical discrimination in housing policy and lending, such as redlining in the mortgage market and segregation in public housing, as well as by current zoning regulations (Rothstein, 2017). Segregation in turn has led to a disproportionate share of racial/ethnic minority families living in high-poverty neighborhoods intergenerationally (Sharkey 2008, 2013).

Relationship to Policy

Policies that aim to increase access to nutrition, housing, or employment are likely to be less effective in places that lack the resources or social networks to support them. For example, families who live in high-poverty neighborhoods tend to eat substantially less nutritious food than their counterparts in low-poverty areas. Although socioeconomic status and limited access to nutritious food in high-poverty areas contribute to unhealthy eating, the vast part of this difference is explained by the concentration of lower levels of education and knowledge about the value of healthy eating in high-poverty neighborhoods as compared to lower-poverty neighborhoods (Allcott, Diamond, and Dube, 2018; Handbury, Rahkovsky, and Schnell, 2015). Thus, the SNAP program may be more effective at increasing nutritional outcomes for families who live in high-poverty neighborhoods if the program is coupled with counseling or education about how to choose and prepare healthy food. States have access to grant funding for such programs through the Supplemental Nutrition Assistance Program—Education

(SNAP-Ed) initiative.[8] While not all states have chosen to implement nutrition education programs, a recent evaluation of the SNAP-Ed program by the Research Triangle Institute suggests that they have the potential to encourage low-income families to make healthier food choices (Hersey et al., 2014).

Geographic location can also play a significant role in creating environments that help break the cycle of intergenerational poverty. In particular, access to high-quality educational experiences, which integrate students from various socioeconomic backgrounds, can improve the likelihood of future success (Rothwell and Massey, 2014).

Housing programs can also have a considerable effect on the level of neighborhood poverty that families experience. The Moving to Opportunity (MTO) experiment, discussed in Chapter 3, demonstrated that offering housing vouchers to families to move to low-poverty neighborhoods (those with less than 10 percent of residents in poverty) led to a reduction in neighborhood poverty by 20 percentage points for families that took up the offer (Gennetian et al., 2012). Although the decrease in their experience of neighborhood poverty led to virtually no improvements in MTO-participating children's well-being in the short term (Sanbonmatsu et al., 2006; Gennetian et al., 2012), the subset of children who moved to a lower-poverty neighborhood at a young age (before age 13) showed longer-term benefits in their college and labor market outcomes (Chetty, 2015). Thus housing programs may be made more effective by targeting families with younger children in high-poverty neighborhoods, as long as the program does not have enough funding to serve all families.

The MTO experiment and corresponding Three-City Study (Cove et al. 2008; Orr et al., 2003) also provide insight into the employment effects on parents of moving from a high-poverty neighborhood to a lower-poverty neighborhood. The effects of this experiment on employment were generally weak and showed that it was difficult for many families to integrate into lower-poverty neighborhoods and take advantage of new social networks and employment opportunities. Thus, policies that require a parent to work to receive benefits may be less effective for families with limited social networks or access to resources.

Rural areas have distinctly different needs where poverty is concerned. Low-income families in some of the nation's rural areas face substantial burdens to employment because of extremely limited public transportation and child care options (Whitener, Duncan, and Weber, 2002). Families in these areas will not benefit from work-based policies in the same way that families with better access to employment will. These rural families may

---

[8] For more information on the SNAP-Ed program, please see https://snaped.fns.usda.gov.

benefit more from income supports that are not based on employment, such as child allowances or child support assurance.

CONCLUSION 8-7: Living in areas of concentrated poverty makes it difficult for parents to lift their children out of poverty; poor Black and Hispanic families face a considerably higher risk of concentrated neighborhood poverty and other forms of neighborhood disadvantage than poor White families.

HEALTH AND DISABILITY

Why It Matters

Across the United States, as in other countries, people living in poverty tend to have worse health than the rest of the population. In the case of U.S. children, this so-called health gradient grows steeper across childhood and adolescence (Case, Lubotsky, and Paxson, 2002), although the gradient has grown flatter in recent years with the expansion of Medicaid coverage for young children (Currie, Decker, and Lin, 2008). In adulthood, the gradient is steeper still: Adults (ages 18 and older) living in poverty in the United States were almost four times as likely in 2016 to report that they were in fair or poor health (28.2%)[9] as adults with family incomes above twice the official poverty line (7.76%),[10] and in 2014–2015 they were several times more likely to report serious psychological distress during the past 30 days (8% vs. less than 2%).[11]

According to the National Council on Disability, approximately 4.1 million parents in the United States live with disabilities, and their number is increasing (National Council on Disability, 2012). Of these 4.1 million parents, 52 percent receive SSI. The Social Security Administration maintains an extensive list of impairments[12] that it has judged to be severe enough to limit or prevent an individual's ability to work. Some examples include cystic fibrosis, multiple sclerosis, cerebral palsy, traumatic brain injury, and schizophrenia (Social Security Administration, 2018). Parents with work-limiting impairments such as these are twice as likely to be

---

[9] National Center for Health Statistics, *Summary Statistics: National Health Interview Survey*, Table A-11a, https://ftp.cdc.gov/pub/Health_Statistics/NCHS/NHIS/SHS/2016_SHS_Table_A-11.pdf.

[10] National Center for Health Statistics, *Summary Statistics: National Health Interview Survey*, Table A-11a, https://ftp.cdc.gov/pub/Health_Statistics/NCHS/NHIS/SHS/2016_SHS_Table_A-11.pdf.

[11] National Center for Health Statistics, *Health, United States, 2016*, Table 46 (page 1 of 2).

[12] For a complete list of qualifying impairments, see https://www.ssa.gov/disability/professionals/bluebook/listing-impairments.htm.

unemployed (48% compared to 22%) and three times as likely to live in poverty as those without disabilities (National Council on Disability, 2012).

Regardless of their own health, parents living below the federal poverty level may have to care for children with physical or mental health conditions or disabilities, which can affect the parents' employability and increase stress on the family (Carlson, Keith-Jennings, and Chaudhry, 2017). According to a secondary analysis of data collected for the National Health Interview Survey (NHIS) from 2001 to 2011, children living in poverty are more likely than other children to have a disability. Results from this analysis also show that the number of children with disabilities living below 100 percent of the federal poverty level increased by 10.7 percent between 2001 to 2011 (Houtrow et al., 2014). Some family members may have to reduce the number of hours they work or stop work altogether to care for relatives with disabilities, which can place an additional strain on family finances (Rupp and Ressler, 2009). This difficult balance between work and caregiving can be especially challenging for single parents (Rupp and Ressler, 2009).

Furthermore, the costs related to caring for a family member with a disability may also create a significant financial burden (Carlson, Keith-Jennings, and Chaudhry, 2017; Stabile and Allin, 2012). An analysis of the period 1996 to 2004 found that people with disabilities had significantly higher health expenditures when compared to those without disabilities[13] (Mitra, Findley, and Sambamoorthi, 2009). Moreover, a more recent examination of administrative and survey data suggests that families with children with disabilities are less likely than other families with children to visit the doctor, more likely to delay paying bills and rent, and more likely to require food assistance[14] (Carlson, Keith-Jennings, and Chaudhry, 2017).

Impacts on the health, employability, and quality of life for persons living with a disability are often further exacerbated if they are Black or Hispanic, are older, have low educational attainment, or are living in poverty (Ross and Bateman, 2018). As an example, Blacks and Native Americans with disabilities have the lowest employment rates (McGrew, Scott, and Madowitz, 2018).

Mental health, developmental, and intellectual disabilities can also create significant barriers to employment (Luciano and Meara, 2014; National Council on Disability, 2012). An analysis of data from 2009 and 2010 found that individuals with a diagnosed mental illness were less likely to work, and 39 percent of those who identified as having a serious mental

---

[13] This was a secondary analysis of the nationally representative Medical Expenditure Panel Survey (MEPS) collected from 1996 to 2004.

[14] This was an analysis of SNAP administrative data and National Health Interview Survey data.

illness had incomes below $10,000[15] (Luciano and Meara, 2014). However, this last analysis also found that when these individuals received employment services such as vocational counseling, their employment rates doubled (Luciano and Meara, 2014). Other studies suggest that families that care for ill or disabled members have an increased risk of emotional, mental, and physical health problems, including increased levels of depression and anxiety.[16]

Substance abuse is also linked to lower levels of employment and wages, although the causal pathway may work in several directions. Adults who abuse drugs or alcohol may seek less work or be less qualified for well-paying jobs (Terza and Vechnak, 2007). Alternatively, the loss of employment or stress of low wages may lead to greater use of substances as a coping mechanism (Badel and Greaney, 2013). Also, injuries that initially limit a person's ability to work may lead to a growing dependency on pain medication (i.e., opioids) that further reduces the person's ability to work or care for himself or herself (National Institute on Drug Abuse, 2018).

Relationship to Policy

A key question for policy is the extent to which poor health is the primary cause of lower employment and earnings, as opposed to poverty causing poor health.[17] However, the fact that health and income are so highly correlated suggests that programs that condition receipt of benefits on employment or that are intended to increase or supplement earnings will not help poor parents who are unable to sustain stable employment due to poor health or a disability. According to a recent National Council on Disability (2012) report, additional family and work supports such as assistance for child care, transportation, and job training may help parents living with disabilities comply with TANF work requirements. Low-income families in which the parents have disabilities that prevent them from maintaining full-time, stable employment are also less likely to be eligible for family and medical leave and less likely to be able to afford to take leave when eligible (Mathur et al., 2017). Further, while the Family and Medical Leave Act guarantees job protection for eligible workers who need to take leave for up to 12 weeks, it does not include wage replacement.[18] Lack of leave time places people with disabilities at extreme risk, because they may

---

[15] Based on data collected from the National Survey on Drug Use and Health between 2009 and 2010.

[16] For more information, see https://www.caregiver.org/caregiver-health.

[17] For reviews of the literature, see Cutler, Lleras-Muney, and Vogl (2008); Evans, Wolfe, and Adler (2012).

[18] For more information about the Family and Medical Leave Act, see https://www.dol.gov/whd/fmla.

experience sporadic health flare-ups or need time off for medical appointments (Vallas, Fremstad, and Ekman, 2015).

Vocational rehabilitation programs have been shown to be effective in helping adults with mental or physical health challenges find and maintain employment (Cullen et al., 2017; Graham et al., 2016; Suijkerbuijk et al., 2017). Despite this, little has been done to connect low-income parents to most of these programs (Farrell et al., 2013; Farrell and Walter, 2013). A recent study conducted by the Office of Planning, Research, and Evaluation at the U.S. Department of Health and Human Services found that there is often only limited collaboration between TANF agencies and Social Security Administration agencies (Farrell et al., 2013). One of the most successful programs included in the study—Families Achieving Success Today, in Ramsey County, Minnesota—found that participants were more likely to receive vocational rehabilitation services and obtain employment than members of the control group and that on average they earned $1,235 more in the first year (Farrell et al., 2013), although this amount may not be enough to enable a family to rise out of poverty.

CONCLUSION 8-8: Because parents who are in poor health or caring for a child in poor health may be less able to work and care for themselves or their children, anti-poverty programs that require employment to maintain eligibility or that have cumbersome eligibility requirements may be less effective for these families.

REFERENCES

Adams, G., and Rohacek, M.H. (2010). *Child Care Instability: Definitions, Context, and Policy Implications*. Washington, DC: The Urban Institute.

Agan, A., and Starr, S. (2018). Ban the box, criminal records, and racial discrimination: A field experiment. *The Quarterly Journal of Economics, 133*(1), 191–235.

Allcott, H., Diamond, R., and Dube, J.P. (2018). *The Geography of Poverty and Nutrition: Food Deserts and Food Choices Across the United States*. Cambridge, MA: National Bureau of Economic Research.

Alsan, M., and Yang, C. (2018). *Fear and the Safety Net: Evidence from Secure Communities*. Cambridge, MA: National Bureau of Economic Research.

Annie E. Casey Foundation. (2010). *Improving Access to Public Benefits: Helping Eligible Individuals and Families Get the Income Supports They Need*. Baltimore, MD: Annie E. Casey Foundation.

Arnold, D., Dobbie, W., and Yang, C.S. (Forthcoming). Racial bias in bail decisions. *Quarterly Journal of Economics*.

Badel, A., and Greaney, B. (2013). Exploring the link between drug use and job status in the U.S. *Regional Economist*, January 7. Available: https://www.stlouisfed.org/publications/regional-economist.

Barr, M. (2009). Financial services, savings, and borrowing among low- and moderate-income households: Evidence from the Detroit Area Household Financial Services Survey. In R.M. Blank and M.S. Barr (Eds.), *Insufficient Funds: Savings, Assets, Credit, and Banking Among Low-Income Households* (pp. 66–96). New York, NY: Russell Sage Foundation.

Barr, M.S. (2012). Introduction. In M.S. Barr (Ed.), *No Slack: The Financial Lives of Low-Income Americans* (pp. 1–21). Washington, DC: Brookings Institution Press.

Batalova, J., Fix, M., and Greenberg, M. (2018). *Chilling Effects: The Expected Public Charge Rule and Its Impact on Legal Immigrant Families' Public Benefits Use*. Washington, DC: Migration Policy Institute.

Bertrand, M., and Mullainathan, S. (2004). Are Emily and Greg more employable than Lakisha and Jamal? A field experiment on labor market discrimination. *American Economic Review*, 94(4), 991–1013.

Bishaw, A. (2014). *Changes in Areas with Concentrated Poverty: 2000 to 2010*. Washington, DC: U.S. Census Bureau.

Broadus, J., Muller-Ravett, S., Sherman, A., and Redcross, C. (2016). *A Successful Prisoner Reentry Program Expands: Lessons from the Replication of the Center for Employment Opportunities*. New York, NY: MDRC.

Burhouse, S., Chu, K., Goodstein, R., Northwood, J., Osaki, Y., and Sharma, D. (2014). *2013 FDIC National Survey of Unbanked and Underbanked Households*. Washington, DC: Federal Deposit Insurance Corporation.

Campbell, A.L. (2014). *Trapped in America's Safety Net: One Family's Struggle*. Chicago, IL: University of Chicago Press.

Capps, R., Fix, M., Ost, J., Reardon-Anderson, J., and Passel, J.S. (2004). *The Health and Well-Being of Young Children of Immigrants*. Washington, DC: The Urban Institute.

Carlson, S., Keith-Jennings, B., and Chaudhry, R. (2017). *SNAP Provides Needed Food Assistance to Millions of People With Disabilities*. Washington, DC: Center on Budget and Policy Priorities.

Carnes, M., Devine, P.G., Baier Manwell, L., Byars-Winston, A., Fine, E., Ford, C.E., Forscher, P., Isaac, C., Kaatz, A., Magua, W., Palta, M., and Sheridan, J. (2015). The effect of an intervention to break the gender bias habit for faculty at one institution: A cluster randomized, controlled trial. *Academic Medicine*, 90(2), 221–230.

Case, A., Lubotsky, D., and Paxson, C. (2002). Economic status and health in childhood: The origins of the gradient. *American Economic Review*, 92(5), 1308–1334.

Caskey, J. (2006). *Can Personal Financial Management Education Promote Asset Accumulation by the Poor?* Terre Haute, IN: Networks Financial Institute.

Castellari, E., Cotti, C., Gordanier, J., and Ozturk, O. (2017). Does the timing of food stamp distribution matter? A panel data analysis of monthly purchasing patterns of U.S. households. *Health Economics*, 26(11), 1380–1393.

Chetty, R. (2015). Behavioral economics and public policy: A pragmatic perspective. *American Economic Review*, 105(5), 1–33.

Chetty, R., Hendren, N., Kline, P., and Saez, E. (2014). *Where is the Land of Opportunity? The Geography of Intergenerational Mobility in the United States*. Cambridge, MA: National Bureau of Economic Research.

Chetty, R., Hendren, N., Jones, M.R., and Porter, S.R. (2018). *Race and Economic Opportunity in the United States: An Intergenerational Perspective*. Cambridge, MA: National Bureau of Economic Research.

Child Trends. (2014). *Immigrant Children: Indicators of Child and Youth Well-Being*. Washington, DC: Child Trends.

Cody, S., Reed, D., Basson, D., Pedraza, J., Martin, E.S., Santos, B., and Smith, E. (2010). *Simplification of Health and Social Services Enrollment and Eligibility: Lessons for California from Interviews in Four States: Final Report.* Washington, DC: Mathematica Policy Research.

Coleman-Jensen, A., Rabbitt, M.P., Gregory, C.A., and Singh, A. (2017). *Household Food Security in the United States in 2016.* Washington, DC: U.S. Department of Agriculture, Economic Research Service.

Congressional Research Service. (2016). *Green Book: Background Material and Data on the Programs within the Jurisdiction of the Committee on Ways and Means.* Washington, DC: Congressional Research Service.

Cove, E., Turner, M.A., Briggs, X.D.S., and Duarte, C. (2008). *Can Escaping from Poor Neighborhoods Increase Employment and Earnings?* Washington, DC: The Urban Institute.

Cullen, K.L., Irvin, E., Collie, A., Clay, F., Gensby, U., Jennings, P.A., Hogg-Johnson, S., Kristman, V., Laberge, M., McKenzie, D., Newnam, S., Palagyi, A., Ruseckaite, R., Sheppard, D.M., Shourie, S., Steenstra, I., Van Eerd, D., and Amick, B.C. (2017). Effectiveness of workplace interventions in return-to-work for musculoskeletal, pain-related and mental health conditions: An update of the evidence and messages for practitioners. *Journal of Occupational Rehabilitation, 28*(1).

Currie, J. (2008). *The Invisible Safety Net.* Princeton: Princeton University Press.

Currie, J., and Grogger, J. (2001). Explaining recent declines in Food Stamp Program participation. *Brookings-Wharton Papers on Urban Affairs,* 203–244.

Currie, J., Decker, S., and Lin, W. (2008). Has public health insurance for older children reduced disparities in access to care and health outcomes? *Journal of Health Economics, 27*(6), 1567–1581.

Curtis, M.A., Garlington, S., and Schottenfeld, L.S. (2013). Alcohol, drug, and criminal history restrictions in public housing. *Cityscape: A Journal of Policy Development and Research, 15*(3).

Cutler, D.M., Lleras-Muney, A., and Vogl, T. (2008). *Socioeconomic Status and Health: Dimensions and Mechanisms.* Cambridge, MA: National Bureau of Economic Research.

Dehlendorf, C., Ruskin, R., Grumbach, K., Vittinghoff, E., Bibbins-Domingo, K., Schillinger, D., and Steinauer, J. (2010). Recommendations for intrauterine contraception: A randomized trial of the effects of patients' race/ethnicity and socioeconomic status. *American Journal of Obstetrics and Gynecology, 203*(4), 319-e1–319-e8.

Desmond, M. (2016). *Evicted: Poverty and Profit in the American City.* New York, NY: The Crown Publishing Group.

Devine, P.G., Forscher, P.S., Austin, A.J., and Cox, W.T. (2012). Long-term reduction in implicit race bias: A prejudice habit-breaking intervention. *Journal of Experimental Social Psychology, 48*(6), 1267–1278.

Doleac, J., and Hansen, B. (2016). *Does "Ban the Box" Help or Hurt Low-skilled Workers? Statistical Discrimination and Employment Outcomes When Criminal Histories Are Hidden.* Cambridge, MA: National Bureau of Economic Research.

Donnelly, E.A. (2018). Do disproportionate minority contact (DMC) mandate reforms change decision-making? Decomposing disparities in the juvenile justice system. *Youth Violence and Juvenile Justice.* doi: https://doi.org/10.1177%2F1541204018790667.

Edin, K., and Lein, L. (1997). *Making Ends Meet: How Single Mothers Survive Welfare and Low-Wage Work.* New York, NY: Russell Sage Foundation.

Enchautegui, M.E. (2013). *Nonstandard Work Schedules and the Well-Being of Low-Income Families.* Washington, DC: The Urban Institute.

Enchautegui, M.E., Johnson, M., and Gelatt, J. (2015). *Who Minds the Kids When Mom Works a Nonstandard Schedule?* Washington, DC: The Urban Institute.

Evans, W., Wolfe, B., and Adler, N. (2012). The SES and health gradient: A brief review of the literature. In *The Biological Consequences of Socioeconomic Inequalities* (pp. 1–37). New York, NY: Russell Sage Foundation.

Farrell, M., and Walter, J. (2013). *The Intersection of Welfare and Disability: Early Findings from the TANF/SSI Disability Transition Project*. OPRE Report 2013-06. Washington, DC: Office of Planning, Research and Evaluation, Administration for Children and Families, U.S. Department of Health and Human Services.

Farrell, M., Baird, P., Barden, B., Fishman, M., and Pardoe, R. (2013). *The TANF/SSI Disability Transition Project: Innovative Strategies for Serving TANF Recipients with Disabilities*. OPRE Report 2013-51. Washington, DC: Office of Planning, Research and Evaluation, Administration for Children and Families, U.S. Department of Health and Human Services.

Floyd, I. (2017). *TANF Cash Benefits Have Fallen by More Than 20 Percent in Most States and Continue to Erode*. Washington, DC: Center on Budget and Policy Priorities.

Gassman-Pines, A., and Bellows, L. (2018). Food instability and academic achievement: A quasi-experiment using SNAP benefit timing. *American Educational Research Journal, 56*(5),897–927.

Gennetian, L.A., and Shafir, E. (2015). The persistence of poverty in the context of financial instability: A behavioral perspective. *Journal of Policy Analysis and Management*, 1–33.

Gennetian, L.A., Sciandra, M., Sanbonmatsu, L., Ludwig, J., Katz, L.F., Duncan, G.J., Kling, J.R., and Kessler, R.C. (2012). The long-term effects of Moving to Opportunity on youth outcomes. *Cityscape, 14*(2), 137–168.

Graham, C.W., West, M.D., Bourdon, J.L., Inge, K.J., Seward, H.E., and Campbell, C. (2016). Employment interventions for return to work in working aged adults following traumatic brain injury (TBI): A systematic review. *Campbell Systematic Reviews 2016:6*. Oslo, Norway. Available: http://www.campbellcollaboration.org.

Gray, K.F., and Cunnyngham, K. (2016). *Trends in Supplemental Nutrition Assistance Program Participation Rates: Fiscal Year 2010 to Fiscal Year 2014*. Washington, DC: Mathematica Policy Research.

Hagan, J., and Foster, H. (2015). Mass incarceration, parental imprisonment, and the Great Recession: Intergenerational sources of severe deprivation in America. *The Russell Sage Foundation Journal of the Social Sciences, 1*(2), 80–107.

Hahn, H., Adams, G., Spaulding, S., and Heller, C. (2016). *Supporting The Child Care and Workforce Development Needs of TANF Families*. Washington, DC: The Urban Institute.

Halpern-Meekin, S., Edin, K., Tach, L., and Sykes, J. (2015). *It's Not Like I'm Poor: How Working Families Make Ends Meet in a Post-Welfare World* (1st ed.). Oakland: University of California Press.

Hamrick, K.S., and Andrews, M. (2016). SNAP participants' eating patterns over the benefit month: A time-use perspective. *PLoS ONE, 11*(7). Available: https://journals.plos.org/plosone/article?id=10.1371/journal.pone.0158422.

Handbury, J., Rahkovsky, I., and Schnell, M. (2015). *Is the Focus on Food Deserts Fruitless? Retail and Food Purchases Across the Socioeconomic Spectrum*. Cambridge, MA: National Bureau of Economic Research.

Hanratty, M.J. (2006). Has the Food Stamp Program become more accessible? Impacts of recent changes in reporting requirements and asset eligibility limits. *Journal of Policy Analysis and Management, 25*(3), 603–621.

Hersey, J.C., Cates, S.C., Blitstein, J.L., and Williams, P.A. (2014). *SNAP-Ed Can Improve Nutrition of Low-Income Amercians Across Life Span*. Research Triangle Park, NC: RTI International.

Hill, H.D., Morris, P., Gennetian, L.A., Wolf, S., and Tubbs, C. (2013). The consequences of income instability for children's well-being. *Child Development Perspectives, 7*(2), 85–90.

Hoffman, L. (2006). *Improving Access to Benefits for Low-Income Families.* Washington, DC: NGA Center for Best Practices.

Holcomb, P.A., Tumlin, K.C., Koralek, R., Capps, R., and Zuberi, A. (2003). *The Application Process for TANF, Food Stamps, Medicaid and SCHIP: Issues for Agencies and Applicants, Including Immigrants and Limited English Speakers.* Washington, DC: The Urban Institute.

Holcomb, P.A., Adams, G., Snyder, K., Koralek, R., Martinson, K., Bernstein, S., and Capizzano, J. (2006). *Child Care Subsidies and TANF: A Synthesis of Three Studies on Systems, Policies, and Parents.* Washington, DC: The Urban Institute.

Holt, S. (2015). *Periodic Payment of the Earned Income Tax Credit Revisited.* Washington, DC: The Brookings Institution. Available: https://www.brookings.edu/research/periodic-payment-of-the-earned-income-tax-credit-revisited.

Holzer, H.J., Raphael, S., and Stoll, M.A. (2006). Perceived criminality, criminal background checks, and the racial hiring practices of employers. *The Journal of Law and Economics, 49*(2), 451–480.

Holzer, H.J., and Wissoker, D. (2001). *How Can We Encourage Job Retention for Welfare Recipients.* Series No. A-49, October. Washington, DC: The Urban Institute.

Horn, K.M., Ellen, I.G., and Schwartz, A.E. (2014). Do Housing Choice Voucher holders live near good schools? *Journal of Housing Economics, 23,* 28–40.

Houtrow, A.J., Larson, K., Olson, L.M., Newacheck, P.W., and Halfon, N. (2014). Changing trends of childhood disability, 2001–2011. *Pediatrics 134*(3), 530–538.

Internal Revenue Service. (2018a). *States and Local Governments with Earned Income Tax Credit.* Available: https://www.irs.gov/credits-deductions/individuals/earned-income-tax-credit/states-and-local-governments-with-earned-income-tax-credit.

_____. (2018b). *Welcome to the Tax Preparer Toolkit: EITC and Other Refundable Credits.* Available: https://www.eitc.irs.gov/tax-preparer-toolkit/welcome-to-the-tax-preparer-toolkit.

Isaacs, J.B., Katz, M., and Amin, R. (2016). *Improving the Efficiency of Benefit Delivery: Outcomes From the Work Support Strategies Evaluation.* Washington, DC: The Urban Institute.

Joshi, P., Ha, Y., Schneider, K.G., and Hardy, E. (2018, January). *Multiple and Interacting Sources of Child Care Subsidy Stability: Complexities of Administrative and Family-Level Factors.* Paper presented at the Society for Social Work and Research Annual Meeting, Washington, DC.

Joshi, P.K., Geronimo, K., Romano, B., Earle, A., Rosenfeld, L., Hardy, E., and Acevedo-Garcia, D. (2014). Integrating racial/ethnic equity into policy assessments to improve child health. *Health Affairs, 33*(12), 2222–2229.

Kabbani, N.S., and Wilde, P.E. (2003). Short recertification periods in the U.S. Food Stamp Program. *The Journal of Human Resources, 38,* 1112-1138.

Kaeble, D., and Bonczar, T. (2016). *Probation and Parole in the United States, 2015.* Washington, DC: Bureau of Justice Statistics.

Kaeble, D., and Glaze, L. (2016). *Correctional Populations in the United States, 2015.* Washington, DC: Bureau of Justice Statistics.

Kaushal, N., and Gao, Q. (2011). Food Stamp Program and consumption choices. In M. Grossman and N. Mocan (Eds.), *Economic Aspects of Obesity.* Chicago, IL: University of Chicago Press.

Keene, D.E., Rosenberg, A., Schlesinger, P., Guo, M., and Blankenship, K.M. (2018). Navigating limited and uncertain access to subsidized housing after prison. *Housing Policy Debate, 28*(2), 199–214.

Kochhar, R., and Cilluffo, A. (2017). How wealth inequality has changed in the U.S. since the Great Recession, by race, ethnicity, and income. *Fact Tank: News in the Numbers*. Available: http://www.pewresearch.org/fact-tank/2017/11/01/how-wealth-inequality-has-changed-in-the-u-s-since-the-great-recession-by-race-ethnicity-and-income.

Kopczuk, W., and Pop-Eleches, C. (2007). Electronic filing, tax preparers and participation in the Earned Income Tax Credit. *Journal of Public Economics, 91*, 1351–1367.

Kornfeld, R. (2002). *Explaining Recent Trends in Food Stamp Program Caseloads: Final Report*. Washington, DC: U.S. Department of Agriculture, Economic Research Service.

Lee, H., McCormick, T., Hicken, M.T., and Wildeman, C. (2015). Racial inequalities in connectedness to imprisoned individuals in the United States. *Du Bois Review: Social Science Research on Race, 12*(2), 269–282.

Leventhal, T., Dupere, V., and Shuey, E.A. (2015). Children in neighborhoods. In H. Bornstein, T. Leventhal, and R.M. Lerner (Eds.), *Handbook of Child Psychology and Developmental Science: Ecological Settings and Processes*. Hoboken, NJ: John Wiley & Sons, Inc.

Looney, A., and Turner, N. (2018). *Work and Opportunity Before and After Incarceration*. Washington, DC: The Brookings Institution.

Loprest, P., Gearing, M., and Kassabian, D. (2016). *States' Use of Technology to Improve Delivery of Benefits: Findings From the Work Support Strategies Evaluation*. Washington, DC: The Urban Institute.

Luciano, A., and Meara, E. (2014). The employment status of people with mental illness: National survey data from 2009 and 2010. *Psychiatric Services, 65*(10), 1201–1209.

Lusardi, A., Schneider, D., and Tufano, P. (2011). *Financially Fragile Households: Evidence and Implications*. Washington, DC: The Brookings Institution.

Lyons, C.J., and Pettit, B. (2011). Compounded disadvantage: Race, incarceration, and wage growth. *Social Problems, 58*(2), 257–280.

Mathur, A., Sawhill, I.V., Boushey, H., Gitis, B., Haskins, R., Holtz-Eakin, D., Holzer, H.J., Jacobs, E., McCloskey, A.M., Rachidi, A., Reeves, R.V., Ruhm, C.J., Stevenson, B., and Waldfogel, J. (2017). *Paid Family and Medical Leave: An Issue Whose Time Has Come*. Washington, DC: The American Enterprise Institute and The Brookings Institution.

Mauer, M., and McCalmont, V. (2015). *A Lifetime of Punishment: The Impact of the Felony Drug Ban on Welfare Benefits*. Washington, DC: The Sentencing Project.

McClure, K., Schwartz, A.F., and Taghavi, L.B. (2015). Housing Choice Voucher location patterns a decade later. *Housing Policy Debate, 25*(2), 215–233.

McDaniel, M., Woods, T., Pratt, E., and Simms, M. (2017). *Identifying Racial and Ethnic Disparities in Human Services: A Conceptual Framework and Literature Review*. OPRE Report No. 2017-69. Washington, DC: Office of Planning, Research and Evaluation, Administration for Children and Families, U.S. Department of Health and Human Services.

McGrew, A., Scott, L., and Madowitz, M. (2018). *The State of the U.S. Labor Market: Pre-March 2018 Jobs Release*. Available: https://www.americanprogress.org/issues/economy/news/2018/04/05/448989/state-u-s-labor-market-pre-march-2018-jobs-release.

McKernan, S.M., Ratcliffe, C., and Vinopal, K. (2009). *Do Assets Help Families Cope with Adverse Events?* Washington, DC: The Urban Institute.

McKernan, S.M., Ratcliffe, C., Steuerle, C.E., and Zhang, S. (2013). *Less than Equal: Racial Disparities in Wealth Accumulation*. Washington, DC: The Urban Institute.

Mendenhall, R., Edin, K., Crowley, S., Sykes, J., Tach, L., Kriz, K., and Kling, J.R. (2012). The role of Earned Income Tax Credit in the budgets of low-income households. *Social Service Review, 86*(3), 367–400.

Meyers, M.K., Gornick, J.C., and Peck, L.R. (2001). Packaging support for low-income families: Policy variation across the United States. *Journal of Policy Analysis and Management, 20*(3), 457–483.

Michalopoulos, C., Lundquist, E., and Castells, N. (2010). *The Effects of Child Care Subsidies for Moderate-Income Families in Cook County, Illinois.* OPRE 2011–3. Washington, DC: Office of Planning, Research and Evaluation, Administration for Children and Families, U.S. Department of Health and Human Services.

Mitra, S., Findley, P.A., and Sambamoorthi, U. (2009). Health care expenditures of living with a disability: Total expenditures, out-of-pocket expenses, and burden, 1996 to 2004. *Archives of Physical Medicine and Rehabilitation, 90*(9), 1532–1540.

Moore, K., Perez-Lopez, D., and Hisnanick, J.J. (2017). *Participation Rates and Monthly Payments From Selected Social Insurance Programs.* Household Economic Studies. Current Population Reports, March. Washington, DC: U.S. Census Bureau.

Mullainathan, S., and Shafir, E. (2013). *Scarcity: Why Having Too Little Means So Much.* New York, NY: Times Books/Henry Holt.

National Council on Disability. (2012). *Rocking the Cradle: Ensuring the Rights of Parents With Disabilities and Their Children.* Washington, DC: National Council on Disability.

National Insitute on Drug Abuse. (2018). *Opiod Overdose Crisis.* Available: https://www.drugabuse.gov/drugs-abuse/opioids/opioid-overdose-crisis.

National Research Council. (2014). *The Growth of Incarceration in the United States: Exploring Causes and Consequences.* Washington, DC: The National Academies Press.

Orr, L., Feins, J.D., Jacob, R., Beecroft, E., Sanbonmatsu, L., Katz, L.F., Liebman, J.B., and Kling, J.R. (2003). *Moving to Opportunity Interim Impacts Evaluation.* Washington, DC: U.S. Department of Housing and Urban Development, Office of Policy Development and Research.

Pager, D., and Shepherd, H. (2008). The sociology of discrimination: Racial discrimination in employment, housing, credit, and consumer markets. *Annual Review of Sociology, 34,* 181–209.

Pager, D., Western, B., and Bonikowski, B. (2009). Discrimination in a low-wage labor market: A field experiment. *American Sociological Review, 74,* 777–799.

Pavetti, L., Schott, L., and Lower-Basch, E. (2011). *Creating Subsidized Employment Opportunities for Low-Income Parents: The Legacy of the TANF Emergency Fund.* Washington, DC: Center on Budget and Policy Priorities.

Perreira, K.M., Yoshikawa, H., and Oberlander, J. (2018). A new threat to immigrants' health—the public-charge rule. *New England Journal of Medicine, 379*(10), 901–903.

Pew Charitable Trusts. (2015). *What Resources Do Families Have for Financial Emergencies? The Role of Emergency Savings in Family Financial Security?* Issue Brief. Available: http://www.pewtrusts.org/en/research-and-analysis/issue-briefs/2015/11/emergency-savings-what-resources-do-families-have-for-financial-emergencies.

Pew Research Center. (2016). *On Views of Race and Inequality, Blacks and Whites Are Worlds Apart.* Washington, DC: Pew Research Center.

Quillian, L., Pager, D., Hexel, O., and Midtboen, A.H. (2017). Meta-analysis of field experiments shows no change in racial discrimination in hiring over time. *Proceedings of the National Academy of Sciences, 114*(41), 10870–10875.

Ratcliffe, C., McKernan, S.M., and Finegold, K. (2007). *The Effect of State Food Stamp and TANF Policies on Food Stamp Program Participation.* Washington, DC: The Urban Institute.

Ross, M., and Bateman, N. (2018). *Disability Rates Among Working-Age Adults Are Shaped by Race, Place, and Education.* Washington, DC: The Brookings Institution.

Rothstein, R. (2017). *The Color of Law: A Forgotten History of How Our Government Segregated America.* New York, NY: Liveright.

Rothwell, J.T., and Massey, D.S. (2014). Geographic effects on intergenerational income mobility. *Economic Geography, 91*(1), 83–106.

Rupp, K., and Ressler, S. (2009). Family caregiving and employment among parents of children with disabilities on SSI. *Journal of Vocational Rehabilitation, 30*, 153–175.

Sanbonmatsu, L., Kling, J.R., Duncan, G.J., and Brooks-Gunn, J. (2006). *Neighborhoods and Academic Achievement: Results From the Moving to Opportunity Experiment.* NBER Working Paper No. 11909. Cambridge, MA: National Bureau of Economic Research.

Schott, L., Pavetti, L., and Floyd, I. (2015). *How States Use Federal and State Funds Under the TANF Block Grant.* Washington, DC: Center on Budget and Policy Priorities. Available: https://www.cbpp.org/sites/default/files/atoms/files/4-8-15tanf_0.pdf.

Selbin, J., McCrary, J., and Epstein, J. (2018). Unmarked: Criminal record clearing and employment outcomes criminal law/criminology. *The Journal of Criminal Law and Criminology, 108*(1).

Sharkey, P. (2008). The intergenerational transmission of context. *American Journal of Sociology, 113*(4), 931–969.

_____. (2013). *Stuck in Place: Urban Neighborhoods and the End of Progress Toward Racial Equality.* Chicago, IL: University of Chicago Press.

Shipler, D.K. (2004). *The Working Poor: Invisible in America.* New York, NY: Vintage.

Social Security Administration. (2018). *Disability Evaluation under Social Security: Part III—Listing of Impairments.* Available: https://www.ssa.gov/disability/professionals/bluebook/listing-impairments.htm.

Stabile, M., and Allin, S. (2012). The economic cost of childhood disability. *Future of Children, 22*(1), 65–96.

Stoll, M.A., Raphael, S., and Holzer, H.J. (2004). Black job applicants and the hiring officers' race. *Industrial and Labor Relations Review, 57*(2), 267–287.

Strawn, J., and Martinson, K. (2000). *Steady Work and Better Jobs: How to Help Low-Income Parents Sustain Employment and Advance in the Workforce.* New York, NY: MDRC.

Sugie, N.F. (2012). Punishment and welfare: Paternal incarceration and families' receipt of public assistance. *Social Forces: A Scientific Medium of Social Study and Interpretation, 90*(4), 1403–1427.

Suijkerbuijk, Y.B., Schaafsma, F.G., van Mechelen, J.C., Ojajarvi, A., Corbiere, M., and Anema, J.R. (2017). Interventions for obtaining and maintaining employment in adults with severe mental illness, a network meta-analysis. *Cochrane Database System Review, 9*, CD011867.

Terza, J.V., and Vechnak, P.B. (2007). *The Effect of Substance Abuse on Employment Status.* University Park: The Pennsylvania State University.

Turner, M.A., Santos, R., Levy, D.K., Wissoker, D., Aranda, C., and Pitingolo, R. (2013). *Housing Discrimination Against Racial and Ethnic Minorities 2012.* Washington, DC: U.S. Department of Housing and Urban Development.

Turney, K., and Goodsell, R. (2018). Parental incarceration and children's wellbeing. *The Future of Children, 28*(1).

U.S. Bureau of Labor Statistics (2018a). *Table A-2. Employment Status of the Civilian Population by Race, Sex, and Age.* Washington, DC: U.S. Bureau of Labor Statistics. Available: https://www.bls.gov/news.release/empsit.t02.htm.

_____. (2018b). *Labor Force Statistics from the Current Population Survey.* August 30. Washington, DC: U.S. Bureau of Labor Statistics. Available: https://www.bls.gov/cps/demographics.htm#race.

U.S. Commission on Civil Rights. (2017). *Targeted Fines and Fees Against Low-Income Communities of Color: Civil Rights and Constitutional Implications.* Washington, DC: U.S. Commission on Civil Rights.

U.S. Department of Education. (2019). *Federal Student Aid: Students with Criminal Convictions.* Washington, DC: U.S. Department of Education. Available: https://studentaid.ed.gov/sa/eligibility/criminal-convictions#incarcerated.

U.S. Department of Housing and Urban Development. (2015). Housing search and leasing. Chapter 8 in *Housing Choice Voucher Program Guidebook*. Washington, DC: U.S. Department of Housing and Urban Development.

Vallas, R., Fremstad, S., and Ekman, L. (2015). *A Fair Shot for Workers with Disabilities*. Washington, DC: Center for American Progress. Available: https://www.americanprogress.org/issues/poverty/reports/2015/01/28/105520/a-fair-shot-for-workers-with-disabilities.

Wagner, J., and Huguelet, A. (2016). *Opportunities for States to Coordinate Medicaid and SNAP Renewals*. Washington, DC: Center on Budget and Policy Priorities.

Whitener, L., Duncan, G., and Weber, B. (2002). *Reforming Welfare: What Does It Mean for Rural Areas?* Washington, DC: U.S. Department of Agriculture.

Wilde, P., Cook, P., Gundersen, C., Nord, M., and Tiehen, L. (2000). *The Decline in Food Stamp Program Participation in the 1990s*. Washington, DC: U.S. Department of Agriculture, Economic Research Service.

Wildeman, C. (2009). Parental imprisonment, the prison boom, and the concentration of childhood disadvantage. *Demography, 46*(2), 265–280.

Wildeman, C., and Turney, K. (2014). Positive, negative, or null? The effects of maternal incarceration on children's behavioral problems. *Demography, 51*(3), 1041–1068.

Wildeman, C., Wakefield, S., and Turney, K. (2013). Misidentifying the effects of parental incarceration? A comment on Johnson and Easterling (2012). *Journal of Marriage and Family, 75*(1), 252–258.

9

Recommendations for Research
and Data Collection

Despite the success of government assistance programs in reducing child poverty in the United States over the past 50 years, an estimated 9.7 million children (13%) still live in families with incomes below 100 percent of the Supplemental Poverty Measure (SPM) poverty threshold. Of these, 2 million are in deep poverty, with family incomes below 50 percent of the SPM poverty line.[1] With this as a backdrop, Congress has asked for expert guidance in ways to achieve greater progress. In 2016, Congress passed legislation directing the National Academies of Sciences, Engineering, and Medicine to establish an expert committee to conduct a comprehensive study of child poverty, with the goal of identifying programs that could achieve further significant reductions in child poverty within 10 years. This report is the fruit of that labor.

In the preceding chapters of this report, our Committee on Building an Agenda to Reduce the Number of Children in Poverty by Half in 10 Years has fulfilled the first four elements of its charge, namely, to: (1) review the literature on the health and social costs of child poverty; (2) evaluate the anti-poverty effectiveness of major assistance programs in the United States and other industrialized countries; (3) identify policies and programs with the potential to further reduce poverty and deep poverty for children by 50 percent within 10 years; and (4) perform analyses to identify combinations of programs that have a strong potential to reduce child poverty and

---

[1] These estimates are for 2015 and use the SPM with income adjusted for underreporting for three large programs—the Supplemental Nutrition Assistance Program (SNAP), Supplemental Security Income (SSI), and Temporary Assistance to Needy Families (TANF) (see Chapter 2).

meet other policy objectives. All of our analyses, as specified in the charge made to us, used the SPM, adjusted for underreporting of major assistance programs, as the standard for assessing program benefits and costs. This chapter addresses the fifth element of our charge from Congress:

> . . . to identify high-priority research gaps, the filling of which would significantly advance the knowledge base for developing policies to reduce child poverty in the United States and assessing their effects.

Substantial evidence undergirds our conclusions in the preceding chapters concerning the effectiveness of programs and combinations of programs at combating child poverty. Owing to gaps in the relevant policy literature and associated data, however, we were unable to assess certain program and policy options as fully as we would have liked. To provide just a few examples:

- In contrast to the wealth of evidence available during the welfare reform debates of the 1990s, today we have very few recent strong evaluations of programs and policies designed to boost the job skills and employment of parents in low-income families receiving public assistance.
- For some assistance programs, such as Supplemental Security Income (SSI) and various types of housing assistance, there is relatively little evidence of their effects on children.
- There is insufficient evidence to assess the potential poverty-reducing effects of programs that do not provide income support, such as family planning and marriage promotion programs.
- Available data sources lack sufficient sample sizes or variables, or both, to assess the poverty-reducing effects of programs for small or specialized population groups, such as American Indians and Alaska Natives, children with disabilities, and children with incarcerated parents.
- Crucial measures of family resources, such as benefits (cash or in-kind) from assistance programs (e.g., Supplemental Nutrition Assistance Program [SNAP] benefits), are underreported or misreported in household surveys. This problem is severe enough that it compromises these measures' use for poverty analysis without substantial investment in data correction and adjustments using administrative data. Fortunately, there is a growing evidence base on ways to make these corrections.

Accordingly, this concluding chapter contains (1) a list of priority areas for research and (2) recommendations for data collection and measurement, which if acted on will fill gaps in the literature and evidence base and make it possible to evaluate program and policy changes that may be made on the basis of our conclusions. In this chapter we also discuss (3) how having high-quality monitoring and evaluation efforts in place will enable a future expert study committee to evaluate progress and identify further steps that may be needed to further reduce child poverty and deep poverty. We could not address the entire field of poverty and well-being research; rather, we focused on areas for which the absence of solid research findings most compromised the committee's ability to assess the effects of alternative programs and policies on child poverty reduction over a 10-year period.

Finally, this chapter concludes by underscoring the importance of a coordinated effort by relevant government agencies to set priorities for research and data collection so that scarce public resources can be used to their greatest effect. The U.S. social safety net is decentralized, with different agencies in charge of administering programs related to food, housing, energy, job training, medical care, and various kinds of income assistance. It is critical for these agencies to work together to provide for cost-effective data collection, monitoring of program administration and child outcomes, and research on the benefits and costs of the nation's current and proposed efforts to reduce child poverty.

PRIORITY AREAS FOR RESEARCH

In this section, we identify four priority areas for research on finding ways to (1) assist parents in obtaining sustained employment; (2) reduce uncertainty and fluctuations in income that make it difficult for low-income families to handle the daily challenges of living; (3) facilitate access for all families to programs for which they are qualified; and (4) help offset the added barriers to poverty reduction encountered by low-income families that are living in urban areas of concentrated poverty or in rural areas lacking transportation and community resources, by low-income families that face pervasive discrimination in housing, employment, and other areas, and by children who have a parent involved in the criminal justice system.

In addition, there are two areas for which we do not make formal recommendations, but which nonetheless deserve attention. First, among the major assistance programs, SSI and various kinds of housing assistance have undergone little evaluation to determine their effectiveness in reducing child poverty and improving child well-being. The agencies with responsibility for these programs need to subject them to rigorous assessment of these impacts.

Second, as we documented in Chapter 7, several family-related issues deserve further research. Despite extensive experimentation, there has been little success in devising programs with positive effects on marriage rates, despite the fact that child poverty would probably decline if more children were living in two-parent households. We are unable to identify specific programs that should be tested. However, we encourage the states, as they are testing work incentives (see next section), to seek out and test ideas for structuring benefits in a way that encourages marriage, or at least does not discourage it by penalizing families with married parents.

Two other family-related issues concern contraception and family leave. There is strong evidence that increasing awareness of and access to effective, safe, and affordable long-acting reversible contraception (LARC) reduces unplanned births, which in turn might reduce child poverty. States therefore have ample evidence that they could use to develop, test, and implement policies that promote the use of LARC. In addition, evidence from a small number of states suggests that paid family and medical leave may promote parental employment and improve child health, although it may reduce employment among women potentially eligible for such leave. It is therefore important to continue evaluating the labor-market, health, and poverty impacts on child poverty of state paid-leave laws.

We stress the importance of randomized controlled methodologies, where feasible, when evaluating the effectiveness of existing or proposed programs and policies for reducing child poverty and deep poverty. These methodologies can also provide evidence to help achieve other program goals that can improve child well-being, such as increasing marriage rates and parents' labor force participation. Such experiments, while not without problems (e.g., missing data, attrition, small samples, high relative cost; see Deaton and Cartwright, 2018; National Research Council, 2010), make it possible to draw causal inferences—and not just correlational associations—concerning the effects of alternative policies.

Although we stress the importance of experiments, we recognize that it is often impossible to carry out controlled experimentation. For example, understanding the longer-term effects of alternative policies might require an experiment lasting far longer than resource constraints, family consent, and attrition from the experiment would allow. When random assignment of families to treatment groups is not an option, alternative methods can often provide compelling evidence on the effects of different regimes. Such methods include regression discontinuity, instrumental variables, propensity score matching, and case control studies, among others.

Analyses of natural experiments can also provide strong evidence of program effects. This approach might be useful, for example, in assessing the poverty-reducing effects of Medicaid expansion based on before-and-after comparisons of states that have and those have not implemented expansion. These before-and-after methods could also be applied to data gathered in health surveys to study policy effects on child and parental biomarkers and mental health. Quasi-experimental methods can be especially helpful for determining the long-term effects of policies to alleviate child poverty on earnings, chronic diseases, and other important components of intergenerational mobility. In fact, much of what we know about long-term outcomes derives from studies with these research designs.

Data from randomized experiments and quasi-experiments often turn up evidence of differential effects of policies on different groups, although these findings should be subject to further testing in cases where analyzing such differences is not part of the original research design. In addition to experimentation and quasi-experimentation, other kinds of research can be used to (1) identify policy features that merit the use of scarce resources for rigorous but expensive research methods; (2) help understand the circumstances and family situations for which a given program might be more or less successful; and (3) help identify aspects of program administration that affect child outcomes. Research methods for these purposes include process analysis, which could look at the details of how programs operate; qualitative analysis, through which community sociologists could examine families' circumstances and behaviors; and correlational analysis, which could suggest promising avenues for poverty reduction and other policy goals, based on ex-postanalysis of multivariate data, that warrant experimentation. (For an assessment of the strengths and weaknesses of various research methods, see National Research Council, 2001, Ch. 4, and National Academies of Sciences, Engineering, and Medicine, 2016, Ch. 6.)

In the recommendations that follow, for the sake of readability, rather than name every agency that could benefit from each proposed action, we call on "relevant agencies" to take appropriate action, on the assumption that agencies will be able to identify those recommendations that are relevant to their missions. The last section discusses the need for a coordination of efforts among the many relevant agencies, including a role for the U.S. Office of Management and Budget (OMB), as well as the need for making administrative data available to qualified researchers outside those agencies for the purposes of program evaluation.

Research on Effective Work-Oriented
Child Poverty-Reduction Programs

Historically, an important goal of programs to reduce child poverty in the United States has been to move low-income families from reliance on government assistance to greater participation in the labor force. If government is to reach appropriate conclusions about which policies will have the largest effects on poverty reduction and labor force participation, it needs a solid and reliable body of research evidence. Much of what is known about the effects of work-oriented features of assistance programs on poverty, government budgets, and society at large (see Chapter 7) comes from many well-run experiments that states conducted before the 1996 welfare reform (Grogger and Karoly, 2005; Haskins and Margolis, 2014; National Research Council, 2001). That research was largely a response to the requirement by the U.S. Department of Health and Human Services that states rigorously assess the effects of program modifications as a condition for obtaining waivers to implement them (Gueron and Rolston, 2013).

In recent years, however, states seeking to test new work-oriented programs, especially those including work requirements, have often chosen evaluations with methodologically weak designs, which have produced unreliable and misleading results (Mitchell, 2018). Low-quality evaluations are a waste of public funds and can harm the public discussion of the merits of new programs. When the government agencies that grant waivers do not prioritize high-quality evaluations, they fail to ensure that the public discussion of the programs' strengths and weaknesses is based on strong evidence. Federal agencies therefore should require states to conduct rigorous and scientifically valid evaluations of any new programs implemented as a result of the waiver process.

> RECOMMENDATION 9-1: Relevant federal departments and agencies, especially those granting waivers to state and local governments to test new work-related programs, should prioritize high-quality, methodologically rigorous research and experimentation to identify ways to boost the job skills and employment of parents of low-income families receiving public assistance. Congress should ensure that sufficient funding is made available to conduct these evaluations.

Research on Features of Assistance Program Administration That Will Enhance the Financial Stability of Low-Income Families

We have documented the financial instability that makes it difficult for many low-income families to juggle everyday challenges and find stable housing, for example when they lack the funds for a deposit and the first month's rent. Low-income families are also vulnerable to financial catastrophe triggered by a loss of employment, a reduction in work hours, the loss of transportation, or other changes in parents' circumstances—which can have dire consequences for children.

We recommend rigorous evaluation of those features of assistance programs that might make it easier for families to obtain and retain benefits. Examples include methods for integrating and streamlining enrollment across multiple program areas (e.g., housing, food, energy) and simplified procedures for updating information so that families retain eligibility. It would also be useful to experiment with different ways of offering short-term financial assistance, such as to enable families to pay a deposit on a rental unit or a large car-repair bill, as well as ways to make existing benefit payments more frequent (e.g., for the Earned Income Tax Credit or EITC), in the interest of accommodating families' needs.

> **RECOMMENDATION 9-2:** Relevant federal departments and agencies should prioritize research and experimentation aimed at finding ways to reduce the financial instability of low-income families participating in assistance programs. Program features that may contribute to this goal and merit evaluation include streamlined program administration, more convenient access to the benefits that families are eligible to receive, provisions for emergency assistance, and flexibility in the frequency of benefit payments.

Research on Features of Assistance Program Administration That Will Reduce Barriers to Access by All Population Groups

The passage of legislation or implementing regulations to improve the government's safety net for low-income families with children is necessary but insufficient to achieve the desired reductions in child poverty and other priority outcomes. In addition to being run as efficiently as possible, programs need to focus on ensuring equitable access to all families who qualify for benefits. In this report we have documented disparities in program take-up rates (e.g., for SNAP benefits) both among states and among demographic groups. While a number of factors may produce such disparities, cumbersome or demeaning enrollment procedures can prevent potential beneficiaries from accessing resources to which they are entitled. Another barrier to access is simply the lack of awareness that programs are available, including awareness of any new program features, such as the provision of emergency assistance. Multifaceted experimentation and other research on ways to reduce these kinds of barriers ought to be high priorities.

> **RECOMMENDATION 9-3:** Relevant federal departments and agencies should prioritize research and experimentation designed to improve the administration of assistance programs, especially to facilitate full and equitable access to the benefits to which low-income families are entitled. Such research should focus not only on streamlining program processes but also on making outreach about programs more effective, enhancing the communication skills of program staff, and strengthening program staff's ability to interact with all population groups.

Research on Reducing Barriers to the Effectiveness of Assistance Programs Resulting from Contextual Factors Affecting Families

Not all low-income families face the same problems as they attempt to climb out of poverty with the help of government assistance programs. Families that live in urban neighborhoods with concentrated poverty (with poverty rates of 40 percent or higher)[2] or in depressed rural areas that lack transportation and community resources are particularly likely to face obstacles to gainful employment and other means of improving their economic situations. Families in which a parent has a chronic disease or is disabled face similar challenges, as do families that routinely encounter discrimination in employment, housing, medical care, and other areas because of their race or ethnicity. Compounding the obstacles to economic betterment that confront minority low-income families is the fact that they are more likely than White families to live in areas of concentrated poverty and to have a parent involved in the criminal justice system.

Income assistance programs, which are the focus of our report, cannot in isolation be expected to significantly reduce neighborhood segregation, discrimination in realms such as employment, or mass incarceration. However, as described in Chapter 8, these programs can help reduce the negative impacts of such conditions on families' access to and use of benefits designed to reduce child poverty. Meanwhile, research is needed to identify and combat discriminatory behaviors, such as neglecting to inform minority families of child care vouchers and other available benefits. Along with that, experimentation is needed to find ways to improve minority families' job prospects. The latter may include providing active assistance in job searches, working directly with major employers to help low-income and formerly incarcerated parents gain a foothold in the labor market, and helping families move to neighborhoods with better public transportation and other supports.

It is also important to note that administrative changes that give more discretion to case workers, for example so they can respond to families experiencing emergencies, may also increase opportunities for discriminatory behavior. This is a tradeoff that needs to be explicitly recognized, studied, and addressed.

RECOMMENDATION 9-4: Relevant federal departments and agencies should prioritize research and experimentation designed to find ways to mitigate the effects of contextual factors that impair the effectiveness of current programs to combat child poverty. These contextual

---

[2] For more information on concentrated poverty, see https://www.cbpp.org/sites/default/files/atoms/files/11-3-15hous2.pdf.

factors include (1) detrimental neighborhood conditions, such as those found in urban areas of concentrated poverty and rural areas with limited transportation and/or access to community resources; (2) racial and social discrimination in employment and housing; and (3) adverse consequences of the criminal justice system, which disproportionately affect poor people, especially minorities. Such research should focus on population groups that are known to be most harmed by discrimination and bias and most likely to face adverse contexts that worsen their families' poverty and their ability to overcome it.

IMPROVEMENTS IN DATA COLLECTION AND MEASUREMENT

Better data can be just as important as closing the research gaps in the effort to assess promising anti-child-poverty initiatives. Improved federal statistics on income and poverty threshold components are also needed to better inform policy makers and the public.

We have prioritized four improvements in data and measures: (1) the addition of relevant variables to surveys and administrative records to better assess the impact of contextual factors on child poverty programs; (2) the expansion of sample sizes for small populations of policy interest; (3) the use of administrative records to correct reported income and program benefits in the Current Population Survey Annual Social and Economic Supplement (CPS ASEC), which is the basis of both the Official Poverty Measure (OPM) and the SPM; and (4) an assessment of the merits of a Health-Inclusive Poverty Measure (HIPM, see Chapter 7) to capture more fully than the SPM does the effects on child poverty of changes to Medicaid and other medical care assistance programs. Improvement of household expenditure data would also be helpful for analyzing consumption patterns and the relationship between income poverty and consumption poverty, and in the longer run it would be helpful for developing a consumption-based measure of poverty.

Collecting Relevant Variables to Analyze Program Effectiveness and Child Poverty

The portfolio of ongoing federal household surveys provides a rich array of data for tracking child poverty and other indicators of child well-being. However, some important variables are systematically missing from both surveys and program administrative records. Having family members involved in the criminal justice system, about which surveys rarely collect information, is a prime example. Surveys rarely ask whether family members are or have been incarcerated or on probation or parole (see National Academies of Sciences, Engineering, and Medicine, 2017a). Similarly, criminal justice records are rarely linked to assistance program records. More generally, it is important for relevant program agencies and statistical agencies to systematically review the extent to which existing and proposed data collections include important variables for the analysis of low-income families' participation in assistance programs, characteristics of parents that are important for understanding child outcomes, and trends in child poverty and other indicators of child well-being. Based on that review, the next step is for agencies to identify priority data gaps and to develop plans, in conjunction with OMB's Statistical Policy Division and relevant OMB budget units, for filling these gaps.

> **RECOMMENDATION 9-5: Relevant federal program agencies and statistical agencies, working with the U.S. Office of Management and Budget, should review relevant data collection programs and proposed programs, including surveys and administrative records, to ensure that they include measures for monitoring and assessing the effects of assistance programs, family characteristics, and contextual factors on child poverty and other child outcomes. For example, surveys on income, wealth, and program participation should obtain information about family members who are currently incarcerated or on parole or probation, using techniques that are known to facilitate response, to support research on how these circumstances may increase child poverty.**

Collecting Data on Small Populations for Analyzing Child Poverty

Household surveys use probability samples to collect information, a method that costs less and imposes less of a burden on respondents than a complete population census would. Surveys intended to yield the data necessary for analyzing income and poverty, such as the CPS ASEC, employ a sufficient sample size for major population groups (the CPS ASEC includes 100,000 households each year), but their sample size is not sufficient to allow the analysis of small population groups that merit particular attention in the context of child poverty. While the American Community Survey, which includes 3 million households each year,[3] can provide poverty estimates for small population groups, it lacks the richness of content to support detailed analysis of program effects on child outcomes.

An important example of this problem concerns the American Indian and Alaska Native (AIAN) population, about which there is a dearth of

---

[3] See https://www.census.gov/topics/income-poverty/poverty/guidance/data-sources/acs-vs-cps.html.

data, particularly on children. Because of the relatively small size of this population, it often goes uncounted in national surveys or is combined with other small racial/ethnic groups. Moreover, evaluations of the effectiveness of programs and policies designed to combat child poverty—whether provided by a tribe or by federal or state governments—have rarely been conducted for this population, even though AIAN families have very high poverty rates and other deficits, such as poor health.

Other groups for which small sample sizes make analysis difficult (assuming the group is identified in the first place) include children with disabilities and children with one or both parents incarcerated or on parole. Data on such small populations can be obtained by adding supplemental samples to existing surveys on a periodic basis. For example, additional samples can be rotated so that one small group, such as AIAN households with children, is oversampled in one year and another group, such as households that have children with disabilities, is oversampled in another. In addition, targeted surveys can be fielded at regular intervals. Finally, program agencies could be required to include relevant variables, such as child disabilities and AIAN status, in their administrative records.

> **RECOMMENDATION 9-6: Federal program agencies and statistical agencies working with the U.S. Office of Management and Budget should explore ways to obtain sufficient sample sizes for the analysis of small population groups of concern for child poverty. Such groups include American Indian and Alaska Native families, families that have children with disabilities, and families with one or both parents involved in the criminal justice system. Methods to consider include adding supplemental samples to existing surveys on a rotating basis, fielding targeted surveys periodically, and ensuring that assistance program records include relevant variables for analysis.**

Improving Measures of Income and Poverty

Estimates of income, poverty, and assistance program participation that are derived from major federal household surveys, including the CPS ASEC, the American Community Survey, and the Survey of Income and Program Participation (SIPP), are followed closely by policy analysts and researchers and serve to inform the public as well as policy makers. However, over time the completeness and accuracy of survey respondents' reports have declined.

When CPS ASEC estimates of recipients and amounts of income from various programs are compared with administrative records, one finds high rates of net underreporting. In 2006–2007, for example, the CPS captured only 83 percent of benefits paid out from the EITC, only 68 percent of unemployment insurance benefits, and only 54 percent of SNAP benefits (Meyer, Mok, and Sullivan, 2009, Tables 3, 8, 10). Similarly, child support receipts reported in the 2017 CPS are only 75 percent of payments distributed to families recorded by the Office of Child Support Enforcement (Grall, 2018; and Office of Child Support Enforcement, 2018). This underreporting has persisted even after the Census Bureau has imputed missing amounts for respondents who say they participated in a program but did not provide an amount, and even after it has reweighted the data to reproduce population estimates by age, gender, and race and ethnicity.

In Chapter 2 we described the TRIM3 model procedures for correcting the underreporting of receipt and amounts of major assistance programs, specifically SNAP, SSI, and Temporary Assistance to Needy Families (TANF), in the CPS ASEC; without such adjustments, the SPM poverty rate for children in 2015 would have been 3.3 percentage points higher. Yet the TRIM3 adjustments, which use published aggregate statistics such as total SNAP beneficiaries, cannot be as accurate as adjustments that could be made by the Census Bureau using administrative records for individuals and households. Moreover, TRIM3 does not attempt to adjust for underreporting of other income types, such as child support, pensions, interest, or dividends (see Chapter 2). Several reports by expert panels of the Committee on National Statistics have recommended that the Census Bureau use administrative records to correct for reporting errors in the CPS ASEC and the SIPP (see, e.g., National Research Council, 1989, 2009). To date, the Census Bureau has used the administrative records to which it has access for statistical purposes to evaluate reporting in its surveys, but not to adjust the data.

One impediment is that the Census Bureau lacks ready access to most state administrative records. (States maintain records for SNAP, Medicaid, unemployment insurance, TANF, and workers' compensation.) Also, the Census Bureau would require additional budget resources to redesign its questionnaires and processes to permit integration of survey responses and administrative records. There are also concerns as to the legal authority for using records to replace survey responses, although Title 13 of the U.S. Code[4] authorizes the Secretary of Commerce (on behalf of the Census Bureau) to obtain and use records to the extent possible in place of direct inquiries.

Over the past decade there has been a growing recognition of the need to use administrative records together with surveys to improve the quality of the data on which important statistics are based by adopting a multiple-data-sources paradigm instead of a survey paradigm (see National Academies of Sciences, Engineering, and Medicine, 2017b, III-3). In 2014,

---

[4] U.S. Code, Title 13, Chapter 1, Subchapter I, § 6.

OMB issued guidance stating that the use of federal administrative records should be routinely considered when compiling federal statistics (Office of Management and Budget, 2014). The more recent report of the Commission on Evidence-Based Policymaking (2017, Ch. 2) includes several recommendations for enhancing the government's ability to use administrative records for evidence-based program evaluation and policy research.[5]

We add our voice to those of other institutions underscoring the importance of producing high-quality statistics that accurately reflect levels of and trends in household income, poverty, and program participation. Organizations such as the Urban Institute (in producing its TRIM3 model) and the Congressional Budget Office have done invaluable service by producing adjusted income statistics to inform policy debate. Nonetheless, it ought to be the role of the responsible federal statistical agency, which can gain access to microlevel administrative records for statistical purposes, to regularly produce authoritative income statistics to ensure that everyone is using the same high-quality information for public discussion and policy analysis.

It would also be useful for the Census Bureau to conduct or commission research on the OPM, anchored SPM, unanchored SPM, and consumption-based measures of poverty to see which of these measures more accurately track other measurements of disadvantage and hardship, such as food insecurity, both over time and across space.

RECOMMENDATION 9-7: Relevant federal departments and agencies, together with the Office of Management and Budget, should work with the Census Bureau to obtain and use administrative records in conjunction with household surveys to improve the quality of the official income, poverty, and program participation estimates that are needed by the public, policy makers, program analysts, and researchers. It is understood that research access to microdata for linked datasets would be governed by relevant laws and regulations for protecting data confidentiality and individual privacy.

Developing a Health-Inclusive Poverty Measure (HIPM)

Extensive evidence points to the positive effects of Medicaid and the Children's Health Insurance Program (CHIP) on child outcomes. Yet the SPM measure used throughout this report, while a significant improvement on the OPM, provides no way to translate the resources transferred to low-income families by health insurance coverage into a trustworthy estimate of poverty reduction. While the SPM takes into account medical

---

[5] Available: https://www.whitehouse.gov/wp-content/uploads/2018/06/Government-Reform-and-Reorg-Plan.pdf.

out-of-pocket (MOOP) expenses, such as premiums and copayments, its thresholds do not include an allowance for medical care needs, and its measurement of family resources does not directly capture the benefits of Medicaid or other health insurance coverage.

In Chapter 7, we describe an approach that seeks to turn the SPM into an HIPM by adding needs for health care insurance to the SPM poverty thresholds and adding health insurance coverage benefits (net of MOOP) to SPM-defined family resources. The proposal uses the Affordable Care Act's Silver Plan provisions as the basis for the threshold amounts and benefits, including caps on premium and nonpremium MOOP expenses, so that families never have benefits added that exceed what the Affordable Care Act deems to be acceptable cost-sharing. Using this HIPM, Medicaid is estimated to have reduced child poverty by over 5 percentage points in 2014 (Korenman, Remler, and Hyson, 2017).

We urge the agencies that produce the SPM—namely, the Bureau of Labor Statistics, which produces the thresholds, and the Census Bureau, which measures family resources and produces poverty estimates—to work with OMB and the Department of Health and Human Services on a plan to evaluate and move toward implementation of an HIPM.

> **RECOMMENDATION 9-8: The Bureau of Labor Statistics and the U.S. Census Bureau, working with the U.S. Office of Management and Budget and the U.S. Department of Health and Human Services, should move expeditiously to evaluate a Health-Inclusive Poverty Measure (HIPM) of the kind illustrated in this report. Using the evaluation results, these agencies should proceed to implement an HIPM that builds on the Supplemental Poverty Measure. Such a measure would permit a fuller assessment of the effectiveness of health insurance programs, such as Medicaid, in reducing measured child poverty.**

CONTINUED MONITORING AND PROGRAM EVALUATION

Provided that the above-described improvements can be made in research and data sources to fill important gaps in what is known about effective child anti-poverty programs, executive branch agencies and Congress (when legislation is needed) should be able to identify promising program features to implement at scale. It is important that program budgets, whether for new or current programs, include sufficient resources for data collection to enable continuous monitoring of program operations and child outcomes.

Needed data may require the inclusion of additional variables in ongoing federal household surveys, additional variables collected in the course of program administration, and new targeted surveys. Budgets also need to include sufficient resources for regular program evaluation and research to support further improvements in program effectiveness. Similarly, budgets for block grant programs like TANF—which allow state governments considerable latitude in their design and administration—need to include resources for data collection, program evaluation, and research.

In other words, implementation of a new or modified income assistance program, whether at the federal or state level, should not signal an end to relevant data collection and research, as occurred to some extent following welfare reform in the mid-1990s. Instead, it ought to be standard practice for policy makers to require continued monitoring and evaluation and to ensure that resources are available to determine where program innovations are and are not working and what further improvements may be possible.

Our recommendation in this regard comports with recommendations for program evaluation contained in the 2017 report by the Commission on Evidence-Based Policymaking. Recommendations 5-1 through 5-6 from that 2017 report call for each department to have a chief evaluation officer, a trained evidence-building workforce, and a multiyear learning agenda; for OMB to coordinate evidence-building activities across departments; for streamlined procedures for approving data collection to support evidence-based policy; and for sufficient resources to support evidence-based program design, implementation, and evaluation. Several of these recommendations by the Commission are adopted in the administration's June 19, 2018, report, *Delivering Government Solutions in the 21st Century— Reform Plan and Reorganization Recommendations*, which includes a section on strengthening federal evaluation.[6] They are also included in the recently passed Foundations for Evidence-Based Policymaking Act of 2018.[7]

> RECOMMENDATION 9-9: Federal and state executive agencies and legislatures should ensure that child anti-poverty assistance programs require and include adequate resources for regular monitoring of program operations and child outcomes, as well as for rigorous program evaluation and research on ways to improve program effectiveness.

COORDINATING RESEARCH AND DATA PRIORITIES ACROSS DEPARTMENTS

Our report lays out packages of anti-poverty programs that have the potential to cut child poverty and deep poverty by one-half within 10 years.

---

[6] Available: https://www.whitehouse.gov/wp-content/uploads/2018/06/Government-Reform-and-Reorg-Plan.pdf.

[7] Available: https://bipartisanpolicy.org/blog/congress-provides-new-foundation-for-evidence-based-policymaking.

It also identifies priorities for research and data collection to fill important gaps in the evidence base, thereby paving the way for further improvements in the effectiveness of programs designed to combat child poverty. We hope the relevant agencies and the U.S. Congress will take our conclusions and recommendations seriously and act on them.

As we noted earlier, however, responsibilities for administering the federal safety net are spread among half a dozen cabinet departments: the U.S. Departments of Agriculture, Energy, Health and Human Services, Housing and Urban Development, Labor, and Treasury, as well as the U.S. Social Security Administration. Responsibilities for data collection, program evaluation, and research on program improvements are similarly dispersed. State agencies, working with their federal counterparts, play an important role in the administration of many assistance programs.

Assuming that stakeholders—Congress, federal and state agencies, and the public—agree that further reduction of child poverty is a priority goal for U.S. policy, we offer a final recommendation: A coordinating mechanism should be put in place to ensure that our report is followed up and that well-considered decisions are made establishing priorities for new and improved assistance programs and supporting the associated research and data needed for monitoring, evaluation, and further improvement. We believe that the Office of Management and Budget is the appropriate agency to coordinate the assessment of our conclusions and recommendations and to put together an action plan.

In response to the 1995 National Research Council report calling for a new approach to poverty measurement, OMB acted on the report's recommendation that it play a lead role by establishing a technical working group of relevant agencies to assess and refine the panel's recommendations. The result of that action was the SPM. Similarly, OMB regularly leads interagency committees on such matters as the content of the decennial census, the American Community Survey, and SIPP. In its 2017 report (p. 6), the Commission on Evidence-Based Policymaking specifically assigned a lead role to OMB to coordinate evidence-based policymaking in the federal government:

> REC. 5-3: The Congress and the President should direct the Office of Management and Budget (OMB) to coordinate the federal government's evidence-building activities across departments, including by undertaking any necessary reorganization or consolidation within OMB and by bolstering the visibility and role of interagency councils.

We conclude our report with a similar recommendation:

RECOMMENDATION 9-10: The Office of Management and Budget (OMB) should convene working groups of appropriate federal program, research, and statistical agencies to assess this report's conclusions about program packages that are capable of reducing child poverty by half within 10 years of adoption. OMB should also convene working groups charged with assessing the report's recommendations for research and data collection to fill important gaps in knowledge about effective anti-child-poverty programs. These working groups should be tasked with recommending action steps, and OMB should work with the relevant agencies to draw up implementation plans and secure appropriate resources. The working groups should consult with the relevant state agencies and outside experts, as appropriate, to inform their deliberations.

REFERENCES

Commission on Evidence-Based Policymaking. (2017). *The Promise of Evidence-Based Policymaking.* Washington, DC. Available: https://cep.gov/content/dam/cep/report/cep-final-report.pdf.

Deaton, A., and Cartwright, N. (2018). Understanding and misunderstanding randomized controlled trials. *Social Science & Medicine, 210,* 2–21.

Grall, T. (2018). *Custodial Mothers and Fathers and Their Child Support: 2015.* Current Population Reports. Washington, DC: U.S. Census Bureau.

Grogger, J., and Karoly, L.A. (2005). *Welfare Reform: Effects of a Decade of Change.* Cambridge, MA: Harvard University Press.

Gueron, J.M., and Rolston, H. (2013). *Fighting for Reliable Evidence.* New York: Russell Sage Foundation.

Haskins, R., and Margolis, G. (2014). *Show Me the Evidence: Obama's Fight for Rigor and Results in Social Policy.* Washington, DC: Brookings Institution Press.

Korenman, S., Remler, D.K., and Hyson, R. (2017). *Accounting for the Impact of Medicaid on Child Poverty.* Washington, DC: The National Academies Press.

Meyer, B., Mok, W.K.C., and Sullivan, J.X. (2009). *The Under-Reporting of Transfers in Household Surveys: Its Nature and Consequences.* NBER Working Paper No. 15181. Cambridge, MA: National Bureau of Economic Research. Available: https://doi.org/10.3386/w15181.

Mitchell, T. (2018). *Some House Leaders Ignore Evidence, Cite Flawed Reports to Justify Taking Basic Assistance Away from Needy Individuals.* Washington, DC: Center for Budget and Policy Priorities. Available: https://www.cbpp.org/sites/default/files/atoms/files/4-18-18tanf.pdf.

National Academies of Sciences, Engineering, and Medicine. (2016). *Commercial Motor Vehicle Driver Fatigue, Long-Term Health, and Highway Safety: Research Needs.* Washington, DC: The National Academies Press.

_____. (2017a). *Improving Collection of Indicators of Criminal Justice System Involvement in Population Health Data Programs: Proceedings of a Workshop.* Washington, DC: The National Academies Press. Available: https://doi.org/10.17226/24633.

_____. (2017b). *Principles and Practices for a Federal Statistical Agency, Sixth Edition.* Washington, DC: The National Academies Press. Available: https://doi.org/10.17226/24810.

National Research Council. (1989). *The Future of the Survey of Income and Program Participation.* Washington, DC: National Academy Press. Available: https://doi.org/10.17226/2072.

_____. (1995). *Measuring Poverty: A New Approach.* Washington, DC: National Academy Press.

_____. (2001). *Evaluating Welfare Reform in an Era of Transition.* Washington, DC: The National Academies Press. Available: https://doi.org/10.17226/10020.

_____. (2009). *Reengineering the Survey of Income and Program Participation.* Washington, DC: The National Academies Press. Available: https://doi.org/10.17226/12715.

_____. (2010). *The Prevention and Treatment of Missing Data in Clinical Trials.* Washington, DC: The National Academies Press. Available: https://doi.org/10.17226/12955.

Office of Child Support Enforcement. (2018). *Preliminary Report FY 2017.* Washington, DC: U.S. Department of Health and Human Services. Available: https://www.acf.hhs.gov/css/resource/fy-2017-preliminary-data-report.

Office of Management and Budget. (2014). *Guidance for Providing and Using Administrative Data for Statistical Purposes.* OMB Memorandum M-14-06. Washington, DC: Office of Management and Budget. Available: https://obamawhitehouse.archives.gov/sites/default/files/omb/memoranda/2014/m-14-06.pdf.

Appendix A

Biosketches of Committee Members and Project Staff

COMMITTEE MEMBERS

Greg Duncan *(Chair)* is a distinguished professor of education at the University of California, Irvine. Duncan spent the first 25 years of his career at the University of Michigan, working on and ultimately directing the Panel Study of Income Dynamics project. He held a faculty appointment at Northwestern University between 1995 and 2008. His recent work has focused on assessing the role of school-entry skills and behaviors on later school achievement and attainment and the effects that increasing income inequality has on schools and children's life chances. He was president of the Population Association of America in 2008 and of the Society for Research in Child Development between 2009 and 2011 and was elected to the National Academy of Sciences in 2010. Duncan holds a B.A. in economics from Grinnell College and a Ph.D. in economics from the University of Michigan. He has an honorary doctorate from the University of Essex.

J. Lawrence Aber is the Willner family professor of psychology and public policy at the Steinhardt School of Culture, Education, and Human Development and university professor at New York University, where he also chairs the board of the Institute of Human Development and Social Change and is co-director of Global TIES for Children, an international research center. Aber is the former director of the National Center for Children in Poverty at Columbia University. An internationally recognized expert in child development and social policy, he has co-edited a number of

275

books on the intersection of these fields. Aber's basic research examines the influence of poverty and violence, at the family and community levels, on the social, emotional, behavioral, cognitive, and academic development of children and youth. He also designs and conducts rigorous evaluations of innovative programs and policies for children, youth, and families. He has served on numerous National Academies committees. Aber holds a Ph.D. in clinical-community and developmental psychology from Yale University.

Dolores Acevedo-Garcia is Samuel F. and Rose B. Gingold professor of human development and social policy and director of the Institute for Child, Youth, and Family Policy at the Heller School for Social Policy and Management, Brandeis University. Her research focuses on the social determinants of racial/ethnic inequities in health, the role of social policies in reducing those inequities, and the health and well-being of children with special needs. She is also project director for diversitydatakids.org, a comprehensive research program and indicator database on child well-being and opportunity by race and ethnicity across multiple sectors (such as education, health, and neighborhoods) and geographies, which is funded by the W.K. Kellogg Foundation and the Robert Wood Johnson Foundation. She was a member of the MacArthur Foundation Research Network on How Housing Matters for Families and Children (2009–2014). She is a member of the editorial board of the journals *Social Problems; Cityscape* and the *Journal of Health and Social Behavior.* Acevedo-Garcia holds a B.A. in public administration from El Colegio de Mexico (Mexico City) and both a master's degree in public administration/urban and regional planning and a Ph.D. in public policy with a concentration in demography from the Woodrow Wilson School of Public and International Affairs at Princeton University.

Janet Currie is the Henry Putnam professor of economics and public affairs at Princeton University and the co-director of Princeton's Center for Health and Wellbeing. She also co-directs the Program on Families and Children at the National Bureau of Economic Research. She has served as the vice president of the American Economic Association, is an incoming president of the American Society of Health Economics, and is a member of both the National Academy of Medicine and the American Academy of Arts and Sciences. She is a fellow of the American Academy of Political and Social Science, the Society of Labor Economists, and the Econometric Society, and has honorary degrees from the University of Zurich and the University of Lyon. She has served on the Board of Reviewing Editors of *Science* and as the editor of the *Journal of Economic Literature,* as well as serving on the editorial board of the *Quarterly Journal of Economics* and many other economics journals. Her research focuses on health and well-being, especially concerning children. She has written about early intervention programs, programs to expand health insurance and improve health care, public housing, and food and nutrition programs. Her current research focuses on socioeconomic differences in health and access to health care, environmental threats to health, and mental health. Currie holds a Ph.D. in economics from Princeton University.

Benard P. Dreyer, past president (2016) of the American Academy of Pediatrics (AAP), is a general and development-behavioral pediatrician who has spent his professional lifetime serving poor children and families. He is also professor of pediatrics at New York University, where he leads the Division of Developmental-Behavioral Pediatrics, and director of pediatrics at Bellevue, where he works as a hospitalist. For more than 30 years he led a primary care program at Bellevue, including co-located mental and oral health services and clinics in homeless shelters. His research focuses on interventions in primary care to improve early childhood outcomes, including early brain development and obesity. Dreyer has held numerous positions on AAP task forces and executive and research committees and is also the medical director of policies for the AAP, which produces more than 80 policies and clinical reports each year. He was president of the Academic Pediatric Association and founded and chairs the association's Task Force on Childhood Poverty and its Research Scholars Program. He also hosts a weekly radio show, On Call for Kids, on the Sirius XM Doctor Radio channel. He has served on multiple roundtables, committees, and planning committees for the National Academies. Dreyer holds an M.D. from the New York University School of Medicine.

Irwin Garfinkel is the Mitchell I. Ginsberg professor of contemporary urban problems and co-founding director of the Columbia Population Research Center. Previously, Dr. Garfinkel was the director of the Institute for Research on Poverty (1975–1980) and the School of Social Work (1982–1984), both at the University of Wisconsin. Between 1980 and 1990, he was the principal investigator of the Wisconsin child support study. His research on child support and welfare influenced legislation in Wisconsin and other states in the United States, in the U.S. Congress, and in Great Britain, Australia, and Sweden. A social worker and an economist by training, he has authored or coauthored more than 200 scientific articles and 16 books and edited volumes on poverty, income transfers, program evaluation, single-parent families and child support, and the welfare state. He was a member of the committee for the Workshop on Design of the National Children's Study Main Study and a member of the Panel on Data and Methods for Measuring the Effects of Changes in Social Welfare Programs. Garfinkel holds a Ph.D. in social work and economics from the University of Michigan.

Ron Haskins is a senior fellow and holds the Cabot Family Chair in Economic Studies at the Brookings Institution, where he co-directs the Center on Children and Families. He is also a senior consultant at the Annie E. Casey Foundation and was president of the Association for Public Policy Analysis and Management in 2016. He is the coauthor of several books on welfare reform social policy. Beginning in 1986, he spent 14 years on the staff of the House Ways and Means Committee, and subsequently he was appointed to be the senior advisor to President George W. Bush for welfare policy. He and his Brookings colleague Isabel Sawhill were recently awarded the Moynihan Prize by the American Academy of Political and Social Science for being champions of the public good and advocates for public policy based on social science research. He was recently appointed by House Speaker Paul Ryan to cochair the Commission on Evidence-based Policymaking. Haskins holds a B.A., M.A., and Ph.D. in developmental psychology, all from the University of North Carolina at Chapel Hill.

Hilary Hoynes is a professor of public policy and economics and holds the Haas Distinguished Chair in Economic Disparities at the University of California, Berkeley, where she also codirects the Berkeley Opportunity Lab. She is a member of the American Academy of Arts and Sciences and a fellow of the Society of Labor Economists. She has served as co-editor of the *American Economic Review* and the *American Economic Journal: Economic Policy* and is on the editorial board of the *American Economic Review: Insights*. Hoynes currently serves on the American Economic Association's Executive Committee and on the State of California Task Force on Lifting Children and Families out of Poverty, while her many previous appointments include membership on the Commission on Evidence-based Policymaking. In 2014, she received the Carolyn Shaw Bell Award from the American Economic Association. Her research focuses on poverty and inequality and the impacts of government programs on low-income families. Current projects include evaluating the effects of access to the social safety net in early life on outcomes in later life, as well as the role of the safety net in mitigating income losses. Hoynes holds a Ph.D. in economics from Stanford University.

Christine James-Brown became president and chief executive officer of the Child Welfare League of America (CWLA) in April 2007, assuming the leadership of the nation's oldest and largest membership-based child welfare organization. She came to CWLA from United Way International, where she had served since 2004 as the organization's fifth president and CEO. As president and CEO, she was responsible for the efforts of the world-wide network of United Way nonprofit member organizations spanning six continents and five regions and serving communities in 45 countries and territories. She has served as a member of the boards of the School District of Philadelphia, Community College of Philadelphia, the Samuel S. Fels Fund, the Greater Philadelphia Chamber of Commerce, Citizens Bank, Public/Private Ventures, and the Pennsylvania Bar Association Judicial Evaluation Commission. She has received numerous awards and recognition throughout her career, including the National Council of Negro Women's Mary McLeod Bethune Award, B'nai B'rith's Humanitarian Award, and Operation Understanding's Distinguished Community Leadership Award. In 1996, she received an honorary doctorate from Drexel University in Philadelphia, Pennsylvania. James-Brown holds a B.A. in cultural anthropology from Rutgers University.

Vonnie C. McLoyd is the Ewart A. C. Thomas collegiate professor of psychology in the College of Literature, Science, and the Arts at the University of Michigan. McLoyd's scholarship helped shape the field of developmental psychology by focusing on how a child develops socially and how social interactions influence cognitive development, shedding light on the ways in which the environment and social context, especially race, ethnicity, and poverty, influence development. Her work has helped change the perspective of the field and has led to a widespread recognition of how socio-environmental factors influence the health, well-being, and developmental experiences of children, adolescents, and their families. Most notable among the many honors McLoyd has received is a MacArthur Fellowship, which was awarded in 1996. Other scholarly activities include participation in the MacArthur Network on Transition to Adulthood, the Council of the Foundation of Child Development, and the advisory board of the National Center for Children in Poverty. She has also served as a member of the Board on Children, Youth, and Families at the National Academies. McLoyd holds a Ph.D. in psychology from the University of Michigan.

Robert Moffitt is the Krieger-Eisenhower professor of economics at Johns Hopkins University, where he has worked since 1995. He also holds a joint appointment at the Johns Hopkins School of Public Health. His research interests are in the areas of labor economics and applied microeconometrics. He is a fellow of the Econometric Society, a fellow of the Society of Labor Economists, a national associate of the National Academy of Sciences, a recipient of a MERIT Award from the National Institutes of Health, a recipient of a Guggenheim fellowship, a fellow of the American Academy of Arts and Sciences, and past president of the Population Association of America. He has served as chief editor of the *American Economic Review* and the *Journal of Human Resources* and as co-editor of the *Review of Economics and Statistics*. He has also served on multiple

National Academies panels, including the Committee for the Behavioral and Social Sciences and Education, the Panel on Data and Methods for Measuring the Effects of Changes in Social Welfare Programs, the Panel to Evaluate Microsimulation Models for Social Welfare Programs, and the Panel to Evaluate Welfare Reform, which he chaired. Moffitt holds a Ph.D. in economics from Brown University.

Cynthia Osborne is an associate professor and director of the Center for Health and Social Policy at the Lyndon B. Johnson School of Public Affairs at the University of Texas at Austin. She is also the director of the Child and Family Research Partnership, an in-house research group that conducts rigorous research on policy issues related to young children, adolescents, and their parents. Her teaching and research interests include social policy issues, poverty and inequality, family and child well-being, and family demography. Osborne has extensive experience leading long-term evaluations of state and national programs, with the aim of helping organizations understand what works and how to ensure sustainable implementation of effective policies. Her work includes evaluations for the Texas Home Visiting Program, the largest home visiting program in the country; for critical child welfare programs of the Texas Department of Family and Protective Services; and for key child support programs of the Texas Office of the Attorney General. She previously was director of the Lyndon B. Johnson School of Public Affairs' Project on Education Effectiveness and Quality, an initiative that measured state educator preparation programs' influence on student achievement. Osborne holds a Ph.D. in demography and public affairs from Princeton University.

Eldar Shafir is the Class of 1987 professor of behavioral science and public policy at Princeton University, the inaugural director of Princeton's Kahneman-Treisman Center for Behavioral Science and Public Policy, and cofounder and scientific director at ideas42, a social science research and development lab. He studies decision making, cognitive science, and behavioral economics. His recent research has focused on decision making in contexts of poverty and on the application of behavioral research to policy. He is past president of the Society for Judgment and Decision Making, and a member of the World Economic Forum's Global Council on Behavioural Science. He was a member of President Barack Obama's Advisory Council on Financial Capability. He has received several awards, most recently a Guggenheim fellowship, as well as the William James Book Award. He was named one of *Foreign Policy Magazine*'s 100 Leading Global Thinkers of 2013. Books he has edited or coauthored have addressed fundamental issues in understanding poverty and social policy. Shafir holds a Ph.D. in cognitive science from the Massachusetts Institute of Technology.

Timothy M. (Tim) Smeeding is the Lee Rainwater distinguished professor of public affairs and economics at the University of Wisconsin–Madison. He was director of the Institute for Research on Poverty from 2008 to 2014 and the founding director of the Luxembourg Income Study from 1983 to 2006. Smeeding's recent work has examined social and economic mobility across generations, inequality of income, consumption and wealth, and poverty in national and cross-national contexts, and he has authored several books on those topics. He is a member of the National Academy of Sciences' Standing Committee on the American Opportunity Study, and in the past has served on the Committee for Behavioral, Social Sciences and Education as well as multiple planning, steering, and other committees for the National Academies. He is also a member of the American Pediatrics Association Taskforce on Child Poverty. Smeeding holds a Ph.D. in economics from the University of Wisconsin–Madison.

Don E. Winstead, Jr., founded Don Winstead Consulting, LLC, a Tallahassee, Florida, health and human services consulting practice in 2011. He is a nationally recognized expert on federal funding issues and has negotiated ground-breaking federal waivers in welfare reform and child welfare. Winstead began his career as a front-line caseworker and has worked in a variety of direct service, administrative, and managerial positions ranging from social worker to deputy secretary of the Florida Department of Children and Families. He served as deputy secretary for a total of 8 years, serving under four secretaries and three governors. From late 2001 to early 2005, he served as deputy assistant secretary for human services policy at the U.S. Department of Health and Human Services. He is a member of the advisory board for the National Poverty Centers and is a past member of the board of directors of Child Trends, a nonprofit, nonpartisan research center that studies children at all stages of development. Winstead holds a B.A. in English from the University of South Florida.

PROJECT STAFF

Suzanne Le Menestrel (*Study Director*) is a senior program officer with the Board on Children, Youth, and Families at the National Academies, where her responsibilities have included directing four consensus studies focused on children and adolescents, from birth to age 21. Prior to her tenure with the National Academies, Le Menestrel was the founding national program leader for youth development research at 4-H National Headquarters, served as research director at the Academy for Educational Development's Center for Youth Development and Policy Research, and was a research associate at Child Trends. She was a founder of the *Journal of Youth Development: Bridging Research and Practice* and chaired its

Publications Committee. She has published in numerous refereed journals and is an invited member of several advisory groups, including a research advisory group for the American Camp Association, a Girl Scouts of the Nation's Capital STEM Strategy advisory group, and the National Leadership Steering Committee for the Cooperative Extension System–Robert Wood Johnson Foundation Culture of Health Initiative. Le Menestrel holds an M.S. and a Ph.D. in human development and family studies from the Pennsylvania State University, a B.S. in psychology from St. Lawrence University, and a nonprofit management executive certificate from Georgetown University.

Pamella Atayi has served since 2009 as a program coordinator on the Board on Children, Youth, and Families of the National Academies. She currently coordinates and oversees the work of support staff handling clerical, administrative, and logistical aspects of meetings. Atayi provides work direction and assists with the daily supervision of support staff. She also compiles and summarizes information for the development and revision of a variety of documents and participates in research efforts. She serves as a liaison between programs and boards of the National Academies and related external customers, members, and sponsors concerning clerical and administrative matters. She was awarded the Sandra H. Matthews Cecil Award by the Institute of Medicine (now Health and Medicine Division) in 2013 and the DBASSE Espirit de Corps Award in 2017. Atayi earned her B.A. in English from the University of Maryland University College and holds a diploma in computer information systems from Strayer University.

Constance F. Citro is a senior scholar with the Committee on National Statistics (CNSTAT) of the National Academies. She previously served as CNSTAT's director (2004–2017), acting chief of staff (2003–2004), and senior study director (1986–2003). She began her career with CNSTAT in 1984 as study director for the panel that produced *The Bicentennial Census: New Directions for Methodology* in 1990. Prior to joining CNSTAT, she held positions as vice president at both Mathematica Policy Research, Inc., and Data Use and Access Laboratories, Inc. Citro was an American Statistical Association/National Science Foundation/Census research fellow in 1985–1986 and is currently a fellow of the American Statistical Association and an elected member of the International Statistical Institute. She co-edited the 2nd through 6th editions and edited the 7th edition of *Principles and Practices for a Federal Statistical Agency* and contributed to studies on measuring racial discrimination, expanding access to research data, the usability of estimates from the American Community Survey, the National Children's Study research plan, and the Census Bureau's 2010 census program of experiments and evaluations. Citro holds a B.A. in political science from the University of Rochester and an M.A. and Ph.D. in political science from Yale University.

Christopher Mackie is a study director with the Committee on National Statistics of the National Academies, where he specializes in economic measurement and statistics. Mackie served most recently as study director for the Panel on the Economic and Fiscal Consequences of Immigration. His prior projects were on the measurement of self-reported well-being and on measuring civic engagement and social cohesion. He was study director for the expert committees that produced the reports, *At What Price? Conceptualizing and Measuring Cost-of-Living and Price Indexes*; *Beyond the Market: Designing Nonmarket Accounts for the United States*; *Understanding Business Dynamics: An Integrated Data System for America's Future*; *Accounting for Health and Health Care: Approaches to Measuring the Sources and Costs of Their Improvement*; *Improving Measurement of Productivity in Higher Education*; and *Subjective Well-being: Measuring Happiness, Suffering, and Other Dimensions of Experience*. He is author of *Canonizing Economic Theory: How Theories and Ideas Are Selected in Economics*. Mackie holds a Ph.D. in economics from the University of North Carolina and has held teaching positions at the University of North Carolina, North Carolina State University, and Tulane University.

Dara Shefska is a research associate on the Board on Children, Youth, and Families of the National Academies. Shefska supports two consensus studies. She joined the National Academies in 2015 as a research assistant on the Food and Nutrition Board, staffing the Roundtable on Obesity Solutions. In this role, she focused on early childhood obesity prevention, publications, and communications. She was awarded the Health and Medicine Division's Fineberg Impact Award in 2016 for her efforts to increase the visibility of roundtable workshops and publications. She holds a B.A. in urban geography from McGill University in Montreal, Quebec.

Elizabeth Townsend serves as an associate program officer on the Board on Children, Youth, and Families, supporting two consensus studies. Prior to joining these studies, Townsend was a research associate for the Board on Behavioral, Cognitive, and Sensory Sciences' Decadal Survey on Social and Behavioral Sciences for Applications to National Security. Under the Board on Children, Youth, and Families other studies that she has worked on produced the reports *Ethical Considerations for Research on Housing-Related Health Hazards Involving Children*; *Children's Health, the Nation's Wealth: Assessing and Improving Child Health*; and *Working Families and Growing Kids: Caring for Children and Adolescents*. Townsend holds a B.S. from Radford University and an M.P.H. from the University of Alabama at

Birmingham, where she interned at the Comprehensive Cancer Center and volunteered with the Alabama Vaccine Research Clinic and 1917 Clinic.

Appendix B

Public Session Agendas

PUBLIC INFORMATION-GATHERING SESSION

June 20, 2017

National Academy of Sciences
Lecture Room
2101 Constitution Avenue, NW
Washington, DC

1:00 – 1:05 pm   **Welcome and Goals**
Greg Duncan, Committee Chair, Distinguished Professor, University of California, Irvine

1:05 – 1:15 pm   **Remarks on Study Statement of Task**
Huilan Krenn, Director of Learning and Impact,
W.K. Kellogg Foundation

1:15 – 2:50 pm   **PANEL 1**
Moderator: Greg Duncan

Edgar Olsen, Professor of Economics and Public Policy, University of Virginia; Visiting Scholar, American Enterprise Institute

Isabel Sawhill, Senior Fellow in Economic Studies, Brookings Institution
Douglas Besharov, Professor of Public Policy, University of Maryland
W. Bradford Wilcox, Director, National Marriage Project and Professor of Sociology, University of Virginia; Senior Fellow, Institute for Family Studies; Visiting Scholar, American Enterprise Institute

2:50 – 3:00 pm	**BREAK**

3:00 – 4:30 pm	**PANEL 2** Moderator: Don Winstead, Principal, Don Winstead Consulting, LLC

Miles Corak, Professor of Public and International Affairs, University of Ottawa, Canada; Economist in Residence, Employment and Social Development Canada
Olivia Golden, Executive Director, Center for Law and Social Policy
Arloc Sherman, Senior Fellow, Center on Budget and Policy Priorities
MaryLee Allen, Director of Policy, Children's Defense Fund

4:30 – 4:55 pm	**Open Discussion Period**

4:55 – 5:00 pm	**Closing Remarks and Adjourn** Greg Duncan

PUBLIC INFORMATION-GATHERING SESSION

September 21, 2017

National Academy of Sciences
Lecture Room
2101 Constitution Avenue, NW
Washington, DC

1:00 – 1:05 pm	**Welcome and Goals** Greg Duncan, Committee Chair, Distinguished Professor, University of California, Irvine
1:05 – 2:40 pm	**PANEL 1: Holistic Approaches to Poverty Reduction** **Moderator:** Christine James-Brown, Committee Member; President and Chief Executive Officer, Child Welfare League of America **Jesús Gerena**, Chief Executive Officer, Family Independence Initiative **Marla Dean**, Executive Director, Bright Beginnings **Satira Streeter**, Executive Director, Ascensions Psychological and Community Services **Gary Bonner**, Director of Family Stability and Economic Success Programs, Center for Urban Families
2:40 – 3:00 pm	**BREAK**
3:00 – 4:35 pm	**PANEL 2: Community Contexts** **Moderator:** Dolores Acevedo-Garcia, Committee Member; Professor of Human Development and Social Policy, Brandeis University **Bruce Western**, Professor of Sociology, Harvard University (via WebEx) **Roy Brooks**, President, National Association of Counties; Commissioner, Tarrant County, Texas **Nora Morales**, Diversity Officer, Prince George's County, Maryland Public Schools

Anita Sampson, Title I Instructional Specialist,
Prince George's County, Maryland Public Schools
Tara Lobin, Coordinator of Title I Programs,
Fairfax County, Virginia Public Schools

4:35 – 4:55 pm   **Open Discussion Period**

4:55 – 5:00 pm   **Closing Remarks and Adjourn**
Greg Duncan

Appendix C

Authors of Memos
Submitted to the Committee

INDIVIDUALS

David Brady, University of California Riverside and WZB Berlin Social
    Science Center
Sarah K. Bruch, University of Iowa
Maria Cancian and Daniel R. Meyer, Institute for Research on Poverty
Miles Corak, University of Ottawa
Matthew Desmond, Harvard University
Robert Doar, American Enterprise Institute
Samuel Hammond, Niskanen Center
Jody Heymann and Aleta Sprague, University of California, Los Angeles
Pamela Joshi, Brandeis University, and Yoonsook Ha, Boston University
John H. Laub, University of Maryland, College Park
Ronald B. Mincy, Columbia University School of Social Work
Edgar O. Olsen, University of Virginia
Pia M. Orrenius, Federal Reserve Bank of Dallas, and Madeline Zavodny,
    University of North Florida
James Riccio, MDRC
Isabel Sawhill, Brookings Institution
Arloc Sherman, Center on Budget and Policy Priorities
Mark Shriver, Save the Children Action Network
Eugene Steuerle, The Urban Institute
Laura M. Tach, Cornell University
W. Bradford Wilcox, University of Virginia
James P. Ziliak, University of Kentucky

ORGANIZATIONS

The Children's Defense Fund
First Focus
The Bernard L. Schwartz Rediscovering Government Initiative (RGI) at
    The Century Foundation (TCF)
Youth Development Institute of Puerto Rico

COMMITTEE ON NATIONAL STATISTICS

The Committee on National Statistics was established in 1972 at the National Academies of Sciences, Engineering, and Medicine to improve the statistical methods and information on which public policy decisions are based. The committee carries out studies, workshops, and other activities to foster better measures and fuller understanding of the economy, the environment, public health, crime, education, immigration, poverty, welfare, and other public policy issues. It also evaluates ongoing statistical programs and tracks the statistical policy and coordinating activities of the federal government, serving a unique role at the intersection of statistics and public policy. The committee's work is supported by a consortium of federal agencies through a National Science Foundation grant, a National Agricultural Statistics Service cooperative agreement, and several individual contracts.